For Barbara and Kelsey

CONTENTS

ACKNOWLEDGMENTS

THE DE L'ISLE Mss., which include most of the Sidney family papers, are cited by permission of Viscount De L'Isle. The Du Moulin and Halifax Mss. are cited by permission of the Duke of Devonshire, and the Coventry, Whitelocke, and Portland Papers are cited by permission of the Marquess of Bath.

Financial support for my research in England was provided by the Center for European Studies and by the Committee on General Scholarships and the Sheldon Fund, both of Harvard University, and by the Committee on Research of the University of California. A Mellon fellowship at the Society of Fellows in the Humanities of Columbia University enabled me to begin the process of revising my original manuscript.

John Dunn and Richard Tuck generously shared their time and their thoughts on seventeenth-century political theory during my stays in England. Jonathan Scott lent copies of several French manuscripts. Harvey Goldman provided valuable advice in New York. Tom Scanlon assisted with the final stages of research. Barbara Edwards, Don Herzog, Harry Hirsch, Kyle Hoffman, Stephen Holmes, Istvan Hont, Sanford Lakoff, Wallace MacCaffrey, Victor Magagna, Judith Shklar, Shannon Stimson, and Tracy Strong have read and commented on part or all of the manuscript. Professors Shklar and MacCaffrey advised the dissertation on which this book is based. They are masters at teaching the academic virtues—precision of analysis and independence of thought—and had an uncanny knack for knowing when to prod and when to leave me to my own devices. To all of these friends I offer my heartfelt thanks.

This book could not have been written without the love, patience, and support of Barbara Edwards. It is to her, and to our daughter Kelsey, that it is dedicated.

NOTE ON THE TEXT

EACH REFERENCE to Sidney's *Discourses Concerning Government* gives the chapter and section numbers as well as the page in the first edition of 1698. Thus *Discourses*, III:41, p. 436 refers to chapter 3, section 41, page 436.

Seventeenth-century orthography, punctuation, and emphases have been retained throughout. Dates are given in old style, with the year regarded as beginning on 1 January.

The Bibliography begins with a chronological list of Sidney's writings and correspondence, cross-referenced to the printed and manuscript sources in which they can be found. This is the first complete catalog of Sidney's writings. The Bibliography also includes full citations for all manuscript, primary, and secondary sources used in this study.

ABBREVIATIONS

"Apology"	"The Apology of Algernon Sydney," in *The Works of Algernon Sydney*, ed. Joseph Robertson (London: 1772)
Blencowe	Robert Blencowe, ed., *Sydney Papers* (London: 1825)
CJ	*Journals of the House of Commons*
Collins	Arthur Collins, ed., *Letters and Memorials of State*, 2 vols. (London: 1746)
CSPD	*Calendar of State Papers, Domestic*
CSPI	*Calendar of State Papers, Ireland*
De L'Isle	Historical Manuscripts Commission, *Report on the Manuscripts of Lord De L'Isle and Dudley*, 6 vols. (London: 1925–66)
Discourses	Algernon Sidney, *Discourses Concerning Government* (London: 1698)
Firth	C. H. Firth and R. S. Rait, *Acts and Ordinances of the Interregnum*, 3 vols. (London: 1911)
HMC	Historical Manuscripts Commission
Letters	*Letters of the Honourable Algernon Sydney, to the Honourable Henry Savile* (London: 1742)
LJ	*Journals of the House of Lords*
Maxims	Algernon Sidney, *Court Maxims, discussed & refelled* (Warwickshire Record Office, CR 1886)
Patriarcha	Sir Robert Filmer, *Patriarcha and Other Political Works*, ed. Peter Laslett (Oxford: 1949)
PRO	Public Record Office
Two Treatises	John Locke, *Two Treatises of Government*, ed. Peter Laslett (Cambridge: 1960)

ALGERNON SIDNEY AND THE
REPUBLICAN HERITAGE
IN ENGLAND AND AMERICA

INTRODUCTION

T HE CONCEPT of republicanism is at the heart of a number of important debates in history and political theory. To many historians, it has provided a useful tool for understanding main currents in seventeenth- and eighteenth-century English and American politics; to many political theorists, it has provided the basis for a coherent and attractive theory of citizenship.[1] The relationship between these two projects has been particularly strong in America. As historians have discovered the republican character of the American Revolution and traced it to its seventeenth-century English roots, political theorists have envisioned the rejuvenation of America's seemingly torpid public life through the revival of republican ideals. In both cases it has been assumed that the defining characteristic of republicanism is a classical theory of virtue, and that the republican language of virtue is distinct from and in tension with the liberal logic of rights and interests.[2] Indeed, it is the moral and political distinctiveness of republicanism—its emphasis on civic virtue, its fear of corruption, its aggressive devotion to political participation—that has given it its strength and vitality. It has also opened it to sharp criticism. Historians have charged that classical republicanism was far less important than Lockean liberalism to the intellectual life of early modern America,[3] and political theorists have argued that the culti-

[1] The bibliography of "republican revisionism" is truly staggering; the most influential contributions have been by Bernard Bailyn, J.G.A. Pocock, Caroline Robbins, Quentin Skinner, and Gordon Wood.

[2] These two themes run throughout the contemporary literature on republicanism. Thus J.G.A. Pocock has argued that the republican language of virtue is "discontinuous" and "incommensurate" with the jurisprudential logic of rights, and Quentin Skinner has suggested that "the ideals of classical republicanism" can be understood only if we "turn back to that period before the concept of individual rights attained . . . hegemony" (J.G.A. Pocock, "Virtues, Rights and Manners," in *Virtue, Commerce, and History* [Cambridge: Cambridge University Press, 1985], 39, 47; Quentin Skinner, "The Paradoxes of Political Liberty," in *Tanner Lectures on Human Values*, ed. Sterling McMurrin [Salt Lake City: University of Utah Press, 1986], 7:238).

[3] Among the most sophisticated historical criticisms of republican revisionism are: Joyce Appleby, "The Social Origins of American Revolutionary Ideology," *Journal of American History* 64 (March 1978): 935–58, and "Republicanism in Old and New Contexts," *William and Mary Quarterly*, 3rd ser., 43 (January 1986): 20–34; Isaac Kramnick, "Republican Revisionism Revisited," *American Historical Review* 87 (June 1982): 629–64; John Patrick Diggins, *The Lost Soul of American Politics* (Chicago: University of Chicago Press, 1984).

vation of civic virtue is an unattractive and impractical ideal for large, complex, and heterogeneous societies.[4]

Despite the enormous attention republicanism has received, its specific character has frequently eluded contemporary analysts. The historical and ideological contexts within which republican ideals were first articulated have been inadequately explored, leaving uncertain not only why they had such tremendous appeal in the past, but also why they continue to be appealing today. Key concepts like virtue and corruption or freedom and slavery have been treated in vague and unfocused ways, leaving unclear their precise meaning and the analytical relationships between them. And republicanism as a whole has been treated as a distinct "mode of discourse" or "language of politics," leaving little sense of the wide range of claims advanced by republican writers, or of the relationships between republican, liberal, and democratic theories of government.

Though largely ignored by twentieth-century historians and political theorists, the political writings of Algernon Sidney (1622–1683) shed new and revealing light on these problems in contemporary analyses of republicanism.[5] As soldier, parliamentarian, and radical exile, Sidney played a leading role in the struggle to establish a republic in seventeenth-century England. During the eighteenth century his *Discourses Concerning Government* enjoyed an extraordinarily wide readership in England and America, not least because he had ended his life on the scaffold, an apparent victim of Stuart despotism. More than James Harrington or John Milton, Sidney represents the essence of republicanism in England and America.

Sidney's republicanism was originally and essentially antimonarchical.[6] He wrote with the express purpose of countering the "slavish" principles and practices of the Stuarts. The foundation of his theory was provided by the concept of liberty and the ideal of self-government. In the ideology of seventeenth-century kingship, human relationships were determined according to hierarchy, degree, and place. Rule and subjection, command and obedience, inequality and depen-

---

[4] Don Herzog, "Some Questions for Republicans," *Political Theory* 14 (August 1986): 473–93; Harry N. Hirsch, "The Threnody of Liberalism: Constitutional Liberty and the Renewal of Community," *Political Theory* 14 (August 1986): 423–50.

[5] George Sabine's comment on the *Discourses*—"there is not an original idea in it"— is typical of the status accorded Sidney's writings by twentieth-century historians of political thought (George Sabine, *A History of Political Theory* [New York: Henry Holt, 1937], 514). Even Pocock's magisterial *Machiavellian Moment* devotes but one paragraph to Sidney (J.G.A. Pocock, *The Machiavellian Moment* [Princeton: Princeton University Press, 1975], 420–21).

[6] Thus it is historically and analytically incorrect to characterize republicanism as an essentially anti-liberal doctrine.

dence: these were the ways of nature. The radical potential latent within this ideology of natural subjection was epitomized by the claim "that all Men are born under a necessity derived from the Laws of God and Nature, to submit unto an Absolute Kingly Government, which could be restrained by no Law, or Oath." Against this authoritarian vision Sidney argued "That Man is naturally free; That he cannot justly be deprived of that Liberty without cause, and that he doth not resign it, or any part of it, unless it be in consideration of a greater good, which he proposes to himself."[7]

Monarchy did not rest on moral and theological grounds alone, however. The defenders of the Stuarts contended that "the best order, the greatest strength, the most stability, and easiest government are to be found in monarchy, and in no other form of government." Here was a comparative judgment, designed to demonstrate the superiority of monarchy to all other forms of government. To this claim Sidney retorted that monarchy was typically accompanied by "slavery, misery, infamy, destruction and desolation." Even a cursory examination of the historical record demonstrated that only in a republic was "the publick Safety . . . provided, Liberty and Propriety secured, Justice administered, Virtue encouraged, Vice suppressed, and the true interest of the Nation advanced."[8] It was Sidney's fierce and sometimes violent opposition to monarchy that led contemporaries to decry his "republican principles," and it was his deep-seated belief that "there is no Medium between Tyranny and Popularity" that led radicals in England and America to cite him as an authority on government throughout the eighteenth century.[9]

The importance of Sidney's writings to our understanding of seventeenth-century English republicanism can be highlighted by looking at two leading works on the period, J.G.A. Pocock's *Machiavellian Moment* and C. B. Macpherson's *Political Theory of Possessive Individualism*. According to Pocock, English republicans attempted to resolve the manifold crises of the seventeenth century by introducing "an ethos of civic excellence." Drawing on the writings of Aristotle and Machiavelli, they conceived of man as a political animal whose self-realization occurs through active participation in public life, and England as a "republic of armed proprietors." By encouraging men to bear arms in service to the nation and by involving them in its political affairs, they hoped that an English republic would facilitate "the

[7] Algernon Sidney, *The Very Copy of a Paper Delivered to the Sheriffs, Upon the Scaffold on Tower-Hill* (London: 1683), 2; *Discourses*, I:2, p. 5.

[8] *Patriarcha*, 86; *Discourses*, III:21, p. 351.

[9] "The Trial of Colonel Algernon Sidney," in *A Complete Collection of State Trials*, ed. T. B. Howell (London: 1816), 9:819; *Discourses*, II:30, p. 241.

release of personal virtue" and the realization of man's "political personality."[10]

Pocock's argument is presented with strength and sophistication and has played a leading role in the revival of interest in republicanism. But the complexity and richness of seventeenth-century English republicanism cannot be captured by Machiavellian notions of virtue and corruption. Virtue was not simply or even primarily a matter of displaying certain innately human capacities or qualities in public. As Sidney's writings demonstrate, alongside the classical or Renaissance virtue of self-affirmation, republicans drew on the Christian virtue of self-denial and the contractual virtue of fidelity to promises. Attending each of these virtues was a form of corruption: weakness, licentiousness, and untrustworthiness. These conceptions of virtue and corruption are logically distinct and frequently at odds with each other. To the extent that they cohere, it is through their fusion with the concepts of rights, interests, laws, and contracts.

Sidney used the concepts of virtue and corruption to reveal the weaknesses of monarchy and to draw attention to the strengths of republican government. While monarchy gave free reign to the corrupt passions of a single man, republicanism emphasized the virtue of obeying the law and respecting the rights of others; while monarchy enervated and emasculated nations by subjecting them to the private interests of one man, republicanism made nations strong by linking civic virtue to the preservation of the private interests of ordinary citizens; while monarchy encouraged magistrates to use public power for private purposes, republicanism stressed the virtue of adhering to public trusts. Sidney's theory of government was not intended to facilitate "the release of personal virtue." Rather, it was designed to enable citizens to achieve common goals and to protect their liberty and their interests from the potentially arbitrary actions of magistrates.

If on the one hand seventeenth-century English republicanism was far richer in the language of rights and interests than Pocock has suggested, on the other hand it did not advocate a purely acquisitive individualism, as C. B. Macpherson has argued. According to Macpherson, the distinctive characteristic of seventeenth-century English radicalism was "the conception of the individual as essentially a proprietor of his own person or capacities, owing nothing to society for

[10] Pocock, *Machiavellian Moment*, 390, 386, 394. Thus Harrington "argued as a humanist: he held that there was in the human animal something planted there by God, which required fulfillment in the practice of active self-rule, and to this something . . . [he gave] the altogether crucial name 'virtue' " (Pocock, "Virtues, Rights and Manners," 41).

them." This ideology of "possessive individualism," which Macpherson finds in virtually every writer from John Lilburne to John Locke, legitimated an emerging bourgeois, capitalist order. Where Pocock sees an "ethos of civic excellence," Macpherson sees an ethos of selfishness.[11]

Once again, a careful study of Sidney's writings demonstrates the inappropriateness of this interpretation. To be sure, Sidney argued that "Liberty consists only in being subject to no man's will, and nothing denotes a Slave but a dependence upon the will of another."[12] And like many of his contemporaries, he invoked this distinction to justify economically based restrictions on the franchise. But his arguments for self-government were not class-based. The antonym of "individualism" in Sidney's theory was not civic-mindedness or a sense of community, but patriarchy and the hereditary ascription of power and authority. Against the claim that monarchy was rooted in the immutable laws of God and nature, Sidney posited the idea of an imperfect political system based on reason and subject to revision in light of the changing needs of its members. His conception of freedom was not intended to unleash the acquisitive instincts of a few, but rather was designed to draw attention to the public and private capacities of the many. He wrote for active citizens, not passive subjects.

By introducing Sidney's ideas into the panorama of seventeenth-century English radicalism, it is possible to see the narrowness of contemporary interpretations of this period. The recovery of Sidney's thought also contributes to our understanding of the ideological origins of the American Revolution. As a result of the pioneering work of Caroline Robbins, Bernard Bailyn, and Gordon Wood, we have become attuned to the ways in which English republicanism influenced American radicalism. Building on the foundation established by these historians, subsequent scholars have attempted to reconstruct the American Revolution along republican lines, laying particular stress on the distinctive role played by the concepts of virtue and corruption in American political thought.[13] Where once it was argued that *Locke et praetera nihil*,[14] scholars now routinely treat essentially

[11] C. B. Macpherson, *The Political Theory of Possessive Individualism* (Oxford: Oxford University Press, 1962), 3.

[12] *Discourses*, III:16, p. 317.

[13] The scope of this revision is surveyed by Robert Shalhope in two articles: "Toward a Republican Synthesis: The Emergence of an Understanding of Republicanism in American Historiography," *William and Mary Quarterly*, 3rd ser., 29 (January 1972): 49–80, and "Republicanism and Early American Historiography," *William and Mary Quarterly*, 3rd ser., 39 (April 1982): 334–56.

[14] The most influential example of the Lockean interpretation of American political thought—and the text against which the republican revision was initially directed—is

Lockean ideas like consent, the state of nature, and natural rights as liberal aberrations in an overwhelmingly republican world.[15]

Thomas Jefferson spoke for many Americans when he wrote that the *Discourses* was "a rich treasure of republican principles" and "probably the best elementary book of principles of government, as founded in natural right which has ever been published in any language," and thus Sidney's name has justifiably been cited to verify the impact of English republicanism on American radicalism.[16] But Jefferson's words should give pause, for they suggest a closer connection between "republican principles" and the language of "natural right" than has hitherto been suspected. Without an adequate account of Sidney's writings and the story of his life we have lacked the historical and conceptual tools necessary to establish the precise contours of his impact on American political thought. In particular, it has not been possible to distinguish between Sidney's fame as a martyr and his influence as a political theorist. Sidney's death at the hands of Charles II provided a point of reference against which Americans frequently measured their own devotion to liberty. This generally reinforced his theoretical influence, but on occasion it did not, as when opponents of the Revolution or the Constitution attempted to capitalize on his fame in order to counter his influence. When attention is restricted to instances in which the influence of Sidney's ideas was strongest, a striking conclusion emerges: virtually all of the "republican" principles drawn from Sidney's writings—from the rule of law to the right of revolution—were perfectly compatible with Lockean liberalism. Indeed, the only salient difference between Sidney and Locke in the minds of most revolutionary Americans was that Sidney's violent opposition to the Stuarts made him a more "radical" figure than the esteemed author of *An Essay Concerning Human Understanding*.

Finally, a careful consideration of Sidney's writings contributes to an important contemporary debate over the meaning of citizenship. From a variety of perspectives, both radical and conservative, political theorists have advocated the republican ideal of civic virtue as a tonic

---

Louis Hartz, *The Liberal Tradition in America* (New York: Harcourt Brace & World, 1955).

[15] "The republican . . . discourse of the eighteenth-century . . . made no significant appeal to Lockean formulae, and neither did many of those who constructed the reply or counter-discourse which it encountered" (J.G.A. Pocock, "Between Gog and Magog: The Republican Thesis and the *Ideologia Americana*," *Journal of the History of Ideas* 48 [April–June 1987]: 339).

[16] Thomas Jefferson to Mason Locke Weems, 13 December 1804, in *Catalogue of the Library of Thomas Jefferson*, ed. W. Millicent Sowerby (Washington, DC: Library of Congress, 1953), 3:13.

for the apparently anemic quality of public life in liberal America.[17] This argument is almost always framed in terms of the need to recover lost or neglected modes of thought, and thus its success or failure turns on the strength of the historical reconstruction on which it is based. By challenging the accuracy of contemporary accounts of the republican heritage—particularly the oft-repeated claims that republicanism is based on a classical theory of virtue and that republicanism and liberalism are antithetical modes of thought—this study points to the need to modify the conceptual framework employed by republican revivalists. At the same time, by situating key republican concepts in context, it breathes life and meaning into terms that are frequently treated in abstract and meaningless ways. This is not always to republicanism's advantage. For example, to the extent that classical virtue remains within the intellectual arsenal of republicanism, it is as a martial ethos that manifests itself in a cult of masculinity and in a glorification of conquest and expansion. The republican heritage is neither as coherent nor as attractive as its advocates would suggest, and it is only by understanding it in context, "warts and all," that we will be able to evaluate its relevance to contemporary politics.

Though focused on the writings of one man, this book is not an intellectual biography. That task has been undertaken by a number of writers.[18] Rather, I have attempted to enhance our understanding of

[17] Robert Bellah has argued that "there are elements in our past other than classic liberalism and . . . it is crucial for our future that we know what they are" ("Commentary and Proposed Agenda: The Normative Framework for Pluralism in America," *Soundings* 61 [Fall 1978]: 356), Quentin Skinner has urged the ideal of civic virtue because "contemporary liberalism . . . is in danger of sweeping the public arena bare of any concepts save those of self-interest and individual rights" ("The Paradoxes of Political Liberty," 249), and Michael Sandel has suggested that "if the 'republican school' is right about our ideological origins, then perhaps there is hope for revitalizing our public life and restoring a sense of community. . . . So the debate about the meaning of our past carries consequences for the debate about present political possibilities" ("The State and the Soul," *New Republic* [10 June 1985]: 39–40). One indication of the ideological diversity of this movement to recover America's "lost" heritage is the fact that it appeals both to Senator Orrin Hatch and members of the Critical Legal Studies movement (Orrin Hatch, "Civic Virtue: Wellspring of Liberty," *National Forum* 64 [Fall 1984]: 34–38; Andrew Fraser, "Legal Amnesia: Modernism vs. the Republican Tradition in American Legal Theory," *Telos* 60 [1984]: 18).

[18] The most recent studies are: Paulette Carrive, *La pensée politique d'Algernon Sidney* (Paris: Méridiens Klincksieck, 1989); John Carswell, *The Porcupine: The Life of Algernon Sidney* (London: John Murray, 1989); Jonathan Scott, *Algernon Sidney and the English Republic 1623–1677* (Cambridge: Cambridge University Press, 1988); Blair Worden, "The Commonwealth Kidney of Algernon Sidney," *Journal of British Studies* 24 (January 1985): 1–40. Scott is the most historically detailed study of Sidney's early life, but in many respects it is less reliable than Worden. Carswell is explicitly unconcerned with

republicanism by capturing the range, structure, and influence of Sidney's political arguments. New discoveries make this possible as never before. Just over a decade ago Blair Worden chanced upon the *Court Maxims*, a previously unknown manuscript treatise written by Sidney in the mid-1660s. And Jonathan Scott has recently unearthed a wealth of new information concerning Sidney's financial affairs and his exile in France.

Even with these additional resources, however, the analysis of Sidney's thought is fraught with difficulties. Sidney was not a systematic philosopher, but a skilled and intelligent polemicist. His arguments are scattered across his writings and—as was the style of his day—are often deeply embedded in detailed discussions of ancient and medieval history. As a result, they must be carefully reconstructed if they are to be understood. The dangers associated with this mode of interpretation are well known;[19] but I am persuaded that it is the only reliable way of making sense of a complex structure of analysis.

The process of reconstructing Sidney's arguments is made particularly difficult by two additional facts. First, with the exception of a pamphlet that was coauthored, appeared anonymously, and was singularly uninfluential, Sidney published nothing during his lifetime. Unlike Milton, Harrington, Locke, or the Levellers, Sidney was not forced to temper his arguments in the heat of England's fierce pamphlet wars. We have no knowledge of how he might have responded to criticisms of his views. Second, even the two surviving treatises ascribed to Sidney are of uncertain status. The *Court Maxims* remains in manuscript, and the handwriting is not Sidney's, not even entirely of the seventeenth century;[20] the *Discourses Concerning Government* was first published in 1698 by men well versed in the art of revising texts, and the original manuscript has not been seen since.[21] Though there are strong internal connections between these two texts, we have no way of knowing with certainty the extent to which they resemble Sidney's original versions. Similarly, we do not have an accurate history

---

Sidney's thought. Carrive is closest to the present study but fails to employ recent biographical and textual discoveries; in particular, it makes no reference to the *Court Maxims*.

[19] Quentin Skinner, "Meaning and Understanding in the History of Ideas," *History and Theory* 8 (1969): 3–53.

[20] Some of the problems associated with the text of the *Court Maxims* are discussed in Blair Worden, "Introduction" to Edmund Ludlow, *A Voyce From The Watch Tower*, Camden Fourth Series, vol. 21 (London: Royal Historical Society, 1978), 15–16; and John Carswell, "Algernon Sidney's 'Court Maxims': The Biographical Importance of a Transcript," *Historical Research* (February 1989): 98–103.

[21] Blair Worden, "Edmund Ludlow: The Puritan and the Whig," *Times Literary Supplement* 3,904 (7 January 1977): 15–16.

of the composition of either text. Though each contains references dating it to a particular period, there is no way of knowing whether either incorporated material written or conceived at an earlier time.

In light of these difficulties, I have attempted to formulate an interpretation that lays bare the essential structure of Sidney's thought yet remains sensitive to the many ambiguities and contradictions in it. I begin with a sketch of Sidney's life, based on a thorough study of manuscript and printed sources. Though known to eighteenth-century radicals as "the British Brutus," Sidney emerges as an opportunist as well as a political radical. I then turn to the structure of seventeenth-century English royalist thought, indicating why Sidney, John Locke, and James Tyrrell thought it necessary to respond to Sir Robert Filmer's theory of patriarchal absolutism. The heart of my account is an analysis of three conceptual pairs around which Sidney constructed his arguments for republican government: freedom and slavery, virtue and corruption, and constitutionalism and revolution. Through the concepts of freedom and slavery, Sidney provided the moral foundation for a free government; through the concepts of virtue and corruption, he demonstrated that monarchy was "rooted in" corruption and established the psychological foundations for republican citizenship; and through the concepts of constitutional government and revolution, he described the political forms most likely to preserve liberty and the conditions under which a free people could revolt against its government. To bring the distinctive features of Sidney's republicanism into greater relief, I compare his arguments to those of other leading seventeenth-century radicals, ranging from Civil War figures like James Harrington, John Milton, and the Levellers to members of the Whig opposition like John Locke and James Tyrrell. I conclude by tracing the impact of Sidney's writings and the story of his life on revolutionary America. With the Revolution and the adoption of the Constitution, many of Sidney's most radical ideas were put into practice; what has remained influential since that time are fragments of his original arguments.

PART ONE

BACKGROUND

Part One

ONE

BIOGRAPHICAL SKETCH

IT WOULD be gratifying to learn that Algernon Sidney "had set up Marcus Brutus for his pattern" and that the "firmness and simplicity of [his] character resembled that first of Romans."[1] Unfortunately, Sidney's life did not always match his posthumous reputation. Though Sidney was possessed of a strong sense of integrity and the firm conviction that his causes were righteous, his commitment to republicanism was intermittent and inconsistent. The course of his life was deeply influenced by private concerns, by violent family conflicts and recurrent financial crises. When he did turn to political action, it was with baroque complexity, not classical simplicity. Sidney had an extremely flexible sense of strategy and tactics, born of his belief that the world is governed more by force and fraud than by reason and persuasion. The image of a man selflessly and single-mindedly devoted to the cause of freedom, so carefully crafted by seventeenth- and eighteenth-century Whigs in England and America, is too narrow and too confining. It does not allow us to see the complex and crosscutting personal and political issues that affected Sidney's conduct, nor does it shed adequate light on his intellectual development. The most striking fact about Sidney's life is not that he was martyred for the *Discourses Concerning Government*, but that he wrote it at all. The first step to understanding Sidney's political writings must be the recovery of an accurate sense of his life.

Background and Early Life (1622–1646)

Algernon Sidney was born in 1622 or 1623.[2] A second son, he claimed without exaggeration that "though I am not a peere, I am of

---

[1] Gilbert Burnet, *Bishop Burnet's History of His Own Time*, ed. M. J. Routh, 2nd ed. (Oxford: Oxford University Press, 1833), 2:410; Sir John Dalrymple, *Memoirs of Great Britain and Ireland*, 2nd ed. (London: 1771), 1:79. "In *Algernon Sidney*, we have, in one View, *Brutus* and *Regulus*. As the First, a Destroyer of Tyrants and Tyranny; as the Latter, a Despiser of Banishment, and even Death itself, when they came in Competition with uttering his Sentiments for his Country's Benefit" (Collins, "Introduction").

[2] Surviving records indicate that Sidney was probably born on 14 or 15 January 1623 (Brigid Haydon, "Algernon Sidney, 1623–1683," *Archaeologia Cantiana* 76 [1961]: 111).

the wood of which they are made."[3] His father was Robert Sidney, second earl of Leicester; his mother was Dorothy Percy, sister to Algernon Percy, tenth earl of Northumberland. This was an extraordinarily high birth and placed Sidney at the apex of England's social and political hierarchies. Only the existence of an older brother stood between him and a seat in the House of Lords.

As a family, the Sidneys had for generations shared several characteristics: a fiery temperament, a commitment to military and political service and the cause of international Protestantism, and a devotion to learning.[4] The least endearing trait of the Sidneys was their volatile temper, fueled by a keen sense of personal and family honor. Sir Philip Sidney (1554–1586), a "naturally . . . warm and high Spirit," was "so jealous of his Honour and Reputation, that he could not brook the least Intrenchment on either."[5] When once he discovered that his father's secretary had read some of his letters, he warned that if ever the offense was repeated "I will thruste my dagger into you. And truste to it, for I speak it in earnest."[6] In an age in which gentlemen commonly carried weapons, such threats were neither intended nor taken lightly.

The Sidneys' aggressive spirit made them well suited to the life of the aristocratic warrior. Algernon's great-grandfather Sir Henry Sidney (1529–1586) led a number of campaigns in Ireland during his tenure as lord deputy. Sir Philip Sidney, the great chivalric hero of the Elizabethan age, died of wounds received in the battle of Zutphen in 1586. His brother Sir Robert (1563–1626) lacked Philip's daring and brashness, but he too "took early to a martial life."[7]

Complementing the Sidneys' martial spirit was their devotion to public life. Sir William Sidney (1482?–1554) founded the family's fortune by serving as both tutor and steward of the household for Prince Edward. Sir William's son Henry, one of the greatest statesmen of the Elizabethan age, was both lord deputy of Ireland and lord president of Wales. He gave voice to the family's public spirit in the process of describing the latter position: "Great it is that in some sort I govern the third part of this realm under her most excellent Majesty; high it

---

[3] "Apology," 10.

[4] An abbreviated family tree is presented in Appendix I. These Sidney family characteristics almost perfectly match Lawrence Stone's catalog of the "five overlapping cultural ideals" that governed aristocratic education: "the man of war, the man of learning, the statesman, the polished cavalier, and the virtuoso" (Lawrence Stone, *The Crisis of the Aristocracy 1558–1641* [Oxford: The Clarendon Press, 1965], 693).

[5] Collins, 1:91.

[6] Stone, *Crisis of the Aristocracy*, 224.

[7] Collins, 1:114.

is for by that I have precedence of great personages and by far my betters; happy it is for the goodness of the people I govern; and most happy it is for the commodity I have, by the authority of that place, to do good every day."[8] Patriarchy blended with self-interest, and in ways more complicated than even Queen Elizabeth had imagined high office, proved to be its own reward.

The military and political exploits of the Sidneys were frequently in service to the cause of international Protestantism. Sir Philip Sidney, an ardent defender of the Huguenots, was friend to both Hubert Languet and Philip du Plessis Mornay. A witness to the massacre of the Protestants in Paris on St. Bartholomew's Eve in 1572, he died while defending the Low Countries against the armies of Catholic Spain. Though Sir Philip's relatives did not share his zeal, they too united religious and patriotic concerns under the banner of Protestantism. It was Algernon's father, the second earl of Leicester (1595–1677), who argued that "it is impossible for an English papist to be a true and faithfull subject to the Crowne and State of England" and who ascribed "all the treasons against Q[ueen] Elisabeth throughout her whole reigne" to the machinations of the Jesuits.[9]

If there was anything that drew the Sidneys away from war and politics it was their deep commitment to learning and intellectual growth. Sir Henry Sidney "highly favoured all Men of Letters and Sciences, and greatly encouraged them, oftentimes saying, 'Science was to be honoured, in whomsoever it was to be found.' "[10] It was probably Sir Philip Sidney who founded the library at Penshurst; by the 1670s it contained more than 4,500 volumes.[11] Algernon's father sustained this tradition throughout much of the seventeenth century. At his death he left behind some "forty quires of paper," including painstaking annotations to the first earl's commonplace books; notes on history, medicine, religion, and the constitution; and a treatise on money.[12]

Into this family and these traditions Algernon Sidney was born. In the fall of 1632, at the age of nine or ten, Sidney and his older

---

[8] Quoted in A. L. Rowse, *The England of Elizabeth* (Madison: University of Wisconsin Press, 1978), 290.

[9] Kent Archives Office, De L'Isle MSS. (U1475), Z1/1, fols. 671–72.

[10] Collins, 1:91.

[11] Germaine Warkentin, "Ins and Outs of the Sidney Family Library," *Times Literary Supplement* 4,314 (6 December 1985): 1394.

[12] "The Trial of Colonel Algernon Sidney," in *A Complete Collection of State Trials*, ed. T. B. Howell (London: 1816), 9:878; Kent Archives Office, De L'Isle MSS. (U1475), Z1/1–10. So great was Leicester's devotion to books that Algernon attempted to reconcile with his father in 1660 by offering to send him books from Rome (Sidney to Leicester, 12 December 1660, in Collins, 2:701–2).

brother Philip accompanied their father on a three-month-long diplomatic mission to Denmark. In 1636 the two boys traveled with their father once again, this time on a mission to France that was to last more than five years. Sidney evidently impressed the English community in Paris. As the countess of Leicester wrote her husband from Penshurst, "To Allgernoone I do send a blessing whom I hear much comended by all that comes from you, and Nic: who spoke well of verie few, said he had a huge deall of witt and much sweetness of nature."[13] This was probably the last time that anyone reported that Sidney had "much sweetness of nature." In later life he was more frequently described as thin-skinned, vain, and humorless. But it is clear from her letters that Sidney's mother felt a great deal of affection for him.

Beyond these bare facts, we know virtually nothing about Sidney's childhood and adolescence. Of his education in England and France, of the tutors he studied with, of the books he read and the ideas he was exposed to, no record has survived.[14]

In June 1641 King Charles nominated Leicester to be lord lieutenant of Ireland. When the Irish rebellion broke out in October of that year, Leicester named his eldest son, Philip, lord Lisle, the lord deputy of Ireland; and Lisle, in turn, named Sidney one of the captains of the horse serving under him. Lisle's policy in Ireland was simple but brutal. According to a government dispatch issued 29 September 1642, "he still proceeds in burning, wasting, spoiling, and destroying all the country about him, and all the rebel's corn, hay, and turf, and depriving the rebels of all the cattle he can, so as to take from them all means of lodging, food and fire."[15] In the context of seventeenth-century Anglo-Irish affairs, Lisle's slash-and-burn strategy was unexceptionable, and it was even said that he deserved "very well of the publicke here."[16] His actions did, however, put him in direct conflict with the earl of Ormonde. Though still officially a soldier in the king's army, Lisle increasingly allied himself with the parliamentary sympathizers in Ireland. The tensions between Lisle and Ormonde culminated in court-martial proceedings against Lisle for fleeing the

[13] Countess of Leicester to the earl of Leicester, 10 November 1636, in *De L'Isle*, 6:83.

[14] In early 1636 Leicester noted in his diary that Algernon was "abrod at schoole," and in August of that year either Algernon or Philip was enrolled in the Huguenot academy in Saumur (Robert Sidney, second earl of Leicester, "Diary of Events 1636–1650," in *De L'Isle*, 6:554; Kent Archives Office, De L'Isle MSS. [U1475], C97/1). Given frequent references to Algernon's presence in Paris between 1636 and 1641, the latter undoubtedly refers to Philip.

[15] Quoted in S. R. Gardiner, *History of the Great Civil War 1642–1649* (London: 1893), 1:116.

[16] Sir John Temple to Leicester, 14 January 1643, in *De L'Isle*, 6:416.

scene of battle at New Ross. Though cleared of the charge, Lisle recognized that as long as Ormonde was in command of the English forces "there is no good to be done in this place," and he made arrangements to return to England.[17]

It is to these tensions between the parliamentary and royalist forces in Ireland that we owe the first extant letter from Sidney. Writing to his mother from Dublin on 18 June 1643 about Ormonde's plans for a truce with the Irish rebels, he observed that "this army cannot live in time of peace unless maintained by the Rebbells, that they having little or noe mony we must be contented with provisions. And it is hardly to be doubted but that they will either in the time of truce conclude a final peace, or else, as soone as they have got in their harvest, they will break the truce, to the inevitable losse of this army." Under such conditions "this will be noe fit place for me to stay in . . . not being able to subsist heare but uppon credit, the most sure way to ruine the fortune of one that hath noe stock to rely upon."[18]

Sidney had no fondness for the military life, "and yet it is the only way of living well for those that have not estates." Even it was insecure, however, and left him continually open to "the greatest of all misfortunes," becoming "burdensome to my friends." His was a complaint common to younger sons in the seventeenth century. It was also shared by many radicals. As James Harrington trenchantly argued in 1656, "I must confess I marvel how much it comes to pass that we should use our children as we do our puppies: take one, lay it in the lap, feed it with every good bit, and drown five! Nay, worse, for as much as the puppies are once drowned, whereas the children are left perpetually drowning. Really, my lords, it is a flinty custom!"[19] As a younger son in a world governed by the law of primogeniture, Sidney resented the life of lean credit and frustrated ambitions that stood before him. He yearned for the power, wealth, and independence with which his brother Philip had been blessed.

Despite Sidney's misgivings, he accepted a commission in the parliamentary army in 1644. Within two months he was "dangerously

[17] "Examination of witnesses taken by John Stoughton, Esq . . . the 5th of April, 1643," in De L'Isle, 6:419–28; Dictionary of National Biography, s.v. "Philip Sidney."

[18] [Algernon Sidney] to the countess of Leicester, 18 June 1643, in History of the Irish Confederation and the War in Ireland, 1641–1649, ed. John Gilbert (Dublin: M. H. Gill, 1882–1891), 2:xlviii–xlix.

[19] James Harrington, "The Commonwealth of Oceana," in The Political Works of James Harrington, ed. J.G.A. Pocock (Cambridge: Cambridge University Press, 1977), 237. For a general discussion of the problems of younger sons, see Joan Thirsk, "Younger Sons in the Seventeenth Century," History 54 (October 1969): 358–77.

wounded" at the battle of Marston Moor.[20] Almost simultaneously Leicester beat a hasty retreat from Oxford to Penshurst, disgraced by the king's decision to strip him of his position as lord lieutenant of Ireland.[21] The contrast between the behavior of the father and that of the son is striking. At the same moment that Leicester was inaugurating a retirement from public life, Sidney was energetically embracing the parliamentary cause.

The earl of Clarendon ascribed Leicester's misfortunes to "the staggering and irresolution of his nature."[22] There is a great deal of truth to this characterization.[23] But Clarendon's own capacity for action blinded him to the bewildering choices forced on Englishmen by the outbreak of the Civil War. Like many of his countrymen, Leicester was desperately anxious to trust his king; but the increasingly immoderate and intransigent royalists at Oxford made that impossible. Instinctively loyal to the king, Leicester simply did not know what to do when it appeared that the king had betrayed him.[24]

Unlike his father, Sidney was able partially to sever his ties to the king and make Parliament the object of his allegiance. Unfortunately, the historical record is silent concerning his reasons for making this momentous decision. We simply do not know whether he was moved by political principle or by considerations of expediency. One clue might lie in the motto he had sewn onto his troop's flag, *Sanctus Amor Patriae Dat Animum*. The *Patriae*, or nation, was an abstraction that allowed Sidney to distinguish between the king and the nation, and hence to oppose the king in the name of the public good. To be sure, this distinction required an enormous act of moral and political imagination, and few Englishmen in the early stages of the Civil War would have viewed their actions in precisely this way. It would be a mistake to read too much into Sidney's motto. But in ways the Elizabethan statesman Sir Henry Sidney might not have wanted to ac-

---

[20] *The Parliament Scout* 57 (18–25 July 1644): 560. See also: Kent Archives Office, De L'Isle MSS. (U1475), O101/1; Collins, 1:151; *CJ*, 3:507.

[21] As Leicester explained to the queen, his dismissal brought "instant destruction to my fortune, present dishonour to myself, and the same for ever to my poor family" (Leicester to the queen, December 1643, in Blencowe, xxvi).

[22] Edward Hyde, earl of Clarendon, *The History of the Rebellion and Civil Wars in England*, ed. W. Dunn Macray (Oxford: Oxford University Press, 1888), 2:531.

[23] For example, in September 1642 Leicester wrote that "we are now about the equinoctal, a time which, by natural reservedness, suspends itself from declaring for day or night, for summer or for winter. Methinks the condition of our affaires is not unlike it" (Leicester to Lady Carlisle, 12 September 1642, in Blencowe, xxii–xxiii).

[24] On the problems facing moderate royalists during the early stages of the Civil War, see Robert Ashton, *The English Civil War* (New York: W. W. Norton, 1978), 208–10.

knowledge, Sidney's decision to support Parliament was simply a spirited extension of the family tradition of public service that he had inaugurated more than a century before.

Sidney remained in the army after it was remodeled in early 1645. But the wounds he had received at Marston Moor continued to bother him, and on 14 May he resigned his commission with "extreme unwillingnesse . . . by reason of my lameness."[25] Provision had already been made, however, for him to become the military governor of Chichester.[26] Not until 1646, in the wake of Parliament's decision to fill vacant seats in the House of Commons through recruiter elections, did Sidney begin to make the transition from soldier to politician.

Parliament (1646–1653)

Sidney was elected to the House of Commons on 17 July 1646. By that time Parliament had commissioned Lisle as lord lieutenant of Ireland and had voted to send Sidney along with him as the commander of a regiment of horse and as governor of Dublin. Thus, before Sidney could enter the House, it was decided that he should return to active military service.[27]

Sidney's second tour of duty in Ireland was cut short by political developments in England. In the face of increasingly widespread dissatisfaction with the system of county committees and military rule, the Presbyterian "party" seized control of Parliament in February 1647 and immediately set about disbanding the New Model Army. As part of this program they decided to restructure the government of Ireland, and both Sidney and Lisle were recalled to London.

As the Presbyterians began to carry out their plans, opposition mounted. Outside Parliament the army became increasingly politicized, and the soldiers organized themselves through a system of "agitators." Inside Parliament the conflict came to a head on 25 May, when a series of ordinances to dismantle the army was considered.

---

[25] Algernon Sidney to General Fairfax, 14 May 1645, British Library, Sloane MS. 1519, fol. 112.

[26] *CJ*, 4:136–37; *LJ*, 7:363, 365; *CSPD*, 1644–1645:541; 1645–1647:132, 148, 151, 173, 182, 229.

[27] "Return. Members of Parliament. Part I: Parliaments of England, 1213–1702," *Parliamentary Papers* (London: HMSO, 1872), 62:498; HMC, *Thirteenth Report, Appendix, Part I* (London: HMSO, 1891), 1:395; *CJ*, 6:600, 603; *LJ*, 8:417–18; *De L'Isle*, 6:441. A comprehensive record of Sidney's parliamentary activities can be found in Appendix II.

On the crucial first vote, over whether to dismantle General Fairfax's regiment, a division was called. Sidney stood as a teller against the motion, but it was passed by a vote of 136 to 115 and was followed without challenge by ordinances disbanding all other regiments in the army.[28]

For Sidney, as for so many others, the Presbyterians' plans to disband the army threatened the survival of Parliament itself. He made his beliefs clear in an attack on the moderate Presbyterian Sir Philip Perceval on 2 June. Perceval, he argued, had not only voted to disband the army, but had also assisted the king and encouraged soldiers in Ireland to "come into England to fight the parliament."[29] The core of the Presbyterian program was capitulation to the king.

Following this spate of activity, Sidney's parliamentary record during the chaotic months of late 1647 and early 1648 is sketchy and demonstrates no clear pattern. He evidently retained the good favor of Fairfax, for on 17 June 1648, in the wake of "the last . . . of the great local insurrections of English history," he was commissioned governor of Dover Castle.[30] For a very brief period Sidney exercised his office responsibly. He saw to his soldiers, suggested reforms in the administration of the castle, and even requested that a financial "establishment" be created for him.[31] Sidney's interest in details was limited, however, and as the conflict between Parliament and the king came to a head, he neglected his post at the castle.

On Friday, 1 December 1648, Parliament began to debate the king's answers to the proposals for reconciliation that had been presented to him at Newcastle. Though shocked by the approach of the army, the House ignored the "martial noises" out-of-doors and continued the debate on 2 December. Faced with a motion by moderate MPs to suspend the debate until Parliament was free of the army's influence, radicals pressed for an immediate vote. With dusk approaching, the conflict centered on a motion to bring in candles to permit a resolution of the debate that evening. A division was called, and Sidney stood as a teller in support of the motion. Though the motion was defeated by a healthy margin, Sidney had demonstrated his unwillingness to compromise with the king.[32]

[28] *CJ*, 5:183.

[29] *CJ*, 5:145, 195; HMC, *Report on the Manuscripts of the Earl of Egmont* (London: HMSO, 1905), vol. 1, part 2, p. 440.

[30] Everitt, *Community of Kent*, 241; *De L'Isle*, 6:443.

[31] *CJ*, 5:633; *CSPD*, 1648–1649: 186–87, 189, 217. See also: Sidney to Sir Michael Livesey, 17 July [1648], Kent Archives Office, Q/SB1/45; Sidney to Fairfax, 19 July [1648], University of Durham Library, Mickleton & Spearman MS. 46, fols. 103–6; Sidney to Borough of Sandwich, 16 July [1648], Kent Archives Office, Sa/ZB2/114.

[32] Underdown, *Pride's Purge*, 133–37; *CJ*, 6:93.

Sidney does not appear to have been a supporter of the radical purge of Parliament begun on 6 December, however. He may not even have been present on that fateful day. He was certainly absent after the 20th, when a test oath designed to ferret out remaining moderates was imposed on all MPs.[33] If he was unwilling to compromise with the king, he was also unwilling to side with the hard-line activists who had gained control of the House.

Despite his withdrawal from Parliament, in January he was named one of the commissioners for the trial of Charles I. As he recalled eleven years later:

> I was at Penshurst, when the act for the triall passed, and comeing up to towne I heard my name put in, and those that were nominated for judges weare then in the painted chamber. I presently went thither, heard the act read, and found my owne name with others. A debate was raised how they should proceed upon it, and after having bin sometime silent to hear what thoes would say, whoe had had the directing of that businesse, I did positively oppose Cromwell, Bradshawe, and others, whoe would have the triall to goe on, and drewe my reasons from their tow points: First, the king *could be tried* by noe court; secondly, that *noe man* could be tried by that court. This being alleged in vaine, and Cromwell using these formall words (I tell you, wee will cut off his head with the crowne upon it,) I replied: you may take your own course, I cannot stop you, but I will keep myself clean from haveing any hand in this businesse, immediately went out of the roome, and never returned.

Conscious of the gravity of Parliament's actions, Leicester carefully noted in his journal that "my two sons Philip and Algernon came unexpectedly to Penshurst *Monday* 22d, and stayd there till *Monday* 29th January, so as neither of them was at the condemnation of the King."[34]

Sidney's reasons for withdrawing from the proceedings against the king are ambiguous and need explication. Like the trial of Louis XVI, the trial of Charles I posed "one of the hardest questions faced by the leaders of a new regime. How are they to settle with the leaders of the old?" In particular, how is it possible for regicide to be presented as a legal act? As Michael Walzer has explained: "The king is brought to trial in violation of the laws of the old regime, the only laws that he acknowledges; he is judged in the name of political or legal principles to which he never consented. He is judged, moreover, by a court whose authority he does not recognize . . . a court com-

---

[33] Underdown, *Pride's Purge*, 166 n. 69.

[34] Sidney to Leicester, 12 October 1660, in Blencowe, 237; Leicester, "Journal," in Blencowe, 54.

posed in large part, if not entirely, of his political opponents. How can this be justice done?"[35] This question weighed particularly heavily on the consciences of seventeenth-century Englishmen, among whom devotion to the law was virtually a civil religion.

In this light, Sidney's first claim—that "the king *could be tried* by noe court"—reflected an unwillingness to step outside the legal doctrines of the old regime. The king could not be brought before a court, nor was he subject to the law. At this critical juncture, Sidney explicitly rejected the radical doctrine that was to make his *Discourses Concerning Government* notorious.

Sidney's second claim—"that *noe man* could be tried by that court"—cut against his first, however. In a letter to his father dated 10 January, he reported that "if the House of Commons had not bin very hasty in turning the Ordinances, for the Kings Tryall, into an Act of their owne, and contented themselves with their owne Power, the Lords are now in a Temper to have given their Assent, if they had received a second Message from us."[36] In its haste, the House of Commons had arrogated to itself a power it did not possess, and hence its proceedings were illegitimate. Had it proceeded with more circumspection, Sidney implied, he might have been willing to accept its decision to bring the king to trial.

Sidney's change of heart between writing his father and confronting Cromwell highlights the tentativeness of his radicalism at this crucial juncture. On 10 January it was still uncertain whether the king was to be executed or simply deposed, and whether either of those actions entailed the elimination of the monarchy.[37] Cromwell's response to Sidney's objections—"I tell you, wee will cut off his head with the crowne upon it"—gave proof that the most extreme course of action was to be followed. As had been the case in December, Sidney set limits to his radical zeal and withdrew from the proceedings.

Despite his objections to the trial and execution of Charles I, Sidney was named in early February to a committee charged with bringing in a bill to abolish the monarchy and the House of Lords.[38] But as his behavior on 22 February indicated, he had not yet reconciled himself with the new regime. On that day Henry Ireton proposed an oath of engagement for members of the newly created Council of State, in which they would testify to their approval of the king's execution and the abolition of the House of Lords. Ireton's obvious in-

---

[35] Michael Walzer, *Regicide and Revolution* (Cambridge: Cambridge University Press, 1974), 70.

[36] Sidney to Leicester, 10 January 1649, in Collins, 1:131.

[37] Underdown, *Pride's Purge*, 182–84.

[38] *CJ*, 6:132, 133, 166, 168.

tent was to ensure that control of the new government was vested only in those who were willing to acknowledge and endorse its bloody founding.[39] As Sidney later recalled,

> I opposed that, and having given such reasons as I could to justify my opinion, I chanced to use this expression, that such a test would prove a snare to many an honest man, but every knave would slip through it; the Lord Grey of Grooby tooke great exceptions at this; and sayed I had called all thoes knaves, that had signed the order [for the king's execution]; upon which theire was a hot debate, somme defending, others blaming what I had sayed, but all mistaking the true sense of it.

Sidney was saved by Henry Marten, who explained "that indeed such expressions did sound something harsh . . . but that . . . I had only sayed, that every knave might slip through, and not that every one who did slip through was a knave." Marten's explanation was a rather weak salve for an already festering wound, however, and as a result of his actions during January and February 1649 Sidney gained the permanent enmity of "Cromwell, Bradshawe, Harrison, Lord Grey and others."[40]

It is unfortunate that we do not know more about Sidney's reaction to the string of loyalty oaths imposed by the new regime. In October 1649 MPs and other public figures were required to take an oath of engagement declaring their allegiance to the Commonwealth; in January 1650 this requirement was extended to the entire adult male population. The oath—"I do declare and promise that I will be true and faithful to the Commonwealth of England as it is now established, without a king or House of Lords"—forced each man to proclaim publicly whether or not he thought a government founded in violence could be legitimate.[41] Many of England's sharpest minds, from Thomas Hobbes to Anthony Ascham and Marchamont Nedham, were mobilized in a fierce campaign to prove that the legitimacy of a government rested not on its origins but on its capacity to protect its citizens. As Nedham trenchantly put it, "the power of the sword ever hath been the foundation of all titles to government in En-

---

[39] Blair Worden, *The Rump Parliament 1648–1653* (Cambridge: Cambridge University Press, 1974), 177–81.

[40] Sidney to Leicester, 12 October 1660, in Blencowe, 238–39. Cromwell had, in fact, also been opposed to Ireton's oath. Sidney's faulty recollection, eleven years after the fact, gives testimony to the degree to which he had come to identify Cromwell with all that had gone wrong in the Commonwealth.

[41] "An Act for subscribing the Engagement, 2 January 1650," in J. P. Kenyon, *The Stuart Constitution* (Cambridge: Cambridge University Press, 1966), 341. The moral and political consequences of loyalty oaths are explored in Don Herzog, *Happy Slaves* (Chicago: University of Chicago Press, 1989), 186–93.

gland."[42] Sidney was surely aware of these debates and may even have been prompted by them to consider the extent to which de facto rule created political obligations. By the mid-1660s he was an implacable foe of de facto theories.[43] During the 1650s, however, he was silent on this topic. To understand the development of his thought prior to the Restoration, we must rely on evidence drawn from debates ancillary to the Engagement Controversy.

One of the thorniest problems facing the Rump Parliament concerned its relationship to the English electorate. Though the Rump claimed to represent the nation, it was but the remnant of a body that had been elected in 1640. New elections could not easily be called, however, for the majority of the nation remained resolutely royalist in spite of the regicide and the constitutional revolution of February 1649. As an interim solution to this problem, and in an effort to bolster lagging attendance, the House decided in the fall of 1649 to fill a handful of seats that had been held by men who had been purged in 1648 and had subsequently died. At about the same time the Rump saw the emergence of "an effectively coordinated radical party." Led by the regicides Henry Marten and Thomas Chaloner, "the common feature of the group was its republicanism."[44] On 11 October the issues posed by the recruiter elections came to a head when the republican Henry Neville's by-election from Abingdon was disputed on the floor of the House. Sidney apparently supported the emerging coalition of republicans, for he stood as a teller, along with Henry Marten, in favor of Neville's election.[45] It was Marten who had shocked the earl of Clarendon in 1641 by proclaiming that "I do not think one man wise enough to govern us all,"[46] and Sidney's association with him suggests an increasingly radical perspective on politics.

---

[42] Marchamont Nedham, *The Case of the Commonwealth of England, Stated*, ed. Philip A. Knachel (Folger Shakespeare Library, 1969), 123. The intellectual contours of the Engagement Controversy are described by Quentin Skinner in "The Ideological Context of Hobbes's Political Thought," *Historical Journal* 9 (1966): 286–317, and in "Conquest and Consent: Thomas Hobbes and the Engagement Controversy," in *The Interregnum*, ed. G. E. Aylmer (London: Macmillan, 1972), 79–98.

[43] "He that without law brings a people under his Power I look on as a *Tyrant, Thief, publick Enemy*, against whom every man is a Souldier" (*Maxims*, 11).

[44] Worden, *Rump Parliament*, 218. Worden also identifies Edmund Ludlow, Henry Smyth, Lord Grey of Groby, Augustine Garland, James Chaloner, Henry Neville, Cornelius Holland, and Luke Robinson as members of this group (218–19). The first four of these men were regicides.

[45] *CJ*, 6:305.

[46] Edward Hyde, earl of Clarendon, *Selections from Clarendon*, ed. G. Huehns (Oxford: Oxford University Press, 1978), 27.

Significantly, however, while Neville quickly joined Marten and Chaloner at the center of the coalition, Sidney always remained on its fringes.

Though still nominally governor of Dover Castle, Sidney was increasingly an absentee commander.[47] But for a period of just over a year affairs at the castle dominated his attention. In April 1650 the Council of War initiated an investigation into Sidney's conduct, and in October new charges were brought against him by soldiers at the castle.[48] The original charges were dismissed, but "divers officers of the army" continued to agitate for his court-martial. The precise nature of the soldiers' allegations is shrouded in mystery. Lisle thought Sidney had had a "very hard measure" and ascribed his problems to "his relations to a sort of people who are looked upon with a most jealous eye."[49] The record in the *Journals of the House of Commons* is more complicated and reflects a three-way tug-of-war between the soldiers at the castle, Sidney, and the Council of State. The divisions that increasingly threatened the alliance between the army and the Rump were mirrored in and impinged upon the struggle between Sidney and his soldiers, and the case ultimately came to hinge on the relationship between military and civilian jurisdictions.[50] Though Sidney was able to escape a court-martial, on 13 May 1651 he was replaced as governor of Dover Castle by Thomas Kelsey, Cromwell's "henchman" in Kent.[51]

Freed from the burden of defending his actions at Dover Castle, Sidney embarked on a brief but active career in Parliament.[52] With increasing frequency he was named to important committees, presented reports to the House, and acted as a teller on controversial

[47] *CSPD*, 1649–1650:172, 174, 256, 265; 1650:228; HMC, *Thirteenth Report, Appendix, Part IV* (London: HMSO, 1892), 216.

[48] *CSPD*, 1650:101, 393, 399.

[49] Lisle to Leicester, 29 January 1651, in *De L'Isle*, 6:487. On 26 June 1650 Edmund Ludlow recommended Sidney to Cromwell as a fit man to serve as second-in-command to Ireton in Ireland, but Cromwell "excepted against him by reason of his relation to some who were in the King's interest" (Edmund Ludlow, *The Memoirs of Edmund Ludlow*, ed. C. H. Firth [Oxford: The Clarendon Press, 1894], 1:247).

[50] *CJ*, 6:523, 526, 528, 529, 554, 562–63, 573; *CSPD*, 1651:118, 151, 189. As one of the soldiers pressing charges against Sidney complained, "If inferior officers of the army must and ever had given obedience to immediate Comands of Parliamt and theyre Comittees without aquainting the Gen and Superiour officers, we had ever bine in a sad Condition" ("Correspondence of Captain Adam Baynes," British Library, Add. MS. 21,426, fol. 7).

[51] Everitt, *Community of Kent*, 282.

[52] In addition to his parliamentary responsibilities, on 20 October 1651 Sidney was named one of the JPs for Kent (Kent Archives Office, Q/JC 4).

bills. His career reached a new plateau on 25 November 1652, when he was elected to the Council of State.[53]

Though no record of Sidney's political views during the early 1650s has survived, we can obtain a glimpse of his interests by observing his activities in the Rump Parliament. Like his ancestors, he devoted a great deal of attention to foreign affairs. He frequently sat on committees whose responsibilities ranged from receiving foreign ministers to setting guidelines for the relations between MPs and foreign governments. He chaired a committee created to oversee Anglo-Irish relations, was a part-time member of a committee charged to effect an Anglo-Scottish union, and sat on the committees regulating trade and plantations.[54] Sidney's domestic interests were less clearly focused. He was frequently involved in decisions relating to the seizure and sale of delinquent estates. He helped select and oversee an extraparliamentary commission created to recommend reforms in the law, and at one point he opposed a bill that would have enabled MPs to serve successive terms as committee chairs or as members of the Council of State.[55]

Sidney frequently joined forces with quite radical men in undertaking his responsibilities as an MP; but at no point does he appear to have been a member of an alliance, voting bloc, or coherent movement.[56] The single most important lesson he learned during his years

[53] *CJ*, 7:220–21. Though Sidney's responsibilities increased with his position on the Council of State, there is no evidence to substantiate the claim that it was at this moment "that Sidney decided to commit himself completely to the Republic" (Jonathan Scott, *Algernon Sidney and the English Republic 1623–1677* [Cambridge: Cambridge University Press, 1988], 100).

[54] *CJ*, 7:64, 161ff., 189; *CSPD*, 1652–1653:2, 9.

[55] *CJ*, 6:587; 7:43, 58, 67, 73, 74, 112, 156, 157, 191, 222. It has been erroneously argued that Sidney actually sat on the Hale Committee for Law Reform (K.H.D. Haley, *The First Earl of Shaftesbury* [Oxford: The Clarendon Press, 1968], 68–70; Richard Ashcraft, *Revolutionary Politics & Locke's Two Treatises of Government* [Princeton: Princeton University Press, 1986], 178). As the records of the committee indicate, Sidney was not a member nor did he attend a single meeting ("Proceedings of the Hale Committee for Law Reform," British Library, Add. MS. 35,683).

[56] Scott has imaginatively argued that Sidney's closest ally in the Rump was Sir Henry Vane the younger (*Sidney*, 94–102). The evidence is more ambiguous than Scott suggests, however. For example, in a division over the highly contentious issue of the drainage of the Holland Fens, Sidney stood as a teller against Vane and in support of one of Vane's chief parliamentary opponents, Henry Marten (*CJ*, 7:118; Violet A. Rowe, *Sir Henry Vane the Younger* [London: Athlone Press, 1970], 153–54). For a similar division between Sidney and Vane, see *CJ*, 5:574. Sidney held Vane in the highest regard, but the theological and political differences between these two men are too significant for Sidney to be accurately characterized as a "Vanist." As Blair Worden observed, "Sidney valued his independence too highly to allow anyone to count on his

in the Rump was practical and not theoretical: that England could be successfully governed without a king. In later years, as he observed the decline in England's fortunes that he thought inevitably accompanied the rule of monarchs, he waxed nostalgically on the wealth, power, and independence of the Commonwealth.

England's brief experiment in republican government was brought to an end in 1653. "Extravagant mistrust and envy" had come "to inform relations between parliament and [the] army" and led directly to Cromwell's dissolution of the Rump on 20 April 1653.[57] Sidney was present on that fateful day, and his account of it—as recorded in his father's journal—captures the drama of the moment:

> The Parlement [was] sitting as usuall . . . [when] the Lord Generall Cromwell came into the House, clad in plain black clothes, with gray worsted stockings, and sate down as he used to do in an ordinary place. After a while he rose up, putt of his hat, and spake; at the first and for a good while, he spake to the commendation of the Parlement . . . but afterwards he changed his style, told them of theyr injustice, delays of justice, self-interest and other faults; then he sayd, Perhaps you thinke this is not Parlementary language, I confesse it is not, neither are you to expect any such from me. . . . After this he sayd to Corronell Harrison (who was a Member of the House) "Call them in," then Harrison went out, and presently brought . . . five or six files of musqueteers . . . then the Generall, pointing to the Speaker in his chayre, sayd to Harrison, "Fetch him downe"; Harrison went to the Speaker and spoke to him to come down, but the Speaker sate still, and sayd nothing. "Take him down," sayd the Generall; then Harrison went and pulled the Speaker by the gowne, and he came downe. It happened that day, that Algernon Sydney sate next to the Speaker on the right hand; the Generall sayd to Harrison, "Put him out," Harrison spake to Sydney to go out, but he sayd he would not go out, and sate still. The Generall sayd again, "Put him out," then Harrison and Wortley putt theyr hands upon Sydney's shoulders, as if they would force him to go out, then he rose and went towards the doore. Then the Generall went to the table where the mace lay . . . and sayd, "Take away these baubles"; so the soldiers tooke away the mace, and all the House went out.

The importance of this event to Sidney's life and ideas can hardly be exaggerated. Sidney had proven his commitment to the preservation of legal forms at the trial of Charles I; but here he, and not a rebel

---

vote" ("The Commonwealth Kidney of Algernon Sidney," *Journal of British Studies* 24 [January 1985]: 7).

[57] Worden, *Rump Parliament*, 285.

king, was the victim of Cromwell's aggressive actions. Sidney's hatred of Cromwell was deeply personal, and it is significant that he later described him as "a tyrant, and a violent one." In a way Charles I never had—perhaps never could have—Cromwell demonstrated the dangers of concentrating too much power in the hands of one man. Unwilling to compromise with the sword Cromwell had unsheathed, Sidney chose instead to enter an internal exile that was to last more than six years.[58]

Internal Exile and Return to Parliament (1653–1659)

Having failed to secure his political fortune, Sidney turned his attention to financial affairs. He purchased fee-farms, developed land-holdings, and attempted to recover funds he felt due from his service at Dover Castle.[59] Sidney's most ambitious undertaking was the management of the affairs of his brother-in-law Philip Smyth, viscount Strangford.[60] Strangford was a profligate man and, having squandered his own resources, constantly called on friends and relatives to relieve him of his debts. Sidney undertook the Herculean task of restoring Strangford's credit in 1655, apparently hoping to secure his own future in the process of meeting family obligations. The challenge proved greater than Sidney's abilities, however, and left him hopelessly bogged down in Strangford's debts. The legal entanglements entailed by Sidney's efforts also made it possible for Strangford to seize Sidney's papers and property when Sidney was out of the country on a diplomatic mission in 1659–60. Far from providing economic security, Sidney's foray into debt management left his future more uncertain than ever.[61]

---

[58] Leicester, "Journal," in Blencowe, 139–41; "Trial of Algernon Sidney," in Howell, *State Trials*, 9:866. See also: Dorothy Osborne to William Temple, 23 April 1653, in *The Letters of Dorothy Osborne to William Temple*, ed. G. C. Moore Smith (Oxford: The Clarendon Press, 1928), 38–39.

[59] Sidney to Richard Sydenham, 4 January 1653, and Sidney to Trustees for Fee Farms at Worcester House, 25 January 1653, British Library, Stowe MS. 184, fols. 269–70, 272–73; John Kellerby to Sidney, 3 June 1654, British Library, Add. MS. 15,914, fol. 118; "Accounts as Kept by John Kellerby, 1654," Kent Archives Office, De L'Isle MSS. (U1500), A14/16; "A note of what Francis Coles hath paide for Collonell Sydney for his worke in Byall Fenn," Kent Archives Office, De L'Isle MSS. (U1475), A74/1; "Petition for Subpoena of Henry Canon," June 1656, PRO, Chancery Court Records, C7 325/2.

[60] For a detailed discussion of Sidney's financial ties to Strangford, see Scott, *Sidney*, 63–67, 121–23, 161–62.

[61] Algernon Sidney, "Suit in Chancery with Philip Lord Strangford," 4 January 1678, PRO, Chancery Court Records, C7 327/50; Algernon Sidney, "Statement of Transac-

Sidney's financial condition was rendered all the more precarious by his declining family relationships. In a letter to Leicester dated 17 June 1656, Lisle—who had only recently been named custos rotulorum for Kent by Cromwell—lashed out at his brother's behavior. To amuse himself and his friends Sidney had put on a play at Penshurst, and in the process he had publicly affronted the lord protector. Legend has it that the play was Shakespeare's *Julius Caesar*, and that Sidney himself played the role of Brutus. This is coherent with Lisle's claim that members of the audience "were exceedingly pleased with the gallant relation of the chiefe actor in it, and that by applauding him they put him severall times upon it," and it resonates with Sidney's later reputation as "the British Brutus."[62] But as with so many of the legends surrounding Sidney's life, there is no evidence to substantiate this story.

Lisle's attack was personal as well as political. In the same letter he complained of the "extraordenary" fact that "the younger sonne should so dominere in your house that . . . at all times I am uncertaine whether I can have the liberty to looke into it or no, for it seames it is not only his chamber but the greate roomes of the house, and purhaps the whole, he commands." Even without Lisle's prodding, cracks and strains had begun to appear in Sidney's relationship with his father. Leicester was outraged by his son-in-law Strangford's behavior, and as Sidney became more and more involved in Strangford's affairs, Leicester's anger affected his feelings for Sidney as well.[63]

Sidney was temporarily rescued from his declining personal and financial affairs by the return of the Rump Parliament in 1659. He was present on 13 May—the first day of sessions recorded in the *Journals of the House of Commons*—and on the 14th was elected to the Council of State. His most important appearance came on 6 June. In one of a series of attempts to "bring the military sword under the power of the civil authority," two bills giving Parliament the sole power to commission army officers were brought before the House.[64] Memories of Cromwell's actions in 1653 haunted the Rump, and Sidney joined Neville and Haselrig in sponsoring the bills. They were opposed by Edmund Ludlow, one of the leading republican MPs,

---

tions with Strangfords," Kent Archives Office, De L'Isle MSS. (U1475), E28/5; Sidney to Leicester, 7 April 1658, in Collins, 2:681–82; Sidney to Leicester, 28 July 1660, in Blencowe, 191–93.

[62] Lisle to Leicester, 17 June 1656, in *De L'Isle*, 6:499.

[63] The breach between Leicester and Strangford is detailed in Julia Cartwright, *Sacharissa* (New York: Charles Scribner's Sons, 1893), 145–48.

[64] Ludlow, *Memoirs*, 2:88–89.

who feared that the bills would shatter the fragile alliance between the army and the Rump. Sidney and his allies carried the day, and the bills were decisively approved; but ultimately neither side proved victorious. During the next six months it became obvious not only that the army and the Rump were incapable of preserving their alliance, but also that neither was capable of ruling the nation by itself.

Sidney's immersion in the affairs of Westminster did not last long, for in early June he was sent as one of four plenipotentiaries to the Baltic to mediate a peace treaty between Sweden and Denmark.[65] Despite the Peace of Roskilde, which had formally ended three years of war in the Baltic in 1658, Sweden and Denmark continued to fight for control of the Sound, the channel linking the North Sea and the Baltic Sea. Because these waters were crucial to both Dutch and English shipping, a loosely organized "Concert" had been established to mediate a new treaty.[66] The "Concert" was fragile, however, for the Dutch had recently "retrieved their commercial ascendancy" over England. The principal subtext of the negotiations was the maneuvering of these two nations to gain permanent control over the valuable Baltic trade.[67]

To complicate matters, royalists in England sought to use the conflict in the Sound to advance the interests of the Orange party in Holland and thereby assist the restoration of Charles II in England. One of their principal agents was Edward Mountagu, Sidney's co-commissioner.[68] Sidney was suspicious of Mountagu's intentions and repeatedly clashed with him during August over the disposition of the En-

[65] The other commissioners were Edward Montagu, Sir Robert Honywood, and Thomas Boone. Bulstrode Whitelock declined the position, explaining that "I was not willing to undertake this service, especially to be joined with those who would expect precedency of me, who had been formerly ambassador extraordinary to Sweden alone, and I knew well the overruling temper and height of colonel Sidney" (Bulstrode Whitelocke, *Memorials of the English Affairs* [Oxford: Oxford University Press, 1853], 4:351).

[66] "Itt beinge notorious, that the Warres in the Sound, and the Balticq Sea is the maine and great obstruction of Trade in Europe" (William Nieupoort to Bulstrode Whitelock, 8 December [1659], Longleat House, Whitelocke Papers XIX, fols. 96–97). See also: Ludlow, *Memoirs*, 2:92–93; Pieter Geyl, *The Netherlands in the Seventeenth Century* (New York: Barnes and Noble, 1964), 2:41–45.

[67] J. R. Jones, *Britain and Europe in the Seventeenth Century* (London: Edward Arnold, 1966), 55–56.

[68] In late June Charles II had offered Mountagu an earldom in exchange for "the return of the Navy to its loyalty." Mountagu, in turn, promised to "venture his interest where most effective" (Charles II to Mountagu, 24 June/4 July 1659, and Mountagu to Charles II, 27 July/6 August 1659, in *Calendar of the Clarendon State Papers*, 5 vols. [Oxford: The Clarendon Press, 1872–1970], 4:246, 297). See also: Chevalier Hugues de Terlon, *Memoires*, 2 vols. (Paris: 1681), 2:475.

glish fleet. In a striking statement responding to Mountagu's plans to return the entire fleet to England, Sidney said that "he was soe much against it, that if his owne father commanded the Fleete, yet if he could any wayes in the world hinder the sayling of it, though by makinge the saylors mutinye against him, he would doe it." The hold of patriarchalism on men's minds in the seventeenth century was so strong that even Sidney, one of its strongest critics, could imagine no greater crime than disobedience to his father. Mountagu succeeded in returning the fleet to England, but his "mortal enemy" proceeded to negotiate for peace in the Baltic all the same.[69]

Like most diplomatic missions, the actual negotiations between Sweden and Denmark were long, painfully slow-moving, and filled with setbacks. Sidney found it "a businesse full of thorns" and was "very uneasy" to be "treating of peace betweene tow forraine kings, when I think I might possible be a littell more serviceable at home."[70] Together with the Dutch, he attempted to hasten the process by threatening the use of force, but it was to no avail.[71] The kings of Sweden and Denmark moved with the speed of glaciers. A series of lengthy letters from the English commissioners to the Council of State provide a wealth of detail about this process, but they reveal very little about Sidney's own political views.[72] Of far more interest are the letters he wrote to his father between 1659 and 1663. In these letters Sidney not only reflected on the negotiations in the Sound, but he also described his reactions to the momentous events taking place in England.

Restoration and Return to Exile (1659–1663)

Sidney was fiercely proud of his efforts to mediate peace in the Sound. Though frustrated by "the tedious ceremonyes and disputes,

---

[69] Edward Mountagu, *The Journal of Edward Mountagu First Earl of Sandwich*, ed. R. C. Anderson (London: Navy Records Society, 1929), 47, 60–61.

[70] Sidney to Bulstrode Whitelock, 24 August [1659], Longleat House, Whitelocke Papers XIX, fols. 74–75.

[71] The king of Sweden accused the English and Dutch negotiators of "mak[ing] Treaties upon your fleetes" (letter to Thurloe, 10 September 1659, British Library, Add. MS. 4,158, fol. 185). See also: Herbert Rowen, *John De Witt* (Princeton: Princeton University Press, 1978), 324–33; *Calendar of State Papers, Venetian*, 1659–1661:63–64, 66.

[72] Reprinted in John Thurloe, *A Collection of the State Papers of John Thurloe* (London: 1742), 7:699, 708–10, 724–27, 731–34, 741–42, 824–25, 881–82, 887. See also the letters from the commissioners to De Witt, and from Sidney to Whitelocke, listed in the Bibliography.

that are usuall in theis northerne courts," he believed that without his efforts "they would dispute and cavill for ever, without concluding anything." This could not be allowed to happen, "this ugly northern part of the world being very considerable unto the rest, and as things now stand, peace or war in the principal places of *Europe* depending upon the settlement of affairs here." Neither Sidney's mission nor the Baltic crisis was as consequential as he imagined, but it was vital to his sense of self-importance that his labors had not been wasted on an insignificant backwater. His was an important job well done; and if his successor "can but write his name, he will be able enough for any thing that remains to be done."[73]

The dissolution of the Rump by the army on 13 October 1659 forced Sidney to consider for the first time the possibility that the monarchy might be restored. He professed unconcern for the abortive royalist uprising in August of that year,[74] but he was baffled and frightened by the Rump's precipitous actions against the army in September. "I cannot imagine what could put them upon so contrary a course, destructive unto themselves, and dangerous to our long defended cause." Being "in the dark as to thoes actions amongst you," he prepared for the worst: "If the government in England doe continue on the good old principles, I shall be ready to serve them; if it returns to monarchy I desire nothing but liberty to retire, finding myself a very unfit stone for such a building." As he unflinchingly proclaimed, "for theis many years, [I] have bin engaged in that cause, which by the help of God I shall never desert."[75]

Sidney shed light on his conception of the "cause" to which he had devoted his energies during his negotiations in the Baltic. Presented with an autograph album at the University of Copenhagen, he inscribed the following motto:

> Manus haec inimica tyrannis
> Ense petit placidam sub libertate quietem.
>
> [This hand, hostile to tyrants,
> seeks by the sword the tranquil peace of freedom.][76]

[73] Sidney to Leicester, 13 September 1659, in Blencowe, 163; Sidney to Downing, 7 April 1660, in Thurloe, *State Papers*, 7:887; Sidney to Leicester, 5 November 1659, in Collins, 2:683–84; Sidney to Leicester, 23 June 1660, in Collins, 2:689–90.

[74] Sidney to Leicester, 13 September 1659, in Blencowe, 167–68. Cf. Sidney to Whitelock, 24 August [1659], Longleat House, Whitelocke Papers XIX, fols. 74–75.

[75] Sidney to Whitelocke, 13 November 1659, in Blencowe, 169–73.

[76] The full text of Sidney's motto was first printed by Molesworth, who embellished on it by adding that the French ambassador to the Danish court tore it out of the album because he considered it "a *Libel* upon the *French* government" ([Lord Molesworth], "Preface," *An Account of Denmark* [London: 1694]). According to Jean Baptiste Lantin,

Less dramatically but no less adamantly, he insisted that "the warre [against Charles I] in which I was engaged" was "undertaken upon good grounds, and . . . it was the part of an honest man to pursue them heartily." As he explained in his "Apology" twenty-three years later, "I had from my youth endeavoured to uphold the common rights of mankind, the lawes of this land, and the true Protestant religion, against corrupt principles, arbitrary power, and Popery." Charles I had threatened each of these causes, and thus he had been justly opposed.[77]

Sidney's radical principles did not lead him to reject the Restoration outright, however. Indeed, just three days after Charles II's landing at Dover, Sidney professed to his father that "since the Parliament hath acknowledged a king, I knowe, and acknowledge, I owe him the duty and the service that belongs unto a subject, and will pay it." At the same time, he knew that "the cause and root of all the bitternesse against me, is from my stiffe adherence to the party they [the royalists] hate. I doe not wonder at it; the reason is sufficient; but that which the King cannot avow, without contradicting the very grounds upon which he doth promise to governe."[78] Therein lay the irony of Sidney's situation. Because the king had been brought to power by Parliament, Sidney was willing to acknowledge his legitimacy. But for Charles II to have admitted that his reign was founded in the actions of Parliament would have been tantamount to accepting the radical doctrines of popular or parliamentary sovereignty. Under the circumstances, the ideological needs of the Restoration overrode its factual basis, and Sidney was unable to reconcile himself to it.

Sidney's reluctance to return to England was not simply the consequence of his radical principles, however. It was also the result of his "stiffe adherence" to "the rules of honour and conscience" and his unyielding determination to be consistent. Sidney would not recant

---

the motto included the ascription "Philippus Sidney" (Bibliotheque Nationale, Fr. MS. 23,254, fol. 101, quoted in Scott, *Sidney*, 133). Even this most sacred of Sidney texts may not be immune to historical criticism, however. It was pointed out in the nineteenth century that Sidney never acknowledged having written anything more than the first line (Chester N. Greenough, "Algernon Sidney and the Motto of the Commonwealth of Massachusetts," *Proceedings of the Massachusetts Historical Society* 51 [1917–18]: 262; cf. Leicester to Sidney, 30 August 1660, and Sidney to Leicester, 21 September 1660, in Blencowe, 210–11, 216). It has also been suggested that the first line was a quotation, since it was apparently granted by patent in 1616 to another man (*Notes and Queries*, 3rd ser., 9 [January–June 1866]: 196–97).

[77] Sidney to Leicester, 21 September 1660, in Blencowe, 222; "Apology," 3.

[78] Sidney to Leicester, 28 May 1660, in Blencowe, 186; Sidney to Leicester, 26 September 1660, in Blencowe, 231.

his past and looked with horror on the "vile and unworthy submissions, acknowledgment of errors, asking of pardon, or the like" that would have been required of him on his return to England. Like his ancestors, he was a man of enormous pride, and he believed himself incapable "of base compliance with fortune."[79]

Supplementing these two reasons for not returning to England was Sidney's fear for his safety. Though General Monck had both publicly and privately expressed his support during the spring and summer of 1660—perhaps, thought Sidney, because of "the ancient friendship that was between us"—Sidney never trusted Monck alone to protect him from the reactionary forces that had gained control of England.[80] Sir Arthur Haselrig's fate had amply proven the limits to Monck's power.[81] Moreover, "many things are more to be apprehended than a hatchet": "I have too well learnt, under the government of the Cromwells, what it is to live under the protection of thoes unto whome I am thought an enemy, to expose myself willingly unto the same . . . I shall be ever suspected, and often affronted, and upon every littell tumult that may happen, be exposed to ruine."[82] Sidney may have exaggerated the dangers he would have faced in Restoration England. But he was convinced that he could not live in peace under the rule of Charles II.

Only gradually did Sidney recognize the insurmountability of these obstacles to his return to England. After concluding the negotiations in the Baltic on 27 May 1660, he drifted between Copenhagen and Stockholm. Having little inclination for France, and disliking "all the drunken countries of Germany, and the north," he finally resolved on traveling to Rome. "I choose this voluntary exile, as the least evil condition that is within my reach. It is bitter, but not soe much soe, as the others that are in my prospect."[83]

In his letters Sidney returned again and again to three explana-

---

[79] Sidney to Leicester, 22 May 1660, in Collins, 2:686–87; Sidney to Leicester, 30 August 1660, in Blencowe, 195; Sidney to Leicester, 21 September 1660, in Blencowe, 223. In late 1660 Sidney wrote that he would "submitte" to the king but would not "recant, renounce, and aske pardon" (Sidney to Leicester, 26 September 1660, in Blencowe, 233).

[80] Sidney to Leicester, 16 June 1660, in Collins, 2:688–89. See also: "Apology," 3; Monck to the States General, 26 April 1660, in Thurloe, *State Papers*, 7:909.

[81] Sidney to Leicester, 21 September 1660, and 19 November 1660, in Blencowe, 226, 241. "The final achievement of Monck's efforts on behalf of Hesilrige was that Sir Arthur died in the Tower instead of upon the scaffold" (Ronald Hutton, *The Restoration* [Oxford: The Clarendon Press, 1985], 164).

[82] Sidney to Leicester, 28 July 1660, and 21 September 1660, in Blencowe, 189–90, 227.

[83] Sidney to Leicester, 28 July 1660, in Blencowe, 190–91.

tions for the bleakness of his exile: his deteriorating relationship with his father, his loss of financial independence, and his desire to live in England. Sidney's relationship with his father had been steadily worsening since the middle of the 1650s. When Sidney departed for the Baltic in the summer of 1659, it ruptured completely. Only one of Leicester's letters to Sidney during this period has survived, and it is petty and abusive. Leicester chided his son for not having written more often; he accused Sidney of having left him "sick, solitary, and sad" following the death of his wife on 20 August 1659; and he cultivated an overwhelming sense of unfulfilled filial obligation by referring to his imminent retirement "to my poor habitation, having for myself no other dessein, than to pass the small remainder of my dayes, innocently and quietly, and, if it please God, to be gathered in peace to my father."[84] Leicester was given to morose self-pity, and he had refined these techniques of emotional blackmail over a lifetime.[85] Their effect was to leave Sidney utterly despondent.[86]

Closely related to Sidney's desire to restore his relationship with his father was his increasing fear of economic dependence and poverty. The Strangfords had stolen the inheritance he had received on his mother's death, and Leicester had withdrawn all financial support. Though he had "a small provision for my maintenance, that will serve me perhaps tow years, in such a condition as I intend to put myself in," one of the primary reasons he had chosen to travel to Rome was his expectation of some sort of "businesse" there.[87]

We have reason to suspect that Sidney was neither as parsimonious nor as impoverished as he reported to his father.[88] But as a middle-aged bachelor in a foreign land he had begun to worry about his future: "At my age, growing very near forty, and giving marks of declining by the colour of my hair, it is time that I had something which

---

[84] Leicester to Sidney, 30 August 1660, in Blencowe, 203–8. Though sworn into Charles II's Privy Council on 31 May 1660, Leicester took leave of the court and returned to Penshurst on 12 October (Leicester, "Journal," in Blencowe, 158–60).

[85] Cf. Leicester to Northumberland, 17 February 1658, in De L'Isle, 6:500–501.

[86] One need only read the opening lines of Sidney's letters to his father during this period to see the impact Leicester's conduct had on him. On 29 January 1661, for example, Sidney wrote that "according to my custom, I give your Lordship this testimony of my being alive; which I think necessary, since your Lordship gives me no sign of remembering I am so" (in Collins, 2:704).

[87] Sidney to Leicester, 21 September 1660, and 26 September 1660, in Blencowe, 226, 234.

[88] From Rome an Englishman wrote, "Here is one Colonel Sidney. . . . He has put himself here into very great equippage, his coach and three lackeys" (Robert Southwell to Sir John Percivalle, 23 December 1660, in HMC, *Report on the Manuscripts of the Earl of Egmont*, vol. 1, part 2, 616).

I may call my own, out of which I may in rest have bread, when fortune hath taken from me all means of gaining it by my industry." Though treated with "humanity and civility" by the Italians, Sidney knew "in a strange land, how farre thoes civilities doe extend, and that they are too aery to feed and cloathe a man."[89] Once again the economic insecurity of which he had first complained in 1643 returned to haunt him.

Finally, Sidney's exile was bitter for the simple reason that he loved his native land and wanted to return to it. Soon after the Restoration he claimed to have "nothing more in my thoughts, then to return into *England* with as much expedition as I can."[90] He never strayed from that hope.

While in Rome Sidney frequented the papal court. Though appalled by Catholic ceremonies,[91] he was charmed by the resident cardinals, among whom he found "some of . . . the most extraordinary persons that ever I met with."[92] The distractions these friendships provided were limited, however, and the emotional strains of exile drove Sidney deeper and deeper into depression. He grew melancholic, complained of headaches, and delighted in solitude and "conversation . . . with birds, trees, and books."[93] Truth itself became a burden: "He that is naked, alone, and without help in the open sea, is lesse unhappy in the night, when he may hope the land is neare, than in the day, when he sees it is not, and that there is no possibility of safety." "Stupidity" was "an advantage" under such conditions, and so he "artificially increase[d] it" so that he might "rest well enough at ease, in a dull indolence."[94]

A temporary respite from this desperate condition was provided in 1661, when an Italian prince invited Sidney to live at his villa in Frascati, just outside Rome. Given his penury, Sidney quickly accepted. Frascati lacked the diversions of Rome—Sidney lived "as a hermite in a palace"—but its solitude brought rewards of its own. As he wrote in early June, "I have applied myself to study a little more than I have done formerly; and though one who begins at my age cannot hope to make any considerable progress that way, I find so much satisfac-

[89] Sidney to Leicester, 23 June 1661, in Blencowe, 248.

[90] Sidney to Leicester, 23 June 1661, in Collins, 2:688–89.

[91] Sidney to Leicester, 29 December 1660, 18 February 1661, 8 April 1661, in Collins, 2:701–11.

[92] Sidney to Leicester, 29 December 1660, in Collins, 2:701–4.

[93] Sidney to Leicester, 3 June 1661, in Collins, 2:718–20. See also: Sidney to Leicester, 22 April 1661, in Collins, 2:716–18; Sidney to Leicester, 19 November 1660, in Blencowe, 242.

[94] Sidney to Leicester, 23 June 1661, in Blencowe, 249.

tion in it, that for the future I shall very unwillingly (though I had the opportunity) put myself into any way of living that shall deprive me of that entertainment." Every day he read from sunrise until "six or seaven of the clock at night," and many of the cramped references that fill the pages of the *Court Maxims* and the *Discourses Concerning Government* no doubt owe their origin to this period in Sidney's life.[95]

Rebellion and Exile in France (1663–1677)

In the fall of 1663 Sidney visited a small band of republican exiles living at Vevey, on the shores of Lake Geneva. According to the leader of the community, Edmund Ludlow, Sidney's motives for leaving Italy were political:

> The Divisions of our Enemyes [in England] began to heighten the hopes of friends touching the Approaching of our deliverance, In so much, that Colonell Algernon Sidney. . . . now [thought] it seasonable to draw towards his Native Country, in Expectation of an opportunity wherein he might be more Active for their Service; and in his way was pleased to favour us with a visit . . . expressing himselfe to us, with much affection & friendship; and to the Publique with much faithfulness not in the least declyning to owne us, & the despised Cause for which we suffered.[96]

Ludlow's "Cause" was Protestant radicalism, and it is clear from Sidney's writings that he was deeply troubled by the persecution of Dissenters in Restoration England. He was also haunted by the execution in 1662 of his friend and parliamentary ally Sir Henry Vane. His mood was signaled by the motto he inscribed in the visitor's book of the Calvinist Academy in Geneva in 1663: "*Sit Sanguinis Ultor Justorum* (Let there be revenge for the blood of the just)."[97] It was not until 1665, however, that Sidney and Ludlow were to foment revolution, and then only as a consequence of England's entry into the Second Dutch War.

Tensions between England and the Low Countries had been escalating since the Restoration. Commercial interests in England provided a great deal of the pressure for war, but they were complemented by political and dynastic considerations. Charles II, strapped by the financial settlement obtained at the Restoration, hoped that

---

[95] Sidney to Leicester, 23 June 1661, in Blencowe, 247; Sidney to Leicester, 3 June 1661, in Collins, 2:718–20; Sidney to Leicester, 23 June 1661, in Blencowe, 248.

[96] Edmund Ludlow, "A Voyce from the Watch Tower," Bodleian Library, MS. Eng. History C487, fol. 977.

[97] Quoted in Scott, *Sidney*, 171.

the destruction of Dutch commercial power would increase the Crown's customs revenues and render him less dependent on parliamentary grants of supply. He also hoped to subvert Holland's republican constitution, thereby enabling the House of Orange—to which he was related by blood—to return to power.[98]

Into this tangled web of national and international affairs stepped the English republicans. On 26 May 1665, several months after the outbreak of the Second Dutch War, Sir George Downing reported from the Hague "that Ludlow, Algernon Sydney and others of that gang are in this country and have private conferences with some in the government." Downing was sufficiently alarmed by the negotiations between the English republicans and John De Witt, the grand pensionary of Holland, that he set about tracking their movements: "I am also trying what I can do to find out what *Ludlow* and his complices are doing. For certain, both he and *Sidney* were very lately *at Amsterdam*; and, by *De Witts advice*, they and the rest of them are scattered for a time severall wayes, to avoyd theyr being too much talked of, and because, as *De Witt* let them know, matters were not yet ripe for them, by reason of the *late defeate* [at Lowestoft]. . . . All is yett in theory, but that *one Captain Philips* is sudainly to *goe for England* to sound and prepare humours there, that so they may have something of grounded to propose to *De Witt*."[99] The promise of an alliance with De Witt was not the only thing that drew Sidney to Holland (Ludlow had, in fact, remained in Switzerland). The combination of religious toleration, a free press, and a lax attitude toward extradition treaties made the Low Countries an ideal refuge for religious and political exiles from England.[100] Among such men there were potent resources for a revolutionary movement.

Unknown to Downing, however, a "bone of contention . . . touching the Tearmes on which to Engage with the Hollanders" had already developed between Sidney and Ludlow. After the Restoration the Dutch had extradited three English regicides, who were subsequently executed for treason. Ludlow was "cleare in [his] conscience" that the Dutch magistrates were "Guilty of that blood, and . . . that whoever confederates & Acts with such a people . . . before that

[98] Geyl, *Netherlands*, 2:54–57; Jones, *Britain and Europe*, 55–58. Sidney discussed both of these aims in *Maxims*, 158–79. See also: Ludlow, "Voyce," fol. 1017.

[99] Downing to Clarendon, 26 May 1665, in *Calendar of the Clarendon State Papers*, 5:487; Downing to Clarendon, 23 June 1665, in T. H. Lister, *Life and Administration of Edward, First Earl of Clarendon* (London: 1837), 3:388.

[100] Keith Sprunger, *Dutch Puritanism* (Leiden: E. J. Brill, 1982), 397–98, and 397–456 passim; James Walker, "The English Exiles in Holland During the Reigns of Charles II and James II," *Transactions of the Royal Historical Society*, 5th ser., 30 (1948): 111–25.

blood be repented of & avenged, become p[ar]taker of their Sin." He would not cooperate with the Dutch until they had cleansed their house of sin. Confessions must be offered, transgressions must be punished, forgiveness must be sought. Sidney recognized that Ludlow's intransigence posed an insurmountable barrier to an alliance with the Dutch and prudentially argued that it was "rediculous to looke backward." But Ludlow was unyielding: in matters of the spirit, there could be no compromise.[101]

The contrast between Ludlow's religion-based ethic of conscience and Sidney's flexible consequentialism is striking and points to a radical divergence in their conceptions of republicanism. For Ludlow, an English republic was to be the new Zion, and hence its origins had to be free of all human corruption; for Sidney, it was to be a nation free of corrupt Stuart monarchs, and any steps necessary to achieve that end were acceptable.

Even had the English republicans been united, De Witt was unwilling to assist them. He feared that the diversion of so many Dutch troops and the threat of a republican concert in northern Europe would induce the French to attack and ruin Holland. And he sincerely doubted that "while the parliament was so firm to the king, any discontents could be carried so far as to a general rising."[102] This left the English republicans with a difficult decision: should they seek the assistance of France, which had entered the war against England in January 1666?[103] Ludlow was suspicious of the French and declined to take part in the trip to Paris; but Sidney plunged ahead, arriving in early May 1666. There he applied to Louis XIV for extensive financial and military support, but he was offered only a small sum of money and the promise of further assistance should the rebels prove successful in their plans.[104] Sidney's willingness to undertake this journey testifies to his desperation and to his complete lack of understanding of French politics. The French had no permanent interest in the creation of an English republic. If Louis XIV often refused to

---

[101] Ludlow, "Voyce," fol. 1056. See also: fols. 1017, 1079–82, 1105; *Maxims*, 168, 172.

[102] Burnet, *History of His Own Time*, 1:414–15.

[103] Though De Witt feigned ignorance of the English republicans' plans for an alliance with France, the idea apparently originated with him (De Witt to Van Beuningen, 4 March 1666 [N.S.], in John De Witt, *Brieven, Geschreven ende gewisselt tusschen de Heer Johan De Witt* [Gravenhage: Hendrick Scheurleer, 1725], 2:205; Ludlow, "Voyce," fols. 1111, 1115).

[104] Ludlow, "Voyce," fol. 1123; Louis XIV, *Memoires pour les années 1661 et 1666* (Paris: Editions Bossard, 1923), 213. But compare the judgment of Van Beuningen, the Dutch ambassador in Paris: "Het is't gevoelen van meest alle Heeren hier, Angliam secure debellari posse conctando, quod Lionne & Turenne & Sidney videtur. Nisi commode conjunctio fieri possit" (Van Beuningen to De Witt, in De Witt, *Brieven*, 2:267).

help Charles II suppress his domestic opponents, it was simply because he saw that the pressure they applied cemented the English monarch to him all the more firmly.[105] Louis XIV's sole aim with regard to England was to render it weak and dependent, so that he would have a free hand to act on the Continent. A revolution, particularly a republican one, could have no place in such plans.

Several months after Sidney traveled to Paris an informant in Holland reported that "Sidney is att present writinge a Treatise in defence of a Republique, & against Monarchy, & designes it soone or late for the presse."[106] This may have been a reference to Sidney's *Court Maxims*, a collection of dialogues between "Eunomius the Commonwealthman" and "Philalethos a morall Honest Courtier & Lover of State Truth."[107] The *Court Maxims* is a curious document. Though Sidney may have intended it for publication, the surviving manuscript is ungainly and incomplete. Its style is ragged, and its arguments are alternately skeptical or dogmatic, finely honed or obtuse. The apparent polemical purpose of the *Court Maxims* was to convince Ludlow and others that the English and the Dutch had a common interest in the advance of republicanism, but its arguments were pitched at a level of abstraction far beyond the needs of an incidental tract. The contents of the *Court Maxims* will be explored in Part 2 of this book. What needs emphasis here are two related facts revealed by the *Court Maxims*: that Sidney tended to think of local or specific events in global or universal terms; and that he sought to justify his actions and mobilize the support of others through the composition of a political treatise.

The same informant who drew attention to Sidney's "Treatise" also reported "that Colonel Sidney is in great esteem with Dewitt, and often in consultation with Benjamin Turly [*sic*] the quaker."[108] Furly was evidently a man of great parts. He assisted William Penn in his fight for religious toleration, provided shelter to John Locke during his exile in Holland, and was a close friend of the third earl of Shaftesbury. He was also inclined to religious mysticism. At the time Sidney first met him, Furly was engaged in "the Hat Controversy," a war against all external formalities in Quakerism. As Furly wrote a friend in 1662, "Are we not called unto liberty from all yoakes & bonds in all outward things, ought we to suffer our selves to be thus judged in

---

[105] David Ogg, *England in the Reign of Charles II* (Oxford: Oxford University Press, 1934), 1:289.

[106] William Scot to Lord Arlington, c. 18–21 August 1666, in W. J. Cameron, *New Light on Aphra Behn* (Auckland: University of Auckland Monograph No. 5, 1961), 47.

[107] *Maxims*, 1.

[108] Scot to Arlington, 12 September 1666, in Cameron, *Aphra Behn*, 73.

meats, drinkes, times, places, Cloths, gestures, or postures in the worship of God?"[109] Furly's extreme individualism and his emphasis on the priority of inner light over outward form may have resonated with Sidney's own belief in the importance of personal integrity.[110] Furley's spiritual doctrines may also have made sense of Sidney's intense inner struggles. Sidney was evidently anxious to believe that his actions originated in a higher source than his own tortured soul. In a letter to Furly that was probably written in 1665 or 1666 Sidney asked that "you and all our friends . . . seeke God for me, praying him to defend me from outward enemyes, but more especially from thoes that are within me, and that he would give me such a steady knowledge of truth, as I may be constantly directed in seeking that which is truly good. This being obtained, all other things will followe." Somewhat more bizarrely, in 1666 Sidney sent Furly a copy of a medieval prophecy. Annotated to establish its relevance to the conflict in northern Europe, it predicted that a cataclysmic war would destroy "the greatest part of the World," leaving "the Son of Man" (England) and "the Eagle" (the Emperor) victorious, establishing "Peace over all the World," and permitting "the sonne of man" to "passe to the land of promise."[111]

Sidney's communications to Furly are difficult to fathom. He appealed to God's active hand in history throughout his life, and it is quite possible that during his difficult years of exile he found solace in Furly's radical Protestantism. At the same time, Sidney's spiritual confessions have a chameleon-like quality to them: they are strongest in those letters and documents directed at men known to be receptive to such ideas. Sidney was undoubtedly sincere in his professions of faith in God, and he clearly sympathized with the plight of Dissenters in England. But it is difficult to escape the conclusion that at least some of his statements were strategic and that he tapered his arguments to suit his audience.

Despite the efforts of the English radicals, revolution in England was not forthcoming. Renouncing all hope, Sidney withdrew to the

---

[109] Quoted in William I. Hull, *Benjamin Furly and Quakerism in Rotterdam* (Swarthmore, PA: Swarthmore College Monograph on Quaker History No. 5, 1941), 14.

[110] According to Burnet, Sidney "seemed to be a Christian, but in a particular form of his own; he thought it was to be like a divine philosophy of the mind; but he was against all public worship, and every thing that looked like a church" (Burnet, *History of His Own Time*, 2:351). In the *Court Maxims* Sidney drew a distinction between "exteriour Unction" and "true spiritual unction" (44).

[111] Sidney to Furly, [1665/1666?], in Blencowe, 260; Algernon Sidney, "A Prophesy of St. Thomas the Martyr," Bodleian Library, MS. Eng. Letters C200, fol. 24. On the medieval origin of this prophecy, see Keith Thomas, *Religion and the Decline of Magic* (Harmondsworth: Penguin Books, 1973), 468.

south of France, pursuing the "half burial" he had once described to his father. He was to remain there for almost eleven years, punctuating his retirement with brief bursts of activity. Despite recent discoveries—most notably a letter written by Sidney in 1677—it is virtually impossible to obtain a clear or convincing portrait of Sidney's life during this period. The knowledge we have is too sketchy, too often based on brief comments and on second- or thirdhand reports, to permit any but the most tentative of interpretations. The bare facts are these: By late 1666 Sidney was in hiding in Montpellier. His contacts in Brussels alternately thought him a potential asset to the English government and a dangerous man with whom to be associated.[112] In 1670 Sidney briefly surfaced in Paris. According to Marshal Turenne, a prominent Huguenot and leading figure in the French army, Sidney desired to be of assistance to Charles II. Among the many views Sidney expressed, Turenne found two particularly noteworthy: that freedom of conscience was the only means of binding English Dissenters to their monarch;[113] and that the English people eagerly anticipated the destruction of the Dutch.[114] On learning of these remarks, Charles II stated that they were consonant with his own views. He declined Sidney's offer of service, however, arguing that Sidney posed too great a threat to be permitted to return to England. Instead, at his behest Sidney was banished to the town of Nerac, in the province of Languedoc.[115]

Despite Charles II's misgivings, in July 1673 he granted Sidney a

[112] [?] to Sam Cottington, 26 April 1667, PRO, SP77/36, fol. 205; Sir William Temple to [Arlington], 29 April 1667, PRO, SP77/36, fol. 208. See also: Temple to Sidney, 29 April 1667, in *The Works of Sir William Temple, Bart.*, 4 vols. (Edinburgh: 1754), 3:70–71.

[113] Turenne's conversation is reported in Louis XIV to Colbert, 29 July 1670, Ministere des Affaires Étrangeres Correspondance Politique Angleterre 99, fol. 270. Scott mistranslates the second half of the following quotation, falsely reporting it as Sidney's view and not that of the Dissenters: "Que les Presbiteriens et independans ne soufriront jamais tranquilement de n'avoir pas de liberté de conscience et qu'ils ont moins de hayne pour la religion catholique que pour le gouvernement des Évesques" (Scott, *Sidney*, 233).

[114] Sidney also stated that among the principal aims of the Rump had been "la ruine des holandois" and "une estroite union avec la france" (Louis XIV to Colbert, 29 July 1670, Ministere des Affaires Étrangeres Correspondance Politique Angleterre 99, fol. 270). As Scott rightly notes, this is difficult to square with every other known statement of Sidney's concerning the interests of the English and Dutch republics (Scott, *Sidney*, 233–34). Without additional information, however, it is impossible to determine whether either statement was intended to persuade Charles II to adopt a pro-French, anti-Dutch policy.

[115] Colbert to Louis XIV, 4 August 1670, PRO, 31/3/125, fol. 227; Colbert to Louis XIV, 25 August 1670, in Dalrymple, *Memoirs*, Vol. 2, Appendix to Part 1, p. 61.

pass to return to England. Neither the reasons for the king's change of heart nor Sidney's motives for refusing to take advantage of the pass have been preserved.[116] All that is known with certainty is that Sidney remained in southern France for another four years.

Though Sidney was involved in the local life of Nerac and was familiar with the leading aristocrats of the region—he advised the duc du Buillion on the management of his estate and may have known the duc de la Rouchefoucauld—he evidently found his exile painful.[117] By late 1676 he had overcome all his reservations and aggressively sought permission to return to England. As he explained to Henry Savile, younger brother of the marquis of Halifax, "there is hardly any worldly thing . . . that I doe soe earnestly desire [as to return to England], both in regard of seeing my freinds and setting my private affaires."[118] Through Savile's efforts a pass was issued on 19 May 1677 "for Algernon Sidney to repair into England about his lawful occasions." Crossing through the Channel Islands, Sidney arrived in England in early September. Of the debt he felt to Savile, "I so far acknowledge it to be the greatest that I have in a long time received from any man, as not to value [it] . . . at a lower rate than the saving of my life."[119]

Return to Politics (1677–1683)

Sidney returned to England in hopes of seeing his friends, restoring his inheritance, and "rendering summe service unto my old father." Revolution appears to have been the furthest thing from his mind. As he explained to Benjamin Furly, "If it please God to give successe

[116] *CSPD*, 1673:459. The latter may have had something to do with the machinations of Sidney's brother, Henry, who was attempting to use Sidney's absence to cement his control over their father's will (Sidney, "Notes concerning an action in chancery," Kent Archives Office, De L'Isle MSS. [U1475], L5).

[117] Sidney to Bafoy, January [1677], Archives Nationales, R2/82. Two radically different interpretations of this recently discovered letter have been published: Scott, *Sidney*, 239–45, and John Carswell, *The Porcupine: The Life of Algernon Sidney* (London: John Murray, 1989), 156–61. I am inclined to Carswell's reading, which is more sympathetic to Sidney, though in distinction to both of these scholars I believe that the letter demonstrates Sidney to be anxiously outside of or marginal to the lives of the great aristocrats of Languedoc. Additional evidence of Sidney's loneliness in exile can be found in: Du Moulin to Halifax, 21 October 1676, Chatsworth House, Du Moulin Letters, 21.9.

[118] Sidney to Savile, 5/15 February 1677, Longleat House, Coventry Papers, Appendix, vol. 2, fol. 134. See also: Mountagu to [?], [November 1676], Longleat House, Coventry Papers, 34, fol. 226.

[119] *CSPD*, 1677–1678:136; Sidney to Savile, 18 December 1676, in *Letters*, 169–70.

unto my endeavours in composing them, I shall have nothing relating unto this world soe much at heart, as the desire of retiring from hence, without any thought of ever returning, and carrying with me that which may be sufficient to purchase a convenient habitation in Gascony, not farre from Bordeaux, where I may in quiet finish thoes dayes that God hath appointed for me."[120] God did indeed "give successe unto" Sidney's "endeavours," but only after he had required Sidney to endure a stint in jail and a series of "vexatious" lawsuits. Sidney even purchased "a small parcell of ground" in France "with an intention of going immediately unto it."[121] But soon he was drawn into a series of political and religious controversies that rocked the nation and brought him to the scaffold.

Though the Restoration had been intended to bring order to the nation, England's "political life was chronically unhealthy during almost the whole period between 1660 and 1688." Englishmen "inhabited a world of change and uncertainty, of sensational plots and conspiracies, of endless personal intrigue and maneuvering, of widespread corruption and almost universal cynicism."[122] Two crises begun in 1678 set in motion a chain of events that raised fundamental constitutional questions and threatened to topple the regime: Parliament's attack on Charles II's leading minister, the earl of Danby; and the revelation of the Popish Plot.

Danby's assertion of the prerogative, his efforts to free the court from its financial dependence on Parliament, his strict and intolerant Anglicanism, his corruption of Parliament: all these had made him an object of anger and resentment during the 1670s. Even so manifestly moderate a politician as the marquis of Halifax felt a burning hatred toward him. Danby's ministry was particularly important because it helped give shape to an emerging opposition movement. As one of the principal architects of "the Church and Cavalier Party,"[123] Danby aggressively pursued a set of policies based on the proposition

---

[120] Sidney to Furly, 29 November 1677, in *Original Letters of Locke; Algernon Sidney; and Anthony Lord Shaftesbury*, ed. T. Forster (London: J. B. Nichols and Son, 1830), 79–81.

[121] "Apology," 4. The details of Sidney's lawsuits are contained in: "Notes concerning a bill to be exhibited in Chancery," Kent Archives Office, De L'Isle MSS. (U1475), L5; "Suit in Chancery with Philip Lord Strangford," PRO, Chancery Court Records, C7 327/50; "The Case of Algernone and Henry Sydney, referred to Sir William Jones," British Library, Egerton MS. 1049, fol. 9.

[122] J. R. Jones, *Country and Court: England, 1658–1714* (Cambridge, MA: Harvard University Press, 1979), 1. "It was no accident that the word 'sham' was coined during this period" (3).

[123] The phrase is Keith Feiling's (*A History of the Tory Party* [Oxford: The Clarendon Press, 1924], 136).

that strict loyalty to the established order was the only effective bul-wark against the return of civil war. It was Danby's proposed Test Oath of 1675—which required MPs to swear that they would not "at any time endeavour the Alteration of the Government, either in Church or State"—that led the earl of Shaftesbury and his supporters to decry the existence of "*a distinct Party*" composed of "the High Episcopal Man, and the Old Cavalier." To an increasing number of Englishmen, Danby's ministry presaged the erection of "an *Absolute* and *Arbitrary* Government" on the twin rocks of Church and Crown.[124]

The political maelstrom engulfing Danby's ministry was strength-ened by the discovery of the Popish Plot. In August 1678 Titus Oates, a man gifted in the art of fabricating conspiracies, revealed to the horror of all England that the Jesuits planned to assassinate Charles II, massacre large numbers of Protestants, and place the king's Cath-olic brother James, duke of York, on the throne. Oates's lurid tale was filled with inconsistencies, but it confirmed long-held English be-liefs about Catholics and conveniently played into the hands of op-position politicians. As the earl of Shaftesbury once remarked, "I will not say who started the Game, but I am sure I had the full hunting of it."[125]

By his own admission Sidney was "infected" with the common be-lief that the Popish Plot was true.[126] He was also deeply implicated in the campaign against Danby. According to the Comte D'Avaux, the French ambassador to the Netherlands, Sidney was instrumental in mobilizing opposition to the Anglo-Dutch alliance pursued by Danby in early 1678. D'Avaux himself took credit for convincing Sidney that "nothing could be more prejudicial to the parliament of England, and the republic of Holland, than to allow the King of Great Britain, to make an alliance with the Prince of Orange, for it was certainly intended to hurt the common liberty."[127] Sidney did not need to be persuaded of that fact, however, for he had long feared that an alli-ance between the houses of Orange and Stuart would permit both kings to reign without benefit of representative institutions. This be-

[124] [Anthony Ashley Cooper], *A Letter From a Person of Quality, To His Friend In the Country* (1675), 9, 1, 29. Danby's place in Anglican royalism is detailed in Mark Goldie, "Danby, the Bishops, and the Whigs," in *Conscience and Authority*, ed. T. Harris, P. Sea-ward, and M. Goldie (Oxford: Blackwell, 1990).

[125] Quoted in J. R. Jones, *The First Whigs: The Politics of the Exclusion Crisis 1678–1683* (London: Oxford University Press, 1961), 23.

[126] Sidney to Savile, 7 April 1679, in *Letters*, 24.

[127] Jean Jacques de Mesmes, Count D'Avaux, *The Negotiations of Count D'Avaux* (Lon-don: A. Millar, D. Wilson, T. Durham, 1754), 1:9–10.

lief remained a polestar for his political conduct throughout the coming constitutional crisis.[128]

Unknown to D'Avaux, Sidney had a much more profound reason for opposing Danby's ambitions, for according to Sidney it was Danby, along with his predecessors Hyde and Clifford, who had engineered the corruption of England's constitutional government. As even the "weakest of all Ministers" could see, the "lewd young men" first elected to Parliament in 1660 were "such as . . . might be easily deluded, corrupted, or bribed. . . . Many knew not what they did when they annulled the Triennial Act, voted the Militia to be in the king, gave him the Excise, Customs and Chimney-mony, made the Act for Corporations . . . pass'd the five mile Act, and that for Uniformity in the Church. This embolden'd the Court to think of making Parliaments to be the instruments of our Slavery, which had in all Ages past bin the firmest pillars of our Liberty."[129] Sidney was particularly distressed by the plight of Dissenters in Restoration England, but his bill of complaints spanned the whole of the monarchy. With even greater vehemence than Shaftesbury, he identified Danby with a lengthy, violent, and partisan campaign of religious and political repression.

It was undoubtedly this deep-seated animus against the Restoration monarchy that led Sidney into closer cooperation with the French. According to Paul Barillon, the French ambassador to England, in late 1678 Sidney helped to manage the correspondence between the French and members of the opposition concerning plans to impeach Danby.[130] This was probably not the first time, and certainly not the last, that Barillon and Sidney worked together. To Barillon, Sidney was "a man of great views and very high designs, which tend to the establishment of a republick." Because he had "a great deal of credit amongst the independents and [was] also intimate with those who are the most opposite to the court in parliament," he was a useful tool for advancing Louis XIV's plan "to prevent England from being re-united by an accomodation between his Britannick Majesty and his parliament." To Sidney, in turn, Barillon was a potent ally in the undeclared war against the union of the Orange and Stuart monarchies. Sidney even hoped to use his contacts with Barillon to convince Louis XIV that he had been mistaken when he re-

---

[128] Barillon to Louis XIV, 14 December 1679 and 30 September 1680, in Dalrymple, *Memoirs*, 2:261, 313; D'Avaux, *Negotiations*, 1:62.

[129] *Discourses*, III:45, pp. 456–57. See also: II:20, p. 153; II:25, p. 205; III:28, p. 385.

[130] Dalrymple, *Memoirs*, 2:198; Barillon to Louis XIV, 5 December 1680, in Dalrymple, 2:285.

fused to help the English republicans topple the monarchy in 1666.[131]

Barillon's letters also indicate that he paid Sidney a small subsidy for his efforts, and the charge that Sidney was a "pensioner" of France has proven a stumbling block to almost all of Sidney's interpreters. How could "the British Brutus" have been on the payroll of England's greatest rival? Either the evidence must be faulty, or Sidney must be considered an unprincipled opportunist. The question of whether or not money changed hands is misplaced, however. There is no evidence to suggest that Sidney was either a witting or unwitting instrument of the French. Indeed, he thought Barillon an uncultured fool who grossly overestimated his influence on English politics.[132] In the stalemate between the Whigs and the Crown that emerged during the Exclusion Crisis, men on both sides looked to France for assistance,[133] and the interesting question is not whether Sidney worked with the French, but why he thought their aims coherent with his own. In point of fact France had no interest in toppling the regime of Charles II, but a subtle understanding of French ambitions had never been Sidney's strong suit.

On 19 December 1678 Danby was impeached by the House of Commons. Once he had been removed from power it was possible to focus the nation's attention on the implications of the Popish Plot. Under Shaftesbury's guidance one wing of the opposition coalesced around a proposal to exclude the duke of York from the throne. Such a plan would have removed from power a man known to have extreme views concerning the rights of the Crown, and it would have frustrated the efforts of European Catholics to dominate England's political and religious life. To a great many Englishmen it appeared that nothing less than England's survival as a free and Protestant nation was at stake in the ensuing Exclusion Crisis.[134]

[131] Barillon to Louis XIV, 14 December 1679, 5 December 1680, and 30 September 1680, in Dalrymple, *Memoirs*, 2:261–62, 288, 313.

[132] "You know Monsieur de Barillon governs us (if he be not mistaken) but he seems not to be so much pleased with that, as to find his Embonpoint encreased by the moistness of our air, by frequently clapping his hands upon his thighs, shewing the delight he hath in the sharpness of the sound that testifies the plumpness and hardness of his flesh; and certainly if this climate did not nourish him better than any other, the hairs in his nose, and the nails of his fingers could not grow so fast as to furnish enough of the one to pull out, and of the other to cut off in all Companies, which being done he picks his ears with as good a grace as my Lord La[uderdale]" (Sidney to Savile, 10 July 1679, in *Letters*, 130–31).

[133] Jones, *First Whigs*, 147–51.

[134] "I have seriously considered the danger we are in from Popery. To make a long discourse of it would be unnecessary. . . . This Parliament must either destroy Popery,

Faced with an increasingly strident opposition, Charles II dissolved Parliament on 24 January 1679. Within days Sidney had joined a group of men "well known for their Commonwealth principles," including the former Leveller John Wildman and the former Rumper Henry Neville, in seeking election to the new Parliament.[135] With the help of William Penn, Sidney stood for the borough of Guildford in Surrey. In a pamphlet anonymously published in 1679 Penn had called on his countrymen to advance men who will protect "your True and Just Interest," "Men of Industry and Improvement," men of courage, "Sincere Protestants." Penn evidently regarded Sidney as just such a man. As he wrote in a letter expressing his disgust at the electoral intrigue that had been used to defeat Sidney in Guildford, "thou (as thy Friends) had a conscientious Regard to England; and to be putt aside, by such base Ways, is really a Suffering for Righteousness."[136]

The Parliament to which Sidney had sought election sat for the first time on 6 March 1679. Contrary to the king's hopes and expectations, it was even more inflexible than its predecessor. The lines were hardened when the king pardoned Danby on 22 March. In a letter to Henry Savile, Sidney crisply summarized the constitutional question involved: Could the king "pardon a man impeached by Parliament upon a publick account?" If the answer were "yes," then the doctrine of ministerial responsibility would be destroyed, and Parliament would lose one of its primary tools for influencing the Crown. Though he never directly stated his own views—"letters are soe often opened, that noe man in his senses will write any thing that is not fit for the publike view"—Sidney clearly implied that he believed that the king did not have the power to pardon Danby.[137]

It was not Danby's pardon that split the nation, however. On 27

---

or they will destroy us; there is no middle way to be taken, no mincing the matter" (William Lord Russell, 26 October 1680, in *Debates of the House of Commons*, ed. Anchitell Grey [London: T. Becket and P. A. DeHonde, 1769], 7:357–58).

[135] Mulys to the earl of Ossory, 28 January 1679, in HMC, *Calendar of the Manuscripts of the Marquess of Ormonde*, N.S. (London: HMSO, 1906), 4:311.

[136] William Penn [Philanglus, pseud.], *Englands Great Interest In The Choice of this New Parliament* (1679?), 3–4; Penn to Sidney, 1 March 1679, in *The Papers of William Penn*, ed. Mary Maples Dunn and Richard S. Dunn (Philadelphia: University of Pennsylvania Press, 1981), 1:587. On the Guildford election, see: Basil Duke Henning, *The House of Commons 1660–1690* (London: Secker & Warburg, 1983), 1:410; "Algernon Sidney, Esq.; his Case concerning the Election for the Towne of Guildford in Surrey," in Collins, 1:153–54.

[137] Sidney to Savile, 28 April 1679, in *Letters*, 40; Sidney to Furly, 23 March 1679, in Forster, *Original Letters*, 94. See also: *Discourses*, III:42, p. 444.

April the House issued a proclamation declaring "that the Duke of York being a Papist, the hopes of his succeedings unto the Crown had been the principal ground and foundation of the Plot against the king's life and the Protestant Religion." London was ablaze in speculation over whether James would be impeached or excluded and over "who is fittest to succeed." A petition thanking Parliament for its proceedings against popery was rumored to have more than a hundred thousand signatures.[138] Tensions reached a peak when, on 21 May, the House passed the first Exclusion Bill by the extraordinary vote of 207 to 128. "When I have said what I can upon this business," Sidney wrote Savile, "I must confess I do not know three men of a mind, and that a spirit of gidiness reigns amongst us, far beyond any I ever observed in my life." The king did not share his opponents' irresolution, however, and on 27 May he prorogued Parliament. "All men's wits have been screwed ever since that day to find out the consequence."[139]

Events during the summer of 1679 only confirmed Sidney's distaste for and distrust of the court. The Scottish Covenanters revolted against their English masters, and Sidney thought that "it is not fallen out by chance." He believed that the revolt had been encouraged by the court in order to provide a pretext for raising an army that could be used against the king's rebellious English subjects.[140]

The defeat of the Scottish "Conventicle-men" by the duke of Monmouth gave Sidney the opportunity to reflect more generally on the nature of monarchy:

Some did think that they [the Covenanters] being a poor people, brought unto despair by the most violent persecution, pitied by all both in England and Scotland, helped by none, without head or conduct, were to be spared; and that in so doing, he [Monmouth] might have made himself very popular in both Kingdoms . . . and best to have provided for the King's interest. Others, who look upon it as a fine thing to kill a great many men, and believe Monarchies are best kept up by terrour, extol the action, and say there is no other way of suppressing old rebellions, or preventing new ones, than by force and rigour; looking

---

[138] Sidney to Savile, 28 April 1679, in *Letters*, 46; Sidney to Savile, 19 May 1679, in *Letters*, 74.

[139] Sidney to Savile, 5 May 1679, in *Letters*, 52–54; Sidney to Savile, 2 June 1679, in *Letters*, 77.

[140] Sidney to Savile, 9 June 1679, in *Letters*, 90. See also: Sidney to Savile, 12 May 1679 and 23 June 1679, in *Letters*, 66, 112–14. The locus classicus for this argument is Shaftesbury's speech in Parliament of 25 March 1679 (Anthony Ashley Cooper, *The Compleat Statesman* [London: Benjamin Alsop and Thomas Malthus, 1683], 66).

upon Caligula as a great Statesman, and *oderint dum metuant* as a good maxim.[141]

The abstractness of this passage, so different from the bulk of Sidney's letters to Savile, is striking. This is the only surviving letter in which he invoked a historical figure to analyze a contemporary problem. That he chose Caligula leaves it beyond a shadow of a doubt that he identified himself with the first of these two paths.

In the same letter Sidney reflected on the behavior of the Scottish lords who had initiated the rebellion: "It is probable enough they may have the fortune that ordinarily accompanies them that pretending to be very subtile and keep well with both sides, ever do too much or too little." Their half measures, having neither kept the peace nor reformed the state, "ruined these poor people by stirring them up, and by leaving them to themselves." He could have said—indeed, might have said—the same thing concerning the earl of Shaftesbury. Though the two men shared a wide range of contacts, they "were at no time on good terms."[142] As Sidney's reference to "the knowne dislikes which he had unto me, and I unto him and his wayes" indicates, their differences were both personal and political.[143] Among the latter undoubtedly the most important was their disagreement over the proper response to the problem of the succession.

As noted above, Shaftesbury organized one wing of the opposition around the demand that the duke of York be excluded from the throne. Though the evidence is sketchy, it would appear that during the critical debates of 1679 and 1680 Sidney threw his weight behind a radical version of the alternative proposed by Halifax, that James be permitted to assume the throne but that his powers be circumscribed. Two distinct accounts of Sidney's views in late 1680 survive. According to D'Avaux, Sidney reported to his Dutch contacts that

> the Parliament of England would not come to a reconciliation with the King of England, but upon these terms. That his Britannic Majesty should renounce all right to prorogue his Parliament, by his sole authority; because they pretended this was a power usurped for some years.

[141] Sidney to Savile, 30 June 1679, in *Letters*, 120–21.

[142] Haley, *Shaftesbury*, 718n. Dorothy Sidney's letter of 29 July 1680 does not sustain Ashcraft's claim that "Sidney, Monmouth, Shaftesbury, and Hampden were once again cooperating with one another." In addition, Ashcraft mistakenly identifies Dorothy as Algernon's mother (she was his sister) and thus confuses Algernon with her real son, the earl of Sunderland, who *did* in fact cooperate with Shaftesbury in late 1680 (Ashcraft, *Revolutionary Politics*, 179; Dorothy Sidney to Halifax, 29 July 1680, and Dorothy Sidney to Henry Sidney, 19 November [1680], in Cartwright, *Sacharissa*, 276, 281–82, 295–96).

[143] "Apology," 14.

That his Majesty should also give up to Parliament the right of choosing general officers, by sea and land. And, that he should likewise grant them the liberty of naming commissioners for the management of the treasury, and payment of the army.[144]

A similar set of "limitations" had been proposed by Halifax as early as 1679, and they continued to be debated throughout 1680.[145] In Halifax's hands these limitations were meant to apply only to a popish successor. Though D'Avaux's account is inconclusive, it suggests that Sidney advocated the much more radical proposition that limitations should be imposed on all English monarchs regardless of their religious beliefs.

A second and substantially different account of Sidney's political views was recorded by the duke of York at roughly the same time:

> The duke to be banished for the King's life to some place five hundred miles from England; to forfeit his revenues if he came nearer, and his life if he returned to any of the King's dominions; and whoever received him, in England or Ireland, should be guilty of high treason. In case of his accession to the crown, that the whole power of government should be vested in a council of forty-one: all foreign treaties and negotiations to be transacted by commissioners taken out of the said council: Ireland to be governed by it also: and it should have power to fill up all vacancies, or remove any from employments; yet to be subject to disallowance or approbation of parliament, which, while sitting, was to exercise all the authority vested in the other, during the interval of sessions. This, as Mr. Algernon Sidney and his party thought, was a gentle way of dropping the government into a commonwealth.[146]

York's reference to "a council of forty-one" may simply have indicated the size of the body of men to govern in the event he succeeded to the throne. But in the highly charged rhetoric of Restoration royalism it may also have been meant to invoke memories of the governing councils advocated by the Long Parliament in the "Grand Remonstrance" and "Nineteen Propositions" of 1641 and 1642. As every schoolboy knew, 1641 led directly to 1649 and the elimination of the monarchy itself.

We have no way of knowing with certainty which, if either, of these programs Sidney favored. The answer may be both; though distinct,

---

[144] D'Avaux, *Negotiations*, 1:62–63.

[145] Burnet, *History of His Own Time*, 2:201–2, 244–48, 252–53; Haley, *Shaftesbury*, 517–18, 531, 601–3.

[146] James II, "The Life of James the Second, Written by Himself," in *Original Papers*, ed. James Macpherson (London: W. Strahan and T. Cadell, 1776), 1:109–10.

they are not mutually exclusive. Their common feature is an emphasis on the constitutional restriction of the powers of the Crown. Unlike Shaftesbury, Sidney evidently believed that the only foolproof way of protecting the nation against the dangers of absolutism was to alter drastically the powers of the monarchy, or to abolish it altogether. His "limitations" were a root-and-branch solution to the problem of a popish successor. York was not the only person to accuse Sidney of "republican" leanings at this time; the charge was also leveled by Sidney's sister, the countess of Sunderland, by Barillon, and by the king himself.[147]

Sidney's increasingly visible radicalism reflected the escalating tensions of 1679 and 1680. Despite the debacle of the previous Parliament, Charles II issued writs for new elections at the end of the summer in 1679. An insufficient number of men loyal to the king were returned, however, and Charles II repeatedly prorogued Parliament from 7 October 1679 to 21 October 1680. This policy had a traumatic effect on the nation. According to Sidney, "We are heare in the strangest confusion that I ever remember to have seene in English business. There never was more intrigues, and lesse truth. . . . Things are so entangled, that liberty of language is almost lost; and noe man knowes how to speake of any thing, least he that is spoken unto may be of a party contrary unto him, and that endeavours to overthrow what he would set up." As one historian has put it, "there seemed no limit to the insanity through which the nation was passing."[148]

Sidney remained active despite the extended silence in Westminster. According to Barillon, it was "through the intrigues of the Sieur Algernoon Sidney that one of the two sheriffs [of London], named [Slingsby] Bethel," was elected in 1680.[149] Because the sheriffs impaneled juries, they played a pivotal role in the legal system. By carefully choosing jurors it was possible either to frustrate or to further criminal prosecutions. As the Whigs were to discover in 1681, this power provided a vital check on the king's ability to stage political trials. Bethel was a Nonconformist who had recently gone on record as a staunch advocate of the advancement of trade and the toleration of Dissenters. He was deeply anti-Catholic and anti-French.[150] He was

---

[147] Dorothy Sidney to Halifax, 29 July 1680, in Cartwright, *Sacharissa*, 282; Barillon to Louis XIV, 30 September 1680 and 5 December 1680, in Dalrymple, *Memoirs*, 2:313, 287; James II, entry for 7 December 1680, in "Life," 1:111.

[148] Sidney to Furly, 13 October 1680, in Forster, *Original Letters*, 98; Ogg, *England in the Reign of Charles II*, 2:595.

[149] Barillon to Louis XIV, 5 December 1680, in Dalrymple, *Memoirs*, 2:287.

[150] Slingsby Bethel [J. B., pseud.], *An Account of the French Usurpation upon the Trade*

also a republican.[151] The court considered his selection "extremely dangerous to the king" and even entertained thoughts of electoral fraud in order to overturn it.[152] Sidney had known Bethel at least since 1665, when they fomented revolution in the Netherlands, and so it comes as no surprise to find them allied fifteen years later. Unfortunately, we have no further evidence concerning the extent of their cooperation during the Exclusion Crisis.

Sidney also continued to lobby the French, arguing with "force" and "openness" that it was in France's best interest to support the republican cause in England.[153] Shaftesbury was deeply troubled by Barillon's contact with members of the opposition and went so far as to declare publicly that Sidney was "a French pensioner." The two men "railed at one another" throughout the summer.[154] The schism between Shaftesbury and Sidney may even have cost the latter a seat in Parliament. In August 1679 Sidney stood for the borough of Amersham in Buckinghamshire, where he was elected on a double return. When Parliament was finally allowed to sit in the fall of 1680 it was asked to determine both the extent of the franchise in Amersham and the validity of either of the polls taken. On the general question of the franchise, which had ramifications for the whole kingdom, the House decided in favor of Sidney. But on the specific question of the election in Amersham it voted overwhelmingly against the poll that would have returned him. As John Carswell has recently argued, it may not have been coincidental that one of the tellers against Sidney's election was William Harbord, at that time one of Shaftesbury's lieutenants in the campaign for Exclusion.[155]

Sidney was defeated in the runoff for Amersham, and again in the elections for the Oxford Parliament in January 1681, through sham elections.[156] Though frustrated by his own electoral misfortunes, he

---

of England (London: 1679); [Slingsby Bethel], *The Interest of Princes and States* (London: John Wickins, 1680).

[151] Russell "was sorry" Bethel was elected sheriff, "for he was as great a Commonwealth's man as Algernon Sidney" (Dorothy Sidney to Halifax, 19 July 1680, in Cartwright, *Sacharissa*, 278). Bethel had cooperated with Sidney during the revolutionary campaign in the Netherlands in 1665–66.

[152] *CSPD*, 1679–1680:558–59. See also: *The Tryal of Thomas Pilkington . . . Slingsby Bethel . . . for the Riot at Guild-Hall* (London: Thomas Dring, 1682), 17–18.

[153] Barillon to Louis XIV, 30 September 1680, in Dalrymple, *Memoirs*, 2:313.

[154] Dorothy Sidney to Halifax, 8 July 1680 and 29 July 1680, in Cartwright, *Sacharissa*, 274, 281.

[155] Henning, *House of Commons*, 1:137–38; Algernon Sidney, *The Case of Algernon Sidney Esq.* (1680); Anchitell Grey, *Debates*, 7:127–28; Carswell, *Porcupine*, 182–83.

[156] Henning, *House of Commons*, 1:137–38; Sidney to Savile, 3 February 1681, in *Letters*, 10–11.

was evidently pleased to report to Henry Savile that "Parliament-Men are for the most part chosen by the Parties most contrary to the Court." Conscious of the frequency with which letters were opened by government spies, he described the nation's mood elliptically. Adopting the tone of a strong supporter of the court, he wrote that "notwithstanding what is said, we good Subjects hope all will go perfectly well." He then praised several of the most egregious of Charles II's ministers, anticipated the day "when things shall be brought into such order, that a Papist may appear open-faced," and stated that "civil and military affairs being thus settled, Treasures flowing in unto us on all sides, and all Foreign Princes, concerned in our affairs, being sure unto us; we need not fear a few *discontented Lords*, a *mutinous City*, or *murmering Counties*."[157] As Sidney clearly saw, the nation was on the verge of another civil war. So stiff was the opposition to the court that the king was forced to dissolve the Oxford Parliament eight days after it was assembled. He was resolved never to call another.

With the ordinary machinery of government in shambles, Charles II enlisted the support of the nation with exceptional skill. In April 1681 he issued a declaration "Touching the Causes and Reasons That moved Him to Dissolve The Two last Parliaments," in which he decried "the restless Malice of ill Men, who are labouring to poyson Our People, some out of fondness for their Old Beloved Commonwealth-Principles and some out of anger at their being disappointed in the particular Designs they had for the accomplishment of their own Ambition and Greatness." With practiced precision he mobilized memories of the Civil War to defend the monarchy and undermine all forms of opposition: "And who cannot but remember, That Religion, Liberty, and Property were all Lost and gone, when the Monarchy was shaken off, and could never be revived till that was restored."[158]

An anonymous answer to the king's declaration, entitled *A Just and Modest Vindication of the proceedings of the Two last Parliaments*, was published in 1682. Bishop Burnet thought it "much the best writ piece that came out in all these Embroilments" and attributed partial authorship to Sidney. Lord John Somers, Sir William Jones, Major John Wildman, and Silius Titus may also have had a hand in its composition.[159] With so many layers of writing and editing it is impossible to

[157] Sidney to Savile, 10 February 1681, in *Letters*, 17; Sidney to Savile, 3 February 1681, in *Letters*, 12–14.

[158] Charles II, *His Majesties Declaration To All His Loving Subjects* (London: 8 April 1681), 9–10.

[159] Gilbert Burnet, "History of My Own Times," British Library, Add. MS. 63,057, vol. 2, fol. 58; Burnet, *History of His Own Time*, 2:283. These two versions of Burnet's

determine how much the final pamphlet reflected Sidney's own ideas. Though extremely sophisticated, most of its arguments were the common property of the Whigs, and it could have been written by almost any member of the opposition with a sharp quill and a flair for writing.[160]

Alongside his efforts as a political pamphleteer, Sidney tried his hand at constitution writing. In the summer of 1681 William Penn sought his advice concerning Penn's "Frame of Government" for the colony of Pennsylvania. The two men had disagreed, Penn recalled that fall, "about my drawing Constitutions, not as proposals, but as if fixt to the hand." Sidney strenuously objected to the creation of an unalterable constitution and apparently felt that Penn had not sufficiently liberated himself from that idea, for he accused Penn behind his back of having had "a good County [Country] but the basest laws in the world, not to be endured or lived under, and that the Turk was not more absolute" than Penn was. "If it be true," Penn wrote, "I shall be sorry we were ever so well acquainted."[161]

After this bitter parting of friends we have only a few fleeting glimpses of Sidney's activities for almost two years. In 1681 an anonymous royalist pamphleteer indicted Sidney, along with Shaftesbury, Wildman, Neville, and others, for subverting England's independence. "We are made Tools and Instruments for *French* purposes, betray'd by their Cunning and Address, to forward and act with our own hands, our Slavery and Ruine."[162] Though wildly inaccurate, the charge that Sidney enjoyed a "French connection" was impossible to deny. In September of the same year Barillon reported to Louis XIV that Sidney was strongly opposed to any accommodations with the

---

History differ in their ascription of authorship of this pamphlet: the former assigns it to Sidney, Wildman, Jones, and Titus, while the latter assigns it to Sidney, Jones, and Somers. *Just and Modest* has also been claimed by Robert Ferguson ("M[r] F[erguson's] account of the bookes, good & bad, published by him," Bodleian Library, MS. Smith 31, fol. 30). Ferguson's word is sufficiently untrustworthy, and the style of the pamphlet is sufficiently unlike tracts from this period that can be safely attributed to him, that I am unpersuaded by his boast.

[160] Two passages bear such a striking resemblance to Sidney's arguments in the *Discourses*, however, that they are almost surely from his hand; see the invocation of Bracton, and the defense of "Commonwealth Principles" as the provenance of "every Wise and Honest man," at the conclusion of the pamphlet (*A Just and Modest Vindication of the proceedings of the Two last Parliaments* [London: 1682], 43–44). Compare also the discussion of Sweden and France in *Just and Modest*, 19, with that in the *Discourses*, III:29, pp. 394–95.

[161] Penn to Sidney, 13 October 1681, in Penn, *Papers*, 2:124–25.

[162] *A Seasonable Address to both Houses of Parliament Concerning the Succession* (London: 1681), 7–9.

king and that he would be of great service were a new Parliament to be called.[163]

In February 1682 a government spy reported that Sidney had been heard speaking "treasonable expressions." It was at this time that he helped secure the release of Lord Howard of Escrick from the Tower. According to Burnet, Sidney "had a great kindness for lord Howard . . . for that lord hated both the king and monarchy, as much as he himself did."[164] The relationship was to prove fatal the following year. Sidney's actions were sufficiently threatening for Secretary Jenkins to warn Lord Hyde in May of that year, "For God's sake have a strict eye to Mr. S[idney]. The Whigs have great expectations from him." Not until June 1683, however, did Sidney step once more onto the public stage.[165]

Trial and Execution (1683)

On 26 June 1683 Sidney was arrested at his home in London for his participation in the Rye House Plot, a conspiracy to assassinate Charles II and his brother James, duke of York, along a remote and narrow stretch of road between London and Newmarket. William Lord Russell, Lord Grey, and John Wildman were arrested on the same day. Soon thereafter the earl of Essex, John Hampden—the grandson of the Civil War hero—and a number of lesser figures were also arrested. A warrant was issued for the arrest of the duke of Monmouth.

The nature and significance of the Rye House Plot can be understood only in the context of the "Stuart revenge" that followed the dissolution of the Oxford Parliament on 28 March 1681. Both Whigs and Tories had been guilty of using the law as a political weapon. But after 1681 Charles II received sufficient subsidies from Louis XIV to

[163] "J'ai trouvé le Sieur Algernon Sidney fort disposé a rejetter toute sorte d'accommodement avec le cour. Il craint d'avantage le Prince d'Orange que le Duc de York. Il est plus acredité qu'il n'a encore este parmi les independans, et je crois en pouvoir tirer de grands services si le Parlement s'assemble" (Barillon to Louis XIV, September 1681, PRO, 31/3/150, fol. 261b).

[164] *Dictionary of National Biography*, s.v. "William Howard, third Baron Howard of Escrick"; Burnet, *History of His Own Time*, 2:351. See also: Burnet, *History of His Own Time*, 2:288–89; *Discourses*, III:42, pp. 442–43.

[165] *CSPD*, 1682:190. In addition to his political activities Sidney continued to be consumed by financial matters (Kent Archives Office, De L'Isle MSS. [U1475], L5; PRO, C6/244/2).

free him from his financial dependence on Parliament, and his agents were able to proceed against his enemies almost unimpeded.[166]

The first victim of the campaign to crush the opposition was Stephen College, who was tried and executed in August 1681 for seditious behavior during the Oxford Parliament. On 2 July Shaftesbury himself was arrested for treason. The Whigs were able to stymie this move against their leader because they were still in control of the government of London and hence were able to pack the grand juries called to indict him.[167] In time this bulwark collapsed, however, for the second prong of the "Stuart revenge" was a campaign to subvert the independence of the city corporations. Despite strenuous efforts and a good deal of electoral chicanery, the Whigs lost control of the London city government in 1682.[168] In October 1683 the city's charter was remodeled, and "Shaftesbury's stronghold" became "a royal demesne."[169] Lest any centers of sedition remain, an unprecedented offensive against Dissenters—who had so frequently supported the opposition—was mounted at the same time.[170]

In the face of this carefully orchestrated campaign, opposition to the king narrowed and became more extreme.[171] The pivotal event appears to have been the sheriffs' elections of July 1682, for once the Whigs lost control of the London juries they had no means of protecting themselves from partisan abuse of the law.[172] Plans were laid

---

[166] Ogg, *England in the Reign of Charles II*, 2:620–56. "By the end of 1681 the decision of no quarter for Whigs was taken at Court" (Feiling, *Tory Party*, 200).

[167] Ogg, *England in the Reign of Charles II*, 2:626–31; Jones, *First Whigs*, 189–94; Haley, *Shaftesbury*, 654–83.

[168] Longford to [?], 27 June 1682, Bodleian Library, MS. Carte 216, fol. 86; *The Tryal of Thomas Pilkington*. See also: A. F. Havighurst, "The Judiciary and Politics in the Reign of Charles II," *Law Quarterly Review* 66 (1950): 242–52.

[169] Ogg, *England in the Reign of Charles II*, 2:639.

[170] "It seems clear that [after 1681] the recusancy laws were . . . used mainly against Dissenters. . . . There were also many more convictions for attending conventicles; there survive nearly 750 certificates of conviction for 1682–83 and 111 for 1684 from Middlesex alone. . . . The only other convictions in the county in Charles II's reign were forty-eight in 1664–5, after the first Conventicle Act, five in 1670, after the second Conventicle act and ten in 1674–5, during Danby's drive against nonconformity" (John Miller, *Popery and Politics in England 1660–1688* [Cambridge: Cambridge University Press, 1973], 191).

[171] The pioneering account of the Whig conspiracies of 1682–83 is Ashcraft, *Revolutionary Politics*, 338–405. Though I do not agree with all of Ashcraft's conclusions, I wish to acknowledge my debt to his painstaking research.

[172] Robert Ferguson, "Ferguson's MS. Concerning the Rye House Business," in James Ferguson, *Robert Ferguson the Plotter* (Edinburgh: David Douglas, 1887), 414–15; Ford Lord Grey, *The Secret History of the Rye-House Plot* (London: Andrew Millar, 1754), 16; "Testimony Concerning Rye House Plot," PRO, SP29/426, fol. 15. According to Robert West, in October 1682 Sidney said "that many tricks had been played in the

for an uprising in November, with Shaftesbury at the head of "ten thousand brisk boys" in London and the duke of Monmouth—who was to be placed on the throne—drawing on his popular support in Cheshire. The rising never took place, however, because of the "cowardliness" of one of the conspirators. Within days Shaftesbury and his chief assistant, Robert Ferguson, fled the country, and the plotters fell into disarray.[173]

In early January leadership of this increasingly militant wing of the opposition was assumed by a "Council of Six," composed of Monmouth, Russell, Essex, Lord Howard of Escrick, Hampden, and Sidney.[174] Though Monmouth and Russell had been key figures in the aborted uprising of the previous November, this was the first time that Sidney, Hampden, Howard, or Essex played an active role in the conspiracy. It is not clear why Sidney joined the movement at precisely this moment. His first meeting with Monmouth was engineered by Howard just days before the council met, but we have no record of their conversation.[175] Undoubtedly both men were influenced by the changes in the political landscape brought about by Shaftesbury's flight and subsequent death on the 21st of January.

Sidney's presence on the council did not bode well for its unity. According to Ford Lord Grey, who was invited to the council in March, Russell and Monmouth hoped that the rebellion would "end in a happy accomodation between the king and his people in parliament," while Sidney and Essex "had set their hearts upon a commonwealth."[176] Given the conduct of these men during the previous four years, Grey's description of their aims is a bit droll. But it suggests

---

scrutiny of the Poll for the Lord Mayor, and that Sʳ William Pritchard was declared tho not duly shown, but sayd he, all that I can say to it is what a Justice of Peace of Essex sayd lately to a Country fellow brought before him for killing a Highway man that would have robd him. Friend says the Justice you have done well, but you might have been robd if you would, and so we may be enslaved if wee will, or else need not" (PRO, SP29/426, fol. 131).

[173] Ford Lord Grey, *Secret History*, 29–32, 41; Robert West, "Full Confession to the King—The Rye House Plot," British Library, Add. MS. 38,847, fols. 90–94.

[174] *The Tryals of Thomas Walcot, William Hone, William Lord Russell, John Rouse & William Blagg, For High-Treason* (London: Richard Royston, Benjamin Took and Charles Mearn, 1683), 44.

[175] "Apology," 11.

[176] Ford Lord Grey, *Secret History*, 45–46, 54–56. Prior to his execution Russell proclaimed that he had supported Exclusion but had opposed limitations because they would have "quite altered" the government and left "little more than the Name of a King. . . . [I] thought it better to have a King with his Prerogative, and the Nation easy and safe under him, then a King without it, which must have bred perpetual Jealousies, and a continual Struggle" (William Lord Russell, *The Speech of the late Lord Russel, To the Sheriffs* [London: John Darby, 1683], 3).

that Russell and Monmouth continued to operate within the basic logic of exclusion, while Sidney and Essex favored a much more radical limitation (if not elimination) of the powers of the Crown. As Sidney forcefully stated his position, "he had heard, when wise men drew their swords against their king, they laid aside the thoughts of treating with him."[177]

The split between these two factions in the council was partly responsible for the failure of the planned rebellion. In January the council decided to strengthen their prospects by arranging a joint rising with rebels in Scotland, and Sidney was given the responsibility of managing the relationship with the earl of Argyll and his compatriots. After lengthy negotiations the plan was abandoned, largely because the English could not afford even the £5,000 "bargain basement" package offered by the Scots. But deeper issues were at play, for Sidney had done his best to subvert the operation once he had determined that the Scotsmen were unwilling to declare themselves in favor of a commonwealth.[178] The collapse of the negotiations with the Scots crushed all hope for a successful rising in the spring of 1683.

Beneath the Council of Six was a second tier of rebels, a band of desperadoes composed of tradesmen, ex-soldiers, sectaries, a tavern-keeper, and at least one disaffected lawyer. It was apparently these men—Robert Ferguson, Francis and Richard Goodenough, Josiah Keeling, John Rumsey, Thomas Walcot, and Robert West, among others—who hatched the plan to assassinate Charles and James Stuart as they passed by the Rye House on their return from Newmarket. Though many of these men had been affiliated with Shaftesbury for years, the relationship between this "lesser" council and the Council of Six was tenuous.[179] The only effective link between them was Ferguson, who had returned from Holland following Shaftesbury's death. The two groups clashed repeatedly, over everything from the content of the "Declaration" justifying their actions to the English

---

[177] Ford Lord Grey, *Secret History*, 56. Compare *Discourses*, II:24, p. 173: "He that draws his Sword against the Prince, say the *French*, ought to throw away the Scabbord; for tho the design be never so just, yet the Authors are sure to be ruin'd if it miscarry."

[178] Ford Lord Grey, *Secret History*, 42, 51–52; "Testimony Concerning Rye House Plot," PRO, SP29/426, fol. 131; West, "Confession," British Library, Add. MS. 38,847, fols. 97, 113; *Tryals of Thomas Walcot, William Hone, William Lord Russell*, 16, 46; *The Tryal and Process of High-Treason . . . against Mr. Robert Baillie* (Edinburgh: 1685), 50.

[179] Even Ashcraft, who has argued for the unity of these two groups, is forced to admit that "it was the threat" of the assassination scheme cooked up by Rumsey, West, and others "that gave the grandees the impetus to resume their meetings about the insurrection" (Ashcraft, *Revolutionary Politics*, 363 n. 108).

people to the speed and violence with which they should act.[180] There are even signs indicating that the Council of Six either was not apprised of or did not endorse the planned assassination.[181] Many contemporaries noted the distinctions between these two strata of the revolutionary movement, but for strategic reasons both the members of the lesser council and their royal accusers emphasized the links between them.[182]

As reports of the plot began to appear in late June and early July 1683, petitions began streaming into the court from all England decrying "the late Horrid and Damnable Conspiracy" and abjectly pledging allegiance to England's "Most Dread Soveraign."[183] Gentlemen anxiously waited on the king and duke of York in an attempt to prove themselves "faithfull and loyall" subjects.[184] The dons of Oxford University, ever ready to provide an intellectual and moral foundation for the Crown's campaign against dissidents, issued a decree thanking "the Divine Providence, which by extraordinary Methods brought it to pass, that the Breath of our Nostrils, the Annointed of the Lord, is not taken in the Pit which was prepared for Him, and that under his shadow we continue to live and enjoy the blessings of his Government." They then condemned twenty-seven propositions concerning the nature of government, beginning with the claim that "all Civil Authority is derived originally from the People."[185]

Against this background the prosecution against Sidney and the other members of the Council of Six began to take shape.[186] As early

[180] West, "Confession," British Library, Add. MS. 38,847, fols. 96, 113; *Tryals of Thomas Walcot, William Hone, William Lord Russell*, 16; Nathaniel Wade, "Confession," British Library, Harleian MS. 6845, fol. 267; Holloway, *Confession*, 4–5.

[181] Ford Lord Grey, *Secret History*, 61; Holloway, *Confession*, 4; Wade, "Confession," British Library, Harleian MS. 6845, fols. 267, 268; West, "Confession," British Library, Add. MS. 38,847, fol. 98.

[182] *Tryals of Thomas Walcot, William Hone, William Lord Russell*, 4; *An Antidote Against Poison* (London: Charles Mearne, 1683), 4; Sir John Lauder of Fountainhall, *Historical Observes of Memorable Occurrents in Church and State* (Edinburgh: Thomas Constable, 1840), 102–3.

[183] Virtually every edition of the *London Gazette* between July and November 1683 contained several petitions from the provinces. As one contemporary noted, "Tho' the doing it signifies little, the omission might signify much" (quoted in Doreen Milne, "The Results of the Rye House Plot and Their Influence upon the Revolution of 1688," *Transactions of the Royal Historical Society*, 5th ser., 1 [1951]: 102).

[184] Edward Dering, *The Diaries and Papers of Sir Edward Dering*, ed. Maurice Bond (London: HMSO, 1976), 145.

[185] "Judgment and Decree of the University of Oxford," *London Gazette* 1845 (23–26 July 1683).

[186] On 13 July, the first day of Russell's trial, the earl of Essex was found in his cell in the Tower, his neck slit with his own razor. Whig propagandists later charged that

as 30 June reference was made to "Col. Sydney's paper," a large treatise discovered in his study at the time of his arrest.[187] This was undoubtedly the manuscript for the *Discourses Concerning Government*. Though begun before Sidney's entrance into the Council of Six and ill suited to the immediate need of rousing the nation, it fully justified resistance to the unlawful exercise of political power.[188] Sidney privately acknowledged his authorship of the manuscript, explaining to Hampden that it was not "like to be [finished] in a long time," and that he had no "other thought concerning it, then when I had finished, and examined it, if I was satisfied with it, to shew it to somme prudent freinds, and then either to publish, keep, or burne it, as they should advise." With a touch of bravado, he even claimed that he was "much inclined to avowe them, and taking the utmost nature, meaning and intention of them, to put it upon a speciall plea, that if such papers, soe written are treason, I am guilty if not not. In this I shall have god to be the defender of my innocence."[189] Publicly, however, he was much more circumspect, and he never directly acknowledged that the manuscript was his.

Sidney's disavowal of the *Discourses* was motivated by prudence. His co-conspirator Lord Howard—who had promised the king's agents in July that "if any expedient can be chalked out, that he may do his Majesty service and take care of his own preservation, he will be glad of it"[190]—provided the sole witness to his wrongdoing. But under English law a man could not be convicted of treason unless there were two witnesses. Thus, acting on the novel principle that *scribere est agere*, the prosecution introduced Sidney's treatise as a second "witness" to his guilt. That the manuscript had never been published was considered irrelevant: "A man convinced of these principles, and that walks accordingly, what won't he do to accomplish his designs?" In a divinely ordained monarchy there could be no such thing as "private" thoughts. As Chief Justice George Jeffreys threatened, "curse not the

---

he had been murdered. Eight days later, on the scaffold at Lincoln's Inn Fields, Russell's own neck was severed by the king's executioner.

[187] *CSPD*, 1683: January–June, 384; 1683: July–September, 57, 223, 412; October 1683–April 1684, 49.

[188] At his trial, Sidney claimed that "these papers may be writ, perhaps, these twenty years, the ink is so old" ("Trial of Colonel Algernon Sidney," in Howell, *State Trials*, 9:866). This is either a mistaken reference to the text of the *Court Maxims*, or it is a patent lie. As Blair Worden has carefully observed, internal evidence "shows that the early part of the *Discourses* was not written before August 1681 and that the later part was composed in 1682 or 1683" ("Commonwealth Kidney," 15).

[189] Algernon Sidney to [John Hampden], 5 November [1683] and 31 October [1683], East Sussex Record Office, Glynde Place Papers 794 (unfoliated).

[190] *CSPD*, 1683: July–September, 80.

king, not in thy thoughts, nor in thy bed-chamber; the birds of the air will carry it." Lest the evidence presented during the trial not prove convincing enough, after directing the jury in public, Jeffreys "retired upon pretence of taking a glasse of sack, to . . . give them more particular instructions." Within a few short minutes they returned with the appointed verdict.[191]

There were some, like Sir John Lauder of Fountainhall, who believed that Sidney deserved his fate.[192] But to many Englishmen it appeared that Sidney's trial had been "a piece of most enormous injustice."[193] In the weeks following Sidney's conviction it became clear that much more than the guilt or innocence of one man was at stake. During the early autumn, as Sidney languished in jail, remnants of the Whig opposition of 1679–81 took up his cause. Though English law prevented Sidney from having benefit of counsel during his trial, he was given detailed written advice by Sir William Williams, Speaker of the House in 1680 and one of the Whigs' chief constitutional litigators.[194] Following Sidney's conviction, members of the opposition vigorously lobbied for his pardon.[195] Though no doubt moved by sympathy, they were also terrified by the sweeping implications of the legal procedures adopted during Sidney's trial. If a man's private papers could be used as evidence against him, then "no man's life or property was safe."[196] One need not have endorsed Sidney's revolutionary actions to have seen the dangers latent in his prosecution.

Public opposition to Sidney's conviction was apparently strong enough to check a similar prosecutorial effort against John Hampden.[197] But in the war between the Whigs and the Tories most of the

---

[191] "Trial of Colonel Algernon Sidney," in Howell, *State Trials*, 9:889, 887, 868; "Apology," 24.

[192] " 'Tho he was a gallant man, yet he had been so misfortunat as ever to be on the disloyall syde, and seimed to have drunk in with his milk republican principles, and was a Collonell against King Charles the 1ˢᵗ, and continued a sworn ennemy to monarchy, which justified the taking of his life very much: see his Speach" (Fountainhall, *Historical Observes*, 109–10).

[193] Burnet, *History of His Own Time*, 2:408. See also: John Evelyn, *The Diary of John Evelyn*, ed. Austin Dobson (London: Macmillan, 1906), 3:117–18; Milne, "Rye House Plot," 97–98.

[194] "Trial of Colonel Algernon Sidney," in Howell, *State Trials*, 9:823–35.

[195] Barnardiston to Skippon, 29 November 1683, and Barnardiston to Cavell, 4 December 1683, reprinted in "The Trial of Sir Samuel Barnardiston," in Howell, *State Trials*, 9:1335–36. See also: [?] to Ellis, 8 December 1683, British Library, Add. MS. 28,875; Burnet, *History of His Own Time*, 2:408.

[196] Milne, "Rye House Plot," 97.

[197] The government's decision not to prosecute Hampden for treason in turn bred skepticism concerning the very existence of the Rye House Plot (Fountainhall, *Historical Observes*, 119). See also: Milne, "Rye House Plot," 98–99.

weapons were in the hands of the government, and it was the immediate needs of the latter that determined Sidney's fate. To Secretary of State Jenkins, Sidney's condemnation was a way to frighten rebellious subjects into cooperation with the government.[198] To the duke of York, Sidney's execution was one more means of crushing his opponents. "The Whigs are growne very insolent . . . yett now that Algernon Sidney is to be beheaded . . . they will not be so high."[199] To the lord chief justice, the verdict was a symbol of his loyalty to the king. On hearing that Sidney had sent Charles II a petition asking him to review his trial, Jeffreys was reported to have said to the king, "either Sidney must die, or [I] must die."[200]

To the king himself, Sidney's death was part and parcel of the pardon he granted to Monmouth on 24 November for his part in the plot. Had Sidney and Monmouth both been pardoned, it might have appeared that the stories of the plot had been fabricated. By executing Sidney it was possible to both "mortify" the king's opponents and "raise the spirits" of "the well affected."[201] With the London coffeehouses abuzz with speculation over Sidney's fate, Charles II rejected Sidney's petition for permission "to goe beyond the seas as he had long desired to doe" and "resolved that the judgment against Algernon Sidney be put in execution."[202]

At half past ten on the morning of 7 December 1683, Sidney ascended the scaffold on Tower Hill. Declining the sheriffs' invitation to speak to the crowd that had assembled, he handed them a brief paper protesting his innocence and outlining the principles he had defended in his treatise. The first four of Sidney's nine tenets indicate the scope of his argument:

That God had left Nations unto the Liberty of setting up such Governments as best pleased themselves.

[198] *CSPD*, October 1683–April 1684, 105.

[199] York to Lord Queensberry, 6 December 1683, in HMC, *Fifteenth Report, Appendix, Part VIII* (London: HMSO, 1897), 200. To William of Orange James wrote that Sidney's execution "will give the lie to the Whigs, who reported he was not to suffer" (York to Orange, 4 December 1683, in Dalrymple, *Memoirs*, vol. 2, Appendix to Part 1, p. 54).

[200] Burnet, *History of His Own Time*, 2:408. See also: "Apology," 23; Evelyn, *Diary*, 3:117.

[201] Lord Ormond to the earl of Arran, 13 December 1683, in HMC, *Calendar of the Manuscripts of the Marquess of Ormonde*, N.S. (London: HMSO, 1912), 7:169; *London Gazette* 1880 (22–26 November 1683); [H. Ball] to Lord Preston, 26 November 1683, in HMC, *Seventh Report*, 375.

[202] Algernon Sidney, "Petition for Transportation," PRO, SP29/434, fol. 116; *CSPD*, October 1683–April 1684, 127. See also: Fountainhall, *Historical Observes*, 110–11.

That Magistrates were set up for the good of Nations, not Nations for
the honour or glory of Magistrates.

That the Right and Power of Magistrates in every Country, was that
which the laws of that Country made it to be.

That those Laws were to be observed, and the Oaths taken by them,
having the force of a Contract between Magistrate and People, could
not be Violated without danger of dissolving the whole Fabrick.

Against the claim "that all Men are born under a necessity derived
from the Laws of God and Nature, to submit unto an Absolute kingly
Government, which could be restrained by no Law, or Oath," Sidney
defended the right of a people to resist an unjust magistrate.[203]

Within days the contents of Sidney's "Paper" were being discussed
in England. Whig exiles in Holland had it printed in the *Harleem
Courant*, where it attracted the attention of William of Orange.[204] Ac-
knowledging that Sidney's "treasonable and insolent" declaration of
principles could not be ignored, the government had it printed at
public expense and initiated a pamphlet crusade against it.[205] Sidney
was accused of having written "for the understanding of the Rabble"
and of having laid "an eternal Foundation for perpetual Changes and
Alterations in Government."[206] He was a "Pseudo-Protestant and Je-
suitical Casuist" who had ungratefully and unnaturally betrayed the
class to which he belonged, "Persons of Noble Birth, and great Estates, the Favourites of Heaven and Earth."[207] The case against Sidney was neatly summarized in an anonymously published tract entitled *The Royal Apology*: "Particularly here in *England*, he who designs
to be truly instructed" concerning the location of "the *Supreme* Power
in any *Government* . . . must not receive his notice from the Discourses
of *private* men (which are many times fallacious, partial and uncertain)."[208] As a private man, a mere subject, Sidney had no moral, political, or intellectual ground on which to stand in treating of the
power and authority of the government. His "republican principles"

[203] Algernon Sidney, *The Very Copy of a Paper Delivered to the Sheriffs, Upon the Scaffold
on Tower-Hill, on Friday Decemb. 7. 1683* (London: 1683), 2.

[204] [?] to Ellis, 11 December 1683, British Library, Add. MS. 28,875, fol. 313; Walker,
"English Exiles," 124; York to Orange, 4 January 1684, in Dalrymple, *Memoirs*, vol. 2,
Appendix to Part 1, pp. 55–56.

[205] York to Orange, 4 January 1684, in Dalrymple, *Memoirs*, Vol. 2, Appendix to Part
1, p. 56; [?] to Ellis, 20 December 1683, British Library, Add. MS. 28,875, fol. 322.

[206] [Elkanah Settle], *Remarks on Algernoon Sidney's Paper* (London: 1683), 2; [John
Nalson], *Reflections Upon Coll. Sidney's Arcadia* (London: 1684), 11.

[207] *Some Animadversions on the Paper Delivered to the Sheriffs . . . By Algernon Sidney* (London: 1683), 3; [Edmund Bohun], *A Defence of Sir Robert Filmer, Against . . . Algernon
Sidney* (London: 1684), 1.

[208] *The Royal Apology: Or, An Answer To the Rebels Plea* (London: 1684), 7.

had no place in the divinely inspired monarchy of seventeenth-century England.[209]

The sentiments expressed by Sidney's critics—contempt for the moral and political capacities of the people, resistance to change, belief in the existence of natural hierarchies among men, unquestioning acceptance of the superiority of monarchy—were reflective of the royalist mind in seventeenth-century England. They were precisely the sentiments Sidney had attempted to refute in the *Court Maxims* and the *Discourses Concerning Government*, and they constitute the backdrop against which his "republican principles" can best be viewed.

[209] "Trial of Colonel Algernon Sidney," in Howell, *State Trials*, 9:840.

TWO

ENGLISH ROYALISM AND THE PLACE OF

SIR ROBERT FILMER

> The greatest liberty in the world (if it be duly considered)
> is for a people to live under a monarch . . . all other shows
> or pretexts of liberty are but several degrees of slavery.
> *(Sir Robert Filmer)*[1]

THE RADICAL doctrines of the *Discourses Concerning Government* were designed to justify rebellion against the illegitimate actions of Charles II. But Sidney's immediate target was Sir Robert Filmer's *Patriarcha*, a royalist tract first published in 1680. The core of Filmer's argument was the concept of patriarchy: "I see not," he wrote, "how the children of Adam, or of any man else, can be free from subjection to their parents. And this subordination of children is the fountain of all regal authority, by the ordination of God himself." As Adam had had the power of a "Father, King and Lord over his family," so kings possessed unlimited dominion over their people. No moral or political alternative existed within the fabric of nature. Mixed government was "a mere impossibility or contradiction," the people "a headless multitude."[2]

Filmer's arguments seem quaintly absurd to twentieth-century readers. But they were sufficiently threatening to seventeenth-century radicals to prompt three lengthy and profound responses: James Tyrrell's *Patriarcha non Monarcha*, John Locke's *Two Treatises of Government*, and Algernon Sidney's *Discourses Concerning Government*. Filmer's distinctiveness lay in his unhesitating affirmation of the most extreme aspects of royalist thought. By streamlining and simplifying orthodox justifications for monarchy, he was able to reach extremely radical conclusions. Like Charles and James Stuart, he revealed a dangerous potential lurking within traditional doctrines and institutions.

Filmer's patriarchal absolutism was particularly menacing because it was gaining currency in the nation. If universally accepted, it would

[1] *Patriarcha*, 55.
[2] *Patriarcha*, 57, 188, 93, 94.

have undermined any attempt to question, much less challenge or resist, the actions of the monarch. Even disasters like the spread of popery and the rise of arbitrary government would have to be weathered without complaint. As Sidney caustically commented, "if it be Liberty to live under such a Government, I desire to know what is Slavery."[3] If we are to understand this claim, and the moral and political beliefs on which it was based, then it must be set against the background of English royalism and the thought of Sir Robert Filmer.

Royalist Thought, 1675–1685

Seventeenth-century English royalist thought was diffuse, unchanging, and frequently incoherent. These are striking characteristics for a mode of thought whose avowed purpose was the vigorous and persuasive defense of monarchy against its critics, and they need explanation. Like their opponents, royalists generally expressed their views in "incidental" tracts designed to have an immediate impact on the conduct of their countrymen. In the heat of battle they tended to deploy any and all possible weapons, rather than patiently searching their intellectual arsenals for those arguments that carried the greatest analytic weight. The nervous quality of their writings was also a reflection of the extreme instability of seventeenth-century English politics. J. R. Jones has written of the period between 1660 and 1688 that "it was as if a whole generation of Englishmen had been subjected to the traditional Chinese curse, that they should 'live in interesting times.' "[4] The same might be said of the seventeenth century as a whole. It was a period of unprecedented demographic change, of religious conflict and political collapse, and of seemingly endless turmoil and anxiety. Men were obsessed with the thought that England might rapidly devolve into the lawless condition of its neighbors to the north and west, Scotland and Ireland. Royalist writers were engaged in a fierce polemical battle over the established order, and they saw their task in an essentially conservative light. Preservation and stability, not innovation and change, were the hallmarks of a well-turned argument. Finally, though there were a few royalist writers of great depth and imagination, and though there were many events of profound historical significance, there were no watersheds,

---

[3] *Discourses*, I:5, p. 12. Cf. *Two Treatises*, I:1; James Tyrrell, *Patriarcha non Monarcha* (1681), "Preface to the Reader."

[4] J. R. Jones, *Country and Court: England, 1658–1714* (Cambridge, MA: Harvard University Press, 1979), 1.

no ideas or events that set the whole of royalist thought on a new and elevated plane. One of the favorite tropes of royalists seeking to describe the ambitions of their opponents was that of a cardplayer attempting to reshuffle the deck in hopes of obtaining a new and better set of cards. The metaphor is appropriate for the life of the royalist mind as well, for it repeatedly drew new hands from the same well-worn deck.

Symbolic of the relatively unchanging character of seventeenth-century royalist thought is the recent controversy over the dating of Sir Robert Filmer's *Patriarcha*. Strong arguments have been made that the original manuscript was written in 1628, between 1635 and 1642, and in 1648.[5] Each of these arguments places the composition of *Patriarcha* in a period of crisis, either during the conflicts surrounding the Petition of Right, or during the years between the Ship Money Controversy and the outbreak of the Civil War, or during the early months of the "second" Civil War. That Filmer's text could plausibly have been written during any of these periods, and that it was equally at home during the Exclusion Crisis of 1679–81, is symptomatic of the complex yet essentially static character of royalist thought throughout the seventeenth century.[6]

Restricting attention to the immediate intellectual context within which *Patriarcha* was published and Tyrrell, Locke, and Sidney composed their rejoinders to it, it is possible to isolate five general arguments used by royalists to justify monarchy: that it was by divine right; that it was in accord with the law of nature; that it was in accord with the traditional English constitution; that it had de facto legitimacy; and that it was politically superior to all other forms of government.[7] Though the decision to focus exclusively on the ten years between 1675 and 1685 is in some sense arbitrary, the arguments that emerge are not. A virtually identical catalog could be composed for the years between 1603 and 1640, or between 1640 and 1660.[8]

---

[5] For 1628, see Richard Tuck, "A New Date for Filmer's Patriarcha," *Historical Journal* 29 (1986): 183–86; for 1635–42, see Peter Laslett, "Introduction," *Patriarcha*, 3–4; for 1648, see John M. Wallace, "The Date of Sir Robert Filmer's Patriarcha," *Historical Journal* 23 (1980): 155–65.

[6] I do not mean to imply that the date of composition of *Patriarcha* is irrelevant to our understanding of Filmer's objectives in writing it. Rather, I wish to highlight the fact that royalist discourse was sufficiently stable for Filmer's arguments to have had salience throughout the seventeenth century.

[7] Contemporaries were well aware of the different facets of royalist thought. For example, in 1680 John Somers identified four basic arguments for monarchy: patriarchalism, the law of nature, conquest, and the ancient constitution ([John Somers], *A Brief History of the Succession* [London: 1680], 15–17).

[8] There is no study of royalist ideas during the years surrounding the Exclusion

The most common claim advanced by royalists to justify monarchy was that it had been ordained by God: "Kings Reign by a Divine Right"; "Monarchy is of *Divine* Institution"; "our Monarchs derive not their Right from the People, but are absolute Monarchs deriving their Royal Authority immediately from God Almighty."[9] But there were varying levels of agreement and disagreement concerning the precise meaning to be attached to the claim that a monarch was "God's Minister and Vicegerent."[10] These can be usefully divided into explanations of why God instituted monarchs and descriptions of the mechanisms he uses to transmit his authority to them.

According to one school of thought, monarchs were necessary to control the lusts and passions of fallen men. God created governments "to bridle the Extravagancies of restless Mankind."[11] Political Augustinianism of this sort was frequently paired with the further claim that "God is not a God of sedition, of mutinye, and confusion, but of unity, order, and of peace."[12] Even this expanded argument was not inherently monarchical, however, and so it had to be filled out and reinforced in other ways. Most commonly, this involved a secular appeal to the nature of sovereignty, and in particular to the need for a final judge of controversies to ensure peace and order.

A seemingly more direct route to the divine right of kings could be found in Paul's Epistle to the Romans: "Let every soul be subject unto the higher powers. For there is no power but of God: the powers that be are ordained of God."[13] It was the duty of every Christian subject

---

Crisis comparable to the work that has been done on the Whigs. For the period between 1603 and 1640, see J. P. Sommerville, *Politics and Ideology in England 1603–1640* (London: Longman, 1986), 9–56.

[9] John Nalson, *The Common Interest of King and People: Shewing the Original, Antiquity and Excellency of Monarchy* (1677), 236; [Matthew Rider], *The Power of Parliaments in the Case of Succession* (1680), 12; George Mackenzie, *Jus Regium* (1684), 13.

[10] William Sherlock, *The Case of Resistance of the Supreme Powers . . . According to the Doctrine of the Holy Scriptures* (1684), 205.

[11] Mackenzie, *Jus Regium*, 123, 91, 101, 172–73. See also: *Captain Thorogood His Opinion of the Point of Succession* (1679), 8; *The True Protestant Subject, or, the Nature, and Rights of Sovereignty Discuss'd, and Stated* (1680), 5–11, 15–17; [George Hickes], *The Harmony of Divinity and Law, In a Discourse About Not Resisting of Soveraign Princes* (1684), 68.

[12] [Dudley Digges], *The Unlawfulnesse of Subjects taking up Armes against their Soveraigne, in what case soever* (1643), 12. The quotation is a gloss on a biblical verse favored by royalists, I Corinthians 14:33. Digges's pamphlet was only one of many royalist tracts from the Civil War that were reprinted during the Exclusion Crisis—in this case, in 1679.

[13] Romans 13:1. For example, see: *Great and Weighty Considerations Relating to the D., Or Successor of the Crown* (1679), 6; Edmund Bohun, "Preface to the Reader," *Patriarcha: or the Natural Power of Kings. By the Learned Sir Robert Filmer*, 2nd ed. (1685), chap. 1, pars. 31–39.

to submit to the rule of the monarch, to render unto Caesar those things that were Caesar's.[14] This too, however, was a perilously unstable argument. It provided no clear indication of what actually belonged to Caesar; and like the Augustinian argument, it was not inherently monarchical. These problems were frequently addressed by drawing attention to the history of the Israelites and to God's decision to set a king over them as revealed in Deuteronomy 17 and I Samuel 8. Thus John Nalson, an Anglican clergyman and historian, argued in 1677 that "what was Canonical Scripture to the Primitive Ages must be so to us, and if Kings had then a Divine Right they have so still."[15] "Genetic" arguments of this type, assuming that "there was a direct and discernable relationship between political duty and the way civil authority began," were quite common during the seventeenth century.[16] That Nalson belabored the point, however, suggests that there were widespread qualms about the validity of genetic arguments. This may have been particularly true when the gospel was applied to political affairs. More important, this kind of argument did not definitively identify the person of Caesar. To answer that question, royalists generally turned either to patriarchal or to providential arguments.

Patriarchalism held that the authority of a monarch was either identical or analogous to the authority of a father over his family. Royalists who emphasized the identity of political and paternal authority drew on the book of Genesis, with its account of "the traduction of Mankind from one single Man."[17] As Adam had had dominion over the whole of the Creation, so monarchs, by the logic of primogeniture and proximity of blood, had dominion over their kingdoms.[18] Political authority was an integral part of their biblical patrimony. Given the frequency with which the bloodline of the English monarchy had been broken, not to mention the virtual impossibility of actually proving that any given monarch was the rightful heir of Adam's dominion, this strong claim was frequently jettisoned

---

[14] [George Hickes], *Jovian* (1683), 283–96; Mackenzie, *Jus Regium*, 99–106.

[15] Nalson, *The Common Interest*, 216, 87. See also: [Rider], *The Power of Parliaments*, 26; Edmund Bohun to George Hickes, 5 November 1683, Bodleian Library, MS. Eng. Letters C12, fol. 159.

[16] Gordon Schochet, *Patriarchalism in Political Thought* (Oxford: Basil Blackwell, 1975), 9.

[17] [Hickes], *Harmony of Divinity and Law*, 15. See also: [John Northleigh], *Remarks Upon the most Eminent of our Antimonarchical Authors* (1699), 616–17.

[18] E.F., *A Letter From A Gentleman of Quality In The Country, To His Friend* (1679), 2–3; [Rider], *The Power of Parliaments*, 9, 18; Mackenzie, *Jus Regium*, 23–25; Bohun, "Preface to the Reader," chap. 1, pars. 31–39; [Northleigh], *Remarks Upon . . . Antimonarchical Authors*, 620–23.

in favor of a weaker one that simply asserted that there existed an analogy between political and paternal authority. Monarchs were *Pater Patriae*, fathers of the fatherland, and possessed all the powers, privileges, affections, and responsibilities that natural fathers did.[19] It was possible to draw support for this claim from a panoply of hierarchical relationships in society, ranging from those between fathers and sons or husbands and wives to those between masters and servants.[20] Moreover, it was possible to buttress this analogy with what was perhaps the most important passage in the Bible for seventeenth-century English men and women, the injunction to "honour thy father and thy mother." "What can be more *Express* in favor of this *Assertion* of Natural Bondage, than the *Fifth Commandment*[?]"[21]

Even analogical patriarchalism fell prey to skeptical criticism, however, and largely for the same reasons that identical patriarchalism had. There were simply too many jumps and starts in the royal line within recent memory to make the analogy entirely plausible, and there was the nagging and unavoidable fact of the Norman Conquest to be dealt with. As a result, most patriarchalists propped up their arguments with references to God's active hand in history. At its most naïve, providentialism asserted that "God's overruling Providence" protected his subjects by placing power in the hands of good and just men.[22] For all but the most rabid of royalists this was an absurd and unpalatable claim, however, and so it was more commonly asserted that over the long run, and not at each step of the way, God ensured that power and authority rested in the hands of righteous monarchs. Short and turbulent reigns indicated that it was God's will that power be lodged elsewhere, while long and peaceful reigns were the fruits of God's blessings.[23] It was even possible to assert that over time God preserved the logic of patriarchy. Thus the Stuarts, as rightful heirs to the throne, were finally brought to power in spite of the "interregnum" of the Tudors.[24]

[19] Nalson, *The Common Interest*, 6, 112; [Northleigh], *Remarks Upon . . . Antimonarchical Authors*, 623–27.

[20] [Marchamont Nedham], *A Pacquet of Advices and Animadversions, Sent from London To the Men of Shaftesbury* (1676), 43; *True Protestant Subject*, 25; [Hickes], *Harmony of Divinity and Law*, 14; Sherlock, *Case of Resistance*, 205; Bohun, "Preface to the Reader," chap. 1, pars. 51, 66; chap. 2, par. 47. The analogy worked both ways; Nedham referred to fathers as "you that are Kings of those little Kingdoms called Families" (*Pacquet of Advices*, 27).

[21] *True Protestant Subject*, 11. On the place of the fifth commandment in seventeenth-century thought, see Schochet, *Patriarchalism*, 79.

[22] *Great and Weighty Considerations*, 3. See also: *True Protestant Subject*, 5, 15.

[23] Bohun, "Preface to the Reader," chap. 2, par. 2.

[24] E.F., *A Letter From A Gentleman Of Quality*, 4–5, 11–15.

Regardless of the justness with which a monarch ruled, the lesson taught by both patriarchalism and providentialism was passivity in the face of political power. According to Edmund Bohun, a virulent Anglican layman who issued a corrected edition of Filmer's *Patriarcha* in 1685, "if the government hath injur'd me, I ought to take it as the injuries of the weather, and not rage and fret at it."[25] The wily Tory pamphleteer and newspaperman Sir Roger L'Estrange agreed: "he that can say Heartily [*Thy Will Be Done*] has conn'd his Lesson."[26]

Closely related to divine-right justifications of monarchy were arguments based on the law of nature. Indeed, during the seventeenth century writers rarely referred to the laws of nature *simpliciter*, but almost always to "the Laws of God and Nature." Where the laws of God emphasized the place of faith and the Bible, however, the laws of nature drew on the powers of human reason.[27]

The most sophisticated arguments for monarchy to make use of the laws of nature were developed by Thomas Hobbes. But Hobbesian arguments found little favor among royalists, in part because they appeared to sever the ties between monarchy and its traditional religious justifications. In fact, the first invocation of the law of nature during the period under consideration was in an explicitly anti-Hobbesian tract. According to John Nalson, it was not Hobbesian fear but self-love and natural sociability that led men to form governments. The "Two great Principles of Nature" were "Self-preservation and the ardent Desire of Happiness."[28] That Nalson misunderstood

---

[25] [Bohun], *Address to the Free-Men*, 30. See also: [Hickes], *Jovian*, passim; Mackenzie, *Jus Regium*, 99–106.

[26] Roger L'Estrange, *The Observator, in Dialogue* (1687), 2:15 (15 February 1683/4). In 1663 L'Estrange wrote in the official government newspaper that "Supposing the press in order, the people in their right wits, and news or no news to be the question, a public mercury should never have my vote, because I think it makes the multitude too familiar with the actions and counsels of their superior, too pragmatical and censorious, and gives them not only a wish, but a kind of colourable right and license to the meddling with the government" (quoted in *Dictionary of National Biography*, s.v. "Roger L'Estrange").

[27] There is no evidence to support Richard Ashcraft's assertion that *Patriarcha* "acted as a catalyst in forcing the ideological battle [during the Exclusion Crisis] onto the terrain of natural law," or that the decision of Sidney and others to frame their arguments in terms of the law of nature meant that they "were following or responding to the natural law argument advanced by Filmer" (*Revolutionary Politics & Locke's Two Treatises of Government* [Princeton: Princeton University Press, 1986], 189, 190 n. 26). The law of nature was invoked by royalists and antiroyalists throughout the seventeenth century, and no discernible shift in the incidence of references to it following the publication of Filmer's writings can be detected. In the case of Sidney and Locke, an examination of their early writings indicates that they were both committed to the law of nature prior to their encounter with Filmer.

[28] Nalson, *The Common Interest*, 23.

Hobbes's arguments and intentions is, in this context, less interesting than that he felt no qualms about countering Hobbes's portrait of the state of nature with one of his own.

Impervious to analysis, the law of nature provided an effective shield behind which controversial yet cherished beliefs could be protected. In response to the first bill to exclude the duke of York, an anonymous pamphleteer argued that the order of succession was "inseparably annexed to proximity and nextness of Blood" by the "Laws of God and Nature."[29] Somewhat more typically, Matthew Rider argued that the law of nature could be defined as "the innate propensity of all Creatures to that, which is most agreeable to their respective natures. . . . Thus it is *Natural* to all Beings, to preserve themselves; to all *Sensitive Creatures* to propagate their *Species* or kind; and to *Rational Agents*, to live in *Society*, and do *as they would be done unto*." Since "all disinterested people acknowledge, [and] experience, reason, and authority confirms," that monarchy is "the best, the ancientest, and most agreeable to man's original," it must be in accord with the laws of nature.[30]

In the same breath that royalists appealed to God and nature, they also invoked the traditional English constitution. The rights of monarchy rested equally upon "the fundamental constitution of our Government, upon our old Laws, upon the Laws of God, of Nature, of Nations, and particularly of the Civil Law."[31] Where arguments based on the law of nature permitted appeals to the universal dictates of reason, however, arguments based on the traditional constitution drew attention to the unique contours of the English political system.

In his seminal study of the ancient constitution, J.G.A. Pocock emphasized the distinction between customary and command theories of law in seventeenth-century English political thought.[32] Customary theories relied on the unchanging and immemorial nature of the common law; command theories relied on the feudal or sovereign capacity of the lawmaker. Coke and Hobbes are archetypes of these two modes of thought. Royalists ultimately relied on a command theory of the law; but the fulcrum of their arguments was not a historical claim about the origins of the traditional constitution, but a simple belief that England's was a *"Well-order'd-Monarchy."*[33] Claiming presumptive validity for the existing constitution, they asserted that

[29] E.F., *A Letter From A Gentleman of Quality*, 2.

[30] [Rider], *The Power of Parliaments*, 11, 15. See also: 12, 37.

[31] Mackenzie, *Jus Regium*, 145.

[32] J.G.A. Pocock, *The Ancient Constitution and the Feudal Law* (Cambridge: Cambridge University Press, 1957).

[33] [Nedham], *Pacquet of Advices*, 40.

there was no happier spot on the globe than England under her monarchs. As one pamphleteer put it, "here are priviledges sufficient to prove the goodness of our Laws."[34] Origins were far less important than the simple fact that "the Known Laws and Statues those *Authentick Records* of the Kingdom" could be invoked to prove that England's traditional constitution was monarchical.[35]

An excellent example of the way royalists invoked the traditional constitution to justify monarchy can be seen in their treatment of Parliament. It was universally agreed that "the supposition, of the Parliaments representing the people, is a fiction of Law." The franchise was restricted to forty-shilling freeholders and citizens in certain boroughs, and its distribution bore no relation to the population as a whole. One need only have looked at Old Sarum, Cornwall, or London to have seen that fact. Parliament was "not at all the Representative of the People," but an organ of the body politic, created by the king to assist him in preserving its health.[36] By presuming the legitimacy of the traditional constitution, royalists were able to turn the very features of the political system that most angered radicals to the advantage of monarchy. It was a viciously circular argument, but as polemic it was brilliant.

In a second and related claim, royalists argued that although Parliament was formally composed of King, Lords, and Commons, this did not mean that its power or authority arose from the coordination of these three estates. In fact, the king was not one of the estates of the realm, but as head of the body politic he presided over them.[37] This argument directly contradicted the "Answer to the Nineteen Propositions" issued by Charles I in 1642, which had proclaimed that the English Constitution rested on a "Balance" of the three estates of monarchy, aristocracy, and democracy.[38] But the doctrine of "Co-or-

[34] Nalson, *The Common Interest*, 158, 136, 151–52. See also: [Rider], *The Power of Parliaments*, 1.

[35] *The Royal Apology: Or, An Answer To the Rebels Plea* (1684), 7, 14–18.

[36] *Captain Thorogood*, 3–5. See also: [Rider], *The Power of Parliaments*, 3–4; *Three Great Questions Concerning the Succession and the Dangers of Popery* (1680), 12–13; [Northleigh], *Remarks Upon . . . Antimonarchical Authors*, 605–11; W.W., *Antidotum Britannicum* (1681), 66.

[37] [Roger L'Estrange], *The Free-born Subject: Or, The Englishman's Birthright* (1679), 5; [Roger L'Estrange], *Citt and Bumpkin. In a Dialogue over a Pot of Ale* (1680), 24; "The Judgment and Decree of the University of Oxford," *London Gazette* 1845 (23–26 July 1683); [Laurence Womock?], *A Short Way To A Lasting Settlement* (1683), 3; [Hickes], *Harmony of Divinity and Law*, 36; *Royal Apology*, 16; [Northleigh], *Remarks Upon . . . Antimonarchical Authors*, 559; W.W., *Antidotum Britannicum*, 122.

[38] Charles I, "His Majesty's Answer to the Nineteen Propositions of both Houses of Parliament," 18 June 1642, in *Historical Collections of Private Passages of State*, ed. J. Rushworth (1659–1701), 5:731.

dinate Powers" was an innovation in constitutional theory, and royalists feared it not only for the independence it gave the two Houses—it implied that they possessed two-thirds of the nation's sovereign power—but also for the indeterminacy it introduced into political decision making. What, after all, was to be done when the three estates disagreed with each other? Unity required unanimity, and that could be guaranteed only if the monarch stood outside of or above the various estates of the realm. The only "balance" late-seventeenth-century royalists permitted was the traditional one between "the *Liberty* and *Property* of the *Subject*, and the *Grandeur* and *Majesty* of the *Sovereign*."[39]

Historical evidence for these claims could be found in the research of antiquarians. Depending on one's sources, the origins of Parliament could be traced to the reigns of Henry I, Henry III, or Edward I; but of the fact that kings had temporally preceded parliaments, and were the authors of them, there could be no dispute.[40] The same body of historical evidence could be used to prove that kings were the authors of the law. As one writer put it, "the Legislative and Architectonick Power of making Laws . . . does solely reside in the King, the Estates of Parliament only consenting."[41]

One awkward fact from the perspective of royalist theories of the traditional constitution was the conquest of the Normans. Though willing to use a command theory of law, most royalists were unwilling to go so far as to claim that the power to command obedience in itself legitimated those commands. *De facto* arguments collapsed the distinction between right and power and were notorious among men steeped in legalist and legitimist traditions of thought. But as a means of reconciling men to the powers that be, de facto arguments were powerful and seemingly unavoidable. As Marchamont Nedham put it in an influential tract written in 1650 to convince reluctant Englishmen to accept the rule of the Rump Parliament, "the power of the sword ever hath been the foundation of all titles to government in

---

[39] [Rider], *The Power of Parliaments*, 1. See also: *Captain Thorogood*, 5; [Womock?], *Short Way*, 29; *Royal Apology*, 19; W.W., *Antidotum Britannicum*, "Epistle Dedicatory." Two pamphlets significantly altered this traditional concept of the balance. One argued that the king held the balance "between the power of Lords and Commons" (*Three Great Questions*, 16); the other held that the king acts to prevent "a Jarring between the three Estates" ([John Dryden?], *His Majesties Declaration Defended* [1681], 19). The presence of fundamental social conflict implicit in both these claims would have been unacceptable to most royalists.

[40] [Nedham], *Pacquet of Advices*, 42; Nalson, *The Common Interest*, 13, 214; *Captain Thorogood*, 6; [Rider], *The Power of Parliaments*, 4; *Three Great Questions*, 5, 9.

[41] Mackenzie, *Jus Regium*, 67. See also: Nalson, *The Common Interest*, 13–14; [Womock?], *Short Way*, 24; Sherlock, *Case of Resistance*, 196–98.

England both before and since the Norman Conquest." Being possessed of the sword, the government not only "may," but "must," be obeyed.[42]

Royalists remained wary of de facto arguments throughout the seventeenth century. But for complicated historical and ideological reasons, they found it difficult to avoid endorsing Hobbes's dictum that "there is scarce a Common-wealth in the world, whose beginnings can in conscience be justified." Thus Roger L'Estrange asserted that if usurpation gave no right to rule then all the governments in the world would be thrown "off the hinges," and Matthew Rider held that "there is hardly any *Monarch* now upon earth, but is either an *Usurper*, or at least his *Heir* and *Successor*." Such bold endorsements of conquest or usurpation were frequently sugarcoated with references to God's active hand in history: "as no usurpation can succeed without God's permission," the sheer fact of its success is a sign of its providential legitimacy.[43] But royalists also relied, as Hobbes had, on the claim that legitimacy was a function of the sovereign's capacity to keep the peace, and not of his (or its) genesis. In so doing, they made use of a distinctly secular, "political" argument for monarchy.

The most important political argument for monarchy rested on the concept of sovereignty. According to George Hickes, who was chaplain to the king's Scottish minister Lauderdale during the late 1670s, the rights of the monarch were "those Prerogatives and Pre-Eminences of Power and Greatness, which are involved in the formal Conception of Sovereignty." Those rights were: to be "accountable to none except God"; to have the "sole Power & Disposal of the Sword"; "to be free from all *Coercive*, and *Vindictive* Power"; "Not to be resisted or withstood by Force upon any pretence whatsoever"; and "to have the Legislative Power, or, the Power that makes any form of Words a Law." The centerpiece of these rights was the claim that monarchs were "accountable to none except God."[44] Monarchs were bound by the laws in conscience only; in the parlance of the day, they were subject to the "directive," but not the "coactive," power of the law. The author of *The Royal Apology* explained the logic of sovereignty in

[42] [Marchamont Nedham], *The Case of the Commonwealth of England, Stated*, ed. Philip A. Knachel (Folger Shakespeare Library, 1969), 25, 28.

[43] Thomas Hobbes, *Leviathan*, ed. C. B. Macpherson (Harmondsworth: Penguin Books, 1981), 722; [L'Estrange], *Observator*, 1:467 (4 January 1684); [Rider], *The Power of Parliaments*, 25; Bohun, "Preface to the Reader," chap. 2, par. 2. On the connections between Bohun's providentialism and his use of conquest theory, see Mark Goldie, "Edmund Bohun and *Jus Gentium* in the Revolution Debate, 1689–1693," *Historical Journal* 20 (1977): 569–86.

[44] [Hickes], *Jovian*, 200–202.

1684: "*Appeals* must not be *Infinite*. . . . There must be some *Supreme Power*, in whose final Determination (be it *right*, or be it *wrong*) all *Inferiors* must acquiesce and submit, otherwise, no *Controversies* could be decided; nay, there could be no *Government*, nothing but Disorder and Confusion in the World."[45] Over and over this message was hammered home: "no man is judg'd but by his Superior, and that which is Supream can have no Superior"; monarchy provided "one Person, from whose Definitive sentence there shall lye no appeal"; the sovereign power of judgment was "the nail, which fastens the whole Fabrick in every Government." "Consider," chided Roger L'Estrange, "how ridiculous it were to *Appeal Downward*; or from *Sovereign Princes*, to any other Power, than to the *King of Kings*, who alone is above them."[46]

While it may be true, as Mark Goldie has observed, that English royalists had great "reverence for . . . and dependence upon" the writings of the great French theorist Jean Bodin,[47] the inspiration for and essence of their theory of sovereignty was strictly English: the common-law maxim that an inferior court cannot judge a superior court. So long as judgment was taken to be the essence of government, there could be no escaping the implications of the theory of juridical sovereignty. In each nation there must be a final voice definitively resolving all controversies. Without such an authority there could be no end to legal or political disputes. But as Hobbes had argued, this sovereign power of judgment need not be placed in the hands of a monarch; it could as easily be lodged in an assembly of notables, or in an elective body representative of the whole nation. Royalists achieved closure in this otherwise underdetermined doctrine by appeal to a second common-law maxim: a man must not be a judge in his own cause. With suitable presuppositions, notably the existence of a monarch with roughly sovereign powers—as was so often the case, circularity was unavoidable—it was possible to pronounce unequivocally that only the monarch was capable of independent and disinterested judgment in controversies. Thus implicitly the argument from sovereignty relied on a second "political" claim, that only in the person of a monarch were public and private interests united.

Like most seventeenth-century English men and women, royalists

[45] *Royal Apology*, 35–36.

[46] Mackenzie, *Jus Regium*, 78; Nalson, *The Common Interest*, 97; [Hickes], *Harmony of Divinity and Law*, 5–6; [L'Estrange], *Free-born Subject*, 3. See also: Sherlock, *Case of Resistance*, 8, 193; Bohun, "Preface to the Reader," chap. 2, par. 47; [Northleigh], *Remarks Upon . . . Antimonarchical Authors*, 504–5, 525.

[47] Mark Goldie, "John Locke and Anglican Royalism," *Political Studies* 31 (1983): 69.

did not distinguish between partial or private interests and factional interests, between interests coherent with or opposed to the public interest. The first charge fired against an opponent was almost always the accusation that he was a member of a party or a faction and that his interests were private and not public. The simple observation that Whigs conducted their business in taverns, clubs, and coffeehouses during the Exclusion Crisis was taken as a self-evident criticism.[48] When it was further noted that some distinguished themselves with green ribbons, and that they were organized into committees and subcommittees, their status as a faction or cabal was confirmed.[49] And as every man knew, "government by Faction can never be for the general good of any Community."[50]

Religious nonconformists were equally subject to attack for their "factional" ideas and conduct. In typically vitriolic fashion, Roger L'Estrange described a Dissenter as "not of *This*, or of *That*, or of *Any Religion*; but *A Member Politique of an Incorporate Faction*."[51] Presbyterians were particularly vulnerable to the charge of being "Corporated parcels of the *Body Politick* . . . march[ing] counter to the publick Interest of the Government."[52] Long before the radical Whigs, royalists had developed a "language of 'invasion' " of their own.[53] Where opponents of Charles II relied on the analogy between a foreign invasion and a domestic betrayal of trust, however, royalists pointed to the role of the Scottish Kirk in the Civil War. There could be no mistaking the aims of the conventicles: they were laying the groundwork for an invasion of England and a return to conditions not seen since the 1640s. That was the ideological intent behind royalist attempts to link English Presbyterians in the 1670s and 1680s with the "Solemn League and Covenant" of 1643.[54]

Only in the person of the monarch, royalists universally agreed, were public and private interests united. In a republic or an aristocracy, the private interests of the rulers need not be identical with the

---

[48] [L'Estrange], *Citt and Bumpkin*, 1, 19; [Dryden?], *His Majesties Declaration*, 5, 17; [John Nalson], *The Complaint of Liberty & Property Against Arbitrary Government* (1681), 2; [Hickes], *Jovian*, 1–2.

[49] *A Seasonable Address to both Houses of Parliament Concerning the Succession* (1681), 19.

[50] Nalson, *The Common Interest*, 64.

[51] [L'Estrange], *Observator*, 1:1 (13 April 1681).

[52] [Nedham], *Pacquet of Advices*, 17.

[53] According to Richard Ashcraft, after the dissolution of the Oxford Parliament radical Whig arguments coalesced around the claim that the king was no different from a usurper or invader (Ashcraft, *Revolutionary Politics*, 395, and generally, 338–405).

[54] [Nedham], *Pacquet of Advices*, 20–22, 34; Nalson, *The Common Interest*, 241, 259–60; [Bohun], *Address to the Free-Men*, 4–5, 10–20.

public interest. But a hereditary monarch "has no separate interest, or distinct design from the good of the public; for whether it be peace, plenty, glory, riches, trade, war, happiness or misfortune, the people can have none of these in general, but the Prince must have his share of them too, so that the Prince cannot be miserable and his people truly happy, nor the Prince happy whilst his people are really miserable."[55] "Salus Regis *Is* Salus Populi."[56] This simple yet dubious claim was repeated ad nauseam. No desire or passion was capable of overriding the basic identity of interests between a prince and his subjects. To royalists, this was the lesson to be learned from the maxim that "interest will not lie."

While the interests of individual Englishmen did not easily fit into royalist arguments, the character of the English people did, and it provided a third political argument for monarchy. According to the author of *The Nations Interest*, "our *English Nature* is not like the *French*, supple to *Oppression*, and apt to delight in that *Pomp* and *Magnificence* of their *Lords*, which (they know) is supported with their *Slavery* and *Hunger*; Nor like the *Highland Scots*, where the *Honour* and *Interest* of the *Chief* is the Glory of the whole *Clan*: So doth it as little (or less) agree with the *Dutch* humour, addicted only to *Traffick*, *Navigation*, *Handicrafts*, and sordid *Thrift*, and (in defiance of *Heraldry*) every man fancying his own *Scutcheon*." No, the genius of the English people was sturdy, robust, and eminently suited to monarchy. This could be proven by means of a simple thought experiment: "[Can you] imagine, that our *Nobility* and *Gentry* (as now in Power) will ever be induc'd to admit a *Parity*; will level their *Degree* and *Domination* to a Proportion with their *Copy-holders*? Nay, will renounce the *wearing of a Sword*, and learn to *make* one?"[57] English gentlemen were aristocrats at heart, linked by their ambitions, their vanity, and their pride to the ideology and practice of hierarchy, degree, and place. It was sheer folly to imagine that they would rest content with anything less than monarchy.

Finally, royalist writers were surprisingly willing to provide contextual and comparative justifications for monarchy. No single form of government was suited to all places or conditions, and "even *Monar-*

[55] Nalson, *The Common Interest*, 109. See also: Mackenzie, *Jus Regium*, 57–58; Bohun, "Preface to the Reader," chap. 2, par. 51; [Northleigh], *Remarks Upon . . . Antimonarchical Authors*, 504–5, 662–63.

[56] [L'Estrange], *Observator*, 1:464 (29 December 1683).

[57] *The Nations Interest: In Relation to . . . the Duke of York* (1680), 10. See also: Sir William Temple, "An Essay Upon the Original and Nature of Government," in *The Works of Sir William Temple, Bart* (1754), 3:55–56; [Hickes], *Harmony of Divinity and Law*, 16–17.

chy itself is but as *Earthen Ware* (though of the *finest* and *strongest Sort*) and liable to sundry *Contingencies*."[58] But by any standard of measurement, it was superior to all other forms of government. This claim was implicit in arguments based on the nature of sovereignty, the public interest, or the genius of the English people. But it was frequently made explicit as well. The most common argument, undoubtedly intended to provoke memories scorched by the Civil War, was framed in terms of comparative atrocities: nonmonarchical governments were a hundred, a thousand, even ten thousand times more brutal than the most tyrannical of monarchs. As George Mackenzie rhetorically wondered, "did not *De Wit* find little of that Justice which he magnified in Republicks?" Mackenzie was a vigorous champion of the prerogative, and as king's advocate in Scotland earned the moniker "Bloody Mackenzie" for his persecution of the Covenanters. But the belief that the only alternative to monarchy was anarchy and desolation was almost universal.[59]

Less gruesome bases of comparison between monarchy and other forms of government ranged from the superior capacity of a monarchy to act with unity, secrecy, and speed, to the fact that monarchs were more qualified, by birth and education, to assume the reins of power.[60] One of the most striking features of these comparisons is the willingness of royalist writers to use classical authors to substantiate their arguments. From Aristotle and Thucydides to Tacitus, Livy, and Cicero, the history and ideas of Greece and Rome were a constant presence in royalist tracts.[61] In a society of classically educated men and women, the writings of the ancients provided a common set of reference points for royalists and antiroyalists alike.

The Ideology of Natural Subjection

These five general arguments—that monarchy was by divine right; that it was in accord with the law of nature; that it was in accord with

[58] *Nations Interest*, 5. See also: Temple, "Essay Upon the Original and Nature of Government," 3:50; Nalson, *The Common Interest*, 21; Sherlock, *Case of Resistance*, 215.

[59] Mackenzie, *Jus Regium*, 61, 40. In 1672 John De Witt and his brother Cornelius were brutally murdered by a popular mob in the Hague. For similar arguments, see also: *Seasonable Address*, 10; [L'Estrange], *Observator*, 1:465 (31 December 1683); [Hickes], *Harmony of Divinity and Law*, 18–20; Bohun, "Preface to the Reader," chap. 1, par. 51.

[60] Nalson, *The Common Interest*, 59–60, 65, 68, 113; Mackenzie, *Jus Regium*, 46–47, 58, 60, 62; [Northleigh], *Remarks Upon . . . Antimonarchical Authors*, 534, 665.

[61] For example, see: [Nedham], *Pacquet of Advices*, 4; Nalson, *The Common Interest*, 73; *True Protestant Subject*, 6–11, 15, 31; [Rider], *The Power of Parliaments*, 12, 16, 17, 19–21, 37–38; [Hickes], *Harmony of Divinity and Law*, 4, 15.

the traditional English constitution; that it had de facto legitimacy; and that it was politically superior to all other forms of government—defined the boundaries of royalist thought during much of the seventeenth century. No single thread runs throughout them; they form a patchwork stitched together over time, rather than a single piece of fabric woven as a whole. There is no "essence" of royalist thought. That is not to say that royalist arguments are unrelated, however. To borrow a metaphor from Wittgenstein, they bear a "family resemblance" to each other, "for the various resemblances between members of a family: build, features, colour of eyes, gait, temperament, etc. etc. overlap and criss-cross in the same way."[62] And as a family, they were devoted to the proposition that "the People of any Nation . . . [are] the natural subject of Obedience, and Subjection."[63]

Virtually everyone living in seventeenth-century England believed that humans were subject to God's commands. But there was great disagreement over what human institutions were entailed by that belief; and in the process of explicating it, royalists tended to draw on a wider and less explicitly theological body of beliefs and prejudices. These habits of the heart rested largely on the evidence of custom and tradition, of metaphor and analogy. The most commonly invoked of these beliefs was that nature itself was built around relationships of rule and subjection, of hierarchy and degree, and that monarchy was an integral part of the natural order. The "similitudes" made possible by "the great chain of being" were virtually limitless.[64] As head, the king gave direction to the body of the nation; as sun, he was the focal point around which the stars, those "plebeians of the sky," revolved; as father and husband of the nation, he benevolently guided his wife and children in their daily lives.[65] These were not accidental or voluntary relationships, and they could not be violated without the direst of consequences. In the words of Shakespeare's Ulysses,

> The heavens themselves, the planets, and this centre
> Observe degree, priority and place

[62] Ludwig Wittgenstein, *Philosophical Investigations*, trans. G.E.M. Anscombe, 3rd ed. (New York: Macmillan, 1958), par. 67.

[63] [Hickes], *Harmony of Divinity and Law*, 14. See also: E.F., *A Letter From A Gentleman of Quality*, 4; [Rider], *The Power of Parliaments*, 2; Bohun, "Preface to the Reader," chap. 1, par. 72.

[64] A wealth of examples can be found in Arthur O. Lovejoy, *The Great Chain of Being* (Cambridge, MA: Harvard University Press, 1964), and E.M.W. Tillyard, *The Elizabethan World Picture* (New York: Vintage Books, n.d.).

[65] Nalson, *The Common Interest*, 126–29. See also: [Rider], *The Power of Parliaments*, 3; [L'Estrange], *Observator*, 1463 (27 December 1683); Mackenzie, *Jus Regium*, 22; [Northleigh], *Remarks Upon . . . Antimonarchical Authors*, 523–25.

. . . .
> Take but degree away, untune that string,
> And, hark! what discord follows.

Differentiation, inequality, and hierarchy were woven into the fabric of the Creation. Were they to be removed, the very seas would "make a sop of all this solid globe."[66]

Coherent with though analytically distinct from the vision of the great chain of being was the belief that "the people" were by nature in need of authority and that their freedom came from being subject to the laws. By "the people" seventeenth-century Englishmen often meant the commonalty, those who were neither noblemen nor members of the clergy. But they also used this term to refer more specifically to those who lived without estates: servants, paupers, and day laborers, artisans, tradesmen, and shopkeepers. Taken together, these men and women (and their dependents) constituted some two-thirds of the nation's population.[67] Their political status was succinctly described by Charles I in his speech on the scaffold in 1649: "For the people . . . their Liberty and their freedom, consists in having of Government; those Laws, by which their life and their goods, may be most their own. It is not for having share in Government (sir) that is nothing pertaining to them. A Subject and a Sovereign are clean different things."[68] The only power permitted to the people was "the *Power* of *Submission*, and *Resignation*." The alternative was "nothing but Cutting of *Throats* to the End of the Chapter."[69] The term most frequently used by royalists to describe the people was "the *Mobile*." They were "restless," "giddy," "freakish," "as changeable, unconstant, and variable as the weather."[70] Their very being posed a threat

---

[66] *Troilus and Cressida*, act 1, sc. 3, lines 84–124. The polemical usefulness of the great chain of being was not missed by Sidney's contemporaries: "If the account of time should be Regulated not by the Sun alone (who is the *Prince* and *Monarch* of the *Heavens*) but by the joynt Motion of the other *Planets* which were a kind of *Oligarchie*, or by the Stars of the first Magnitude (which are *Optimates Coeli*) and were an *Aristocracy*, what Disorders would creep into the Kalendar? But how great would the Confusion be, if those *Plebeian Sparks*; those lesser Stars (which People the Sky, and only glymmer by the Contribution of Light which they receive from the greater Luminaries) should have a Predominant Influence upon our Seasons?" (W.W., *Antidotum Britannicum*, "Preface"). See also: *The Character of a Rebellion, and what England may expect from one* (1681), 10–11.

[67] This figure is rough and is meant only to be illustrative of the magnitude of this group. It is based on Gregory King's income tables of 1688, reprinted in Peter Laslett, *The World We Have Lost—Further Explored*, 3rd ed. (London: Methuen, 1983), 32–33.

[68] Charles I, *King Charles His Speech made upon the Scaffold* (1649), 6.

[69] [L'Estrange], *Observator*, 1:463 (27 December 1683), 1:464 (29 December 1683).

[70] *A Funeral Sermon on the Occasion of the Death of Algernon Sidney* (1683), 45–46. See

to the delicate balance of hierarchy and degree that held society together. Only by constantly reminding the people that the gospel itself "positively asserts *Rule* and *Obedience*, as the *only* means to preserve *Peace* among *Mankind*" was it possible to avert a complete breakdown of the moral and political order.[71]

If only to exaggerate the problems created by the disorderly nature of the people, they were also believed to be incapable of authoring the laws needed to contain them. Contempt for the moral and cognitive capacities of "private men" was an integral part of the royalist outlook. In Roger L'Estrange's savagely satiric vision, the people was composed of porters, cobblers, and tinkers, "*Whistling Politiques*, and *Reformation*, to the *Underlaying of a Shoe*, or the *Footing of a Pair of Stockings*."[72] They could be expected to know "their own wants, fears and dangers," but they were not "sufficiently qualified" to judge matters of state. That was what was meant when it was said that "private men" ought not meddle in public business.[73]

Given these beliefs, royalists viewed resistance and rebellion not simply as challenges to existing authorities, but as efforts to unhinge and overturn the order God had established in the universe. Rebellion was "as ancient as the Creation," coeval with the fall from grace. Brought on by "the Serpent of Sedition," by "the sin of Witchcraft," it was an attempt to reform heaven and earth.[74]

When Whigs began to agitate against the government of Charles II and the threat posed by the duke of York, royalists mobilized the ide-

---

also: [J. Dean], *The Wine-Cooper's Delight* (1681), 2; [Rider], *The Power of Parliaments*, 2; *Some Animadversions on the Paper Delivered to the Sheriffs . . . By Algernon Sidney* (1683), 2–3; *An Exact Account of the Tryal of Algernon Sidney* (1683), 2–3; S. Ward, *The Animadversions and Remarks Upon Collonel Sydney's Paper Answered* (1684), 1; [L'Estrange], *Observator*, 2: "Preface"; Mackenzie, *Jus Regium*, 21.

[71] *True Protestant Subject*, 11. "The generality of men can scarce be contained in their Duty by the severest Laws that can be made" (Mackenzie, *Jus Regium*, 91); "consider what a wild Desert of unmanageable Brutes must this City [London] of necessity be without Laws and Government" (*Character of a Rebellion*, 12). See also: Nalson, *The Common Interest*, 20.

[72] [L'Estrange], *Observator*, 1:463 (27 December 1683). See also: [Rider], *The Power of Parliaments*, 2–3.

[73] *An Impartial Account of the Nature and Tendency of the Late Addresses*, in *State Tracts* (1693), 1:426. See also: *True Protestant Subject*, 15; [L'Estrange], *Observator*, 1:464 (29 December 1683); Mackenzie, *Jus Regium*, 55; *Royal Apology*, 7. Closely connected to this view was the belief that there existed "mysteries" or "secrets" of state that were beyond the comprehension of mere mortals.

[74] *Captain Thorogood*, 7; [Northleigh], *Remarks Upon . . . Antimonarchical Authors*, sig. B2; Sherlock, *Case of Resistance*, 221. See also: *An Exact Account of . . . the Execution of Algernon Sidney*, 4; [Elkanah Settle], *Remarks on Algernoon Sidney's Paper* (1683), 2; [John Nalson], *Reflections Upon Coll. Sidney's Arcadia* (1684), 5, 16.

ology of natural subjection against them. As early as 1676 the earl of Shaftesbury was described as an unprincipled man, motivated solely by ambition and a desire for revenge. According to Marchamont Nedham, "having Jugled himself out of all at Court; and being past hope of Jugling himself in again (all his Feats being well understood there—) he sets up at t'other end o'th' Town, to Jugle up a Mutiny in the City; in hope to find combustible matter there to set Fire in the Country; and, at length, inflame a Party for his purpose in this Parliament, or rather in a *New One*."[75] Demythologizing Whig claims was a staple activity for Tory pamphleteers throughout the Exclusion Crisis.[76] But there was more to the accusation that the Whigs were "ambitious" men than the simple observation that behind their populist mask the Whigs were a group of disgruntled "outs" attempting to get themselves "in." Among men who accepted the ideology of natural subjection, the concept of ambition carried strong moral and religious overtones. It was almost always qualified with adjectives like "covetous" or "prideful." In the eyes of royalists, Whigs were guilty of something far worse than the sin of wanting to get ahead; they desired to taste "the forbidden Apple of State."[77] Matthew Rider gave forceful expression to this argument in 1680: "The World is now come to this pass, that the meanest Coblers dare censure the greatest *States-Men*. . . . There is no *Mystery* of State, no Policy or Intregue, of weight or importance soever it be, but the *Mobile* must have it discussed and examined before the *Infallible Tribunal* of their *Vertiginous* Brains, and the whole matter must either stand or fall according to their well-digested *Verdict* and profound judgment . . . this *presumption* be altogether insufferable, as being wholly destructive of all good Order and Government."[78] Presumption: this was the crime of which the Whigs were most guilty. They were attempting to claim a power and an authority that neither God nor nature had intended them to possess. Even Shaftesbury was guilty of ambition, for he had attempted to impose conditions on the Crown. Like Daedalus of legend, his fate was determined by his desire to rise above his station.[79]

---

[75] [Nedham], *Pacquet of Advices*, 6; cf. 11, 29–34, 40. See also: [Thomas Sprat], *A True Account and Declaration of the Horrid Conspiracy Against the late King*, 2nd ed. (London: Thomas Newcomb, 1685), 6.

[76] L'Estrange's *Observator* was dedicated to "the Undeceiving of the People" (1:1 [13 April 1681]). See also: [L'Estrange], *Citt and Bumpkin*, passim; Nalson, *The Common Interest*, 25, 35, 219, 258; *Nations Interest*, 3; [Dryden?], *His Majesties Declaration*, 9; *Seasonable Address*, 7–9, 12.

[77] Nalson, *The Common Interest*, 169, 35. See also: *Nations Interest*, 3; *Funeral Sermon*, 22, 34; [Northleigh], *Remarks Upon . . . Antimonarchical Authors*, "Introduction."

[78] [Rider], *The Power of Parliaments*, 2. See also: *Funeral Sermon*, 35–36.

[79] "Men, when they leave the Calling that Providence hath allotted them, and would

Closely related to "ambition" was a second term fraught with moral and religious connotations, "arbitrary." Just as the Whigs were thought to be ambitious, so also were they considered "the most Arbitrary principled persons in the World."[80] This did not simply mean that they desired uncontrolled power and authority. On the royalists' own terms that was an accurate, if incomplete, description of monarchy. Rather, it referred to the ends to which that power and authority were to be applied. "Arbitrary principled persons" were "restless" and "turbulent." Like ambitious men, they aspired to ends that were unconnected with and contrary to the purposes of God and nature.[81]

Recognition of the idiosyncratic way royalists used the terms "ambition" and "arbitrary" also sheds light on their reasons for describing their Whig opponents as "Levellers."[82] It was not simply that Whigs agitated for many of the same causes that the Levellers had, or even that many Whigs were former Levellers. Both these charges were true, but they do not sufficiently explain the use of this epithet. Royalists applied this odious label to Whigs for the same reason that they had applied it to Lilburne, Walwyn, and Overton: it was believed that they intended to dismantle the structure of hierarchy, degree, and place that gave coherence to an otherwise anarchic world. The Whigs were at war with the Creation. And as one pamphleteer warned, "what is Sauce for a Goose is Sauce for a Gander . . . he that practiseth Disobedience to his Superiors, teacheth it to his Inferiors."[83] Once the floodgates were opened, the whole moral and political infrastructure of society would be swept away by a sea of destruction.

A similar point might be made about the treatment of "Church Levellers" in royalist tracts.[84] The "tremendous unifying force" behind the Restoration had been "the determination of the English and Welsh gentry that never again would they go through an experience such as the civil wars and the Interregnum had been." In alliance with

---

soar into a sphere above them, they very rarely miss the fate of *Daedalus*, their Molten Wings deceive them, and their fall too late gives them notice of their ruine" (*Some Reflections on the Paper Delivered unto the Sheriffs of London by James Holloway* [1684], 2).

[80] [Nalson], *Complaint of Liberty*, 1. See also: [Womock?], *Short Way*, 15.

[81] Nalson, *The Common Interest*, 167; Charles II, *His Majesties Declaration* (1681), 9; *Funeral Sermon*, 21; [Hickes], *Jovian*, 264–65.

[82] Nalson, *The Common Interest*, 189, 234; [Nedham], *Pacquet of Advices*, 50–52; [Rider], *The Power of Parliaments*, 6, 8; [L'Estrange], *Observator*, 1:464 (29 December 1683); *Funeral Sermon*, 2–4; Mackenzie, *Jus Regium*, 134.

[83] *Seasonable Address*, 12.

[84] *Funeral Sermon*, 46. See also: [Bohun], *Address to the Free-Men*, 12; [Womock?], *Short Way*, 18.

the Anglican clergy they enacted the Clarendon Code, a series of harshly repressive measures designed to eliminate religious dissent, on "the assumption that religious uniformity was a necessary prerequisite for political unity."[85] This was no aberrant belief, but one that had long informed English practice. It was widely agreed that religious diversity led to political division and that a consensus on fundamental values was a precondition to the existence of social order.[86] The only alternative to unity was chaos.

Given this faith in the moral and political virtues of religious uniformity, Dissenters posed a distinct danger to the polity. Conventicles were "Corporated parcels of the *Body Politick*."[87] Independent of the national church and governed by their own rules, they introduced discontinuities into the otherwise seamless fabric of society. Like a weak link in a chain, or a fragile stone at the base of a building, they threatened the whole with destruction. Bruised memories of the Civil War painfully reminded the Churchman and the Cavalier of the consequences of religious diversity.[88] Within the royalist ideology of natural subjection, the differentiation of religious and political life was not possible.[89]

Before turning to consider the place of Sir Robert Filmer's political writings in this matrix of ideas, it is important to recall the polemical purpose of English royalist writings. The arguments discussed above were not neutral or universally shared descriptions of social reality. They were attempts to persuade men and women to accept certain basic yet increasingly controversial structures of moral, political, and religious authority. It was once thought that seventeenth-century English society was like a lake in the middle of a forest: stable, placid, and unchanging.[90] In such a society, the royalist vision of harmonious vertical integration might have been uncontested. But we now know that that metaphor is inappropriate and that beginning in the sixteenth century "England was subjected to a series of interlocking,

[85] Ronald Hutton, *The Restoration* (Oxford: The Clarendon Press, 1985), 147; Jones, *Country and Court*, 147.

[86] Conrad Russell, "Arguments for Religious Unity in England, 1530–1650," *Journal of Ecclesiastical History* 18 (October 1967): 203–5.

[87] [Nedham], *Pacquet of Advices*, 17.

[88] [Nedham], *Pacquet of Advices*, 12; [John Nalson], *The True Liberty and Dominion of Conscience Vindicated*, 2nd ed. (1678), 58–64, 115; *Character of a Rebellion*, 4; W.W., *Antidotum Britannicum*, "Preface."

[89] For an illuminating discussion of this problem, see: Don Herzog, *Happy Slaves* (Chicago: University of Chicago Press, 1989), 156–81.

[90] Laslett, *World We Have Lost*, passim. Laslett's revised interpretation of English society incorporates many of the discoveries that have been made since his first edition of 1965, but he remains committed to the claim that England was a "one-class society."

dimly understood yet profoundly unsettling social and economic changes."[91] If England was a lake, it was a lake whose depths were moved by turbulent demographic, economic, and cultural currents, and whose surface was capped by rebellious white-topped waves. Throughout the countryside there were "masterless men," men (and women) who either failed or refused to be integrated into the traditional networks of power and authority.[92] In the cities there were increasing numbers of conventicles, each filled with Nonconformists who preferred to risk punishment and even death rather than remain within the soulless confines of the Anglican church. Most striking of all, the nation itself had endured for eleven years without benefit of a king. Though most were horrified by the execution of Charles I, there were those—including Sidney—who were inspired by the consequences of that bloody act. "English society in the late seventeenth century was still in many respects what it had been in the reign of Elizabeth. . . . But it was also a society which had been irreversibly altered."[93] The ideology of natural subjection was not simply the intellectual wing of an offensive to retain control over society; it was also part of an effort to re-create a world that, if it had ever existed, had long since disappeared.

The Place of Sir Robert Filmer

Sir Robert Filmer's political writings were published during the Exclusion Crisis as a contribution to the matrix of ideas and arguments, beliefs and prejudices, outlined above. In 1679 and again in 1680 a collection of essays that had appeared individually during the Civil War was printed, and in 1680 *Patriarcha* was made public for the first time.[94] Filmer's arguments were swiftly, powerfully, and painstakingly met by three of the most important political theorists of the seventeenth century: James Tyrrell, John Locke, and Algernon Sidney.[95] No other royalist writer was accorded this distinction, and it

[91] David Underdown, *Revel, Riot, and Rebellion* (Oxford: The Clarendon Press, 1985), 18.

[92] Herzog, *Happy Slaves*, 39–71.

[93] Keith Wrightson, *English Society 1580–1680* (New Brunswick: Rutgers University Press, 1982), 13.

[94] Laslett, "Introduction," *Patriarcha*, 33–34, 44–48.

[95] In addition to the book-length responses of Tyrrell, Locke, and Sidney, see Thomas Hunt, *Mr. Hunt's Postscript for Rectifying some Mistakes in some of the Inferiour Clergy* (1682), 35–83. Ironically, though only Tyrrell and Hunt published their rejoinders to Filmer in time to have an impact on the debates surrounding the Exclusion

remains to be seen why Filmer became the bête noire of radical Whig-gism.

Filmer's argument was devastatingly simple. In his "Observations Upon Aristotles Politiques" he summarized it in six points:

1. That there is no form of government, but monarchy only.
2. That there is no monarchy, but paternal.
3. That there is no paternal monarchy, but absolute, or arbitrary.
4. That there is no such thing as an aristocracy or democracy.
5. That there is no such form of government as a tyranny.
6. That the people are not born free by nature.[96]

These were strong claims, even by the standards of English royalist thought. Filmer based them on the Bible and the writings of Jean Bodin. From his study of the Bible, Filmer learned that God had des-ignated kings as the rightful heirs of Adam's paternal dominion. From his study of Bodin, he learned that there were no viable alter-natives to the sovereign rule of one man. On these two pillars he con-structed the surprisingly sturdy if ramshackle edifice known as patri-archalism.

The foundation of Filmer's argument was the biblical account of the Creation:

In the beginning God created the heaven and the earth. And the earth was without form, and void; and darkness was upon the face of the deep. And the Spirit of God moved upon the face of the waters. . . . And God said, Let there be light: and there was light. . . . And God said, let the earth bring forth grass, the herb yielding seed, and the fruit tree yielding fruit after his kind, whose seed is in itself, upon the earth: and it was so. . . . And God said, Let the waters bring forth abundantly the moving creature that hath life, and fowl that may fly above the earth in the open firmament of heaven. . . . And God said, Let the earth bring forth the living creature after his kind, cattle, and creeping thing, and beast of the earth after his kind: and it was so. . . . And God said, Let us make man in our image, after our likeness: and let them have dominion over the fish of the sea, and over the fowl of the air, and over the cattle, and over every creeping thing that creepeth upon the earth. . . . And God saw everything that he had made, and behold, it was very good.[97]

The importance of this story to Filmer's political theory cannot be overemphasized. The book of Genesis revealed that humans had

---

Crisis, they have received far less attention from historians and political theorists than Locke and Sidney.

[96] *Patriarcha*, 229.

[97] Genesis 1.

been created by a beneficent and purposive God. Like the birds in the air and the fish in the sea, they have a specific part to play in the symphony of creation. It was blasphemous to believe that the order God had created was not perfect; and hence political inquiry properly understood was an exploration of his creation.[98]

From the book of Genesis Filmer learned that humans are not like mushrooms: they do not "all on a sudden . . . [spring] out of the earth without any obligation one to another." Rather, "the scripture teacheth us . . . that all men came by succession, and generation from one man."[99] As Adam was the first man, so he was the father of all men. And "by the appointment of God" he was "monarch of the world." His family was a commonwealth, and no distinction existed between his paternal and his political power. He was "Father, King and Lord over his family: a son, a subject and a servant or a slave, were one and the same thing at first."[100] All were equally and naturally subject to his unlimited paternal power.

Though humankind is no longer united in a single family, kings retain the power and authority of the first patriarch. Filmer recognized the peculiarity of this claim: "It may seem absurd to maintain that Kings now are the fathers of their people, since experience shows the contrary. It is true, all Kings be not the natural parents of their subjects, yet they all either are, or are to be reputed, as the next heirs of those progenitors who were at first the natural parents of the whole people, and in their right succeed to the exercise of supreme jurisdiction."[101] Filmer's use of the qualifier "are to be reputed" suggests that he viewed the biblical account of Adam's patriarchy as a metaphor or analogy for the office of kingship. But no metaphoric or analogical argument could justify Filmer's belief that "there is, and always shall be continued to the end of the world, a natural right of

---

[98] "It were impiety, to think, that God who was careful to appoint judicial laws for his chosen people, would not furnish them with the best form of government: or to imagine that the rules given in divers places in the gospel, by our blessed Saviour and his Apostles for obedience to Kings should now, like almanacs out of date, be of no use to us" (*Patriarcha*, 278).

[99] *Patriarcha*, 241. "It is not possible for the wit of man to search out the first grounds or principles of government . . . except he know that at the creation one man alone was made, to whom the dominion of all things was given, and from whom all men derive their title" (*Patriarcha*, 203–4).

[100] *Patriarcha*, 289, 189. Genesis 3:16, "where God ordained Adam to rule over his wife . . . [is] the original grant of government, and the fountain of all power placed in the Father of all mankind; accordingly we find the law for obedience to government give in the terms of honour thy Father" (283). See also: 63.

[101] *Patriarcha*, 60–61.

a supreme Father over every multitude."[102] The story of the Creation was not metaphoric, it was true; and Adam's patriarchy provided an archetype and foundation for all subsequent "supreme Father[s]." As Sidney, Locke, and Tyrrell were to prove, this was not a claim that could stand up to careful scrutiny. But to many seventeenth-century Englishmen it would have been unexceptionable. Steeped in the stories of the Bible, they were accustomed to viewing their world through the lens of Scripture.

Reinforcing Filmer's biblical patriarchalism was the theory of sovereignty he drew from the writings of

> the great modern politician Bodin: hear him touching limited monarchy: "Unto majesty or sovereignty (saith he) belongeth an absolute power, not subject to any law. . . . sovereignty being of itself indivisible, how can it at one and the same time be divided betwixt one prince, the nobility and the people in common? . . . Where the rights of the sovereignty are divided betwixt the prince and his subjects, in that confusion of state there is still endless stirs and quarrels for the superiority, until that some one, some few, or all together, have got the sovereignty."[103]

According to Bodin, sovereignty is the power to make laws and command obedience to them. It is the power of final judgment, of making decisions that cannot be appealed. Filmer's debt to Bodin's account of sovereignty was second only to his debt to the biblical account of the Creation. He repeatedly cited Bodin in his writings, and in 1648 he even published a tract composed entirely of extracts from Bodin's *Six Books of the Commonwealth* in order to prove that "a pure absolute monarchy is the surest commonweal, and without comparison, the best of all."[104] But the lessons Filmer learned from Bodin were quite simple and are fully contained in the passage quoted above: sovereignty is indivisible; it is best contained within the framework of monarchy; and it is a necessary precondition to peace.[105] As the Bible taught that kings are patriarchs, so Bodin taught that they are necessarily sovereign.

Filmer's fusion of biblical patriarchy and Bodinian sovereignty

[102] *Patriarcha*, 62. See also: 188, 231.

[103] *Patriarcha*, 304–6.

[104] *Patriarcha*, 326.

[105] "The supreme power being an indivisible beam of majesty, cannot be divided among, or settled upon a multitude"; "to have two supremes is to have none, because the one may destroy the other, and is quite contrary to the indivisible nature of sovereignty"; "if unity in government, which is only found in monarchy, be once broken, there is no stay or bound, until it come to a constant standing army" (*Patriarcha*, 189, 219, 199).

yielded a theory shot through with tensions and inconsistencies. The theory of sovereignty emphasized the need for centralized and concentrated power, while the theory of patriarchy placed a premium on the genealogy of power; the theory of sovereignty was essentially secular and directed at the maintenance of peace, while the theory of patriarchy called on men to carry out the revealed will of God. Filmer made no attempt to avoid these sandy shoals; he simply averted his eyes and winced when his theory touched bottom. For in his heart he knew that all truths cohered and that the basic lessons of the Bible and Bodin were the same: there could be no diminution of or resistance to the supreme power of the king. Subjection to the rule of absolute, patriarchal monarchs was the natural condition of humankind.

Historians of political thought have differed widely in their estimates of the nature and significance of Filmer's writings. To Peter Laslett, Filmer's modern editor, Filmer was a "codifier of conscious and unconscious prejudice," and his writings were "the *ipsissima verba* of the established order" in the 1680s. Gordon Schochet echoed this view in his study of *Patriarchalism in Political Thought*: during the Exclusion Crisis, "the Filmerian position very nearly became the official state ideology." It was "the backbone of the Tory ideology." These views have been strongly challenged by James Daly: "it is no exaggeration to say that, for the majority of royalist and Tory writers, neither Filmer nor Filmerism seems to have existed."[106]

The differences between these two interpretations can be traced to the frameworks within which the authors analyze Filmer's writings. To Laslett and Schochet, Filmerism has to be studied anthropologically as well as textually; the Convocation Book of 1606, or the structure of seventeenth-century English households, is at least as important to an understanding of Filmerism as are the texts of Dudley Digges, John Nalson, or George Mackenzie. *Patriarcha* was a powerful book just because it resonated with deep structures and beliefs in English society. To Daly, on the other hand, Filmerism has to be studied in the context of the stream of political and theological tracts that flooded the bookstalls of London throughout much of the seventeenth century. *Patriarcha* was a weak book just because its arguments were not shared by any other major royalist writer.

This difference in focus is reflected in the pictures of Filmerism that these authors paint. To Laslett and Schochet, the essence of Fil-

[106] Laslett, "Introduction," *Patriarcha*, 41, 34; Schochet, *Patriarchalism*, 193, 130; James Daly, *Sir Robert Filmer and English Political Thought* (Toronto: University of Toronto Press, 1979), 124.

merism is patriarchalism, the identification of political and paternal authority. It was patriarchalism that united Filmer's writings with a whole host of everyday beliefs and practices.[107] To Daly, on the other hand, the essence of Filmerism is a theory of undivided and unlimited sovereignty; it was this that distinguished Filmer from virtually every other royalist writer in seventeenth-century England.[108]

Neither of these interpretations, however, yields a satisfactory explanation of why Sidney, Locke, and Tyrrell chose to devote a great deal of time and energy in the midst of a profound constitutional crisis to refuting Filmer's arguments. Laslett and Schochet, by making Filmer an archetype of conservative and royalist thought, provide no sense of the uniqueness of Filmerism, or of why Filmer in particular was chosen as an object of attack. Daly, by contrast, presents a Filmer so radically unique that the only possible explanation for condemning his views was that he was "the perfect straw man . . . had he not existed, the Whigs would have had to invent him."[109]

A satisfactory answer to the basic question "Why Filmer?" lies somewhere between these two extremes and requires attention to the multiple levels on which Filmer's arguments operated. Filmer was, as Laslett and Schochet have demonstrated, a "codifier of conscious and unconscious prejudice." He was unquestioningly committed to the ideology of natural subjection, and virtually every royalist argument outlined above can be found in his writings. He was also an innovator, though—*pace* Daly—in a very special sense. Filmer was a hedgehog and not a fox, and his single-minded devotion to the principles of patriarchy and sovereignty led him to streamline and simplify orthodox doctrines in new and radical ways. He was a force to be reckoned with precisely because he was both a traditionalist and an innovator. He revealed, as Sidney, Locke, and Tyrrell recognized, a dangerous potential latent within traditional royalist doctrines.

An excellent example of the way Filmer streamlined and radicalized orthodox royalist arguments can be seen in his treatment of the

[107] "The patriarchal defense of absolutism can be reduced to two propositions and a conclusion that allegedly followed from them: (1) Familial authority is natural, divinely sanctioned, and—in its pristine form—absolute and unlimited. (2) Political power is identical to the power of fathers. Therefore, political power is natural, divinely sanctioned, and—because it still enjoys the ancient and original rights of fatherhood—absolute and unlimited" (Schochet, *Patriarchalism*, 269).

[108] "At its [Filmerism's] heart was a concept of omnicompetent sovereignty, sovereignty unrestricted, unlimited, unbounded, from which there was no appeal and within which there was a radical simplicity, an undiluted singleness of will. This sovereignty was the only political binding force that could exist, or ever had existed" (Daly, *Sir Robert Filmer*, 13).

[109] Daly, *Sir Robert Filmer*, 160.

question of whether the powers of the English monarch were "absolute" or "arbitrary." To most royalists, the distinction was critical. Though the monarch's powers were absolute, they were not unbounded; though the monarch's will gave being to the law, it was not itself the law. Like the banks of a river, the traditional constitution created a channel within which the monarch's power flowed.[110] It was the presence of those banks that distinguished England's absolute yet limited monarchy from the arbitrary and tyrannical monarchies of Turkey or France.[111]

The distinction between absolute and arbitrary power proved far easier to endorse than to articulate, however. Royalists wanted to maintain both that the king was the author of the laws and that kingship was a juridically defined office, that the king's powers were absolute and yet that they were also limited. They were torn between their profound commitment to the rule of law and the traditional constitution, and their acceptance of the logic of sovereignty. The difficulties posed by these two conflicting commitments came into focus when they attempted to define the boundaries of the monarch's powers. It was generally agreed that Parliament had been created by the command of the king. It was also believed that the king had "condescended and promised" not to "repeal old, nor make any new Statutes" without the "Consents and Approbations" of Parliament.[112] But what bound the king to this promise? What kept him from changing his mind, from deciding to rule by royal proclamation, as Charles I had done between 1629 and 1640, or as Charles II threatened to do after 1681? The very authors who proclaimed the English monarchy to be limited also held that "the sovereign power," that is to say the king, "made the laws, and can repeal them, and dispense with them, and make new laws." In none of these activities was the king obligated to consult either the nobility or the commons.[113] It did little good to assert, as Matthew Rider did, that kings are bound by the law in the same way that "Divines are limited to the plain Text of the *Holy Scriptures*."[114] It would have been blasphemous to have asserted that di-

---

[110] [Hickes], *Harmony of Divinity and Law*, 29–30, 38–48. See also: [Nedham], *Pacquet of Advices*, 43; Nalson, *The Common Interest*, 116; [L'Estrange], *Free-born Subject*, 3; *Three Great Questions*, 9; [Dryden?], *His Majesties Declaration*, 10; Sherlock, *Case of Resistance*, 210.

[111] Nalson, *The Common Interest*, 151–52; [Dryden?], *His Majesties Declaration*, 10; [Hickes], *Jovian*, 193, 209–11; Mackenzie, *Jus Regium*, 50.

[112] *Three Great Questions*, 9.

[113] Sherlock, *Case of Resistance*, 196–99; Nalson, *The Common Interest*, 15; Mackenzie, *Jus Regium*, 37.

[114] [Rider], *The Power of Parliaments*, 37.

vines were the authors of the Bible; but that was precisely the relationship between the king and the law.

In Filmer's hands the complications and confusions that surrounded this issue dissolved: "For as Kingly power is by the law of God, so it hath no inferior law to limit it"; "the King is the sole immediate author, corrector and moderator" of both statute and common laws; Parliament exists solely by the king's "favour and grace."[115] Though bound "by the natural law of a Father" to "ratify the acts of their forefathers and predecessors in things necessary for the public good of their subjects," kings are subject to no earthly restraint. And subjects, like servants and slaves, have "no authority or liberty," no "commission" or "power," to judge the actions and commands of their master.[116] "We do but flatter ourselves, if we hope ever to be governed without an arbitrary power."[117]

Filmer's conflation of the categories of absolute and arbitrary monarchies is typical of his style of analysis. Virtually every doctrine and dogma discussed in this chapter can be found in his writings, and in every case they are integrated into an account of Adam's paternal dominion over the Creation. Even among royalists Filmer's conclusions were extreme, and many refused to follow in his footsteps. Two features of the crisis that enveloped England during the late 1670s and early 1680s, however, gave them extraordinary salience: they crystallized ideas that were gaining sway throughout the country, and their publication coincided with the discovery of the absolutist pretensions of Charles and James Stuart.

According to Locke, Filmer's doctrines had been "publickly owned" by "the Pulpit, of late Years." Tyrrell concurred: "this Notion of the Divine and Patriarchal Right of absolute Monarchy hath obtain'd . . . much among some modern Church-men, who cry it up as their *Diana*."[118] This charge was not without foundation. Though we do not know precisely who decided to publish Filmer's writings or why they did so, the best evidence points toward the Anglican hierarchy.[119] The most striking feature of this allegation is not that it attributed absolutist values to the clergy—a common Whig accu-

---

[115] *Patriarcha*, 96, 113, 118.

[116] *Patriarcha*, 103, 105.

[117] *Patriarcha*, 277.

[118] *Two Treatises*, "Preface"; Tyrrell, *Patriarcha non Monarcha*, "Preface." "In this last age a generation of men has sprung up among us, who would flatter princes with an Opinion, that they have a Divine Right to absolute Power" (*Two Treatises*, "Preface").

[119] In 1685 the Archbishop of Canterbury sponsored a revised and corrected edition of *Patriarcha* (Edmund Bohun, *The Diary and Autobiography of Edmund Bohun* [Beccles: Read Crisp, 1853], 67–68). See also: Gordon Schochet, "Sir Robert Filmer: Some New Bibliographical Discoveries," *The Library* 26 (1971): 154–60.

sation[120]—but that it credited the Church with responsibility for the spread of Filmerian ideas throughout the nation. In the 1660s, when Sidney was composing the *Court Maxims*, he dismissed patriarchalism as irrelevant to political matters.[121] By the 1680s he could no longer afford to do so. As he explained at the very start of the *Discourses*, "A People from all Ages in love with Liberty, and desirous to maintain their own Privileges, could never be brought to resign them, unless they were made to believe that in Conscience they ought to do it; which could not be, unless they were also perswaded to believe, that there was a Law set to all Mankind which none might transgress, and which put the examination of all those Matters out of their power." Filmer's writings were published as part of just such a campaign of persuasion. As Tyrrell nervously observed, "the Poyson [of patriarchalism] hath spread . . . far among the men of Letters, and in the Country among divers of the Gentrie and Clergie." It had even "infected" the universities, from which vantage point it might shape men's minds for generations to come.[122] Through the agency of the Church a subtle yet profound shift in English political sensibilities was being effected.

The high cost of accepting Filmer's arguments was manifest during the Exclusion Crisis. Throughout the 1670s Charles II pursued an "absolutist" policy designed to "free him from having to rely on the cooperation of parliament" in the conduct of national affairs.[123] At first with the assistance of the earl of Danby, and then later with ample subsidies from Louis XIV, he moved closer and closer to that goal. In the background, immeasurably complicating any consideration of Charles's conduct, stood his younger brother James. Were Charles to die first, James would become king; and as a Catholic he was thought capable of and inclined to the most hideous of crimes. Awaiting the nation on James's ascension were "French Auxiliaries, and a Stack of Faggots in Smithfield."[124] Exclusion was the only thing

---

[120] See, for example: J.D., *A Word without Doors Concerning the Bill for Succession* [1679], 1; [John Somers], *A Brief History of the Succession* [1680], 15; C.B., *An Address to the Honourable City of London* (1681), 5; Hunt, *Mr. Hunt's Postscript*, "Preface," 33–35, 50–54; Edmund Hickeringill, "The History of Whiggism," in *The Works of Mr. Edmund Hickeringill*, 2 vols. (London: John Baker and R. Burleigh, 1716), 1:17, 100, 115, 123, 140–41, 151.

[121] "The Paternall Government extends only to a family and so belongs not to the matter of our discourse" (*Maxims*, 10).

[122] *Discourses*, I:1, p. 4; Tyrrell, *Patriarcha non Monarcha*, "Preface."

[123] Jones, *Country and Court*, 164.

[124] [Thomas Hunt], *The Great and Weighty Considerations, Relating to the Duke of York* (1680), 29. For a representative sample of Whig fears concerning the duke of York, see [Elkanah Settle], *The Character of a Popish Successor* (1681).

that stood between the nation and a campaign of political and religious persecution the likes of which had not been seen since the days of Queen Mary. And yet if Filmer were to be believed, the nation was powerless to protect itself. Sidney was incredulous: "Having for a long time lain unregarded, [Filmer's *Patriarcha*] has bin lately brought into the light again, as an introduction of a Popish Successor, who is to be established, as we ought to believe, for the security of the Protestant Religion, and our English Liberties."[125] To men infected with anti-Catholic sentiment, men tempered and hardened by the rough brawls over religious toleration, the impeachment of Danby, and the prosecution of the Popish Plot, the notion that James should be welcomed with open arms was ludicrous. The intellectual farce it represented was matched only by the political and religious tragedy it presaged.

Unlike almost any other writer of his time, Filmer demonstrated an astounding capacity for squeezing a few more trump cards out of the well-worn deck of royalist ideas. This made him a powerful polemicist, for it meant that his dramatic conclusions were deeply rooted in orthodox beliefs. As both his proponents and his detractors clearly recognized, he crystallized a claim latent in a wide range of royalist arguments: that the nation was and ought to be powerless to examine the actions of its monarchs. In the charged conditions of late-Stuart England this argument had momentous implications. It was no accident that Sidney, Locke, and Tyrrell were terrified by the spread of Filmer's ideas.

[125] *Discourses*, III:43, p. 448.

PART TWO

SIDNEY'S ARGUMENT

THREE

FREEDOM AND SLAVERY

Liberty solely consists in an independency upon the Will
of another, and by the name of Slave we understand a
man, who can neither dispose of his Person nor Goods,
but enjoys all at the will of his Master.
(Algernon Sidney)[1]

S IR ROBERT FILMER placed men and women within a dense,
interlocking network of hierarchical relationships. Sons were
subject to fathers, wives and servants were subject to husbands
and masters, and everyone was subject to the king. Patriarchal authority was the God-given glue that held together the social and political universe. Algernon Sidney rejected this vision of natural subjection, replacing it with an ethic of individual freedom and a politics
of consent. Where Filmer saw the natural and legitimate exercise of
power, Sidney saw force and coercion; where Filmer saw subjects integrated into a coherent social whole, Sidney saw slaves dependent
on their master's arbitrary will. Though born within a few miles of
each other in the community of Kent, the two men inhabited radically different mental worlds.

The intellectual distance between Filmer and Sidney can be measured by their respective answers to a simple question: "Whether one
form of Government be prescribed to us by God and Nature, or we
are left according to our understanding, to constitute such as seem
best to our selves."[2] To Filmer, "the true grounds and principles of
government" were uniquely and comprehensively revealed in the
book of Genesis. Adam's dominion over the whole of the Creation
was "the fountain of all government."[3] It provided an archetype from
which men should not diverge, and upon which they could not im-

---

[1] *Discourses*, I:5, p. 12.

[2] *Discourses*, II:16, p. 130.

[3] *Patriarcha*, 278, 71. "It is not probable that any sure direction of the beginning of
government can be found either in Plato, Aristotle, Cicero, Polybius, or in any other
of the heathen authors, who were ignorant of the manner of the creation of the world:
we must not neglect the scriptures, and search in philosophers for the grounds of
dominion and property, which are the main principles of government and justice"
(187). See also: 73, 203.

prove. But to Sidney, the notion that "God and Nature have put us into a way from which we are not to swerve" was ludicrous. It was inconceivable that God, "who disposes all things in Wisdom and Goodness," would have exposed humanity to "a multitude of . . . Absurdities and Mischiefs; subjecting the Aged to be governed by Children; the Wise, to depend on the Will of Fools; the Strong and Valiant, to expect defence from the Weak or Cowardly." And yet that was precisely the consequence of Filmer's doctrine, for it subjected every inhabitant of every nation to the arbitrary rule of patriarchal monarchs. "I cannot believe God hath created Man in such a state of Misery and Slavery."[4]

Against the claim that absolute monarchy was rooted in the immutable laws of God and nature, Sidney posited the idea of an imperfect political system based on consent and subject to revision in light of the changing needs of its members. There were no timeless blueprints governing human conduct.[5] Instead, "God in Goodness and Mercy to Mankind, hath with an equal hand given to all the benefit of Liberty, with some measure of understanding how to employ it."[6] The key moral and political question facing seventeenth-century Englishmen was not "What are God's comprehensive plans for mankind?" but rather "What is the nature of man's liberty, why is it valuable, and what form of government most adequately protects and advances it?"[7]

Sidney's answer to this question was complex and richly textured, and it spans the whole of his theory of government. His starting point was a distinction between freedom and slavery: "Liberty consists only in being subject to no man's will, and nothing denotes a Slave but a dependence on the will of another."[8] The concept of freedom expressed Sidney's highest ideals and aspirations and provided the moral foundation for his theory of self-government; the concept of slavery captured his deepest fears and justified his opposition to the principles and practices of absolute monarchy. Sidney's analysis of these contrasting conditions can best be understood by organizing it

[4] *Discourses*, I:1, p. 4; I:6, p. 17; I:11, p. 24.

[5] "No Government is imposed upon men by God or Nature" (*Discourses*, II:20, p. 151). See also: I:6, p. 14.

[6] *Discourses*, I:6, p. 14. "A Faculty as well as a Liberty was left to every one, and will be to the end of the world, to make use of his Wit, Industry, and Experience, according to present Exigencies, to invent and practise such things as seem convenient to himself and others in matters of least importance" (II:8, p. 94).

[7] "What makes you believe that in civil things God has not left us a liberty of chosing & constituting such a Government as according to the time & nature of the place & people we find most Convenient?" (*Maxims*, fol. 32).

[8] *Discourses*, III:16, p. 317.

along four different axes: the freedom of having power over one's own life, versus slavery to the commands of another; the freedom of conscience, versus slavery to the religious beliefs of another; the freedom of following reason, versus slavery to the passions; and the freedom of a nation to direct its own affairs, versus slavery to the dictates of foreign powers. Each of these contrasts was designed to demonstrate the value of liberty, highlight the connection between monarchy and slavery, and provide justification for the claim that free governments are based on the consent of the governed.

The Patriarch Unmonarch'd

Sidney's dismay at the publication of Filmer's political writings in 1679 and 1680 was shared by James Tyrrell and John Locke. All three men rejected the doctrine of patriarchalism as absurd and illogical. They also agreed that Filmer was "an Advocate for Slavery," though they disagreed over the precise significance of that claim.[9] Because Tyrrell's *Patriarcha non Monarcha* and Locke's *Two Treatises of Government* were composed at roughly the same time as the *Discourses Concerning Government*, shared the objective of refuting Filmer's arguments, and operated within the same general matrix of ideas, they provide an invaluable point of reference from which to measure the unique contours of Sidney's theory.[10] By charting the intellectual ground common to all three, it will be possible to isolate the distinctive features of Sidney's conception of freedom and slavery.

Filmer's critics heaped scorn upon his abilities as a political theorist. Sidney thought *Patriarcha* "a heap of Incongruities and Contradictions." Filmer demonstrated "a most supine stupidity" and "hath not used one Argument that is not false, nor cited one Author whom he hath not perverted and abused." Locke agreed: "there was never so much glib Nonsense put together in well sounding English." Full of "mistakes, Inconsistencies, and want of . . . Scripture-proofs," *Patriarcha* was "nothing but a Rope of Sand."[11]

Despite their withering contempt for Filmer's treatises, Sidney,

---

[9] *Two Treatises*, "Preface."

[10] The strong similarities between the arguments of Sidney, Locke, and Tyrrell were not entirely accidental. All three men were members of the Whig opposition during the Exclusion Crisis. Locke and Tyrrell were friends and collaborated on a number of topics at this time (J. W. Gough, "James Tyrrell, Whig Historian and Friend of John Locke," *Historical Journal* 19 [1976]: 581–610). There is, however, only weak circumstantial evidence to suggest that either of these men ever met Sidney.

[11] *Discourses*, II:20, p. 151; II:18, p. 144; I:1, p. 5; *Two Treatises*, "Preface," I:1.

Locke, and Tyrrell took great pains to demonstrate the irrationality of patriarchalism. All three men began their treatises by rejecting Filmer's central claim, that Adam had had a *"natural and private dominion"* over the whole of the Creation.[12] Sidney, relying on bluster and a vaguely Aristotelian distinction between the family and civil society, asserted that "no Dream was ever more empty, than his [Filmer's] Whimsey of *Adam's* Kingdom."[13] Locke and Tyrrell relied on the Bible itself to deflate Filmer's claims. Locke was particularly effective at this strategy, and in a series of chapters in his *First Treatise* he demonstrated that Adam could not have had dominion either by creation, by donation, by the subjection of Eve, or by the rights of fatherhood.[14] "And if God made all Mankind slaves to *Adam* and his Heirs, by giving *Adam* Dominion over *every living thing that moveth on the Earth* . . . methinks Sir *Robert* should have carried his Monarchical Power one step higher, and satisfied the World, that Princes might eat their Subjects too, since God gave as full Power to *Noah* and his Heirs . . . to eat *every Living thing that moveth*, as he did to *Adam* to have Dominion over them, the *Hebrew* words in both places being the same."[15] Locke was being facetious, but his sarcasm was intended to make a serious point. No consistent reading of the Bible could lend support to patriarchalism without also reducing humankind to the status of brute animals.

Like skilled lawyers, all three men followed this initial rejection of patriarchalism with a series of descending hypothetical counterarguments designed to block Filmer's claims at every turn. Even if God had made Adam "monarch of the whole world,"[16] there was no reason to suspect that he had intended Adam's heirs to inherit his power. As Sidney pointed out, "the Creation is exactly described in the Scripture; but we know so little of what passed between the finishing of it and the Flood" that it is hard to believe that God intended the Bible to provide a record of the transmission of Adam's dominion.[17]

Even if God had intended Adam's dominion to be transmitted to his heirs, it was impossible to determine who was currently entitled to it. Filmer had claimed that "if Adam himself were still living, and now ready to die, it is certain that there is one man, and but one in the

---

[12] *Patriarcha*, 71.

[13] *Discourses*, I:7, pp. 17–18. See also: II:2, pp. 67–68.

[14] *Two Treatises*, I:15–72. Cf. James Tyrrell, *Patriarcha non Monarcha* (London: 1681), 11–13.

[15] *Two Treatises*, I:27.

[16] *Patriarcha*, 188.

[17] *Discourses*, I:8, pp. 19–22; I:14, p. 30. See also: I:7, p. 17; *Maxims*, 33–35; *Two Treatises*, I:82–83.

world, who is next heir, although the knowledge who should be that one man be quite lost."[18] But this was patently absurd. In the first place, the laws of inheritance were municipal, not natural. "Tho the Law of *England* may make one man to be sole Heir of his Father, yet the Laws of God and Nature do not [do] so."[19] Second, even if the law of primogeniture was natural, it was radically incomplete. It did not provide any guidance for deciding between the claims of "the Grand-Son by a Daughter" and "a Nephew by a Brother."[20] Yet without a canonical set of rules capable of covering this and similar cases, no monarch could lay an unquestionable claim to the dominion of Adam. "The Right must fall if there be none to inherit."[21] As Tyrrell parodied, "*Adam* being dead, and his right Heir not to be known, it is all one as if he had none; for ought I know to the contrary, the Authors Footman may be the Man."[22] If ever there was a principle guaranteed to produce political instability, it was Filmer's doctrine of patriarchalism. In the absence of clear rules and incontrovertible evidence, it could only lead to the equation of right and power, of consent and conquest.[23]

Independent of the plausibility of Filmer's "Adamite" argument, Sidney, Locke, and Tyrrell thought patriarchalism fundamentally flawed because it was based on a faulty theory of paternal authority. Filmer had maintained that the power of a father over his children arose because he was their creator; with the seed of life came the power of death.[24] But as Locke remonstrated, "They who say the *Father* gives Life to his Children, are so dazled with the thoughts of Monarchy, that they do not, as they ought, remember God, who is *the Author and Giver of Life: 'Tis in him alone we live, move, and have our Being.*"[25] We are the workmanship of God, not man, and fathers have

[18] *Patriarcha*, 61.

[19] *Discourses*, II:4, p. 72. See also: I:17, p. 44; III:18, pp. 331–32; *Two Treatises*, I:123–24; Tyrrell, *Patriarcha non Monarcha*, 50–51, 54–60. Filmer was not the only royalist to rely on the "natural" status of primogeniture; cf. [Matthew Rider], *The Power of Parliaments in the Case of Succession* (London: 1680), 9, and George Mackenzie, *Jus Regium* (London: 1684), 25.

[20] *Two Treatises*, I:123. See also: *Discourses*, II:24, pp. 187–89.

[21] *Discourses*, I:12, p. 26. See also: III:18, p. 332.

[22] Tyrrell, *Patriarcha non Monarcha*, 45. See also: *Discourses*, I:12, p. 25.

[23] *Discourses*, I:19, p. 53; II:24, pp. 189–200; III:18, p. 339; III:21, p. 353; Sidney, *Very Copy of a Paper* (1683), 2; *Two Treatises*, I:78–80. Filmer made no effort to hide this fact: "It skills not which way Kings come by their power, whether by election, donation, succession or by any other means, for it is still the manner of the government by supreme power that makes them properly Kings, and not the means of obtaining their crowns" (*Patriarcha*, 106).

[24] *Patriarcha*, 231–33.

[25] *Two Treatises*, I:52. As Locke further observed, creation would at best "give the

power over their children solely because they are instruments in God's creation. Paternal authority is not inherent and irrevocable, but is always held in trust. As a result, "fatherhood" itself is only incidentally a biological category. The foster father who performs "the Office and Care of a Father" to a "forlorn and Perishing Infant" has a greater claim to *"Paternal Power"* than the natural father who has neglected the child. Moreover, the authority of a father ceases when his "Office and Care" are no longer necessary. According to Tyrrell, once children attain their majority they are "in all actions free, and at their own dispose."[26]

Unlike Locke and Tyrrell, Sidney did not rely on God's workmanship in man to refute Filmer's theory of paternal authority. Indeed, he explicitly embraced the claim that "the obedience due to Parents arises from [the fact] . . . that they are the instruments of our Generation."[27] By "Generation" he meant more than mere paternity, however, for he also argued that "the duty of Children to Parents . . . proceed from the benefits received from them." Chief among those benefits were moral, intellectual, and physical sustenance. According to Sidney, "every man doth perpetually owe all love, respect, service, and obedience to him that did beget, nourish, and educate him."[28] This did not mean that the rights of a father were unlimited. Experience had taught men that fathers were capable of abusing their power, and consequently it "has long since bin much restrain'd in all civilized Nations."[29] It did mean, however, that the rights of fatherhood could be held only by those who were, quite literally, fathers. No similitude or approximation could generate the vast debt of gratitude children owed those who had given them life.[30] As a result, the power of a father over his children was neither heritable nor transferable: "The same Law that gave to my Father a Power over me, gives me the like over my Children; and if I had a thousand Brothers, each of them would have the same over their Children."[31] In each

---

Father but a joynt Dominion with the Mother," since the mother had as much or more to do with the creation of the child as the father (I:55).

[26] *Two Treatises*, I:100, II:65; Tyrrell, *Patriarcha non Monarcha*, 20. Similar arguments can be found in Thomas Hunt, *Mr. Hunt's Postscript* (1682), 62–63.

[27] *Discourses*, III:33, p. 406.

[28] *Discourses*, III:1, pp. 255, 250. See also: I:20, p. 54.

[29] *Discourses*, III:1, p. 255. See also: III:1, pp. 251–52.

[30] "No man can be my Father but he that did beget me; and 'tis as absurd to say I owe that Duty to one who is not my Father, which I owe to my Father, as to say, he did beget me, who did not beget me; for the obligation that arises from benefits can only be to him that conferred them" (*Discourses*, I:17, p. 44). See also: I:19, p. 54; III:1, p. 250.

[31] *Discourses*, I:6, p. 16. "The character of a Father is indelible, and incommunicable"

generation the rights of fathers and the obligations of children are created anew.

The different conceptions of paternal power held by Locke and Sidney reflect a deeper disagreement over the nature of freedom and will be discussed below. They also reflect different attitudes toward the family. By depriving fathers of those powers that made them sovereigns in their own households, Locke sought to provide a more egalitarian standard by which to evaluate family relationships.[32] As there must be reform in the polity, so also must there be change in the household. Sidney, by contrast, showed little interest in disrupting the structure of authority within the patriarchal family. His eyes were exclusively focused on the political world, a realm inhabited by the male heads of households.[33]

Both men, however, argued that once paternal power was properly understood it ceased to provide support for patriarchal theories of government. According to Filmer, "Adam was the Father, King and Lord over his family: a son, a subject and a servant or a slave, were one and the same thing at first."[34] Collapsing the distinctions between paternal, political, and economic power, patriarchalism yielded a single, homogeneous form of authority that structured all human relationships. For all of his professed regard for Aristotle, Filmer was engaged in an essentially anti-Aristotelian project; the household and the polis were identical in the patriarchal worldview. His critics, though no more Aristotelian than he, followed Aristotle on this point. They insisted that these types of power be differentiated. Paternal and political power were *"perfectly distinct and separate"*; they had

---

(I:19, p. 54). See also: I:17, p. 44; II:31, p. 243; III:1, p. 250; *Two Treatises*, I:74; Hunt, *Mr. Hunt's Postscript*, 72.

[32] For example, Locke argued that child-rearing and education should follow the path "likeliest to produce vertuous, useful & able Men in their distinct Callings" (John Locke, "Some Thoughts Concerning Education," in *The Educational Writings of John Locke*, ed. James Axtell [Cambridge: Cambridge University Press, 1968], par. 112).

[33] "The question is not concerning the power that every Housholder in *London* hath over his Wife, Children and Servants; but whether they are all perpetually subject to one man and Family; and I intend not to set up their Wives, Prentices, and Children against them, or to diminish their Rights, but to assert them, as the gift of God and Nature, no otherwise to be restrained than by Laws made with their consent" (*Discourses*, II:9, p. 101). See also: I:11, p. 24; II:4, p. 74. Sidney showed no theoretical interest in the family or education, and the few comments concerning women that are found in his writings show him to have been a thoroughly conventional man of the seventeenth-century (I:18, p. 47; II:2, p. 68; III:1, p. 254; *Maxims*, 55; Algernon Sidney, "Of Love," in *A Collection of Scarce and Valuable Tracts . . . of the Late Lord Somers*, ed. Sir Walter Scott, 2nd ed., 13 vols. [London: 1809–15], 8:618–19). The place of women in Sidney's analysis of virtue and corruption will be discussed in Chapter 4.

[34] *Patriarcha*, 188.

"different Foundations" and "different Ends."[35] Once this claim had been accepted it was possible to reopen a set of questions Filmer had attempted to close through his theory of patriarchal absolutism: What are the origins of legitimate political power? At what point has a government exceeded its rightful authority? And who is entitled to call it back to its proper functions? These questions were of decisive importance to the opponents of Charles and James Stuart, for the legitimacy of resistance hinged on the answers to them. Sidney and Locke subtly but significantly parted company in their answers to these questions; in order to see this, it is necessary to turn to the claim that patriarchalism led to slavery.

The Language of Freedom and Slavery

Sidney, Locke, and Tyrrell agreed that Filmer was "an Advocate for Slavery." Tyrrell accused him of "taking away all distinctions between Kings and Tyrants, and between Slaves and Subjects." Locke noted with disdain that "Slavery is so vile and miserable an Estate of Man, and so directly opposite to the generous Temper and Courage of our Nation; that 'tis hardly to be conceived, that an *Englishman*, much less a *Gentleman*, should plead for't." And Sidney rhetorically wondered, "If it be Liberty to live under such a Government [as Filmer proposes], I desire to know what is Slavery."[36] In making this claim they adapted a familiar and richly textured concept to new and radical purposes.

The concept of slavery played an important role in seventeenth-century English thought. This is particularly noteworthy because the institution of slavery was virtually nonexistent. For a small number of men and women—colonists in the British West Indies, traders in Bristol and Liverpool, and members of the Royal African Company—slaves and slavery were a part of everyday life, and of great commercial interest.[37] For a smaller number, forcibly transported to the col-

[35] *Two Treatises*, II:71. See also: *Two Treatises.*, II:2; *Discourses*, I:14, p. 31; II:2, p. 68.

[36] *Two Treatises*, "Preface"; Tyrrell, *Patriarcha non Monarcha*, "Preface"; *Two Treatises*, I:1; *Discourses*, I:5, p. 12.

[37] Though small by eighteenth-century standards, the slave trade was brisk and quickly drew the attention of the Restoration monarchy. The Royal African Company, chartered in 1663 and then rechartered in 1672, was presided over by the duke of York and included among its stockholders both Charles II and the earl of Shaftesbury (*Calendar of State Papers, Colonial Series, America and West Indies*, 1661–1668:120–22; 1669–1674:409–12). By the mid-1680s, more than three thousand slaves a year were being sent to Jamaica alone (A. P. Thornton, "The Organization of the Slave Trade in

onies for the commission of crimes, for participation in failed rebellions, or for religious nonconformity, slavery was a matter of personal experience.[38] And for a few unfortunate souls, indentured servitude was the only alternative to starvation in the face of severe economic distress.[39] But for the vast majority of English men and women, slaves and slavery were far beyond the pale of ordinary experience.

As a moral and political abstraction, however, slavery would have been quite familiar to seventeenth-century English men and women. Had they seen or read a Shakespearean play, they would have noted Othello's having been "taken by the insolent foe and sold to slavery," Hamlet's search for the man that "is not passion's slave," and Northumberland's determination to "shake off our slavish yoke."[40] Had they received an education, they would have studied the histories of Greece and Rome, Aristotle's defense of natural slavery, and Tacitus's description of slaveholding in Germania.[41] Were they philosophically inclined, they would have been familiar with the controversies surrounding Grotius's arguments for contractual slavery in *De Juri Belli ac Pacis*.[42] And regardless of their background, as members of a Christian commonwealth they would have been nursed on stories recounting the slavery of the Israelites in Egypt, Jesus's admonition that "every one who commits sin is a slave to sin," and Peter's warning against those who promise freedom but "themselves are slaves of corruption."[43]

In seventeenth-century English political discourse, the concept of slavery was used to define forcefully and graphically the outer boundaries of acceptable behavior. With its roots in the distinction between man's "higher" and "lower" nature—as when it was said that a man was a slave to his passions—it played neatly into the ideological needs of a hierarchical society. For members of the gentry obsessed with status, for example, it could be used to define and reinforce so-

---

the English West Indies, 1660–1685," *William and Mary Quarterly*, 3rd ser., 12 [1955]: 399–409).

[38] C. M. MacInnes, *England and Slavery* (Bristol: Arrowsmith, 1934), 21–22.

[39] According to an eighteenth-century Maryland minister, indentured servants were for "three, four or five years . . . to all Intents & Purposes Slaves" (quoted in T. H. Breen, review of *The Peopling of British North America and Voyagers to the West*, by Bernard Bailyn, *New York Review of Books* 34 [29 January 1987]: 27–29).

[40] *Othello*, act 1, sc. 3, lines 137–38; *Hamlet*, act 3, sc. 2, line 77; *Richard II*, act 2, sc. 1, line 291.

[41] Aristotle, *The Politics*, 1253b–1255b; Tacitus, *Germania* (Loeb Classical Library, 1970), pars. 20, 25.

[42] Richard Tuck, *Natural Rights Theories: Their Origin and Development* (Cambridge: Cambridge University Press, 1979), 78–79, and passim.

[43] Exodus; John 8:34; 2 Peter 2:19.

cial distinctions, since it was felt that "gentlemen ought not to be shamed by 'slavish' punishments like whipping or the stocks."[44] More commonly, however, the concept of slavery was used to describe the condition of an individual, a group, or a nation that lived without the benefit of legal, constitutional government. Thus in 1610, in the face of James I's warning not to question his actions, Thomas Wentworth argued in Parliament that "if we shall once say that we may not dispute the prerogative, let us be sold for slaves."[45] With no less certainty or passion the brewers of London proclaimed themselves in 1660 to be "Free-men Inslaved" because the imposition of an excise tax on beer and ale was "contrary to the Fundamental Law of this Land."[46]

Sidney and Locke drew on the resonant power of this familiar and plastic concept in their attacks on Filmer's patriarchalism. But they added an important and revolutionary twist to its conventional meaning: they declared that men were by nature free, and therefore that men were made slaves whenever they were subjected to powers to which they had not given their consent. It was here that Sidney and Locke diverged in their arguments against Filmer, and in their conceptions of freedom and slavery. According to Sidney, the moral foundation of government lay in the belief

> That Man is naturally free; That he cannot justly be deprived of that Liberty without cause, and that he doth not resign it, or any part of it, unless it be in consideration of a greater good, which he proposes to himself.

Locke's definition of freedom was characteristically more precise. It was also subtly but significantly different:

> The *Natural Liberty* of Man is to be free from any Superior Power on Earth, and not to be under the Will or Legislative Authority of Man, but to have only the Law of Nature for his Rule. The *Liberty of Man, in Society,* is to be under no other Legislative Power, but that established, by consent, in the Common-wealth, nor under the Dominion of any Will, or

[44] David Underdown, *Revel, Riot, and Rebellion: Popular Politics and Culture in England 1603–1660* (Oxford: The Clarendon Press, 1985), 21. In a gloss on I Samuel 8:1–15, James I described the terrors of the monarchy set over the Israelites by God as including the "redacting noble houses, and men, and women of noble blood, to slavish and servile offices" (James I, "The Trew Law of Free Monarchies," in *Political Works of James I,* ed. C. H. McIlwain [Cambridge, MA: Harvard University Press, 1918], 59).

[45] Quoted in J. P. Sommerville, *Politics and Ideology in England 1603–1640* (London: Longman, 1986), 101.

[46] *Free-men Inslaved: Or, Reasons humbly offered . . . for the taking off the Excise upon Beer, and Ale* [London: 1660].

Restraint of any Law, but what the Legislative shall enact, according to the Trust put in it.[47]

Both men emphasized the importance of consent to the creation of legitimate authority. But Locke added an element missing in Sidney's account: man's freedom is connected to his adherence to the laws of nature.

The significance of this distinction can be highlighted by drawing on a recent interpretation of Locke's political theory tendered by John Dunn and James Tully. According to these scholars, the bedrock of Locke's moral theory was his belief that humans are the "Workmanship" and "Property" of a benevolent and purposive God: "For Men being all the Workmanship of one Omnipotent, and infinitely wise Maker; All the Servants of one Sovereign Master, sent into the World by his Order and about his business, they are his Property, whose Workmanship they are, made to last during his, not one anothers Pleasure."[48] On the basis of this and similar passages in Locke's writings, Tully has argued that "Locke's political philosophy hinges on this one-way dependency relation between God and man."[49] Only God's "Workmanship" ensured the validity of the law of nature; only God's "Property" in men and women obliged them to obey "the main intention of Nature . . . the increase of Mankind, and the continuation of the Species in the highest perfection."[50] This followed from a particular conception of the nature of law. According to Locke, "The originall & foundation of all Law is dependency. A dependent intelligent being is under the power & direction & dominion of him on whome he depends & must be for the ends appointed him by that being. If man were independent he could have no law but his own will noe end but himself. He would be a god to himself, & the satisfaction of his own will the sole measure & end of all his actions."[51] The rights and duties of men derive from the fact that they are God's creation. In the words of John Dunn, "theology was the key to a coherent understanding of human existence" in Locke's philosophy.[52]

Filmer was no less theologically oriented than Locke; he too believed that all the world was God's creation. But his belief that "*the*

---

[47] *Discourses*, I:2, p. 5; *Two Treatises*, II:22.

[48] *Two Treatises*, II:6. See also: I:52–54, 86; I:56; and Locke, "Some Thoughts Concerning Education," par. 136.

[49] James Tully, *A Discourse on Property: John Locke and His Adversaries* (Cambridge: Cambridge University Press, 1980), 36.

[50] *Two Treatises*, I:59.

[51] John Locke, "Ethica: Morality," Bodleian Library, MS. Locke c.28, fol. 141.

[52] John Dunn, *The Political Thought of John Locke* (Cambridge: Cambridge University Press, 1969), 263. See also: 93–95, 127, 266.

natural and private dominion of Adam" was "the fountain of all government and propriety" destroyed the moral foundations of society by making men Adam's, and not God's, property.[53] As many commentators have noted, Locke's theory of property in chapter 5 of the *Second Treatise* was historically and analytically linked to his reading and refutation of Filmer.[54] Locke's argument was designed to rebut Filmer's attack on the Grotian theory of contractual property rights,[55] and it can be seen as part of a European debate over "the 'modern' theory of natural law."[56] It also provided the foundation for Locke's theories of freedom and authority. What Locke distrusted was not political power per se, but "human beings left to their own devices, human beings who no longer grasp their dependence on their divine Creator."[57] So long as Filmerian monarchs had a private and unconstrained property in their subjects, they were gods unto themselves, free to satisfy their own "Ambition, Revenge, Covetousness, or any other irregular Passion."[58] The legacy of Adam's dominion destroyed the law of nature, making Filmerian subjects slaves and Filmerian monarchs creatures to be feared as men feared beasts and wild animals. The concept of God's "Workmanship" or "Property" in men provided an important counter to the theory of patriarchal ownership by directly linking freedom to God's purposes for men.

Like Locke, Sidney believed that God created the world and that significant moral and political consequences flowed from that fact. But unlike Locke, he did not rely on the fact of God's creation to counter Filmer's patriarchalism. Or, perhaps more accurately, he viewed God's creation in a different way: where Locke drew attention to the sheer fact that God created men and women, Sidney pointed to the fact that he created them to be free; where Locke relied on God's workmanship to link men and women to a fairly robust theory

---

[53] *Patriarcha*, 71. See also: 203–4.

[54] Peter Laslett, "Introduction," in *Two Treatises*, 81; Dunn, *Political Thought of John Locke*, 66; Tully, *Discourse on Property*, 56; Istvan Hont and Michael Ignatieff, "Needs and Justice in the *Wealth of Nations*: An Introductory Essay," in *Wealth and Virtue*, ed. Hont and Ignatieff (Cambridge: Cambridge University Press, 1983), 36.

[55] "In place of the crude antithesis between everything belonging to everybody (with its logical incoherences so doggedly mocked by Filmer) or everything belonging to Adam or his heir, the world is presented [by Locke] as belonging to nobody but available for the appropriations of all" (Dunn, *Political Thought of John Locke*, 67).

[56] The phrase is Richard Tuck's: "The 'Modern' Theory of Natural Law," in *The Languages of Political Theory in Early-Modern Europe*, ed. Anthony Pagden (Cambridge: Cambridge University Press, 1987), 99–119. Locke's contribution to this debate is succinctly described in Hont and Ignatieff, "Needs and Justice," 36–41.

[57] John Dunn, *Locke* (Oxford: Oxford University Press, 1984), 53.

[58] *Two Treatises*, II:199.

of natural law, Sidney pared the claims of "God and Nature" to a minimum.[59] Sidney's conception of freedom was much more individualistic than that of Locke. Its essence was negatively summarized by his claim that "every one must bear the penalty of his own crimes." We are each responsible for our own actions.[60] Positively, Sidney's argument was captured by the claim that "the Liberty God & nature gave me . . . is the power over my self."[61] "As an ingenious Person not long since said, [God has not] caused some to be born with Crowns upon their heads, and all others with Saddles upon their backs."[62] Every man was born with the power, authority, and independence of a king; no man was born a natural subject. Indeed, "that which is Dominion, if in one, when 'tis equally divided among all men, is that universal Liberty which I assert."[63] Filmerism was wrong because it deprived men and women of their natural freedom. By subjecting them to the absolute dominion of one man, it dealt them benefits and burdens independent of their actions and prevented them from directing their own lives.

The different analytic frameworks within which Locke and Sidney operated help to explain their reactions to Filmer's theory of property.[64] The concept of property was integral to Locke's moral and political theory, and his discussion of it has justly been considered one of his greatest innovations. It was through his analysis of prop-

[59] For example, from the fact that "God is our Lord by right of creation, and our only Lord, because he only hath created us," Sidney concluded that no man had the right "to play the Lord over his Brethren" (*Discourses*, II:9, p. 101). See also: I:12, p. 26.

[60] *Discourses*, III:40, p. 435. Sidney viewed his own life in these terms: "I did not make myself, nor can I correct the defects of my own creation. I walk in the light God hath given me; if it be dimme or uncertaine, I must beare the penalty of my errors" (Algernon Sidney to the earl of Leicester, 30 August 1660, in Blencowe, 197).

[61] *Maxims*, 28.

[62] *Discourses*, III:33, p. 406. This was a popular expression among supporters of the Bill of Exclusion. In a parliamentary speech of 6 November 1680 Sir Henry Ford noted that "They say, no man is born with a Crown on his head, or a saddle on his back" (Anchitell Grey, ed., *Debates of the House of Commons*, 10 vols. [London: 1769], 7:426–27).

[63] *Discourses*, I:12, p. 26. Cf. *Two Treatises*, II:123.

[64] There are historical and textual reasons for this difference as well. Locke read and made use of the whole of Filmer's printed writings, while Sidney shows signs of having read only *Patriarcha*. Thus Sidney did not read Filmer's "Observations . . . Upon H. Grotius," or his "Observations Upon Aristotles Politiques." Both of these tracts contained significant discussions of Filmer's theory of property. Moreover, the lengthy discussions of "natural community and voluntary propriety" and "the dangerous conclusions of Grotius," printed as chapters 8 and 9 of the Laslett edition of *Patriarcha* (pp. 63–73), were not included in the 1680 edition of *Patriarcha*. They were, however, included in the "Grotius," and hence they too were available to Locke but not to Sidney.

erty that Locke was first able to make use of the normative implications of God's workmanship in man. Slavery was a secondary category, graphically describing the condition of an individual or a nation that had been deprived of its capacity to act rationally, to incur obligations, to own property, and to obey the laws of God and nature. For Sidney, by contrast, the nature of and justification for property were secondary, while the concept of slavery was primary. To be sure, he thought it "impossible for a man to have a right to Lands or Goods, if he has no Liberty."[65] But that was simply a reflection of the dangers latent in absolute monarchy. Without benefit of a well-ordered system of laws, men lacked the security and stability that made the ownership of property meaningful. Property was a consequence of freedom, and not a constitutive element in its definition. As Locke could not have stated his case against patriarchalism without a sophisticated concept of property, Sidney could not have done so without reference to the contrasting conditions of freedom and slavery. The differences between Locke and Sidney are often a matter of emphasis, but they also reflect fundamentally different approaches to the problem of legitimacy.

"Power Over My Self"

At the heart of Sidney's analysis of freedom and slavery was a simple definition: "Liberty solely consists in an independency upon the Will of another, and by the name of Slave we understand a man, who can neither dispose of his Person nor Goods, but enjoys all at the will of his Master."[66] Sidney amplified this definition in two ways. First, liberty was "an exemption from the dominion of another."[67] It characterized a life lived without reference to the commanding will of a superior. Second, liberty was natural, "written in the heart of every Man." It was as obvious as the axioms of Euclid and could be denied by none who possessed reason or common sense.[68] Taken together,

[65] *Discourses*, III:16, p. 318.

[66] *Discourses*, I:1, p. 12. See also: III:16, p. 317.

[67] *Discourses*, III:33, p. 406. See also: I:12, p. 26; I:17, p. 44; II:31, p. 243.

[68] *Discourses*, I:2, pp. 5–6. This was a common trope, indicating that a belief or statement was beyond question; thus, for example, Locke argued that "where there is no Property, there is no Injustice, is a Proposition as certain as any Demonstration in Euclid" (John Locke, *An Essay concerning Human Understanding*, ed. Peter H. Nidditch [Oxford: The Clarendon Press, 1975], 4.3.18, p. 549). Sidney's use of geometric and mathematical analogies in no way justifies the claim that he was a Platonist (Jonathan Scott, *Algernon Sidney and the English Republic* [Cambridge: Cambridge University Press, 1988], 22, 201).

these claims stood patriarchalism on its head: "every Man is a King till he divest himself of his Right, in consideration of something that he thinks better for him."[69]

Beyond these simple claims and definitions, Sidney wrote very little about the abstract meaning of the concepts of freedom and slavery. He was not a systematic thinker, and there is no place in his writings where one can turn to find a "theory" of liberty. That is not to say that his use of these concepts was incoherent or unintelligent. Nor does it imply that he was uninterested in their meaning. It does, however, affect the tools and techniques that must be used to analyze his account of them. The enormous power of the concepts of freedom and slavery arose from their ability to express a wide range of ideals and aspirations and from their resonance with a radical interpretation of the dangers posed by the government of Charles and James Stuart. To understand them we must pay careful attention not only to Sidney's abstract or conceptual claims, but also to the ends and activities he sought to protect.

According to Sidney, "the end of all Government" is "the publick Good."[70] At a number of points in both the *Court Maxims* and the *Discourses Concerning Government*, he attempted to put flesh on this bare-bones claim by describing the ends that guided men in the creation of governments. These ranged from providing for "the prosperity and happiness of the People" to increasing their "Number, Strength, Power, Riches, and Courage."[71] Governments were created "for the good of the People, and for the defence of every private man's Life, Liberty, Lands and Goods. . . . If the publick Safety be provided, Liberty and Propriety secured, Justice administered, Virtue encouraged, Vice suppressed, and the true interest of the Nation advanced, the ends of Government are accomplished."[72] Governments were not woven into the fabric of nature, nor were they expressive of deep cosmic principles. Rather, they were tools or instruments created to serve the changing needs of the nation. Those governments were best that were best able to advance the public good.

[69] *Discourses*, I:7, p. 18. See also: III:33, p. 406. "He that pretends a power over me must show how I have lost the Liberty God & nature gave me; That is the power over my self for I am naturally equal to him in freedom" (*Maxims*, 28).

[70] *Discourses*, III:7, p. 281. Though seemingly banal, this premise precluded alternatives like carrying out the revealed will of God.

[71] *Discourses*, III:14, p. 313; II:26, p. 209. "That Government is evidently the best, which, not relying upon what it dos at first enjoy, seeks to increase the number, strength, and riches of the people" (II:23, p. 165).

[72] *Discourses*, III:21, p. 351. Governments are constituted "that in a society wee may live free, happy and safe" (*Maxims*, 13; see also: 4, 6, 20).

In listing the ends of government Sidney placed special emphasis on the preservation and advancement of individual liberty. He was particularly concerned with the extent of an individual's power over his own life. As he argued in the *Court Maxims*, "the most important temporall interests of all honest men are to preserve life, liberty and estate, to be preserved from suffering evill unless they deserve it, by disobeying a known and just Law, and to have a way open, by honest industry to provide everyone for his own family, according to his vocation."[73] This argument was underscored in the *Discourses*. In matters of concern to the public, an individual's actions might be constrained; but each

> still retains to himself the right of ordering according to his own will all things merely relating to himself, and of doing what he pleases in that which he dos for his own sake. . . . My Land is not simply my own, but upon condition that I shall not thereby bring damage upon the Publick, by which I am protected in the peaceable enjoyment and innocent use of what I possess. But this Society leaves me a liberty to take Servants, and put them away at my pleasure. . . . Nay, the State takes no other cognizance of what passes between me and them, than to oblige me to perform the contracts I make, and not to do that to them which the Law forbids.[74]

Sidney's example—the hiring and firing of servants—is somewhat bizarre and carries distinctly aristocratic overtones. But the principle behind it is universal: governments are legitimate, and citizens are free, only to the extent that each man "retains to himself the right of ordering according to his own will all things merely relating to himself."[75]

Sharply contrasting with this state of freedom was the condition of slavery. A slave was "a man, who can neither dispose of his Person nor Goods, but enjoys all at the will of his Master." Sidney was careful to note that it was the fact of dependency, and not the degree of suffering, that defined slavery: "The weight of Chains, number of Stripes, hardness of labour, and other effects of a Master's cruelty, may make one servitude more miserable than another: but he is a slave who serves the best and gentlest man in the world, as well as he who serves the worst; and he dos serve him if he must obey his commands, and depends upon his will."[76] Freedom and personal depen

---

[73] *Maxims*, 144. See also: 177; *Discourses*, I:5, p. 13.

[74] *Discourses*, III:41, p. 437.

[75] Sidney's preferred method for adjudicating between public and private actions will be discussed in Chapter 5.

[76] *Discourses*, III:21, pp. 349–50.

dence were mutually exclusive. This was partly an analytical claim: one might compare the fruits of liberty with the benefits of serving a kind master, but they were distinct modes of living nonetheless.[77] It was also an empirical observation: no matter how benevolent a ruler might seem, there was ample historical evidence to suggest that he would not always be so.[78] But first and foremost it was a declaration of independence: what mattered most about a man's actions was that he, and not someone else, had chosen them. "I am not afraid to say, that naturally and properly a man is the judg of his own concernments."[79]

In many respects Sidney's argument for individual freedom was a straightforward expression of the desire for "negative liberty," for an "area within which a man can act unobstructed by others."[80] This was liberty as Hobbes above all others had envisioned it: "Liberty, or Freedome, signifieth (properly) the absence of Opposition (by Opposition, I mean externall Impediments of motion)."[81] Sidney differed from Hobbes in one crucial respect, however, for he argued that "he is a free man who lives as best pleases himself, under Laws made by his own consent."[82] The latter claim was violently anti-Hobbesian, and it goes to the heart of Sidney's radicalism.

According to Hobbes, "Liberty in the proper sense" is "corporall Liberty; that is to say, freedome from chains, and prison." Consequently, "the Liberty of a Subject, lyeth . . . only in those things, which in regulating their actions, the Soveraign hath prætermitted: such as is the Liberty to buy, and sell, and otherwise contract with one another; to choose their own aboad, their own diet, their own trade of life, and institute their children as they themselves think fit; & the like."[83] Men are free if and only if the law is silent. Hobbes

[77] "For this reason the Poet [Claudian] ingeniously flattering a good Emperor, said, that Liberty was not more desirable, than to serve a gentle Master; but still acknowledged that it was a service, distinct from, and contrary to Liberty: and it had not bin a handsom complement, unless the evil of servitude were so extreme, that nothing but the virtue and goodness of the master could any way compensate or alleviate it" (*Discourses*, III:21, p. 350).

[78] "As 'tis folly to suppose that Princes will always be wise, just and good, when we know that few have bin able alone to bear the weight of a Government, or to resist the temptations to ill, that accompany an unlimited power, it would be madness to presume they will for the future be free from infirmities and vices" (*Discourses*, III:21, p. 350).

[79] *Discourses*, III:46, p. 436.

[80] Isaiah Berlin, *Four Essays on Liberty* (Oxford: Oxford University Press, 1969), 122.

[81] Thomas Hobbes, *Leviathan*, ed. C. B. Macpherson (Harmondsworth: Penguin Books, 1981), 261.

[82] *Discourses*, III:21, p. 349. See also: I:2, p. 6.

[83] Hobbes, *Leviathan*, 264.

made no attempt to hide the polemical purpose of this conception of liberty. Many of his contemporaries, having read "the Histories, and Philosophy of the Antient Greeks, and Romans," had mistakenly concluded that political participation was a constituent part of freedom. As a result they "have gotten a habit (under a false shew of Liberty,) of favouring tumults, and of licentious controlling the actions of their Sovereigns." But as Hobbes remonstrated, the citizens of a republic were no more free than the subjects of a monarch; neither possessed the right to challenge the commands of the sovereign.

> There is written on the Turrets of the city of *Luca* in great characters at this day, the word LIBERTAS; yet no man can thence inferre, that a particular man has more Libertie, or Immunitie from the service of the Commonwealth there, than in *Constantinople*. Whether a Commonwealth be Monarchicall, or Popular, the Freedome is still the same.[84]

Hobbes even intimated that the onerous duties of republican citizenship actually diminished the extent of a man's freedom. The Lucchese were more tightly bound by their laws than were their brethren in neighboring monarchies. The liberty of the ancients—the right to participate in political decision making—was a chimera and could not be used to undermine the authority of modern sovereigns.

Sidney's contrary assertion, that freedom and political participation were intimately linked, was partly a consequence of the polemical task he assigned himself in writing the *Discourses*. At stake in his debate with Filmer—and, by extension, with Charles II—was not simply, or even primarily, whether there should be laws, but rather who should control the law. Patriarchalism was only tangentially concerned with liberty; it was above all a theory of rule, and its principal purpose was to justify the exercise of God-given power. Sidney shifted attention away from subjection and onto liberty, but as a practical matter he still had to wrest control of the political system from the hands of the monarch. The logic of patriarchalism—and the behavior of Charles II—did not permit him to separate questions concerning the degree to which Englishmen were governed from questions concerning the authority by whom they were governed.

Reinforcing these polemical considerations was a complex set of claims concerning the relationship between individual freedom and the patterns of history, the powers of reason and the purposes of government. The nature and extent of an individual's power over his life were profoundly influenced by the political institutions under which he lived. The possibilities open to an individual were not pre-

---

[84] Hobbes, *Leviathan*, 266.

determined, and hence the location of authority over those institutions was critical to the structure of freedom. While royalists fixed this power in the hands of the king, Sidney argued that only the public was adequate to the task.[85]

The starting point for Sidney's argument was an anti-Aristotelian portrayal of the state of nature: "Men were sent into the World rude and ignorant. . . . The bestial Barbarity in which many Nations, especially of *Africa, America* and *Asia*, do now live, shews what human Nature is, if it be not improved by art and discipline."[86] There was an enormous gap between the poverty of unimproved nature and the riches of civilization. Primitive men lacked the beliefs and conventions necessary to collective life.[87] They also lacked the material and intellectual resources that made life pleasant. While few questioned the legitimacy of innovations in food and housing,[88] many—including Sir Robert Filmer—drew the line when it came to matters moral and political. It was for these men that Sidney reserved his most withering scorn: "If it be lawful for us by the use of that understanding to build Houses, Ships and Forts better than our Ancestors, to make such Arms as are most fit for our defence, and to invent Printing, with an infinite number of other Arts beneficial to mankind, why have we not the same right in matters of Government, upon which all others do almost absolutely depend?" According to Filmer, God's grant of dominion to Adam had determined the correct form of government for all time. "We may as reasonably affirm that Mankind is for ever obliged to use no other Clothes than leather Breeches, like *Adam*; to live in hollow Trees, and eat Acorns, or to seek after the Model of his House for a Habitation, and to use no Arms except such as were known to the Patriarchs, as to think all Nations for ever obliged to be governed as they governed their Families."[89] With a measure of hubris unthinkable to Filmer, Sidney suggested that in certain fundamental respects the world had improved since God cre-

---

[85] My argument in this and the following paragraphs owes a great deal to Stephen Holmes, *Benjamin Constant and the Making of Modern Liberalism* (New Haven: Yale University Press, 1984), esp. 28–78.

[86] *Discourses*, III:7, p. 281.

[87] The significance of this claim for the construction of a nontheological version of the social contract is explored in Quentin Skinner, *The Foundations of Modern Political Thought*, 2 vols. (Cambridge: Cambridge University Press, 1978), 2:340–42; its relevance to Sidney's argument will be discussed below.

[88] Sidney gave no consideration to "the European tradition of nostalgia for the Golden Age of primitive communism" to which Grotius and Pufendorf had directed a similar contrast between nature and civilization (Hont and Ignatieff, "Needs and Justice," 33).

[89] *Discourses*, III:7, p. 281; I:6, p. 16.

ated it. Human nature might not have changed, but the possibilities of human action had been radically altered.[90]

Reinforcing Sidney's argument for change was his appreciation of the limited powers of human reason: "Such is the condition of mankind, that nothing can be so perfectly framed as not to give some testimony of human imbecility, and frequently to stand in need of reparations and amendments."[91] This was particularly true with regard to politics, where "no Law made by man can be perfect," and thus "there must be in every Nation a power of correcting such defects as in time may arise or be discovered." Moreover, as it was impossible for men to design perfect laws, so also was it unlikely that any specific generation of men might imagine all the ends to which laws might be addressed. The flawed powers of reason required the provision of some mechanism by which men could "advance a good that at the first was not thought on."[92] Unlike James Harrington, Sidney thought "an immortal commonwealth" neither possible nor desirable.[93]

Sidney exploited the radical potential of this argument by contending that only the people at large had the moral authority and epistemic insight necessary to judge whether or not these changes were in the public interest. He made this point by drawing an analogy between politics and everyday life:

> A Physician does not exercise his Art for himself, but for his Patients; and when I am, or think I shall be sick, I send for him of whom I have the best opinion, that he may help me to recover, or preserve my health; but I lay him aside if I find him to be negligent, ignorant, or unfaithful; and it would be ridiculous for him to say, I make my self judg in my own case, for I only, or such as I shall consult, am fit to be the judg of it.[94]

[90] "Those who will admit of no change would render Errors perpetual, and depriving Mankind of the benefits of Wisdom, Industry, Experience, and the right use of Reason, oblige all to continue in the miserable barbarity of their Ancestors, which sutes better with the name of a Wolf than that of a Man" (*Discourses*, III:25, p. 366).

[91] *Discourses*, III:25, p. 366. Contrary to Ashcraft's assertion, Sidney demonstrated almost no interest in "the peculiar socioeconomic characteristics of a commercially developed society" (Ashcraft, *Revolutionary Politics*, 224). The core of his argument was moral, not sociological, and rested on a blend of political, theological, and epistemological considerations.

[92] *Discourses*, III:22, p. 357; II:17, p. 136. See also: II:13, p. 117; III:7, p. 281; III:37, pp. 418–19.

[93] James Harrington, "The Commonwealth of Oceana," in *The Political Works of James Harrington*, ed. J.G.A. Pocock (Cambridge: Cambridge University Press, 1977), 209. This distinction draws attention to the uniqueness of Harrington's concerns and calls into question Pocock's attempt to understand republicanism in terms of a common conception of "time."

[94] *Discourses*, III:14, p. 313. See also: III:41, p. 436.

As a maxim that "seems only to have acquired political relevance in the Civil War" put it, "can any man tell better than yourselves, where your shoe pincheth you, and what is most expedient for you to do?"[95] Cobblers might have technical expertise, but only their customers could effectively judge the success of their labors. A full exploration of Sidney's use of this argument will be presented in Chapter 5, in the context of an analysis of his constitutional theory. At this point I would simply draw attention to one of its central implications: even an "absolute" ruler would have to be subject to regular public supervision, for only the public would know whether or not he is doing his job correctly.

The importance of public supervision to the preservation of freedom was reflected in Sidney's characterization of the consequences of slavery. Freedom and slavery were polar opposites, between which lay no neutral ground. Where free men were independent, slaves were dependent on the capricious will of another; where freedom brought "strength, glory, plenty, security and happiness," slavery brought "misery, infamy, destruction and desolation." And "when the people are brought to be few, weak and poor . . . every ones thoughts will be confind to the seeking of necessaries and by extream labour to get a pair of *canvass breeches, wooden shoes, course bread* for his family."[96] This was the point behind Sidney's claim that slavery was worse than civil war: it radically collapsed the "horizon of possible experiences and actions" and gave "the name of Peace to desolation."[97]

The debilitating consequences of slavery were not limited to poverty. Slavery eliminated the very possibility of individual liberty by effacing the distinction between "public" and "private" spheres of life. According to Filmer, "a son, a subject and a servant or a slave,

[95] J.A.W. Gunn, *Politics and the Public Interest in the Seventeenth Century* (London: Routledge & Kegan Paul, 1969), 24–25. Sidney was well aware of this maxim. In response to Filmer's claim that "an implicit faith" ought to be placed in a king, Sidney responded, "Who will wear a Shoe that hurts him, because the Shoe maker tells him 'tis well made? or who will live in a House that yields no defence against the extremities of Weather, because the Mason or Carpenter assures him 'tis a very good House?" (*Discourses*, I:3, p. 9).

[96] *Discourses*, III:21, p. 351; *Maxims*, 64. "The present sense of their wants hinders them from applying their thoughts beyond anything but getting of bread, and their weakness keeps them quiet abasing their spirits: despair of success keeps them from attempting any thing" (*Maxims*, 59–60). See also: *Discourses*, III:5, p. 271.

[97] Holmes, *Benjamin Constant*, 65; *Discourses*, II:26, p. 206. See also: *Maxims*, 17. In 1652 Sidney reported to his father that English slaves in the West Indies preferred death to servitude (Robert Sidney, "Notes on Slavery," Kent Archives Office, De L'Isle MS. [U1475], Z1/9).

were one and the same thing at first."[98] Every inhabitant of the polity was subsumed within the household of the ruler. As a result, no region of life could be shielded from the controlling will of the monarch; absolute monarchy was "an oppressive way of life extending into every sphere of the subject's existence."[99] The politics of slavery were the politics of "Spies, Informers and false Witnesses."[100] As the courtier Philalethos explained in the *Court Maxims*: "We give honours and rewards to accusers and informers, fill all houses with spyes, set division in all familys. . . . If the wife be inclined to Gallantry, or the son debauch'd, we know they are ours. If they do not of themselves fall into these courses, we have baits to allure them. By this means, few can so conceal themselves but we know what they say in their chambers or beds."[101] Absolute monarchy poisoned the world by giving men and women incentives to betray each other. Even the family was not impervious to its effects. This insight was of tremendous importance to the structure of Sidney's theory of liberty. For as he realized, individual freedom and the effective exercise of political rights were inseparable. Without the preservation of a private sphere of life beyond the reach of public powers, political participation—which is based on trust and cooperation—was not possible. Without adequate public supervision of governmental authority, on the other hand, the boundary between public and private life could not be preserved.

Freedom of Conscience

Further insight into the intellectual structure and polemical appeal of Sidney's conception of freedom can be obtained by focusing on his arguments for religious toleration. For most of the seventeenth century, Protestant Dissenters were subject to an array of punishments and disabilities that affected not only their ability to practice their faith but also their freedom to pursue an occupation, choose a domicile, and participate in the political life of the nation. These sanctions were neither random nor the fruit of simple prejudice; as suggested in Chapter 2, they reflected deeply held beliefs concerning the structure of a well-ordered society. After the Restoration they also provided the foundation for a conscious political program. Though Charles II apparently had a taste for toleration—he had promised "a

[98] *Patriarcha*, 188.
[99] Ashcraft, *Revolutionary Politics*, 213.
[100] *Discourses*, II:27, p. 214.
[101] *Maxims*, 190. See also: 158.

liberty to tender consciences" in the Declaration of Breda in 1660 and attempted to give toleration to Dissenters on four other occasions—he was virtually alone among the men who dominated English politics during his reign.[102] During the early 1660s an alliance between the Anglican clergy and the conservative provincial gentry enacted the Clarendon Code, a series of repressive measures designed to ensure political stability through religious uniformity.[103] Sidney was particularly sensitive to the plight of Dissenters in Restoration England, and his devotion to radical Protestantism reinforced and extended his commitment to freedom as "an exemption from the dominion of another."

The key text for understanding Sidney's defense of toleration is the *Court Maxims*. Despite the overwhelming importance of religious belief and practice to the crises of the 1670s and 1680s, Sidney chose not to address the problem of religious uniformity in his attack on Sir Robert Filmer.[104] This may have been a reflection of the extent to which Filmer set the terms of the debate: though his writings presumed the truth of Christianity and neatly dovetailed with High Church teachings, he did not explicitly address theological or ecclesiastical matters. It may also have been a deliberate polemical strategy. Most Englishmen feared popery far more than they sympathized with Dissenters, and the Exclusion Crisis drew its energy from the grave religious and political threat posed by the Catholicism of James duke of York. By treating the church as an instrument of the king's will it was possible to focus attention on the nation's right to restrain its magistrates without raising the potentially divisive question of toleration. As will be suggested below, however, the separation of religion and politics was implicit in the very framework of analysis Sidney employed in the *Discourses Concerning Government*.

Sidney adopted two strategies in attempting to refute the Restoration settlement: he savaged the practices of the Anglican clergy, and he rejected the theological premises justifying uniformity. No insult was spared in his attack on the "Men of that Reveren'd Coat": they were "Lustfull lawn-sleeved Parasites," "Teachers of lies, workers of iniquity, persecutors of saints, and Apes of Rome." Hiding behind the cloak of apostolic authority, they actively subverted the teaching of

---

[102] Charles II, "Declaration of Breda," 4 April 1660, in Samuel Rawson Gardiner, *Constitutional Documents of the Puritan Revolution 1625–1660*, 3rd ed. (Oxford: The Clarendon Press, 1906), 466; Ronald Hutton, *The Restoration: A Political and Religious History of England and Wales 1658–1667* (Oxford: The Clarendon Press, 1985), 147.

[103] J. R. Jones, *Country and Court: England, 1658–1714* (Cambridge, MA: Harvard University Press, 1979), 145–47. See also: Hutton, *Restoration*, 166–80.

[104] This holds for Locke and Tyrrell as well.

the gospel. " 'Tis no matter whether a man be an independent, Presbeterian or Anabaptist, if he can prey or preach he's a fanatick with them. Our prisons are full of such our churches empty."[105] By giving the Anglican clergy a legal monopoly over religious practice, the Clarendon Code had turned the public faith into an instrument of private oppression. True religion languished while the church filled its coffers.

Sidney's conviction that the Clarendon Code served as a spiritual mask for corrupt temporal interests was founded on his unqualified rejection of the premises justifying uniformity. He framed his argument with a set of questions: "First whether it is possible by force or fear to make any man beleive any thing? Secondly, whether acceptable to God that a man worship him when his heart is far from him? Thirdly, whether those who are not spiritual men are fitt to judge of spiritual things? Fourthly, whether a prudent man can have such assurance he is in the right as to dare force others to his way?"[106] Like many radical Protestants, Sidney held that "beleife is not the act of the will" and consequently that "its neither in my power to beleive what I please, nor what pleases another man that is stronger then I."[107] True faith was a matter of inner light, not outward conformity, and was based on an open heart and the grace of God. "Humane impositions may make hypocrites, never Christians."[108]

The absurdity of England's uniform and compulsory national church was made manifest by the fact that it subverted the very orthodoxy that it trumpeted. By virtue of the Act of Supremacy of 1534 the king had the authority to "repress, redress, reform, order, correct, restrain and amend all such errors, heresies, abuses, offences, contempts and enormities" as existed in the Church of England. As Sidney tartly observed, this gave the king almost unlimited power over the doctrinal content and ecclesiastical organization of the church and meant that "I am to be a papist, Jew, Turk, heathen or to sacrifice to the devil if my Prince so comand me." This was no idle speculation; during the sixteenth century England's national faith changed five times in less than thirty years, and the Catholicism of

---

[105] *Maxims*, 8, 78, 80, 41. "The only way to maintain their authority is to keep people from perusing the bible . . . for that discovers the vanity of both their callings and all their fig-leafe pretences" (96).

[106] *Maxims*, 83.

[107] *Maxims*, 83. "I cannot but beleive every thing to be but as it appears to my understanding. I beleive the 3 Angles of a Triangle to be equal to 2 right angles. Torment may perhaps force me to say they are equal to 3 right angles or but to one. But all the tyrants in the world can never make me beleive they are not equal to two" (83–84).

[108] *Maxims*, 84.

the duke of York raised the spectre of its doing so once again. Under such conditions men learned to survive by bending their consciences like willows in a breeze.[109]

The foundation of true faith lay in "a rational and natural right of disputeing whats uncertain, and of not receiving it till convinced that its a certain truth." Each man was the steward of his own soul, and thus it was "madness" to compel another. And though no amount of compulsion could destroy a man's "spiritual interest," it could effectively "hinder" him in the "outward performance of [his] spiritual dutys." So vital was a man's spiritual life to his identity and fate that "no injury . . . offerd to a man can be more justly repell'd than violence offer'd to the conscience."[110]

Sidney's espousal of toleration belies the claim that republican liberty was essentially "civic" in nature.[111] Religious faith was an intensely personal matter and could not be subjected to public determination. By placing toleration at the center of his theory, Sidney indicated the importance of privacy to the content of liberty. Freedom of conscience did, however, serve a vital civic function. The Restoration settlement, with its furious blend of religion and politics, had corrupted both. Priests taught the virtues of obedience, while princes resolved doctrinal questions. The chief beneficiaries of this unholy marriage were the Crown and the clergy; its greatest victims were the English people. Toleration was a vital mechanism for preserving "the true Protestant religion" and for rendering the political life of the nation subject to the will of the people. By separating religion and politics it made it possible to preserve the integrity of each.[112] Ironically, this dimension of Sidney's argument can best be seen by focusing on an aspect of his analysis that would seem to undermine the logic of toleration, his invocation of the language of freedom and slavery associated with Egypt and Canaan.

The book of Exodus played a unique role in the moral imagination of seventeenth-century radicals. With its description of the bondage of the Israelites, its promise of an "end [that] is nothing like the be-

[109] "Act of Supremacy," 1534, in G. R. Elton, ed., *The Tudor Constitution* (Cambridge: Cambridge University Press, 1960), 356; *Maxims*, 85, 89.

[110] *Maxims*, 91, 90, 145, 86. See also: 87.

[111] According to J.G.A. Pocock, "the republican vocabulary . . . articulated the positive conception of liberty: it contended that *homo*, the *animale politicum*, was so constituted that his nature was completed only in a *vita activa* practiced in a *vivere civile*, and that *libertas* consisted in freedom from restraints upon the practice of such a life" (J.G.A. Pocock, "Virtues, Rights, and Manners," in *Virtue, Commerce, and History* [Cambridge: Cambridge University Press, 1985], 40–41).

[112] "Apology," 3. As Sidney rhetorically asked, "Shall a blind man be made judge of colours, or a deaf give his opinion of Musick?" (*Maxims*, 89).

ginning," and its emphasis on the perils of the journey to Canaan, the Exodus narrative provided a powerful pattern of explanation for the hopes and sufferings of the English people in their attempt to leave behind the Stuart monarchy. As Michael Walzer has demonstrated, at almost every turning point during the turbulent middle decades of the seventeenth century someone found need to explain the murmurings of slaves in the wilderness, perhaps never more so than after the restoration of Charles II.[113] For example, in 1644 John Milton thought England a "noble and puissant Nation" to whom God had, "as is His manner," revealed himself first. But by 1660, when the English people had fallen prey to the same false promises of "plentie and prosperitie" that had tempted the Israelites, he could only lament that they were "chusing them a captain back for Egypt."[114] To Algernon Sidney, writing the *Court Maxims* a few years later, the metaphor of Egypt still seemed apposite: "Burnt children dread the fire; but we more childish than children, tho oft scorch'd and burnt, do agen cast our selves into the fire; like moths and gnats, delighting in the flame that consumes us . . . we could never be contented 'til we return'd againe into Egypt, the house of our bondage." But, declared Sidney, "the redeemer of Israel liveth, and many signs perswade us to hope that salvation is near att hand."[115] Given these confessions, it is critical to ask whether Sidney viewed England as an elect nation. Was slavery a state of spiritual bondage, and freedom the realization of God's kingdom on earth? Was his defense of toleration a clever ploy designed to advance sectarian aims?

These questions can be fruitfully approached from two directions: Sidney's biography, and the conceptual structure of his theory. Precious little is known of Sidney's spiritual life. We know that he was a Christian whose views savored of Independency,[116] that he believed

---

[113] Michael Walzer, *Exodus and Revolution* (New York: Basic Books, 1985), 11, 3–4. See also: *The Revolution of the Saints* (Cambridge, MA: Harvard University Press, 1965).

[114] John Milton, "Areopagitica," in *Complete Prose Works* (New Haven: Yale University Press, 1953–82), 2:558; Milton, "The Readie and Easie Way to Establish a Free Commonwealth," in *Complete Prose Works*, 7:462–63.

[115] *Maxims*, 202–3, 93. See also: 78, 85, 193–95.

[116] "He was a Christian at large, as he said himself, but he hated all sorts of Church men, and so he never joyn'd himself to any, but to ye Independents; he kept up very litle of an outward profesion of Religion . . . he seem'd in discourse with me to believe the truth of Christianity very firmly, yet he thought devotions and the worship of God were but slight things, and that good Morality was all that was necessary" (Gilbert Burnet, "History of My Own Times" [British Library, Add. MS. 63,057], 2:137–38). This manuscript version of Burnet's history differs dramatically from the printed version (*Bishop Burnet's History of His Own Time*, ed. M. J. Routh, 2nd ed., 6 vols. [Oxford: Oxford University Press, 1833], 2:351).

himself to be an instrument in God's hands,[117] and that he identified himself with the cause of "God's people."[118] Sidney publicly professed these views in the prayer with which he concluded the paper he handed to the sheriffs at his execution: "Bless thy People, and Save Them. Defend thy own Cause, and Defend those that Defend it. . . . Grant that I may Dye glorifying Thee for all thy Mercies; and that at the last Thou has permitted me to be Singled out as a Witness of thy Truth; and even by the Confession of my Opposers, for that OLD CAUSE in which I was from my Youth engaged, and for which Thou has Often and Wonderfully declared thy Self."[119] Without an explanation of who "God's people" were, or what the "Old Cause" was, however, these expressions of faith are inconclusive. They are consistent with a commitment to the creation of a Christian commonwealth, but they are also consistent with a call for religious toleration. It is worth noting that none of Sidney's contemporaries, not even the wily Tory pamphleteer Sir Roger L'Estrange, ever accused him of religious enthusiasm;[120] and in a nation of men whose ears were finely tuned to theological matters, this absence of evidence cannot be ignored.

Regardless of the importance of these beliefs to Sidney's biography, from the perspective of the history of ideas they should not be taken as determinative. What is at stake is not Sidney's own religiosity, but the arguments he put forward for public consideration. Without making a series of strong assumptions—among others, that Sidney intended his theory to express his religious vision; that his agenda was unaffected by the ideological climate within which he wrote; that he was in complete control of the theoretical machinery he produced; and that he wrote what he believed to be the truth and did not attempt to deceive, cajole, appease, sedate, or intimidate his

---

[117] "I walk in the light God hath given me" (Algernon Sidney to the earl of Leicester, 30 August 1660, in Blencowe, 197). See also: Algernon Sidney to [John Hampden], 6 October [1683] (East Sussex Record Office, Glynde Place Papers 794, letter 4), fol. 6; Sidney to [Hampden], [1683] (letter 6), fol. 3.

[118] "I am certaine I can have no peace in my owne spirite, if I doe not endeavour by all meanes possible to advance the interest of God's people" (Algernon Sidney to Benjamin Furly, n.d., in Blencowe, 258–60). See also: *Maxims*, 203.

[119] Sidney, *Very Copy of a Paper* (1683), 3. See also: Algernon Sidney to [John Hampden], 31 October 1683 (East Sussex Record Office, Glynde Place Papers 794, letter 8), fol. 3.

[120] "There was Nothing of Religion in his Charge; Nothing in his Defense" (Sir Roger L'Estrange, *The Observator, in Dialogue*, vol. 1 [London: J. Bennet, 1684], 469 [7 January 1684]). L'Estrange devoted nine editions of *The Observator* to Sidney's *Paper* (461 [24 December 1683] to 469 [7 January 1684]).

audience—there is little reason to expect a particularly tight fit between his private beliefs and his public arguments.

These considerations are particularly important because the arguments Sidney put forward in the *Discourses* preclude the possibility of viewing freedom and slavery in terms of the bondage of an elect nation. Were Sidney's theory designed to enmesh men in a new, divinely sanctioned order, it would have given pride of place to God's revelation in the Bible. But Sidney explicitly rejected Filmer's claim that "ignorance of the Creation occasioned several errors amongst the heathen philosophers." Religious knowledge was unnecessary for an understanding of the moral foundations of society. Freedom was "written in the heart of every Man, [and] denied by none, but such as were degenerated into Beasts." It had the self-evidence of Euclid's axioms, "which none could deny that did not renounce common Sense."[121] Pagan and Christian alike were capable of freedom; the Romans were no less capable of teaching Sidney's contemporaries than were the Israelites.

Consistent with this essentially secular attitude toward politics is the absence of a religious covenant in Sidney's theory. During the sixteenth century the Huguenot theorists Beza and Mornay had written "of two separate contracts which the people may be said to sign at the inauguration of a commonwealth: the religious covenant or *foedus* by which they promise God to act as a godly people; and the political covenant, embodied in the *Lex Regia*, by which they agree to transfer their *Imperium* to an elected ruler on certain mutually acceptable terms."[122] These men believed that the creation of a commonwealth was an expression of man's religious duty, and hence that it was a matter of grave theological concern. There were no parallels to these views in Sidney's theory of consent; his argument was much closer to that of the radical Scots Calvinist George Buchanan—whom he quoted with some frequency—who saw himself "as talking exclusively about politics, not theology, and about the concept of rights, not religious duties."[123] There was not even any place in Sidney's theory for the mystical Christian communitarianism advocated by his fellow

---

[121] *Patriarcha*, 80; *Discourses*, I:2, p. 5. See also: I:2, p. 6; II:1, p. 59.

[122] Skinner, *Foundations of Modern Political Thought*, 2:341.

[123] Skinner, *Foundations of Modern Political Thought*, 2:341. Failure to distinguish between the arguments of Calvinist resistance theorists, coupled with a tendency to rely on family history and "coincidences of sources, ideas, and examples," vitiates one of the central themes of Scott's *Algernon Sidney*; cf. 17, 23, 28, 51–53, 107, 187, 204, 228. Contrary to Scott's assertions, there is no evidence to indicate that Sidney ever read the work of Beza or Mornay; he did, however, cite Buchanan (*Maxims*, 187, 191; *Discourses*, I:2, p. 6; II:24, p. 196; II:30, p. 233; III:14, p. 314; III:40, p. 435) and Hotman (*Discourses*, II:30, pp. 233–35).

Rumper Sir Henry Vane the younger.[124] The ends and purposes of governments were established by men, not God, and the terms of the social contract were drafted on earth, not in heaven. Once having provided the foundation for government by making men free, God relinquished control over them.

An excellent example of this aspect of Sidney's theory of freedom can be seen in his reflections on the character of the law. He frequently expressed his devotion to "the lawes of this land."[125] But he thought it absurd to think that God's will had "bin more particularly revealed to our Ancestors, than to any other Nation. . . . If it be said that we ought to follow the Customs of our own Country, I answer, that those of our own Country deserve to be observed, because they are of our own Country; But they are no more to be called the Laws of God and Nature than those of *France* or *Germany* . . . I do not believe that any general Law is appointed."[126] English law was valid solely because it had been consented to by the English people. Though directed against the ancient constitution, this argument applied to the concept of an elect nation as well. Neither common lawyers nor religious enthusiasts could find solace in Sidney's theory of legislation.[127]

Sidney's constant reference to the contingent nature of political arrangements served a vital function in the struggle against Charles II. As he noted in both the *Court Maxims* and the *Discourses Concerning Government*, "the Power of Princes cud not be fully established unless they had a power over consciences."[128] The primary weapons employed by the king and his clerical minions to accomplish this goal were the twin doctrines of "implicit faith and blind obedience."[129] By claiming that God had set "a Law . . . to all Mankind which none

[124] See, for example: Sir Henry Vane, *The Retired Mans Meditations* (London: 1655), 383–96. Vane's communitarianism is explored in Margaret Judson, *The Political Thought of Sir Henry Vane the Younger* (Philadelphia: University of Pennsylvania Press, 1969), 21, 30, 56. Judson incorrectly asserts, however, that Vane was concerned with "the problem of man obeying himself" (35–36). Vane's problem was not Rousseau's, but Calvin's: how can an individual obey God?

[125] "Apology," 3. See also: Algernon Sidney to [John Hampden], 31 October 1683 (East Sussex Record Office, Glynde Place Papers 794, letter 8), fol. 3.

[126] *Discourses*, III:18, p. 331. "Our Laws were not sent from Heaven, but made by our Ancestors according to the light they had, and their present occasions" (III:25, p. 368).

[127] Latent within Puritanism was an instrumental attitude toward politics; but the "secular implications" of their arguments were hidden by their belief that God set the terms of the social contract (Walzer, *Revolution of the Saints*, 182–83).

[128] *Maxims*, 81; *Discourses*, I:1, p. 4.

[129] The phrase is William Penn's (*An Address to Protestants upon the Present Conjuncture* [1679], 143). Cf. *Discourses*, I:3, p. 8.

might transgress, and which put the examination of all those Matters out of their power," royalists paved the way for absolutism in both church and state.[130] Religious toleration was designed to break the chains that bound these two realms together. By depriving political arrangements of their divine sanction, it called attention to their conventional origins; by depriving the church of its temporal mission, it highlighted the spiritual nature of "the true Protestant religion." Sidney's friend and campaign manager William Penn once asked of the Nonconformist, "Why may not this Man Sell, Buy, Plow, pay his Rent, be as good a Subject, and as true an *English-man* as any *Conformist* in the Kingdom?" His answer, an answer that Sidney no doubt found congenial, was that there were no good reasons for making citizenship contingent on religious belief. "Religion and Policy . . . are two distinct things."[131] By separating them it was possible both to preserve "God's people" and to permit the pursuit of shared secular ends. The freedom of Canaan was possible only when the slavish principles of the Restoration settlement had been left behind.[132]

Rational Autonomy

At the core of Sidney's theory of freedom was the claim that "he is a free man who lives as best pleases himself, under Laws made by his own consent." Men were free when they had power over their own lives, when they were neither subjected to the arbitrary dominion of another nor deprived of a voice in the affairs of the nation. But the phrase "as best pleases himself" was fraught with moral and theological overtones, for Sidney was insistent that liberty was not the same

[130] *Discourses*, I:1, p. 4.

[131] William Penn, *England's Present Interest Discover'd* (1675), 46; William Penn [Philo-Britannicus, pseud.], *The Great Question to be Considered by the King, and this approaching Parliament* [1680], 4.

[132] Why then did Sidney invoke the language of Egypt and Canaan in the *Court Maxims* and not in the *Discourses Concerning Government*? In all likelihood it was a matter of expedience. As noted in Chapter 1, the *Court Maxims* was written in the context of an acrimonious debate between Sidney and Edmund Ludlow over the feasibility of fomenting revolution during the Second Dutch War. "One of the principal themes" of Ludlow's *Voyce From The Watch Tower*, which includes a record of this debate, was "Ludlow's concern to fortify and unite the godly in England during the period of Egyptian bondage under the 'Pharaoh,' Charles II" (Blair Worden, Introduction to *A Voyce From The Watch Tower*, Camden Fourth Series, vol. 21 [London: Royal Historical Society, 1978], 10). Sidney undoubtedly felt that the best way of bringing Ludlow over to his side was to adopt Ludlow's language. At the time he was writing the *Discourses*, by contrast, the chief danger facing Protestantism was not persecution but the "popish" phenomena of absolutism and idolatry.

thing as licentiousness.[133] Free men were not free to do just anything; there was, after all, such a thing as sin. The distinction between liberty and license hinged on the relationship between reason and passion: free men obeyed reason, while slaves were held captive by their passions. The interplay of reason and passion added depth to Sidney's conception of freedom and played a vital role in his campaign against the principles and practices of absolute monarchy.

Sidney frequently described reason as "the candle of Nature" or "the light of common sense."[134] It was "the Law of man's Nature, . . . an emanation of the divine Wisdom, or some footsteps of divine Light remaining in us."[135] As "man is by nature a rationall creature every thing therefore that's irrational is contrary to mans nature."[136] It was reason that gave man access to "the immutable Laws of God and Nature," to those uniform and universal truths that provided the moral foundation for his conduct.[137] Without reason, men would be no better than beasts.[138] Reason was the voice of freedom and the arbiter of all controversies. The passions, by contrast, were private and partial and tended to deflect men from the correct course of action.[139] "As there is no happiness without liberty," so there is "no man more a slave than he thats overmaster'd by vicious passions."[140]

Revealing though they are, these examples tell us very little about the precise mechanisms linking freedom with reason and slavery with the passions. In the process of articulating his theory, Sidney invoked two distinct but related possibilities: that as an individual matter, freedom is possible only when a person is liberated from the slavish chains of the passions; or, that as a political matter, freedom is possible only when reason, and not the passions, governs public decision making.

Sidney frequently suggested that freedom was synonymous with behavior in accord with the dictates of reason. For example, at the beginning of the *Court Maxims* he argued that "he is not happy that

---

[133] "The Liberty asserted is not the Licentiousness of doing what is pleasing to every one against the command of God; but an exemption from all human Laws, to which they have not given their assent" (*Discourses*, I:2, p. 6).

[134] *Maxims*, 114; *Discourses*, III:21, p. 350.

[135] *Discourses*, III:3, p. 265. See also: *Maxims*, 18.

[136] *Maxims*, 27. See also: *Discourses*, II:4, p. 72.

[137] *Discourses*, I:13, p. 27. Sidney frequently expressed his belief in the existence of a single, harmonious pattern of moral truths that could be discovered by human reason (*Maxims*, 6, 101, 192; *Discourses*, I:13, p. 28; I:19, p. 56; II:23, p. 171).

[138] *Discourses*, I:15, p. 34.

[139] *Discourses*, III:14, pp. 312–13.

[140] *Maxims*, 20. See also: *Discourses*, II:19, p. 146; III:25, pp. 368–69.

hath what he desires but desires what is good and enjoys it."[141] The passions were enslaving because they diverted a man from "the immutable Laws of God and Nature" and subjected his "higher" self to the control of his "lower" self. To be free a man had to attain dominion over his passions. This was a very common idea in seventeenth-century England and reflected the profound influence of Christian and classical moralists on the imaginations of Sidney's contemporaries.

Sidney had strong personal reasons for viewing freedom in these terms. According to Bishop Burnet, he was "a man of boisterous and rough temper" who used "foul language" against any who dared contradict him.[142] Sidney himself noted "the heat and violence of my disposition."[143] In the undated essay "Of Love" he reflected on the grip his passions had over him: "[Love] hath with more violence transported me, than a man of understanding ought to suffer himself to be by any passion. . . . [It] hath made itself master of all the faculties of my mind, and hath destroyed all that is in opposition unto it." Sidney found little to rejoice about in this fact. As he explained: "I write my thoughts at one time, that, in perusing them at another, I may come to the knowledge of myself, that, by seeing without passion that which I write in passion, I may know what I am, how I improve or impair; as one that hath his picture drawn when he is emaciated by sickness, may, in his recovery, by comparing that with his present countenance, judge, in some degree, of the state of his own health."[144] Swept by uncontrollable desires and irrational impulses, Sidney felt no more free than if he had been in the shackles of a mad despot. Only in calm, reflective moments could he recall how he ought to have acted; only then could he remind himself of what it meant to be autonomous, to be the master of his self.[145]

---

[141] *Maxims*, 3.

[142] Burnet, "History of My Own Times" (British Library, Add. MS. 63,057), 2:137.

[143] Algernon Sidney to Benjamin Furly, n.d., in Blencowe, 260. "I knowe the titles that are given me, of fierce, violent, seditious, mutinous, turbulent, and many others of the like nature" (Algernon Sidney to the earl of Leicester, 30 August 1660, in Blencowe, 196).

[144] Sidney, "Of Love," in *A Collection of Scarce and Valuable Tracts of . . . Somers*, 8:612, 616.

[145] "The psychological experience of observing myself yielding to some 'lower' impulse, acting from a motive that I dislike, or of doing something which at the very moment of doing I may detest, and reflecting later that I was 'not myself,' or 'not in control of myself,' when I did it, belongs" to the concept of "freedom as self-mastery" (Berlin, *Four Essays*, 138, 134). My argument in this and the following paragraphs is indebted to, but not dependent upon, Berlin's well-known distinction between "positive" and "negative" liberty.

Sidney's invocation of the ideal of rational autonomy created the potential for significant tension within his theory of freedom. While the concept of freedom as "power over my self" places a premium on the creation of regions of life within which individuals are free to act without interference or supervision, the concept of self-mastery equates freedom with following a specific course of action dictated by reason. The former sets limits to the intrusion of public powers into private life; the latter may positively justify it. As a result, it is vital to determine the precise meaning Sidney attached to the notion that men are free when they obey reason. The key, as was the case in his defense of religious toleration, lies not in the facts of his biography but in the structure of his arguments.

The coherence and persuasiveness of any theory of freedom rest on the detail and precision with which it describes the process of liberation. No matter what the ideal, be it the rule of reason, community, or solidarity, the final test of a theory's strength lies in its provision of techniques for getting from a slavish present to a free (or freer) future. It is here that a surprising aspect of Sidney's theory is revealed. Contrary to what one might expect, the guidelines generated by reason tend to be general and procedural, and not specific and substantive. For example, in discussing the question of religious authority Sidney adopted a skeptical posture and argued that "its madness to obleidge another to think as I doe, if I may be deceaved my self. . . . Every man [has] a rational and natural right of disputeing whats uncertain, and of not receiving it till convinced that its a certain truth." Concerning the political scope of reason, Sidney thought "nothing but the plain and certain dictates of Reason can be generally applicable to all men as the Law of their Nature." And what were those dictates of reason? "Reason enjoins every man not to arrogate to himself more than he allows to others, nor to retain that Liberty which will prove hurtful to him; or to expect that others will suffer themselves to be restrain'd, whilst he, to their prejudice, remains in the exercise of that freedom which Nature allows."[146] Locke drew precisely the same conclusion from the writings of "the Judicious *Hooker*."[147] Given the premise that all men are equal, reason enjoined the Golden Rule.

---

[146] *Maxims*, 90–91; *Discourses*, II:20, p. 152. "The equality in which men are born is so perfect, that . . . I cannot reasonably expect to be defended from wrong, unless I oblige my self to do none; or to suffer the punishment prescribed by the Law, if I perform not my engagement" (III:41, p. 437).

[147] "This *equality* of Men by Nature, the Judicious *Hooker* looks upon as so evident in it self, and beyond all question, that he makes it the Foundation of that Obligation to mutual Love amongst Men, on which he Builds the Duties they owe one another. . . .

Sidney's equation of political reason with the Golden Rule is reflective of his understanding of the psychological basis of the relationship between reason and the passions. His theory assumed the existence of distinct faculties or compartments of the personality that could be labeled "reason" and "the passions," and that were at constant war with each other. The function of the Golden Rule was to provide a decision-making technique that enabled a person to mute the base promptings of his passions.

The unique contours of Sidney's argument can be highlighted by comparing it with Locke's treatment of the same relationship. Locke, too, feared the "strange courses" to which "fancy and passion" could lead a man if "reason, which is his only Star and compass, be not that he steers by. The imagination is always restless and suggests variety of thoughts, and the will, reason being laid aside, is ready for every extravagant project. . . . And when Fashion hath once Established, what Folly or craft began, Custom makes it Sacred, and 'twill be thought impudence or madness, to contradict or question it."[148] In the *Essay Concerning Human Understanding* Locke returned to this theme, arguing that "the greatest part" of mankind "govern themselves chiefly, if not solely, by this Law of Fashion." The central purpose of Locke's *Thoughts Concerning Education* was to chart a course for the education of a young gentleman that would avoid the sandy shoals of custom, habit, and tradition. "A Mind free, and Master of it self and all its Actions" was Locke's ideal.[149] Sidney shared Locke's commitment to rational autonomy, but he lacked Locke's epistemology and the understanding of the social bases of heteronomous behavior that it made possible. He paid no attention to the role of "Fashion" in the play of reason and the passions. His point of reference was the isolated individual, prey to the temptations of his lusts and appetites.

Sidney employed this account of the relationship between reason and the passions to undermine one of the central tenets of English

---

His words are; 'The like natural inducement, hath brought Men to know that it is no less their Duty, to Love others than themselves, for seeing those things which are equal, must needs all have one measure; If I cannot but wish to receive god, even as much at every Man's hands, as any Man can wish unto his own Soul, how should I look to have any part of my desire herein satisfied, unless my self be careful to satisfie the like desire, which is undoubtedly in other Men, being of one and the same nature?' " (*Two Treatises*, II:5).

[148] *Two Treatises*, I:58.

[149] Locke, *An Essay concerning Human Understanding*, 2.28.12, p. 357; Locke, "Some Thoughts Concerning Education," sec. 66. "We are *born Free*, as we are born Rational; not that we have actually the Exercise of either: Age that brings one, brings with it the other too" (*Two Treatises*, II:60).

royalism. One widely accepted version of the Golden Rule held that a man should not be a judge in his own case. This maxim posed a potential threat to the legal supremacy of the Crown, since it challenged the king's ability to prosecute faithfully his own abuses of the law. As noted in Chapter 2, royalists sought to evade the radical implications of this principle by claiming that the interests of the king were identical to those of the nation, and hence that there could be no occasion for passion to sway his judgment. To Sidney, this was an absurd argument. Every man was a slave of his passions.[150] "The question is only, Whether the Magistrate should depend upon the Judgment of the People, or the People on that of the Magistrate; and which is most to be suspected of injustice."[151] Given that even the best of kings "are subject to mistakes and passions," and that the worst "declare their contempt of all human and divine Laws," nothing could be more insane than to subject a nation to the will of one man. "No Liberty can subsist where there is such a Power."[152]

From this insight into the pervasive influence of the passions Sidney drew the following problem: Is it possible to design a commonwealth that maximizes public reason yet at the same time minimizes the influence of private passions? James Harrington argued that the solution to this problem could be found in the wisdom of "two silly girls" sharing a cake. When one divided and the other chose, the corrupting influence of the passions was eliminated.[153] The constitution of Oceana was designed to embody this decision-making procedure and thus guarantee the rule of reason in perpetuity. Unlike Harrington, Sidney did not believe "an immortal commonwealth" either possible or desirable. But he did share Harrington's commitment to "an empire of laws and not of men."[154] Law—not the customary law of the ancient constitution, but the statutory law of a freely consenting nation—was a check on the passions and thus enhanced a nation's capacity to act rationally.[155] "Void of desire and fear, lust and anger,"

[150] "Every man has Passions; few know how to moderate, and no one can wholly extinguish them" (*Discourses*, II:24, p. 186).

[151] *Discourses*, II:24, pp. 178–79. On the problem of a man being a judge in his own case, see: II:30, p. 237; II:32, pp. 247–49; III:14, pp. 312–13; III:21, pp. 348–49; III:41, p. 436.

[152] *Discourses*, III:21, pp. 348–49. See also: II:31, p. 230; III:14, p. 312.

[153] Harrington, "Oceana," in *Works*, 172.

[154] Harrington, "Oceana," in *Works*, 161. "In Common-wealths its not men but laws, Maxims, interests and constitutions that govern" (*Maxims*, 23).

[155] "If the liberty of a man consist in the empire of his reason, the absence whereof would betray him unto the bondage of his passions; then the liberty of a commonwealth consisteth in the empire of her laws, the absence whereof would betray her unto the lusts of tyrants" (Harrington, "Oceana," in *Works*, 170).

the law provided "a more solid foundation" for the public interest than the irregular passions of man.[156] Politically, the solution to the problems posed by the enslaving power of the passions was a theory of legislation.

National Freedom

Sidney did not restrict the concepts of freedom and slavery to individuals, but he applied them to nations as well. He thought it made as much sense to speak of free and slave states as it did to speak of free and slave men. Indeed, he often merged his discussion of these two subjects, writing as if the same vocabulary could be applied to both. This was partly a matter of historical accident: the same forces that threatened to destroy individual freedom—most notably the absolutist ambitions of Charles II and the Catholicism of the duke of York—also endangered England's national freedom. But it was also a consequence of the way he constructed his theory.

As each individual within a nation ought to be free from "the dominion of another," so ought each nation: "Every Nation is to take care of their own Laws; and whether any one has had the Wisdom, Virtue, Fortune and Power to defend them or not, concerns only themselves."[157] From a moral point of view each country ought to take its bearings from the needs and aspirations of its citizens. It ought neither concern itself with nor be concerned by the appeals and imprecations of others. From a practical point of view this meant that all forms of international dependence had to be avoided. In a ruthlessly competitive world, "the State that is defended by one Potentat against another becomes a Slave to their Protector."[158] To Sidney's contemporaries the significance of this claim would have been apparent: by joining in a league with Louis XIV, Charles II had threatened England with the loss of its national independence.[159]

To this commonplace notion Sidney added a second, more stringent condition on the use of the terms freedom and slavery: to be free a nation had to be governed according to the will of its citizens. "We have no other way of distinguishing free Nations and such as are

---

[156] *Discourses*, III:15, p. 316. See also: III:13, p. 307; III:43, p. 445.

[157] *Discourses*, III:26, p. 374. See also: III:25, p. 367.

[158] *Discourses*, II:23, p. 166. See also: *Maxims*, 152–55.

[159] "Whatever Prince seeks assistance from foreign Powers, or makes Leagues with any stranger or enemy for his own advantage against his people, however secret the Treaty may be, declares himself not to be the Head [of the nation], but an enemy to [it]" (*Discourses*, III:39, p. 430). See also: III:7, p. 280.

not so, than that the free are governed by their own Laws and Magistrates according to their own mind, and that the others either have willingly subjected themselves, or are by force brought under the power of one or more men, to be ruled according to his or their pleasure."[160] Without this second qualification, it would have been impossible to distinguish between France and England; both would have been free states. As individual freedom combined a negative exemption from the dominion of others with a positive capacity to act politically and obey the dictates of reason, so national freedom could be described as a combination of sovereignty and rational self-determination.[161]

Though Sidney predicated of nations the capacity to be "free" or "enslaved" in the same way that he predicated these conditions of individuals, he did not think of nations as independent, corporate entities in the same way that individuals are. Analytically this would have been completely out of character, given his uncompromisingly contractual view of the nature and origins of nations. Sidney was an atomizer, not an aggregator.

Nonetheless, a thick vein of nationalism, in the form of an implicit faith in the political capacities of the English people, runs throughout his argument. Sidney lacked the poetic vision that enabled Milton to see "a noble and puissant Nation rousing herself like a strong man after sleep, and shaking her invincible locks."[162] But he thought it rare to find "so well a deserving People as that of England." "Why should not a free nation full of men who excell in wisdom & experience rather keep the power in their own hands of governing themselves or one another by turns than perpetually govern'd by one man and his posterity[?]"[163] Why not indeed? As Sidney was convinced that individuals were capable of planning their own lives, so he was convinced that whole nations were capable of directing their public affairs. The same capacities applied to both; there were no *arcana*

---

[160] *Discourses*, III:21, p. 349. See also: III:31, p. 399.

[161] Quentin Skinner has mapped out a similar argument in his studies of Machiavelli's theory of liberty ("The Paradoxes of Political Liberty," in *Tanner Lectures on Human Values*, ed. Sterling McMurrin, vol. 7 [Salt Lake City: University of Utah Press, 1986], 225–50; and "The Idea of Negative Liberty: Philosophical and Historical Perspectives," in *Philosophy in History*, ed. Richard Rorty, J. B. Schneewind, and Quentin Skinner [Cambridge: Cambridge University Press, 1984], 193–221). Skinner's argument is predicated on a sharp distinction between the "classical republican" language of virtue and the "contractarian" language of rights, however, while Sidney's discussion of virtue is framed by a contractual theory of obligation. Sidney's theory of virtue will be examined in Chapter 4.

[162] Milton, "Areopagitica," in *Complete Prose Works*, 2:557–58.

[163] *Maxims*, 3, 10. See also: *Discourses*, III:33, p. 408; III:44, p. 453.

imperii, no mysteries of state that restricted public life to a small circle of initiates.[164] Sidney never indicated whether he thought these capacities unique to the English, though his occasional references to nations that were incapable of freedom suggest that he did not believe them universal.[165] Ultimately it was a moot point, for despite his wide-ranging historical observations, Sidney's attention never strayed from the immediate circumstances of seventeenth-century England.

The Morality of Consent

Each of the four conceptions of freedom and slavery Sidney appealed to presumed a relationship of trust between a people and its government. Magistrates were "Sentinel[s] of the Publick," "Servant[s] of the Commonwealth."[166] Like any employee "entrusted" with power, they could "be restrained or chastised, if they betray[ed] their Trust."[167]

[164] *Discourses*, I:3, p. 8. Cf. *Patriarcha*, 54–55.

[165] He apparently thought such nations could be found among "the base effeminate Asiaticks and Africans" (*Discourses*, I:2, p. 6; see also: II:1, p. 67; III:4, p. 269; *Maxims*, 9, 11, 205). Sidney's invocation of Aristotle to the contrary, his use of the term "natural slaves" was distinctly non-Aristotelian. Slavery played two distinct yet related roles in Aristotle's theory of the polis. Practically, slaves were "necessary to the existence of the state," living possessions whose "bodies minister to the needs of life" (Aristotle, *The Politics*, in *The Complete Works of Aristotle*, ed. Jonathan Barnes [Princeton: Princeton University Press, 1984], 2:2028 [1278a], 2:1990 [1254a]). Without slavery, classical citizenship would not have been possible. Slavery also served as a vivid example of the organizational structure of the cosmos. "In all things which form a composite whole and which are made up of parts, whether continuous or discrete, a distinction between the ruling and the subject element comes to light" (*The Politics*, 2:1990 [1254a]). As the master ruled his slaves, the soul ruled the body, the mind ruled the appetites, and the principles of harmony ruled music. Sidney rejected both of these arguments, claiming that "men are all made of the same paste" (*Discourses*, III:1, p. 255). Nature was not teleological, and God had not "caused some to be born with Crowns upon their heads, and all others with Saddles upon their backs" (III:33, p. 406). An Aristotelian theory of slavery was far more suited to the ideological needs of the ancien régime than of republican radicalism. Indeed, reference to the limited capacities of "all the people in *Asia* and *Africa*, as well as *Europe*, that lie southerly," was a common trope among European proponents of absolute monarchy (Johan de Witt [and Pieter de la Court], *The True Interest and Political Maxims of the Republick of Holland and West-Friesland* [London: 1702], 8). Sidney's grotesque reflections on the inhabitants of non-European countries are part of a very different stream of ideas, one that emphasized the progressive development of the human species and that culminated in John Stuart Mill's defense of despotism in *Representative Government*. As in so many other cases, Sidney used classical language, even cited classical authors, but argued essentially nonclassical arguments.

[166] *Discourses*, III:39, p. 429; III:16, p. 318. See also: III:38, p. 421; III:43, p. 450.

[167] *Discourses*, III:22, p. 356; I:6, p. 15. See also: III:27, p. 377; III:38, p. 423.

The legitimacy of a government was contingent on its fulfillment of the social contract.

Sidney framed this argument using a matrix of ideas drawn from the natural jurisprudence tradition. The first step to understanding the proper task of government was to imagine a world without political order, a world in which "one man is not bound by the actions of another."[168] In such a world, "no one Man or Family is able to provide that which is requisite for their convenience or security, whilst every one has an equal Right to every thing, and none acknowledges a Superior to determine the Controversies, that upon such occasions must continually arise, and will probably be so many and great, that Mankind cannot bear them. . . . The Liberty of one is thwarted by that of another." The inconveniences of this common condition of "Liberty without restraint" are so great that "we find no place in the world where the Inhabitants do not enter into some kind of Society or Government to restrain it. . . . Every one sees they cannot well live asunder, nor many together, without some Rule to which all must submit."[169] This "collation of every man's private Right into a public Stock" through common consent is "the act of Men (according to natural Reason) seeking their own Good."[170] From it, and from it alone, arose legitimate governments.[171]

Painted with such broad brushstrokes, Sidney's account of the consensual origins of government was indistinguishable from any number of similar portraits produced during the seventeenth century. It was, moreover, neither inherently radical nor essentially republican. As Grotius had demonstrated in his influential *De Jure Belli ac Pacis* (1625), the enslavement of an entire nation could be justified using the language of natural jurisprudence.[172] The concept of consent

---

[168] *Discourses*, III:33, p. 406. Though Sidney did not use the term "state of nature," he made use of a similar construct: "The matter is yet more clear in relation to those who never were in any Society, as at the beginning, or renovation of the world after the Flood; or who upon the dissolution of the Societies to which they did once belong, or by some other accident have bin obliged to seek new habitations" (*Discourses*, III:33, p. 407). See also: II:30, p. 237; III:7, p. 281.

[169] *Discourses*, I:10, p. 23; II:20, p. 151. There could be no exemptions from this rule: "Every man bearing in his own breast Affections, Passions, and Vices that are repugnant to this end, and no man owing any submission to his Neighbour; none will subject the correction or restriction of themselves to another, unless he also submit to the same Rule" (II:1, p. 64).

[170] *Discourses*, II:1, p. 60; II:20, p. 151. "A Civil Society is composed of Equals, and fortified by mutual compacts" (II:2, p. 68).

[171] "A general consent . . . is the ground of all just Government"; "Human societies are maintained by mutual Contracts" (*Discourses*, I:10, p. 23; II:30, p. 236).

[172] "To every man it is permitted to enslave himself to any one he pleases for private ownership, as is evident both from the Hebraic and from the Roman Law. Why, then,

provided a powerful and appealing way of linking freedom, obligation, and authority. But the possibility that an agreement of the people might end in absolutism haunted seventeenth-century radicals and forced them to address a series of difficult questions. What moral obligations could be incurred through consent? What political institutions were consistent with consent? And is an expression of consent given in the past (perhaps even by previous generations) binding on the present? Without carefully crafted answers to these questions, it would have been impossible to exploit the radical potential of consent theory during the manifold crises of the seventeenth century.[173]

The most troubling possibility posed by the jurisprudential tradition was that a nation might permanently and totally alienate its freedom. Were that to happen there would be little practical difference between a government founded in consent and one imposed by conquest or inherited through patriarchy. All three would deprive the people of any legitimate recourse against tyranny.

This possibility was particularly problematic for Sidney, for he was in principle willing to accept the rule of a single virtuous man. As he explained in the *Discourses*,

> *Aristotle* highly applauds Monarchy, when the Monarch has more of those Vertues that tend to the good of a Commonwealth than all they who compose it. This is the King mentioned in his *Ethicks*, and extolled in his *Politicks*: He is above all by Nature, and ought not by a municipal Law to be made equal to others in Power: He ought to govern, because 'tis better for a People to be governed by him, than to enjoy their Liberty; or rather they do enjoy their Liberty, which is never more safe, than when it is defended by one who is a living Law to himself and others. Wheresoever such a man appears, he ought to reign: He bears in his Person the divine Character of a Sovereign: God has raised him above all.[174]

Were it possible to find one man who "hath more virtue, understanding, industry and valour than a whole nation," and were it possible to

---

would it not be permitted to a people having legal competence to submit itself to some one person, or to several persons, in such a way as plainly to transfer to him the legal right to govern, retaining no vestige of that right for itself?" (Hugo Grotius, *De Jure Belli Ac Pacis*, trans. Francis Kelsey [New York: Oceana Publications, 1964], 1.iii.8, p. 103).

[173] One measure of James Harrington's idiosyncratic role in seventeenth-century English political thought is his indifference both to the concept of consent and to the heated debates surrounding it.

[174] *Discourses*, II:10, pp. 102–3. See also: I:13, p. 29; II:9, p. 97; II:20, p. 230; II:1, p. 62; III:23, pp. 358–59; *Maxims*, 29–30. The reference is to Aristotle, *The Politics*, 1284b.

ensure that those qualities would be "transmitted to his posterity," Sidney was willing to accept him as an absolute, hereditary monarch.[175] His rule would be legitimate by virtue of the people's desire to advance "their own Good" through his government.

Republican arguments for the rule of an aristocracy of virtue were common in the seventeenth century. For example, in 1659 and 1660, in the face of strident domestic opposition, the breakdown of relations between the army and Parliament, and the increasing likelihood that Charles II would be restored, John Milton, Sir Henry Vane the younger, and Henry Stubbe each appealed to the well-affected party of men faithful to "the Good *old cause*" to govern England and preserve the republican cause.[176] In the judgment of these men England was not capable of governing itself, and its best hope lay in the rule of the wise and the holy. Sidney's willingness to embrace the possibility of the rule of a single man of superior virtue bears a strong resemblance to these arguments. But unlike Milton, Vane, or Stubbe, Sidney was quick to emasculate this theoretical concession, and in the process he revealed the radical implications of his appeal to consent.

The argument that some men "ought to reign" was irrelevant "till such a Man, or succession of men do appear." But that had not happened since the time of Moses, Joshua, and Samuel.[177] Without denying the principle that had justified the rule of the biblical patriarchs, Sidney refused to allow it to be invoked in the name of seventeenth-century monarchs like Charles II or Louis XIV.[178] The very qualities that were required of such a man served to demonstrate just how remote a possibility the legitimate rule of one man was.[179] As Sidney argued in the *Court Maxims*, "Wee all breath the same aire are composd of the same materials have the same birth, and tho they [monarchs] or their flatterers sometimes say they are Gods they shall die like men they are naturally no more than men

---

[175] *Maxims*, 9, 30. See also: 210.

[176] Henry Stubbe, *An Essay in Defence of the Good Old Cause* (London: 1659), "Preface." See also: Milton, "The Readie and Easie Way," in *Complete Prose Works*, 7:396–463; [Sir Henry Vane], *A Needful Corrective or Ballance in Popular Government* [London: 1660]. In 1654 Milton defended Cromwell's seizure of power by reference to his superior virtue ("Second Defence of the English People," in *Complete Prose Works*, 4:556).

[177] *Discourses*, II:1, pp. 62, 66; II:30, p. 240.

[178] "And if Moses as a type of Christ's Kingly power and spirituall Kingdom had ben a King. . . . what's that to those that have no gifts Politick Moral or divin above the vulgar?" (*Maxims*, 34). See also: *Discourses*, II:9, pp. 101–2; III:21, p. 350.

[179] "By shewing who only is fit to be a Monarch, or may be made such, without violating the Laws of Nature and Justice, [Aristotle] shews who cannot be one" (*Discourses*, III:23, p. 359).

and can justly therefore pretend to no more than others."[180] Sidney repeated this argument in the *Discourses*: "men are all made of the same paste."[181] In the absence of the direct intervention of God, the natural equality of men effectively eliminated the possibility that any man might possess sufficient virtue to justify his wielding absolute power.

Reinforcing this argument from equality were two further constraints on the application of the concept of consent. Both appealed to the conditions under which a nation could be said to have validly consented to a government. First, consent was legitimate if and only if the possibility of not consenting was a "live" option. Filmer had explored the possibility that "the silent acceptation of a governor" implied "the tacit assent of the whole commonwealth," and hence "that every Prince that comes to a crown, either by succession, conquest or usurpation, may be said to be elected by the people." Though Filmer thought this argument "ridiculous,"[182] it had been maintained by de facto theorists during the 1650s and had been revived by apologists for Charles II and the duke of York during the 1670s.[183] To Sidney this equation of conquest and consent was ludicrous; it was no different than saying that "a man approves of being robbed, when, without saying a word, he delivers his purse to a Thief that he knows to be too strong for him. 'Tis not therefore the bear sufferance of a Government when a disgust is declared, nor a silent submission when the power of opposing is wanting, that can imply an Assent, or Election, and create a Right; but an explicit act of approbation, when men have ability and courage to resist or deny."[184] As he had explained in the *Court Maxims*, " 'tis no argument" for the goodness of an act "unless it appear" that the actors "need not doe it unless they thought it good."[185] Consent and coercion were mutually exclusive. Without a set of viable alternatives, an individual could not be said to have meaningfully consented either to a course of action or to a form of

[180] *Maxims*, 30. See also: 28.

[181] *Discourses*, III:1, p. 255. This is undoubtedly a reference to Genesis 2:7 ("And the Lord God formed man of the dust of the ground"). On the equality of all men, see also: I:10, p. 23; I:12, p. 26; I:16, p. 37; I:19, p. 49; II:9, pp. 101–2; II:31, p. 242; III:17, p. 329; III:33, p. 406.

[182] *Patriarcha*, 82. Filmer's reason for rejecting this claim—"in such cases the people are so far from the liberty of *specification* that they want even that of *contradiction*"— should have appealed to Sidney; but rather than acknowledge this common ground, Sidney simply ignored it.

[183] See above, pp. 25–26 and 77–78.

[184] *Discourses*, II:6, p. 84. Cf. *Two Treatises*, II:186.

[185] *Maxims*, 11.

government.[186] One need only "ask the naked, barefooted and half-starved people" of Normandy whether they had consented to the rule of Louis XIV to see the truth of that.[187]

The second condition Sidney identified with the valid use of the concept of consent was even more far-reaching. Many seventeenth-century theorists assumed that the consent of previous generations was binding on the present. This was a troubling thought, for it meant that past actions, no matter how ill conceived, could permanently yoke a nation's future. That was why, for example, the Levellers found it necessary to engage in a detailed analysis of England's constitutional history: if it could be proven that eleventh- or twelfth-century Englishmen had renounced their freedom, then contemporary agitation against the Stuarts was illegitimate.[188] Locke had seen his way around this common problem by appealing to links between freedom, the law of nature, and God's workmanship in man. As "no Body has an absolute Arbitrary Power over himself, or over any other," so "a Man . . . cannot subject himself to the Arbitrary Power of another."[189] Consent, whether past or present, could never be used to justify the rule of a tyrant.

Sidney was no less attentive to the record of England's past than were the Levellers, but like Locke he believed that the claims of history were ultimately irrelevant to the question of a government's legitimacy: "Tho it were confessed [that all power was originally in the hands of the King], (which I absolutely deny, and affirm that our Rights and Liberties are innate, inherent, and enjoy'd time out of mind before we had Kings) it could be nothing to the question, which is concerning Reason and Justice; and if they are wanting, the defect can never be supplied by any matter of fact, tho never so clearly

[186] Sidney used the converse of this claim to explain why princes were bound by their coronation oaths: "there being no colour of force or fraud, fear or error for them to alledg. . . . 'tis hard to find an example of any People that did by force oblige a man to take upon him the Government of them" (*Discourses*, III:17, p. 327). The links between consent and "the principle of alternatives" are fruitfully explored in Don Herzog, *Happy Slaves* (Chicago: University of Chicago Press, 1989), 215–47.

[187] *Discourses*, III:5, p. 271. "Some declare their hatred; others murmur more privately. . . . Many would resist, but cannot" (II:6, p. 82).

[188] Tuck, *Natural Rights Theories*, 149.

[189] *Two Treatises*, II:135. As Richard Tuck has observed, Locke "perceived that it is enough to rule out absolutism that the sovereign ought under no circumstances to act in an arbitrary or unjust way towards his subjects, given a general theory of sovereignty as created by agreement. For if there is such a restriction on possible actions by a sovereign, men cannot put themselves under a ruler who might break it: that would be to consent to another man's acting in an immoral way and would thus go against the fundamental principles of the law of nature" (Tuck, *Natural Rights Theories*, 173).

proved."[190] Unlike Locke, however, Sidney did not rely on the law of nature to establish this claim. Instead, he drew on the resources made available by his theory of historical change.

As noted above, Sidney thought the powers of human reason insufficient to the task of forming "an immortal commonwealth." Over time even the best of constitutions was rendered ineffectual. Improvement was possible, however, and hence

> no man or number of Men was ever obliged to continue in the errors of his Predecessors. The authority of Custom as well as of Law (I mean in relation to the Power that made it to be) consists only in its rectitude: And the same reason which may have induced one or more Nations to create Kings, when they knew no other form of Government, may not only induce them to set up another, if that be found inconvenient to them, but proves that they may as justly do so, as remove a man who performs not what is expected from him. . . . Those who will admit of no change would render Errors perpetual, and depriving Mankind of the benefits of Wisdom, Industry, Experience, and the right use of Reason, oblige all to continue in the miserable barbarity of their Ancestors, which sutes better with the name of a Wolf than that of a Man.[191]

Filmer had castigated consent theorists for their ahistorical and atomistic view of society. As the Bible made clear, men were not "mushrooms . . . all on a sudden . . . sprung out of the earth without any obligation one to another."[192] The cement of society was mixed with the seed of the first father, and each new generation of men was bound to respect the actions of its predecessors. Sidney's radical interpretation of consent theory was designed to undermine this strong theory of intergenerational obligations. Embedded in his analysis were the belief that political mistakes were corrigible and the promise that living generations need not be dominated by the dead weight of the past.

In light of these broad considerations Sidney concluded that the

---

[190] *Discourses*, III:29, p. 393. Sidney did, however, seek to prove that the people of England had never relinquished their freedom; hence his constant references to the histories of Caesar and Tacitus and to the Saxon micklegemots and wittenagemots (e.g., III:8, p. 288; III:237, pp. 380, 383). Though irrelevant to the key moral claims Sidney sought to advance through the concept of consent, these historical facts provided yet another example of the errors contained in *Patriarcha*.

[191] *Discourses*, III:25, pp. 365–66.

[192] *Patriarcha*, 241. The reference is to Hobbes: "Let us return again to the state of nature, and consider men as if but even now sprung out of the earth, and suddainly (*like* Mushroomes) come to full maturity without all kind of engagement to each other" (Thomas Hobbes, *De Cive*, ed. Howard Warrender [Oxford: The Clarendon Press, 1983], 117).

consent of a free people could be used to justify only governments that advanced the public interest: "Nothing obliging [the people] to enter into this Society, but the consideration of their own Good, that Good, or the opinion of it, must have been the Rule, Motive and End of all that they did ordain."[193] This did not mean that any specific form of government would be chosen. "No Government is imposed upon men by God or Nature"; "every Nation acting freely, has an equal right to frame their own Government," and the contract by which they do so "can be of no force or obligation to others."[194] There was no necessary connection between the morality of consent and democratic or republican forms of government. It did mean, however, that the legitimacy of governments founded in consent was radically contingent. Nations consented to particular governments with the expectation of attaining a greater good, and they retained the right to revoke their consent if that good was not realized.

The claim that political power was held in trust was sufficient to establish Sidney's credentials as a radical theorist. It drew attention to the contingency of all political arrangements, and it proclaimed the revocability of all political authority. It directly countered Sir Robert Filmer's patriarchalism, and it provided an effective weapon in the campaign against Charles and James Stuart. Exclusion was but another example of how a free people "restrained" the fury of an unjust magistrate.[195] The concept of trust did not, however, provide Sidney with a sufficiently rich moral psychology to comprehend the manifold dangers to which freedom was subjected. As a result, alongside his analysis of freedom and slavery he devoted a great deal of attention to the parallel concepts of virtue and corruption.

[193] *Discourses*, II:5, p. 76. "It cannot be imagined that men should generally put such Fetters upon themselves, unless it were in expectation of a greater good that was thereby to accrue to them" (I:12, p. 27). See also: II:7, p. 92; III:7, p. 281; *Maxims*, 145. Cf. *Two Treatises*, II:131.

[194] *Discourses*, II:20, p. 151; III:12, p. 304; III:4, p. 267. See also: III:1, pp. 256–57; Sidney, *Very Copy of a Paper* (1683), 2.

[195] *Discourses*, III:43, pp. 448–49.

FOUR

VIRTUE AND CORRUPTION

> All governments are subject to corruption and decay. . . .
> Our inquiry is not after that which is perfect, well
> knowing that no such thing is found among men; but we
> seek that human Constitution which is attended with the
> least, or the most pardonable inconveniences.
>
> *(Algernon Sidney)*[1]

WHY DO free nations fall into slavery? This deceptively simple question was at the heart of Algernon Sidney's analysis of virtue and corruption. While virtuous behavior helped to sustain nations in their freedom, corruption slowly but surely reduced them to slavery. Without virtue, in fact, freedom was not possible.[2]

The pivotal role of virtue and corruption in the moral psychology of republicanism has been the focus of several recent and influential studies in the history of political thought. Contemporary scholars have emphasized two distinct but related theses: that the defining characteristic of republicanism is a classical theory of virtue; and that the republican language of virtue is distinct from and in tension with the liberal logic of rights and interests.[3] A careful examination of Sid-

[1] *Discourses*, II:19, p. 149; II:18, p. 142.

[2] "*Machiavel* discoursing of these matters, finds Vertue to be so essentially necesary to the establishment and preservation of Liberty, that he thinks it impossible for a corrupted People to set up a good Government, or for a Tyranny to be introduced if they be vertuous . . . Which being confirmed by Reason and Experience, I think no wise man has ever contradicted him" (*Discourses*, II:11, p. 105).

[3] Both theses inform the recent and influential work of J.G.A. Pocock and Quentin Skinner. For Pocock, see: *Politics, Language and Time* (New York: Atheneum, 1971), 80–147; *The Machiavellian Moment* (Princeton: Princeton University Press, 1975), passim; "The Machiavellian Moment Revisited: A Study in History and Ideology," *Journal of Modern History* 53 (March 1981): 49–72; "Machiavelli in the Liberal Cosmos," *Political Theory* 13 (November 1985): 559–74; *Virtue, Commerce, and History* (Cambridge: Cambridge University Press, 1985), 37–50; "Between Gog and Magog: The Republican Thesis and the *Ideologia Americana*," *Journal of the History of Ideas* 48 (April–June 1987): 325–46. For Skinner, see: *Machiavelli* (Oxford: Oxford University Press, 1981), 48–77; "Machiavelli on the Maintenance of Liberty," *Politics* 18 (November 1983): 3–15; "The Idea of Negative Liberty: Philosophical and Historical Perspectives," in *Philosophy in History*, ed. Richard Rorty, J. B. Schneewind, and Quentin Skinner (Cambridge: Cam-

ney's writings demonstrates that these theses are incomplete and misleading and that they fail to capture either the polemical purpose or the conceptual structure of English republicanism. In the course of his analysis Sidney employed three different conceptions of virtue and corruption: the virtue of self-control, versus the corruption of licentiousness; the virtue of martial valor, versus the corruption of weakness and effeminacy; and the virtue of integrity, versus the corruption of violating a public trust. In each case his starting point was an aristocratic ethic of character; but that ethic was ultimately overridden by a republican emphasis on the relationship between virtue and laws, rights and interests. The account of virtue and corruption that emerges from Sidney's writings is complex, multilayered, and often at odds with itself.

Sidney's purpose in focusing on these three conceptions of virtue was twofold: to demonstrate that absolute monarchy was "rooted in" corruption, and to describe the psychological foundations of republican citizenship.[4] Sir Robert Filmer had claimed that "the best order, the greatest strength, the most stability, and the easiest government are to be found in monarchy, and no other form of government."[5] Sidney argued to the contrary that monarchy was given to licentiousness, weakness, effeminacy, and frequent violations of the public trust. Only a republic could claim stability, strength, and the pursuit of the public interest, for only a republic was founded on obedience to the law, the defense of common interests, and the keeping of covenants.

Self-control and Licentiousness

The primary meaning of corruption in Sidney's writings is the change in human nature that accompanied the fall from grace in the Garden of Eden. "Man by Sin is fallen from the Law of his Creation," and the evils of the world are a consequence of "our corrupted na-

---

bridge University Press, 1984), 193–221; "The Paradoxes of Political Liberty," in *Tanner Lectures on Human Values*, ed. Sterling McMurrin, vol. 7 (Salt Lake City: University of Utah Press, 1986), 225–50. See also: Zera Fink, *The Classical Republicans* (Evanston: Northwestern University Press, 1945); Felix Raab, *The English Face of Machiavelli* (London: Routledge & Kegan Paul, 1964); Blair Worden, "Classical Republicanism and the Puritan Revolution," in *History and Imagination*, ed. Hugh Lloyd-Jones, Valerie Pearl, and Blair Worden (London: Duckworth, 1981), 182–200. The use of these theses in recent interpretations of the American Revolution will be discussed in Chapter 6.

[4] *Discourses*, II:19, p. 149.

[5] *Patriarcha*, 86.

ture."[6] Corruption led men to a wide range of passions, infirmities, and vices: ambition, anger, arrogance, covetousness, cowardliness, cruelty, debauchery, dishonesty, hypocrisy, ignorance, injustice, lewdness, lust, perfidiousness, pride, slothfulness, rage, and viciousness.[7] With nature itself corrupt, virtue could only be a matter of self-denial, of the repression of nature. It required the cultivation of discipline and control and bore fruit in the exercise of temperance and moderation.

Before exploring the ways Sidney used this conception of virtue and corruption, we should note three things. First, Sidney's catalog of the corrupt passions was entirely conventional. It reflected the distinctive blend of Christian sin and classical vice that had characterized much of Western moral thinking since the time of Augustine and would have been perfectly familiar to any educated Englishman of the sixteenth or seventeenth century. To say that it was conventional is not to say that it was universal, however; it was part of a distinctively aristocratic code and presumed that the people—the *Mobile*—were neither capable of nor inclined to virtue. One measure of Sidney's radicalism, in fact, is the degree to which he attempted to transpose this ethic into a new key, where virtue was a consequence of republican liberty and not aristocratic birth and discipline. Second, like most of his contemporaries, Sidney saw no redeeming value in the corrupt passions.[8] The notion that private vices might yield public benefits, most clearly articulated by Bernard Mandeville at the beginning of the eighteenth century, was completely foreign to Sidney's way of thinking. The degree to which the passions held sway over life provided a thermometer with which the moral health of a society could be measured. Finally, though the passions were inescapably bad, they were also unavoidable. "Every man has Passions; few know how to moderate them, and no one can wholly extinguish them." Even "the best of men have their affections and passions."[9] The crucial question concerning any political system was not whether corrupt

[6] *Discourses*, II:8, p. 95. "The sin of our first Parents on Earth hath brought forth Briars and Brambles, and the nature of Man hath bin fruitful only in Vice and Wickedness" (I:2, pp. 7–8). See also: II:3, p. 71; II:19, p. 149; II:24, p. 180; III:6, p. 275.

[7] Examples of Sidney's use of these terms can be found on virtually every page of the *Court Maxims* and the *Discourses Concerning Government*.

[8] Minor exceptions abound; for example, the poet Ben Jonson argued that "though ambition itself be a vice, it is often the cause of great virtue" (quoted in Keith Thomas, "The Social Origins of Hobbes's Political Thought," in *Hobbes Studies*, ed. K. C. Brown [Oxford: Blackwell, 1965], 207). The only major exception was Hobbes, who argued that fear could be used in politically beneficial ways.

[9] *Discourses*, II:24, p. 186; II:30, p. 230. See also: III:22, p. 356.

passions were present, but rather what role they were permitted to play in public life.

Sidney's case against absolute monarchy was twofold: it gave free rein to the passions of monarchs, and as a consequence it reduced whole nations to a state of corruption. His arguments were designed to reveal a paradox at the heart of absolute monarchy: by concentrating power in the hands of one man, it created weakness and instability, not authority and strength. "An unlimited Prince," he observed, "might be justly compared to a weak ship exposed to a violent storm, with a vast Sail and no Rudder."[10] Only by limiting the power of magistrates was it possible to enable them to traverse politically troubled waters.

The vulnerability of absolute monarchy could be traced to the way it magnified the power of the passions. Like every other member of the human community, an absolute monarch is subject to the corrupting influence of his passions.[11] Unlike everyone else, however, he has the power to act on his passions: "The rage of a private man may be pernicious to one or a few of his Neighbours; but the fury of an unlimited Prince would drive whole Nations into ruin: And those very men who have lived modestly when they had little power have often proved the most savage of all Monsters, when they thought nothing able to resist their rage."[12] Reinforcing and exaggerating the temptations and opportunities of unlimited power are the men and women who surround the monarch, courtiers and courtesans who attach themselves to the throne like leeches hoping to draw blood from the body politic. "The strength of [the monarch's] own affections will ever be against him: Wives, Children and Servants will always join with those Enemies that arise in his own breast to pervert him: if he has any weak side, and Lust unsubdued, they will gain the victory. He has not search'd into the nature of man, who thinks that any one can resist when he is thus on all sides assaulted."[13] In the face of such temptation, "good and wise men know the weight of Sovereign Power, and misdoubt their own strength."[14]

Were the corruption that followed on the heels of absolute monarchy restricted to the court, it might still be tolerable. But "the corruption thus beginning in the Head, must necessarily diffuse it self

---

[10] *Discourses*, III:43, p. 447.

[11] "Men are all made of the same paste," and hence kings are "subject to the same Frailties, Passions, and Vices [as] the rest of Mankind" (*Discourses*, III:1, p. 255; II:9, p. 102). See also: II:27, p. 212.

[12] *Discourses*, III:13, p. 308. See also: II:24, p. 186.

[13] *Discourses*, II:19, p. 148. See also: II:19, p. 149; II:25, p. 204; III:43, p. 446.

[14] *Discourses*, III:40, p. 433.

into all the Members of the Commonwealth." The reason for this cancerous spread was quite simple: a corrupt nation provided the least resistance to the machinations of the court.[15] The mechanism by which it consumed the nation was equally straightforward: "Men are naturally propense to coruption; and if he whose Will and Interest it is to corrupt them, be furnished with the means, he will never fail to do it. Power, Honors, Riches, and the Pleasures that attend them, are the baits by which men are drawn to prefer a personal Interest before the publick Good; and the number of those who covet them is so great, that he who abounds in them will be able to gain so many to his service as shall be suficient to subdue the rest."[16] Corruption fed upon corruption. Like a swirling vortex, the court of an absolute monarch drew the whole nation down with it into the depths.

Portrayals of courts as seedbeds of corruption are probably as old as courts themselves. Among a certain class of seventeenth-century Englishmen—particularly members of the provincial gentry, men increasingly resentful of the encroachment of the central government on their power in the counties—this view of courts played an increasingly important role in their political perceptions. When these men of the "Country" looked at the courts of James I and Charles I, they saw the domination of Inigo Jones's baroque architecture and William Lawes's Italianate music and the vast attention and wealth that were lavished on court masques. That all of these features of court life smacked of Catholicism only heightened the country-man's sense that something was fundamentally wrong. Some historians have even identified the evolution of distinct court and country cultures as a factor contributing to the outbreak of the Civil War.[17]

Algernon Sidney's portrait of absolute monarchy no doubt owed something to this country perspective on English politics. Though his own family cannot accurately be characterized as a country family, the country ethos was an essential element of the Kentish world in which he grew up. Unlike his country compatriots, however, Sidney did not contrast the corruption of court life with the innocence and simplicity of a country Arcadia. No homage to hearth and home inhabits the pages of his writings. His was a much darker world, a world

---

[15] *Discourses*, II:25, p. 204. See also: II:24, p. 182; III:19, p. 343.

[16] *Discourses*, III:6, p. 275.

[17] See, for example: Lawrence Stone, *The Causes of the English Revolution 1529–1642* (New York: Harper & Row, 1972), 105–8; Robert Ashton, *The English Civil War: Conservatism and Revolution 1603–1649* (New York: W. W. Norton, 1978), 1–126. As John Morrill has carefully noted, there were in fact two distinct parts of the "Country": the " 'official' Country" composed of "outs" wanting "in," and the " 'pure' Country" of provincial squires (John Morrill, *The Revolt of the Provinces* [London: Longman, 1980], 17).

in which the corrosive effects of corruption could never fully be escaped. It was closer to the harsh theology of Augustine or John Calvin than to the poetic vision of Ben Jonson's archetypical country poem "To Penshurst."[18] To understand Sidney's argument, it is necessary to examine the sources from which he drew it: his own experiences in royal courts and his wide reading in sacred and profane history.

While serving in the Baltic as English ambassador to the peace negotiations between Denmark and Sweden in 1659–60, Sidney had the opportunity to observe court culture at firsthand. As a Sidney, he was predisposed to be suspicious of courts. The family's relationship to the English court had long been problematic and had led most recently to the humiliating withdrawal of the lord lieutenancy of Ireland from Sidney's father, the earl of Leicester, in 1643.[19] Nonetheless, Sidney's experiences in the Baltic proved eye-opening.[20] Exasperated by "the tedious ceremonyes and disputes, that are usuall in theis northern courts," he firmly believed that without his undivided attention "they would dispute and cavill for ever, without concluding anything."[21]

Sidney vented the extremely cynical view of court life he had developed in a letter to his father in 1661. Following the death of Cardinal Mazarin of France, the courts of Europe were inflamed with speculation over who might be chosen as his successor. After reporting all the rumors he had heard, Sidney noted that "I have no other opinion of my own, than that he will be chosen that can find most favour with the ladies, and that can with most dexterity, reconcile their interests, and satisfy their passions. I look upon their thoughts as more important than those of the king and all his council, and their humour as of more weight than the most considerable interest of France."[22] Sidney's cynicism was not without foundation. Though

---

[18] And though thy walls be of the countrey stone
They are rear'd with no mans ruine, no mans grone,
There's none that dwells about them, wish them downe.

. . . .
Thy lady's noble, fruitfull, chaste, withall
His children thy great lord can call his owne;
A fortune, in this age, but rarely knowne.

[19] Earl of Leicester to the queen, December 1643, in Blencowe, xxvi.

[20] "I am in this year's employment grown much less credulous than I was" (Sidney to Leicester, 8 September 1660, in Collins, 2:695–99).

[21] Sidney to Leicester, 13 September 1659, in Blencowe, 163; Sidney to Downing, 7 April 1660, in *A Collection of the State Papers of John Thurloe* (London: 1742), 7:887.

[22] Sidney to Leicester, 12 March 1661, in Collins, 2:706–8. See also: Sidney to Leicester, 13 September 1659, in Blencowe, 166–67.

an able administrator during the regency of Louis XIV, Mazarin had risen to power by way of the bedchambers of Queen Anne.[23] Passion, not reason, ruled the royal courts of Europe. To a man of Sidney's bent, there could have been no greater reason to condemn the institution of absolute monarchy.[24]

The lessons Sidney learned through practical experience were reinforced, magnified, and multiplied by his reading of sacred and profane history. In the Bible he found evidence for the claim that absolute monarchy was "rooted in" corruption in the description of kingship that Samuel presented to the Israelites. Such a man would "take your sons, and appoint them for himself"; he would "take your daughters . . . and [your] fields, and your vineyards . . . and ye shall be his servants."[25] This passage had provided the centerpiece for James I's essay "The Trew Law of Free Monarchies," where it was glossed as an expression of God's desire to "prepare" the Israelites for "the due obedience of that King, which [He] was to give unto them."[26] Sidney drew a rather different conclusion from Samuel's description of absolute monarchy. Far from being a preparation of the Israelites for the depths to which their divine obligations might take them, it was a warning against the "folly" of subjecting themselves to "the irregular Will of a Man." Such, wrote Sidney with typical intransigence, was "acknowledged by all Interpreters, who were not malicious or mad."[27]

Alongside this conclusion drawn from biblical exegesis stood the vast stockpile of evidence against absolute monarchy that Sidney mined from the annals of profane history. The blood-soaked pages of the *Discourses* pile example on top of example of the depraved and sordid behavior of absolute monarchs, as if sheer weight and volume would prove Sidney's case. That was precisely his intention: he sought to demonstrate that absolute monarchy had everywhere and always been "rooted in" corruption.

To that end, Sidney ransacked the historical record of medieval and early modern Europe. Given the role France played in English

[23] And by "traffick" in "Abbies and Bishopricks" (*Discourses*, II:25, p. 205).

[24] As Sidney noted to Henry Savile in 1680, the French courtiers recently sent to England "spake of nothing so much as *la gloire de leur Maitre*; though perhaps there were more of true glory in the steadiness of a little good common sense, than in all the vanities and whimsies their heads are filled with" (Sidney to Savile, 26 July [1680], in *Letters*, 172–74).

[25] I Samuel 8:11–18.

[26] James I, "The Trew Law of Free Monarchies," in *Political Works of James I*, ed. C. H. McIlwain (Cambridge, MA: Harvard University Press, 1918), 57.

[27] *Discourses*, III:1, p. 257; III:3, p. 266. See also: III:46, p. 458; *Maxims*, 35–36, 39–41.

political and religious demonology, it was only natural that Sidney gave it a prominent place in his survey of the consequences of giving corrupt humans unlimited power. The French religious wars, so frequently on the minds of seventeenth-century Englishmen, provided a particularly brutal example of a general feature of the French political system: "from the first establishment [it has] bin full of blood and slaughter, through the violence of those who possessed the Crown, and the Ambition of such as aspired to it."[28] A similar story could be told wherever absolute monarchy reared its ugly head. No nation was spared in Sidney's litany of horrors, not Spain, not Italy, not even England.

Above all else, however, Sidney rested his case against absolute monarchy on a highly selective reading of Aristotle, Plato, Livy, and Tacitus.[29] His use of classical sources reflected the syllabus of a gentleman's education in seventeenth-century Europe. It also embodied a powerful rhetorical device. As he explained in the *Discourses*:

> If I often repeat these hateful names [of Caligula, Nero and Domitian], 'tis not for want of fresher examples of the same nature; but I use such as Mankind has universally condemn'd, against whom I can have no other cause of hatred than what is common to all those who have any love to virtue, and which can have no other relation to the Controversies of later Ages, than what may flow from the similitude of their causes, rather than such as are too well known to us, and which every man, according to the measure of his experience, may call to mind in reading these.[30]

This was a common polemical strategy and would have been well understood by his contemporaries.[31] Sidney was being more than a little

---

[28] *Discourses*, II:24, pp. 195–96. This general topic is explored in J.H.M. Salmon, *The French Religious Wars in English Political Thought* (Oxford: The Clarendon Press, 1959). There is, however, no textual warrant for Salmon's claim that Sidney allied himself with the French monarchomach writers, or that his "most admired French author was Hotman" (135–36).

[29] Surprisingly, Cicero—whose *De Officiis* was a handbook of moral instruction to Englishmen throughout much of the sixteenth and seventeenth centuries—played only a minor role in Sidney's arguments. See: *Discourses*, I:1, p. 4; I:16, p. 38; I:20, p. 55; II:19, p. 150; III:10, p. 299; III:21, p. 351; III:25, p. 365; III:26, p. 370.

[30] *Discourses*, III:16, p. 320. See also: II:24, p. 179; III:5, p. 273; *Maxims*, 125.

[31] Cf. *An Appeal from the Country to the City* [1679], in *State Tracts* (London: 1693), 1:405. The polemical uses of Tacitus in contemporary moral and political discourse are described in: Alan Bradford, "Stuart Absolutism and the 'Utility' of Tacitus," *Huntington Library Quarterly* 46 (Winter 1983): esp. 147–49; Peter Burke, "Tacitism," in *Tacitus*, ed. T. A. Dorey (London: Routledge & Kegan Paul, 1969), 149–71; Kenneth Schellhase, *Tacitus in Renaissance Political Thought* (Chicago: University of Chicago Press, 1976), esp. 157–65.

disingenuous when, after his conviction for treason, he claimed that "when nothing of particular Application unto Time, Place, or Person could be found" in the manuscript of the *Discourses*, "all was supplied by *Innuendo*."[32] He wrote with the express purpose of exhorting others to see the parallels between the rule of the Stuarts and the tyrannies of Caligula, Nero, and Domitian.

From his reading of Plato and Aristotle, Sidney drew two maxims: that the only justification for absolute monarchy is the superior virtue of the monarch;[33] and that tyranny arises when a man of ordinary or inferior virtue is given the powers of an absolute monarch.[34] Were a man of exceptional virtue to be found, a man possessing "a mind unbiassed by passion, full of goodness and wisdom, firm against all the temptations to ill, that may arise from desire or fear," he might legitimately be given absolute power.[35] Moses and David had proven to be just such men when they led the Israelites. But were such virtue lacking, were a man unable to discipline and control his passions to be given such immense power, he would necessarily become a tyrant.

Sidney invoked Aristotle to justify the claim that no man was sufficiently free of passion to withstand the temptations of unrestrained power.[36] But the real evidence for his argument that absolute power and corruption were inseparable came from the histories of Tacitus. It was Tacitus above all others who had demonstrated, through his studies of imperial Rome, that government by one man could never be in the public interest. "Former writers, says Tacitus ... might delight their readers with great & noble actions; we have nothing to relate but cruel commands, continual accusations, false friendships, and the destruction of the innocent."[37] As Sidney was fond of repeating, it was Caligula who "wished the People had but one Neck, that he might strike it off at one blow."[38] Ruled and in turn ruling by their

---

[32] Algernon Sidney, *The Very Copy of a Paper Delivered to the Sheriffs, Upon the Scaffold* (London: 1683), 2. See also: "Apology," 12, 17, 20, 29.

[33] For Plato, see: *Discourses*, II:1, pp. 63–66; II:9, p. 97; II:30, p. 230. For Aristotle, see: *Discourses*, II:1, pp. 60–62, 65–67; II:10, pp. 102–4; II:30, pp. 230–31; III:23, pp. 358–60.

[34] For Plato, see: *Discourses*, II:3, p. 70. For Aristotle, see: *Maxims*, 146, 210; *Discourses*, II:1, p. 62; III:7, p. 278; III:23, p. 358; III:26, p. 373.

[35] *Discourses*, III:23, p. 359.

[36] *Discourses*, III:23, pp. 358–60.

[37] *Maxims*, 131. For references to Tacitus's histories of Rome, see: *Maxims*, 70–71, 130–33, 186, 188; *Discourses*, I:5, p. 12; I:20, p. 57; II:3, p. 70; II:12, pp. 114–16; II:15, pp. 125, 127; II:18, p. 142; II:21, p. 155; II:24, p. 192; II:27, pp. 210, 212; II:28, p. 216; II:29, p. 225; III:1, p. 227; III:3, p. 264; III:10, p. 293; III:12, pp. 302–3; III:21, p. 349; III:24, p. 360; III:25, pp. 363–64; III:26, p. 369.

[38] *Discourses*, I:20, p. 58. See also: II:24, p. 179; II:27, p. 210; *Maxims*, 65.

passions, the emperors of first-century Rome succeeded in destroying everything of value that had been cultivated during Rome's centuries of republican liberty.

Not all monarchs are as corrupt as Caligula, of course. There have been and might once again be absolute monarchs of great personal virtue. But the sheer unlikelihood of such a monarch appearing, particularly in a hereditary system, only served to strengthen Sidney's argument: "I will not say such a King is a Phenix; perhaps more than one may be found in an Age; but they are certainly rare, and all that is good in their Government proceeding from the excellency of their personal Virtues, it must fail when that Virtue fails; which was the root of it."[39] Filmer had claimed that order and stability were possible if and only if a nation was ruled by an absolute monarch. By focusing on the consequences of corruption, Sidney was able to stand Filmer's maxim on its head: "of all things under the Sun, there is none more mutable or unstable than Absolute Monarchy."[40] Patriarchalism made political order a function of the monarch's character. But the simple truth was that "human Nature is not well capable of Stability": "the nature of man is frail, and stands in need of assistance."[41]

Sidney proposed two forms of "assistance" to cope with the problems posed by corruption: "balancing the Powers in such a manner, that the corruption which one or a few men might fall into, should not be suffer'd to spread the contagion to the ruin of the whole";[42] and creating a regime in which "well-established Laws govern [and] not men."[43] Sidney's commitment to "balancing the Powers" was a concession to the frailty of virtue and reflected his deep distrust of concentrations of power. Every man stood on the edge of a moral and psychological precipice, off which he might gladly tumble if given the opportunity.[44] If it was not possible to eliminate the temptation, at least it was possible to minimize the damage that would be done. So great was Sidney's fear of unchecked power that he refused to permit any room in his theory for prerogative powers. Magistrates were to be strictly confined within the boundaries established by the law. They might be permitted areas of discretion within the law, but they

[39] *Discourses*, II:25, p. 204. "Experience shewing that among many millions of men, there is hardly one that possesses the Qualities required in a King, 'tis so many to one, that he upon whom the Lot shall fall, will not be the man we seek" (II:11, p. 106).

[40] *Discourses*, II:11, p. 106.

[41] *Discourses*, II:11, p. 106; III:43, p. 446.

[42] *Discourses*, III:43, pp. 446–47. See also: I:1, p. 3; II:25, p. 200; II:30, p. 241; III:28, pp. 378–79; III:37, p. 419; III:40, p. 434.

[43] *Maxims*, 200.

[44] "Men have a strange propensity to run into all manner of excesses, when plenty of means invite, and . . . there is no power to deter" (*Discourses*, II:19, p. 145).

could have no powers outside of or above the law.[45] In this Sidney differed sharply from John Locke, who argued that in order to adhere to the law of nature " 'tis fit that the Laws themselves should in some Cases give way to the Executive Power."[46] The reasons for this difference will be discussed in Chapter 5, in the context of an analysis of Sidney's constitutional theory.

The logic of "balancing the Powers" left the concepts of virtue and corruption essentially untouched. Virtue required self-control, and corruption was a consequence of succumbing to the temptations of one's passions. Given the frailty of the former and the vigor of the latter, prudence dictated a kind of constitutional damage control. Sidney's second form of "assistance," however, introduced a significant shift in the meaning of these key concepts. In a passage frequently cited by his eighteenth-century admirers, he explained the relationship between virtue, corruption, and the rule of law:

> 'Tis not therefore upon the uncertain will or understanding of a Prince, that the safety of a Nation ought to depend. He is sometimes a child, and sometimes overburden'd with years. Some are weak, negligent, slothful, foolish or vicious: others, who may have something of rectitude in their intentions, and naturally are not uncapable of doing well, are drawn out of the right way by the subtilty of ill men who gain credit with them. . . . The good of a People ought to be established upon a more solid foundation. For this reason the Law is established, which no passion can disturb. 'Tis void of desire and fear, lust and anger. 'Tis *Mens sine affectu*, written reason, retaining some measure of the Divine Perfection. It dos not enjoin that which pleases a weak, frail man, but without any regard to persons commands that which is good, and punishes evil in all, whether rich or poor, high or low. 'Tis deaf, inexorable, inflexible.[47]

Sidney's vision of the pure rule of law surely underestimates the need for prerogative powers in any government. But his fear of the unbounded power of the passions was so great that he believed that even the best of magistrates ought to take the law, and not their own character, as a guide to action. As the commonwealthsman Eunomius

[45] *Discourses*, II:5, p. 76; III:15, p. 315; III:16, p. 318; III:21, pp. 348–54; III:22, p. 357.

[46] *Two Treatises*, II:159.

[47] *Discourses*, III:15, p. 316. See also: II:30, p. 230; *Maxims*, 200. In an absolute monarchy everything depends "on the person of a man and must therefore necessarily be perpetually wavering and uncertain according to the life of him that gives the Impulse unto them. But in Common-wealths its not men but laws, Maxims, interests and Constitutions that govern" (*Maxims*, 23). The Latin phrase is from Aristotle, *The Politics*, 1287a.

crisply stated the new ethic in the *Court Maxims*, "I think the rule of my actions to be the Law."[48]

Though Sidney nowhere acknowledged it, his dedication to the rule of law entailed a dramatic reconfiguration of the concepts of virtue and corruption. Virtue was no longer defined as self-control, but as obeying the law; corruption was no longer defined as licentiousness, but as deviating from the law. There is obviously a great deal of overlap between these two views. Legalism is a theory of impersonal rule, and strict adherence to the law may require great self-control, particularly by men whose judgment is easily swayed by the passions. But there is an essential difference between a character-oriented ethic that emphasizes heroic self-discipline and a behavior-oriented ethic that emphasizes obedience to the law. The former is essentially aristocratic and links the virtue of a magistrate to his ability to cultivate and exercise personal characteristics like courage, honesty, and liberality. The latter is essentially egalitarian and links the virtue of a magistrate to his ability to adhere to an externally provided set of rules and commands. These two conceptions of virtue need not sanction the same behavior. The former, with its emphasis on character and judgment, elevates the discretionary authority of a magistrate, while the latter positively proscribes it. They also provide very different reasons for behaving virtuously. The former views magistracy as an expression of a man's soul, while the latter views it as the exercise of delegated power and authority. These differences are particularly pronounced when, as in Sidney's theory, the content of the law is contingent, variable, and subject to the consent of the governed.

There is, of course, no necessary connection between the rule of law and justice. Legalism is capable of encompassing a wide range of practices.[49] As Sidney acknowledged, "there have bin and are Laws that are neither just nor commendable."[50] The virtue of law-abidingness was dependent on the content of the law, and to that extent Sidney's conception of virtue was dependent on his theory of legislation.

Martial Valor, Weakness and Effeminacy

Alongside self-control and licentiousness stood a second account of virtue and corruption in Sidney's writings: the virtue of martial valor

---

[48] *Maxims*, 69. "The Law . . . is a help to those who are wise and good, by directing them what they are to do, more certainly than any one mans personal judgment can do" (*Discourses*, III:13, p. 307). See also: II:20, p. 153.

[49] Judith N. Shklar, *Legalism: Law, Morals, and Political Trials* (Cambridge, MA: Harvard University Press, 1964), pp. 29–110.

[50] *Discourses*, III:10, p. 299.

and the corruption of weakness and effeminacy. There is a great deal of overlap between these two accounts. The exercise of martial valor requires personal discipline, particularly since cowardice and irresolution are two of the corrupt passions to which men are most susceptible. But the ideal of martial valor belongs to an essentially different matrix of ideas than the ideals of self-control and law-abidingness. The latter grew out of the Christian belief that nature is corrupt and that it has to be systematically regulated and suppressed. The former, by contrast, is predicated on the pagan belief that nature is strong and vibrant and that it ought to be exercised, cultivated, and displayed. According to the ethic of self-control, virtue is a matter of self-abnegation; according to the ethic of martial valor, it is a matter of self-affirmation. Many of the techniques for developing these two virtues are the same, but their ends are quite different.

Sidney ascribed value to the cultivation of martial valor for two quite different reasons: because it had symbolic or expressive value; and because it was instrumental to the preservation of liberty. In both cases he thought it possible to demonstrate that absolute monarchy maximized the growth of corruption and destroyed all traces of virtue.

The strength of a nation was, according to Sidney, a self-evident indication of its virtue. A weak nation was ipso facto corrupt, while a strong nation was worthy of the highest accolades. And while strength and weakness might be partially measured by a nation's wealth, or by the size of its population, final proof of their presence could be provided only on the battlefield.[51] War provided the ultimate opportunity to display a nation's virtue. This was, of course, a very traditional idea. Deeply rooted in the heroic ideals of the aristocracy, it bore fruit in many of the needless wars that scarred the historical landscape of late medieval and early modern Europe.

Something like this very traditional and aristocratic conception of virtue was at work in Sidney's frequent references to the contrast between republican and imperial Rome. While governed as a republic, Rome conquered every nation within its reach; "the greatest Monarchs of the Earth were as dust before them."[52] But once it came to be ruled by emperors, it "was made a Prey to unknown barbarous Nations, and rent into as many pieces as it had bin composed of."[53]

---

[51] Thus when Sidney cataloged the ends to which free governments devoted themselves—increasing "the Number, Strength, Power, Riches, and Courage of their People"—three of the five ends were related to the cultivation of martial valor (*Discourses*, II:26, p. 209).

[52] *Discourses*, II:15, p. 128. See also: I:16, p. 38; II:12, p. 113; II:15, pp. 128–29.

[53] *Discourses*, II:11, p. 109. See also: II:15, p. 129; II:24, p. 185.

The reason for this shocking decline in Rome's fortune was the loss of its liberty: "Whilst Liberty continued, it was the Nurse of Vertue; and all the Losses suffered in Foreign or Civil Wars, were easily recovered: but when Liberty was Lost, Valour and Virtue was torn up by the roots, and the *Roman* Power proceeding from it, perished."[54] With the loss of its liberty, Rome fell from the bright pinnacle of virtue to the blackest depths of corruption.

Sidney's account of Rome's fall emphasized the instrumental value of liberty. The focus of his attention was not the freedom of Rome's citizens, but the enormous capacity of republican Rome to wage and win wars. That was the true measure of its greatness. It was also a measure of the greatness England had achieved in the few short years that it had been governed as a commonwealth: "Neither the *Romans* nor *Grecians* in the time of their Liberty ever performed any actions more glorious than freeing the country from a Civil War that had raged in every part, the conquest of two such Kingdoms as *Scotland* and *Ireland*, and crushing the formidable power of the *Hollanders* by Sea."[55] Monarchy had reduced England to "weakness, cowardice, baseness, venality, lewdness, and all manner of corruption," while the Commonwealth had elevated it to "Greatness, Power, Riches, Strength, and Happiness."[56]

The heroic character of Sidney's imperial vision can be highlighted by comparing it with similar arguments in the writings of John Milton and James Harrington. Like Sidney, Milton exhorted his countrymen to exhibit the "fortitude and Heroick vertue" that would enable them to build "another Rome in the west." But Milton's Rome was not Sidney's Rome. Writing in 1644, Milton asked "why else was this Nation chos'n before any other, that out of here as out of *Sion* should be proclam'd and sounded forth the first tidings and trumpet of Reformation to all *Europ*." Ten years later England seemed poised to fulfill

[54] *Discourses*, II:15, p. 126. "All that was ever desirable, or worthy of praise and imitation in Rome, did proceed from its Liberty, grow up and perish with it" (II:12, p. 112). See also: *Maxims*, 129–30.

[55] *Discourses*, II:28, p. 220. See also: II:11, p. 112; II:28, p. 222; III:10, pp. 292–93; *Maxims*, 16.

[56] *Discourses*, II:28, p. 220. "And to show, Comon-wealths better employ their Power in war, then Kings, 3 modern examples may suffice. The One of the united Provinces defending themselves against the power of Spain and encreasing in strength and riches during the wars. The other of Venice warring with litle losse for 20 years against the dreadfull Power of the Ottoman Empire. And the English Comon-wealth which in 5 years conquer'd absolutely Scotland & Ireland, and in so many battells broke the Hollanders that they were brought to the uttmost weakness" (*Maxims*, 15–16). See also: *Discourses*, II:27, p. 211.

its religious and political destiny, and Milton heightened the rhetorical pitch of his already shrill prose:

> Now, surrounded by such great throngs, from the Pillars of Hercules all the way to the farthest boundaries of Father Liber, I seem to be leading home again everywhere in the world, after a vast space of time, Liberty herself, so long expelled and exiled. And, like Triptolemus of old, I seem to introduce to the nations of the earth a product from my own country, but one far more excellent than that of Ceres. In short, it is the renewed cultivation of freedom and civic life that I disseminate throughout cities, kingdoms, and nations.[57]

England's empire was to be an empire of liberty, forged in the fires of a Protestant crusade. James Harrington's attitude toward martial valor is extremely complicated, but it is clear that he, too, believed that a "commonwealth for increase" would lead to "the liberty of mankind."[58] As the lord archon explained to Oceana's council of legislators: "If the empire of a commonwealth be patronage, to ask whether it be lawful for a commonwealth to aspire unto the empire of the world is to ask whether it be lawful for her to do her duty, or to put the world into a better condition than it was before." It was the unique mission of "an immortal commonwealth" to foster "the propagation of civil liberty . . . and the liberty of conscience."[59] Of these three leading republican theorists, only Sidney was willing to discuss the value of an English empire without direct reference to the spread of liberty. Only Sidney presented the international display of martial valor as a self-justifying activity.

Tempering and ultimately dominating this heroic vision, however, was an argument that ran in the opposite direction: martial valor was not a self-justifying virtue, but a necessary precondition to the preservation of freedom. Despite his glorification of strength and power, of conquest and expansion, Sidney was wary of the claim that the creation of an empire ought to be the guiding purpose of a commonwealth: "If the end of Government were the enlargement of dominion, he that enlarges the dominion of a Nation may pretend to doe good to it. But if Government be constituted for another end, that in

---

[57] John Milton, "The Tenure of Kings and Magistrates," in *Complete Prose Works*, ed. Don M. Wolfe (New Haven: Yale University Press, 1953–82), 3:191; "The Readie and Easie Way to Establish a Free Commonwealth," ibid., 7:423; "Areopagitica," ibid., 2:552; "Second Defence of the English People," ibid., 4:555–56.

[58] James Harrington, "The Commonwealth of Oceana," in *The Political Works of James Harrington*, ed. J.G.A. Pocock (Cambridge: Cambridge University Press, 1977), 320, 330. See generally: 320–33.

[59] Harrington, "Oceana," in *Works*, 328, 332.

a Society we may live free, happy and safe, he that makes a Conquest is not a benefactor to the Nation unless it conduce to these ends."[60] The exercise of force was acceptable only if it advanced the ends of government, and hence martial valor was of purely instrumental value. With liberty subject to frequent threats, free men had to be ever vigilant. "Swords were given to men, that none might be Slaves, but such as know not how to use them."[61]

The necessity of martial valor for the maintenance of freedom was a consequence of domestic and international factors. "If Mankind were of a temper to suffer those to live in peace, who offer no injury to any," or if "men who have Money to hire Soldiers when they stand in need of them, could find such as would valiantly and faithfully defend them," then a nation might preserve its independence without recourse to violence. "But experience teaching us that those only can be safe who are strong; and that no People was ever well defended, but those who fought for themselves; the best Judges of these matters have always given the preference to those Constitutions that principally intend War, and make use of Trade as assisting to that end: and think it better to aim at conquest, rather than simply to stand upon their own defence."[62] The depth of Sidney's commitment to "Constitutions that principally intend War" is unclear, however, particularly since he found occasion in the pages following this ringing declaration to praise the republican federations of Switzerland and the Netherlands.[63] Seventeenth-century observers considered the Dutch to be extremely bellicose. One pamphleteer went so far as to say that "war is their heaven and peace their hell."[64] But the Dutch were not cut of Roman (or Machiavellian) cloth. As their polemicists repeatedly emphasized, they viewed peace and trade, not empire and annexation, as their primary mode of existence.[65] The Dutch abhorred the military and "intended" war only in the sense that they were prepared to defend their liberty with their wealth and their

[60] *Maxims*, 13.

[61] *Discourses*, III:4, p. 270. See also: II:23, p. 169; III:33, p. 407; III:36, p. 416.

[62] *Discourses*, II:22, pp. 161–62. See also: II:15, p. 124; II:23, pp. 166–68.

[63] *Discourses*, II:22, pp. 162–64; II:23, p. 171.

[64] Quoted in Simon Schama, *An Embarrassment of Riches* (New York: Knopf, 1988), 238.

[65] [Pieter de la Court] and John De Witt, *The True Interest and Political Maxims of the Republic of Holland*, 1662, revised in 1671 (London: J. Nourse, 1746), 199–209, 310; [Pieter de la Court], *Consideratien van Staat, Oder Politische Wagschale*, trans. Christoph Kormarten, 1661 (Leipzig: 1669), 317–18. See also: Schama, *Embarrassment*, 221–57; E. H. Kossmann, *In Praise of the Dutch Republic* (London: H. K. Lewis, 1963); Kossmann, "Dutch Republicanism," in *L'età dei lumi* (Naples: Jovene, 1985), 1:453–86.

lives. It was, they thought, an unfortunate stroke of fate that they were so often called on to do so.

Sidney was aware of Dutch arguments linking freedom and trade,[66] but he refused to endorse their official pacifism categorically. The value of peace was relative to a nation's constitution and to the international threats that faced it. With an eye to Sidney's frequent use of hyperbole, and his tendency to state a position dogmatically and then qualify it in a hundred different ways, his dictum that "that is the best Government, which best provides for War" might be glossed as follows: like the unconscious Hobbesians who lock their doors at night and carry a weapon when they go abroad,[67] the most successful and secure nations have learned that, regardless of their own intentions, it is best to suspect their neighbors of the worst.

Alongside the grave threats to liberty posed by foreign governments stood a number of domestic dangers as well. In every government, regardless of its constitution, there were magistrates who were moved primarily by "injustice, cruelty, and malice"; and with tyranny just around the corner, the only sure protection for liberty was the courage that enabled men to make use of their arms and legs. " 'Tis in vain to say, that this may give occasion to men of raising tumults or civil war; for tho' these are evil, yet they are not the greatest of evils. Civil War in *Macchiavels* account is a Disease, but Tyranny is the death of a State."[68] Given England's experiences during its Civil War, this was an extremely radical and intentionally provocative thing to say. Only in the wake of the Popish Plot and the Exclusion Crisis, and only among men who believed that the king and the duke of York were spearheading an "invasion" of England's liberty, could it have even begun to make sense.[69]

With their links to France and Rome, the two Stuarts embodied the greatest of all possible threats to England's liberty. Whatever defects existed in their own ambitions would be supplied by Louis XIV and the pope. But, Sidney argued, their behavior was not exceptional; they exemplified traits inherent in all monarchs. Sidney drove this point home by exploding one of the oldest and most cherished metaphors for monarchy, that of the shepherd: "[Monarchs] consider Nations, as Grasiers do their Herds and Flocks, according to the

[66] "The hollanders in all business of warr or peace with any nation doe principally consider trade" (*Maxims*, 62). See also: 61, 159.

[67] Thomas Hobbes, *Leviathan*, ed. C. B. Macpherson (Harmondsworth: Penguin Books, 1981), 186–87.

[68] *Discourses*, III:40, p. 434. See also: II:26, p. 206; *Maxims*, 17, 142.

[69] On the language of invasion, see Richard Ashcraft, *Revolutionary Politics & Locke's Two Treatises of Government* (Princeton: Princeton University Press, 1986), 394–402.

profit that can be made of them. . . . Tho he desire to be a good Husband, yet they must be delivered up to the slaughter when he finds a good Market, or a better way of improving his Land."[70] The more docile the flock, moreover, the easier the shepherd's task. As a result, many of the policies pursued by an absolute monarch were designed to reduce his subjects to a condition of passive obedience. The first step in this process was the introduction of poverty. As the courtier Philalethos explained in the *Court Maxims*: "Generally all people grow proud when Numerous and rich, They think themselves masters of all, The least injury putts them into a fury; But if poor, weak, miserable and few they'l be humble and obedient. The present sense of their wants hinders them from Applying their thoughts beyond anything but getting of bread, and their weakness keeps them quiet abasing their spirit: despair of success keeps them from attempting anything."[71] Lest any subjects display the slightest hint of independence or valor, vast networks of "Spies, Informers and False Witnesses" are created to detect and crush them.[72] In order to ensure that their will is done, absolute monarchs surround themselves with weak-willed courtiers, men whose only qualification for public office is their capacity to carry out their master's orders without question or hesitation.[73] And if these stratagems prove insufficient, the assistance of foreign powers can be brought to bear on the task of domesticating the nation.[74] Truly it might be said that for a nation of sheep there can be no freedom or safety.

What was needed for the preservation of liberty was a manly spirit, a capacity to remain "strong," "vigorous," and "stout" in the face of adversity.[75] Absolute monarchy was to be condemned because it destroyed this spirit, because it led to the feminization of men. Distrust of women and of the moral and psychological qualities associated with them is at the heart of republican theories of virtue.[76] Men of

[70] *Discourses*, II:27, p. 213. See also: *Maxims*, 142–43, 185. Cf. Thrasymachus's comment in Plato, *The Republic*, 343b.

[71] *Maxims*, 59–60. "Princes are never so rich as when their subjects are poor. The oppulency of the King of france proceeds principally from the peoples poverty" (64). See also: *Discourses*, II:19, p. 146; II:26, pp. 206–7; III:36, p. 416.

[72] *Discourses*, II:27, p. 214. See also: *Maxims*, 190.

[73] *Maxims*, 56–59, 70; *Discourses*, II:15, p. 129; II:18, p. 143; II:27, p. 214.

[74] "Let him that doubts this . . . [recognize that] he may soon see a man in the Throne, who had rather be a Tributary to France than a lawful King of England" (*Discourses*, II:27, p. 211). See also: III:1, p. 254; III:7, pp. 280–81; III:19, p. 343.

[75] *Discourses*, III:4, p. 269; III:36, p. 414.

[76] This dimension of early modern republicanism has received relatively little attention; two prominent exceptions are: Hanna Fenichel Pitkin, *Fortune Is a Woman* (Berke-

martial valor are firm, unyielding, and self-assertive. Moved by honor and conscience, they are not afraid of standing up for their own rights and the rights of others. As a result, they are the first men an absolute monarch destroys. In their place, absolute monarchs cultivate courtiers, soft and pliable men, passive men, men given to sensuality and luxury. The fate of a nation living under an absolute monarch is determined not by the stern politics of a free Parliament, but by the corrupt passions of a dependent court.[77]

The cumulative effect on a nation of the practices associated with absolute monarchy was to weaken and debase it and to deprive it of the martial valor with which it defended its liberty. Sidney invoked the condition of Florence before and after the Medicis to verify this claim:

> When the family of *Medicis* came to be masters of *Tuscany*, that Country was without dispute, in men, mony and arms, one of the most flourishing Provinces in the World, as appears by *Macchiavels* account, and the relation of what happened between *Charles* the eighth and the Magistrates of *Florence*, which I have mentioned already from *Guicciardin*. . . . Whereas now that City, with all the others in that Province, are brought to such despicable weakness, emptiness, poverty and baseness, that they can neither resist the oppressions of their own Prince, nor defend him or themselves if they were assaulted by a foreign Enemy.[78]

It is important to note that this is one of only a handful of instances in the whole of his writings where Sidney referred to the great Florentine theorist Niccolò Machiavelli.[79] Though familiar with Machiavelli's writings—he briefly quoted from *The Prince*, *The Discourses*, and the *History of Florence*—Sidney did not rely extensively on Machiavelli's arguments. To be sure, he endorsed the Machiavellian doctrine that constitutions "must perish, unless they are timely renewed, and reduced to their first principles"; but as noted in Chapter 3, Sidney framed his theory of change with the language of natural jurispru-

---

ley and Los Angeles: University of California Press, 1984); Ruth H. Bloch, "The Gendered Meanings of Virtue in Revolutionary America," *Signs* 13 (1987): 37–58.

[77] *Maxims*, 55–59, 61; *Discourses*, I:18, p. 47; II:12, p. 114; II:15, p. 129; II:19, p. 145; II:25, pp. 202–4; III:6, p. 275; III:7, p. 277; Sidney to Leicester, 29 January 1661, in Collins, 2:704–5; Sidney to Leicester, 12 March 1661, in Collins, 2:706–8; Algernon Sidney, "Of Love," in *A Collection of Scarce and Valuable Tracts . . . of the Late Lord Somers*, ed. Sir Walter Scott, 2nd ed. (London: 1812), 8:618–19.

[78] *Discourses*, III:36, p. 415; II:26, p. 208. See also: *Maxims*, 60.

[79] See also: *Maxims*, 20, 33, 70, 71, 77, 142; *Discourses*, II:11, p. 105; II:29, p. 226; III:16, p. 319; III:40, p. 434.

dence, not with a classical theory of corruption.[80] No other hallmark of Machiavelli's thought—from the polar concepts of *virtú* and *fortuna* to the emphasis on political foundings, great legislators, and civic religions—can be found in Sidney's writings.[81] There is, of course, no reliable way of interpreting this silence. But it suggests at minimum that the claim that Machiavelli dominated seventeenth-century English republicanism has been vastly overstated.[82]

In sharp contrast to absolute monarchies, commonwealths are relatively free from dissipation and enervation. This notion was implicit in Sidney's Florentine example, but he frequently made it explicit as well. His reasoning is particularly interesting, because it exhibits the same kind of half-conscious transformation of the language of virtue and corruption that was found in his analysis of self-control and licentiousness. There, as was shown above, he resolved the problem of self-control into a problem of law; here he resolved the problem of martial valor into a problem of interests.

The final cause of the destruction of martial valor in absolute monarchies was the inescapable conflict that existed between the private interest of the king and the public interest of his subjects. It was this conflict that led monarchs to debase their subjects and to destroy every vestige of independence in the land. It was this same conflict that made their subjects reluctant to assist them, even in the face of grave crises, for fear of preserving and strengthening the very power that oppressed them.[83] "In a popular or mixed Government," on the other hand, "every man is concerned."[84] The private interest of the magistrate is coherent with the private interest of every other citizen,

---

[80] *Discourses*, II:13, p. 117. The relevance of this claim to Sidney's theory of revolution will be explored at the conclusion of Chapter 5.

[81] Thus I am unable to accept the widely held view that Machiavelli exerted a "tremendous influence" on Sidney (Neal Wood, "The Value of Asocial Sociability: Contributions of Machiavelli, Sidney and Montesquieu," in *Machiavelli and the Nature of Political Thought*, ed. Martin Fleisher [New York: Atheneum, 1972], 293). See also: Worden, "Classical Republicanism," 183; Blair Worden, "The Commonwealth Kidney of Algernon Sidney," *Journal of British Studies* 24 (January 1985): 18; Jonathan Scott, *Algernon Sidney and the English Republic 1623–1677* (Cambridge: Cambridge University Press, 1988), passim.

[82] The "Machiavelli thesis" has been argued most strongly in Felix Raab, *The English Face of Machiavelli* (London: Routledge & Kegan Paul, 1964), and J.G.A. Pocock, *The Machiavellian Moment* (Princeton: Princeton University Press, 1975).

[83] "Tacitus observes . . . [of the Roman people that] when their Spirits were depressed by servitude, they had neither courage to defend themselves, nor will to fight for their wicked Masters; and least of all to increase their Power, which was destructive to themselves: The same thing is found in all places" (*Discourses*, II:21, p. 155). See also: III:36, p. 416.

[84] *Discourses*, II:21, p. 157. See also: II:26, p. 204.

and taken together they are reflected in and advanced by the public interest.[85] As a result, martial valor flourishes: "men are valiant and industrious, when they fight for themselves and their Country." "We every where see the difference between the Courage of men fighting for themselves and their posterity, and those that serve a Master who by good success is often render'd insupportable."[86]

Arguments for civic virtue are frequently couched in terms of a simplistic contrast between a virtuous devotion to the public interest and a base concern for private interests. But as Sidney's analysis of martial valor demonstrates, this can be highly misleading. The point of any coherent theory of interests is to distinguish between those private interests that are in harmony with the public interest and those that are in conflict with it. One of the central purposes of Hobbes's *Leviathan*, for example, was to delegitimate the interest men had in a range of traditional aristocratic ideals—especially glory and honor—that were incompatible with the preservation of peace. Similarly, arguments for religious toleration in the seventeenth century were frequently pitched in terms of the conflict between the private interest of a few in religious conformity and the public interest of the many in religious diversity.

Sidney's case against absolute monarchy hinged on the contention that it sacrificed the public interest to the private interests of a single man. Rome burned while Nero fiddled. The great majority of private interests, however, were not only consistent with the public interest, but also conducive to the cultivation of martial valor. That was why Sidney argued that the best governments were those that "so provide for the good of the People, that they may daily increase in Number, Courage and Strength, and be so satisfied with the present state of things, as to fear a change, and fight for the preservation or advancement of the publick Interest as of their own."[87] Civic virtue did not grow out of the renunciation of private interests, but rather out of the recognition that the vast majority of private interests are encompassed in, indeed are part and parcel of, the public interest. To put the point somewhat baldly, self-interest was the strongest possible foundation for civic virtue. A striking example of this principle was given during Sidney's brief career as governor of Dover Castle. In a letter to the Kent Quarter Sessions Sidney argued that financial assistance for the widow and children of one of his soldiers would not only be "an acte of justice and mercy" but would also be "an courage-

---

[85] "A duly created Magistracy, governing a Nation with their consent, can have no interest distinct from that of the Publick" (*Discourses*, II:19, p. 146).

[86] *Discourses*, II:28, p. 217; II:23, p. 168. See also: II:17, p. 134; II:28, p. 220.

[87] *Discourses*, II:23, p. 168. See also: II:23, p. 165.

ment to others to adventure their lives for the state in hope of the like releife for theirs." By securing the welfare of the families of fallen soldiers, the nation would strengthen the resolve of the men called on to defend it. As Sidney argued in the *Discourses*, "virtuous actions that are profitable to a Commonwealth ought to be made, as far as it is possible, safe, easy, and advantageous."[88]

Sidney provided no independent criteria by which to distinguish constructive and destructive private interests. As a result, the success of his attempt to link martial valor with the preservation of private interests was contingent on his ability to describe a system of government capable of distinguishing between legitimate and illegitimate private interests and then of articulating a coherent and comprehensive statement of the public interest. Without such a system, his argument would remain formal and be of relatively little value. Sidney's constitutional theory will be explored in detail in Chapter 5, but it is worth noting here that he thought absolute monarchy incapable of meeting this need: "Men can no otherwise be engaged to take care of the Publick, than by having such a part in it, as Absolute Monarchy dos not allow; for they can neither obtain the Good for themselves, Posterity and Friends, that they desire, nor prevent the Mischiefs they fear, which are the principal Arguments that perswade men to expose themselves to labours or dangers."[89] Only a commonwealth was capable of engaging men "to take care of the Publick," because only a commonwealth gave men an active role in the articulation and preservation of the public interest. Active citizens, not passive subjects, were the only sure guardians of England's liberty.

Integrity and the Violation of a Public Trust

The final form of virtue and corruption to which Sidney devoted his attention was the virtue of integrity and the keeping of covenants and the corruption of violating a public trust. Like martial valor, the virtue of integrity was closely related to the virtue of self-control. For example, venality could be and was frequently described as the behavior of a man who had succumbed to the base temptations of avarice. It was condemned because it reflected a loss of self-control and in the process revealed a basic flaw in a man's character. Traces of this ethic can be found throughout Sidney's writings, particularly in

[88] Algernon Sidney to Kent Quarter Sessions, 17 July [1648], Kent Archives Office, Q/SB 1/45; *Discourses*, III:43, p. 446.

[89] *Discourses*, II:21, p. 155.

his accounts of his own life. He believed himself to be a man who displayed "stiffe adherence" to "the rules of honour and conscience" and recorded with evident pride that royalist attempts to assassinate him in the early 1660s had been motivated by the fact that "it was knowne that I could not be corrupted."[90] Unlike those atheists who inhabited the court, Sidney understood and practiced "the religion of an Oath."[91]

Overshadowing this ethic of personal integrity, however, was an ethic of public responsibility. The primary reason venality and other forms of corruption were condemned by Sidney was not that they reflected a loss of self-control, but that they entailed the gross violation of a public trust.[92] They were public crimes, not private vices. By virtue of the social contract creating a government, magistrates were "entrusted" with power to act in the public interest.[93] It was consequently "the highest of all delinquencies" when a magistrate "deflect[ed] from the end of his Institution, and set up an interest of his own in opposition to it."[94] By violating his trust, he subverted the ends for which he had been empowered.

Sidney was not the only seventeenth-century Englishman to emphasize the importance of keeping covenants. The concept of trust was central to the legalistic ethos that had arisen around the institutions of Parliament and the common law; and at a very practical level, every man of even the slightest substance was dependent on the maintenance of a dense network of contractual relationships. When Hobbes made the keeping of covenants one of the laws of nature, or when Locke argued that "Truth and keeping of Faith belongs to Men, as Men, and not as Members of Society," they were in many respects simply providing philosophical restatements of a common-sense truth.[95] But they were also pointing to an important problem in the logic of the social contract. As John Dunn has explained in the context of an analysis of Locke's theory of trust, "When men confer power upon other men and establish a legitimate political society by doing so, they seek to provide against the inconveniences of the state of nature, the practical hazards posed by the general partiality of

[90] Sidney to Leicester, 22 May 1660, in Collins, 2:686–87; "Apology," 4. See also: Sidney to Leicester, 21 September 1660, in Blencowe, 222.

[91] *Discourses*, III:17, p. 326.

[92] On the distinction between arguments based on the fallen nature of man and arguments based on the problem of men consciously rejecting the public interest, see J.A.W. Gunn, *Politics and the Public Interest in the Seventeenth Century* (London: Routledge & Kegan Paul, 1969), 268.

[93] *Discourses*, III:22, p. 356.

[94] *Discourses*, III:14, p. 312.

[95] Hobbes, *Leviathan*, 201–8; *Two Treatises*, II:14.

mankind. But they also expose themselves more acutely to the potential partiality of the particular human beings who always in practice constitute the holders of governmental power." The social contract simultaneously removed the threats to freedom posed by men in general and created new threats by entrusting specific men with the powers of government. Thus it was that for Locke "trustworthiness, the capacity to commit oneself to fulfilling the legitimate expectations of others, is both the constitutive virtue of, and the key causal precondition for the existence of, any society."[96] Sidney shared this view: "truth, faithful dealing, [and] due performance of Contracts . . . are bonds of Union, and helps to good."[97] Without integrity and the keeping of covenants, society was not possible. The universality of this idea in seventeenth-century England points to the commonplace origin of many of Sidney's most radical arguments. It also highlights once again the extent to which the language of virtue and corruption was inseparable from the logic of rights, interests, laws, and contracts.[98]

The most egregious violations of the public trust vested in magistrates generally involved money. As befitted men of base motives, courtiers were constantly feeding at the public trough. The great bulk of their time and attention was devoted either to designing schemes for obtaining "monies to supply the vastness of" their expenses or contriving "how to spend with pleasure" their ill-gotten booty.[99] The problems posed by avarice were not limited to the diversion of public funds, however. Ministers in the government frequently treated their power as a commodity to be sold to the highest bidder, even when that meant adhering to the interests of a foreign government.[100] MPs were routinely given pensions and places of preferment in exchange for their support of Crown policies in Parliament.[101] Even the electorate was subject to corruption. As Sidney's friend and campaign manager William Penn complained in 1679, there was hardly an election in which Englishmen were not asked to "make a *Swop* of our *Birthright* (and that of our *Posterities* too) for a

[96] John Dunn, "The Concept of 'Trust' in the Politics of John Locke," in *Philosophy in History*, ed. Richard Rorty, J. B. Schneewind, and Quentin Skinner (Cambridge: Cambridge University Press, 1984), 296, 287.

[97] *Discourses*, III:19, p. 343. See also: III:19, p. 341.

[98] Failure to recognize the interconnections between these concepts vitiates most recent studies of early modern republicanism; for references, see note 3, above.

[99] *Maxims*, 7. See also: 5, 61; *Discourses*, III:39, p. 431.

[100] *Maxims*, 149; *Discourses*, II:25, p. 204; II:27, p. 211.

[101] *Discourses*, III:45, pp. 456–57.

Mess of Pottage, a *Feast* or a *Drinking-bout*."[102] To use a coin newly minted in the intellectual treasury of Restoration England, "sham" politics ruled the day.

The corrosive influence of money on English politics was a particular manifestation of a general problem: the misuse of publicly constituted power. The problem with money was not so much that wealth was in and of itself bad, but that the pursuit of wealth frequently led men to violate public trusts they had undertaken. Money tended to deflect magistrates and the institutions they governed from the ends for which they had been established. Similar problems existed in areas of life relatively unaffected by the ebb and flow of money. Sidney's views on the corruption of religion by the Anglican clergy—those "lustfull lawn-sleeved Parasites"[103]—were explored in Chapter 3, in the context of an analysis of his theory of freedom. Here I would like to examine two further areas to which Sidney devoted particular attention, the corruption of the law by lawyers and the corruption of the national defense by mercenary soldiers.

"Laws," Sidney argued, "are made to keep things in good order without the necessity of having recourse to force."[104] They provide a regular and regulated method by which men can be prevented from doing harm to one another. Such is "the nature of man," in fact, that he "cannot be without [them]"; "there is a vast distance between what men ought to be, and what they are."[105] To fulfill their regulatory function, to serve as "landmarks to warn and prevent dangers," it is absolutely essential that the laws be plain and clear, "that every man may understand them if he will."[106] But that is precisely what the English law of the seventeenth century was not: though once "plain and easy," it had become "so ambiguous, perplext and intricate, that 'tis hard to know when 'tis broken."[107] "The law itself is made a snare; and we, who should be protected, are destroyed by it. These mischiefs arise from the prevalence of a Party, favouring the private interest of one or a few men, to the prejudice of the Commonwealth."[108] The "Party" responsible for the corruption of the law was

---

[102] William Penn [Philanglus, pseud.], *Englands Great Interest In The Choice of this New Parliament* [1679?], 1.

[103] *Maxims*, 78.

[104] *Discourses*, III:13, p. 306. See also: III:36, p. 415; *Maxims*, 110.

[105] *Discourses*, III:1, pp. 253–54. See also: III:13, p. 306; III:40, p. 433.

[106] *Maxims*, 111. See also: *Discourses*, III:26, p. 370.

[107] *Maxims*, 97; *Discourses*, III:37, p.418. See also: *Maxims*, 98–99, 111–12, 122; *Discourses*, III:26, pp. 369–70.

[108] *Maxims*, 121. See also: 97, 100, 105, 128, 140; *Discourses*, III:26, p. 369; "Apology," 8; Algernon Sidney, "The Case of Algernone and Henry Sidney," British Library, Egerton MS. 1049, fol. 9, p. 21.

composed of the English monarch and his minions, the lawyers. By rendering the law a snare to every honest man, the lawyers were able to line their pockets with needless and excessive fees, and the monarch was able to exercise his power unimpeded.

Attacks on the lawyers and their law were commonplaces of seventeenth-century English life. The urge to "kill all the lawyers" was a result of the frustration, anger, and sense of helplessness that many Englishmen, particularly those in the lower ranks of society, experienced when they were caught up in the tangled web of the law.[109] In the 1640s the Levellers launched a massive attack on a system that tended "to nothing but the vexation of the people, and the enriching of Lawyers," and virtually all of Sidney's complaints, ranging from the sheer number of the laws to the fact that legal proceedings were still conducted in Latin and Norman French, can be found in their writings.[110] To be sure, the Levellers mounted their assault on the legal system under the banner of a war on monopolies, and not under the rubric of a theory of virtue and corruption. But both Sidney and the Levellers were outraged that a system of public law had been transformed into an instrument of private oppression. Sharing a deep distrust of sophistication and complexity, they both believed that the only way to ensure that the legal system was fair and free from abuse was to make it simple, comprised of a relatively small number of laws, and coherent with common sense.

A very different problem was posed by the corruption of the national defense by mercenary soldiers. As noted above, Sidney believed that "men are valiant and industrious, when they fight for themselves and their Country." This was because their private interests were interwoven with the public interest of national defense; having a stake in society, they were committed to preserving and protecting it. "Mercenary Souldiers," on the other hand, "always want Fidelity or Courage, and most commonly both. . . . These are the followers of Camps, who have neither faith nor piety, but prefer Gain before Right. They who expose their Blood to sale, look where they can make the best bargain, and never fail of pretences for following their interests." One of the great advantages of a commonwealth was that it was not reliant on such men. Instead, "the body of the People

---

[109] Shakespeare, *Henry VI, Pt. 2*, act 4, sc. 2, line 86.

[110] [William Walwyn], "A Helpe to the right understanding" (1645), 3, in *Tracts on Liberty in the Puritan Revolution*, ed. William Haller (New York: Columbia University Press, 1934), 3:[195]. The range of Leveller arguments is reflected in [John Lilburne], "Englands Birth-Right Justified" (1645), in *Tracts on Liberty*, 3:[258–307], and in the specific reforms embodied in the three "Agreements of the People."

is the publick defence, and every man is arm'd and disciplin'd."[111]
The importance of this distinction was captured in a pamphlet defending the conduct of the New Model Army in 1647: "We were not a meer mercinary Army, hired to serve any Arbitrary power of a State; but called forth and conjured, by the severall Declarations of Parliament, to the defence of our owne and the peoples just rights, and liberties." The men of the New Model Army were guided by the distinctive sense that they were citizen-soldiers, not mercenary warriors. They were not like those base soldiers on the Continent whose courage reflected the size of their pocketbooks. The moral distinctiveness of the New Model Army was the source of its pride, and the guarantee of its fidelity to the public good.[112]

The most famous argument against the use of mercenary soldiers in the literature of early modern political theory was to be found in *The Prince* and *The Discourses* of Niccolò Machiavelli. "Mercenary soldiers are useless," Machiavelli argued, for the simple reason that "they have no cause to stand firm when attacked, apart from the small pay which you give them."[113] The only sure defense of a nation was the self-interest of its own citizens. Though he was familiar with Machiavelli's writings, Sidney did not mention him in this context. One English republican who did was James Harrington: "Mercenaries, who make their arms their trade, must of all others be the most pernicious; for what can we expect less of such whose art is not otherwise so profitable, than that they should (as Machiavel shows) be 'breakers of their faith, given up to rapine, enemies of peace and government'?"[114] Like Machiavelli (and Sidney), Harrington believed that the only secure foundation for a nation's defense lay in its own citizens.

According to J.G.A. Pocock, Harrington's elaborate schemes for organizing the military capacities of seventeenth-century Englishmen were based on "the Machiavellian theory of the possession of arms as

---

[111] *Discourses*, II:23, p. 166; II:21, p. 157. See also: II:21, p. 156.

[112] "A Declaration, or, Representation from his Excellency, Sir Thomas Fairfax, And the Army under his command" (1647), 4, in *The Leveller Tracts 1647–1653*, ed. William Haller and Godfrey Davies (New York: Columbia University Press, 1944), 55. That the soldiers' understanding of their trust did not comport with that of either their commanders or Parliament, and that these divisions repeatedly split the nation between 1647 and 1659, need only prove that the absence of mercenary soldiers was a necessary, but not a sufficient, condition to the preservation of freedom.

[113] Niccolò Machiavelli, *The Discourses*, trans. Leslie Walker, ed. Bernard Crick (Harmondsworth: Penguin Books, 1970), 218. See also: *The Discourses*, 339–41; and Niccolò Machiavelli, *The Prince*, trans. George Bull (Harmondsworth: Penguin Books, 1981), 77–87.

[114] Harrington, "The Prerogative of Popular Government," in *Works*, 445.

necessary to political personality." Harrington's "dominant purpose is the release of personal virtue through civic participation."[115] Pocock argues his case quite powerfully, but his attempt to project an Aristotelian-Machiavellian theory of citizenship onto Harrington's writings fundamentally misconstrues the nature of the debate over mercenaries in seventeenth-century England. Part of the problem lies with the term "mercenary army" itself, for by it Harrington and Sidney meant virtually any form of professional army. And the political problem that was repeatedly posed by professional armies in seventeenth-century England was one of control: who was to direct them, and how were they to be confined to the public interest? How, that is, were publicly constituted forces to be prevented from becoming private armies? Professional armies represented huge and unstable concentrations of power, and, as the New Model Army had repeatedly proven during the Civil War, they could have a tremendous impact on the conduct of the nation's affairs.[116] Harrington once compared sovereignty to gunpowder, "a necessary but formidable creature" that should be "so collected as to be in full force and vigour, and yet so distributed that it is impossible you should be blown up by your own magazine."[117] He might have said the same thing about armies. Like Sidney, Harrington endorsed militias not because they permitted "the release of personal virtue," but because he could not imagine any other way of safely generating the military power necessary to defend England's liberty.[118] Mercenary armies were corrupt because they frequently violated their public trust; militias were virtuous because they rarely lost their integrity. The reason for this difference had nothing to do with "an ethos of civic excellence,"[119] and everything to do with the proper relationship between public and private interests.

Patriot-Heroes and the Limits of Virtue

What would men who embodied virtue and corruption look like? During his years of self-imposed exile in southern France, Sidney composed character sketches of Oliver Cromwell, Charles X of Swe-

[115] Pocock, *Machiavellian Moment*, 386, 390.

[116] The political problems posed by the New Model Army are superbly discussed in Lois Schwoerer, *"No Standing Armies!"* (Baltimore: Johns Hopkins University Press, 1974), 51–71.

[117] Harrington, "Oceana," in *Works*, 229.

[118] *Discourses*, II:30, p. 236; Harrington, "Oceana," in *Works*, 316; Harrington, "The Art of Lawgiving," in *Works*, 658, 683.

[119] Pocock, *Machiavellian Moment*, 390.

den, and Sir Henry Vane the younger.[120] Though only the sketch of Vane has survived,[121] scattered references throughout Sidney's writings permit the other two portraits to be partially reconstructed. With the help of all three, it is possible to put flesh on the theoretic bones of Sidney's account of virtue and corruption.

Oliver Cromwell was the complete anti-hero, the man who had betrayed England's freedom in order to play the part of the tyrant. Sidney's reflections on him were invariably rooted in dramatic personal experiences. In January 1649 Sidney objected to the proposed trial of Charles I, stating that "First, the King *could be tried* by noe court; secondly, that *noe man* could be tried by that court." Cromwell heatedly replied, "I tell you, wee will cut off his head with the crowne upon it," at which point Sidney, proclaiming that he would not have "any hand in this businesse," withdrew from the proceedings.[122] The dangerous potential Sidney saw in Cromwell's actions fully revealed itself four years later when, on 20 April 1653, Cromwell dissolved the Rump Parliament. Sidney was present that fateful day, and it was only after he had been threatened with force that he withdrew from the parliamentary chambers.[123] Sidney never fully recovered from this traumatic and deeply personal event. It shocked him in a way in which even the collective misdeeds of Charles I had not. The violent clash between Cromwell's will and power and the legal institutions of the nation jarred loose any lingering hopes Sidney might have had concerning Cromwell's devotion to the public interest. Without the slightest hint of irony or exaggeration, Sidney likened Cromwell to Caesar: his ambition had transformed him into "a tyrant, and a violent one" at that.[124]

[120] On 12 October 1701, the duke of Shrewsbury recorded in his journal that "My Lord Bernard lent me a MS. of Algernon Sidney's, which he recovered at Montpelier; it is writ in Latin, and is called 'Icon Cromwellij, Icon Caroli Gustavi, Sueciae Regis, & Icon Henrici Vanij Junioris.' It is the character of three persons" (HMC, *Report on the Manuscripts of the Duke of Buccleuch & Queensbury, Vol. II, Part 2* [London: HMSO, 1903], 756).

[121] A translation of the sketch of Vane, in an unknown hand, is deposited among the Cowper manuscripts at the Hertfordshire Record Office, D/EP F45. It has been printed as "Appendix F: The Character of Sir Henry Vane by Algernon Sidney," in Violet A. Rowe, *Sir Henry Vane the Younger* (London: Athlone Press, 1970), 275–83. All references are to this printed version.

[122] Sidney to Leicester, 12 October 1660, in Blencowe, 237.

[123] "Journal of the Earl of Leicester, December 31, 1646–September 8, 1661," in *De L'Isle*, 6:615.

[124] Algernon Sidney, "The Trial of Colonel Algernon Sidney," in *A Complete Collection of State Trials*, ed. T. B. Howell (London: 1816), 9:866. See also: Sidney to Leicester, 28 July 1660, in Blencowe, 189–90; Algernon Sidney, Bibliotheque Nationale, Fr. MS.

In Charles X of Sweden, Sidney found a more balanced mixture of virtue and corruption. As he confessed to his father following Charles X's death in early 1660, "the king of *Sweden* had such qualities, as I did love and admire, though I knew his errors also." The quality Sidney most admired in Charles X was his capacity for action: "I think never any prince had so many and potent enemies as he, that did so well defend himself against them, with a small strength; his greatest was, in his own industry, wit, and courage."[125] Oliver Cromwell had, of course, also been a great man of action, as he had repeatedly proven at the head of the New Model Army. What distinguished Charles X was that he used his strength to advance the public good, not his own power. Even during "the time of his sickness and the certain approaches of death," Sidney reported, "he would not so much as give himself the ease of a bed in the violence of his fever, saying he did not live or reigne for himself, but for his people . . . nothing could make him omitte the duty which he thought he owed to his people."[126] Charles X's virtue was not untarnished, however, for he was incapable of governing his passions. "[He] is soe violently transported with ambition and choller upon every slight occasion, that he doth frequently omitte things that are most for his advantages, and cast himself into thoes extremityes, which would have ruined him, if he had not bin often assisted by his friends, beyond what could in reason be expected."[127] Charles X's virtue could not be gainsaid, but his corruption made him a permanent threat to Sweden's public interest. He provided a perfect example of the tensions within the institution of monarchy that led Sidney to advocate a government of laws and not men.

In Sir Henry Vane the younger, by contrast, virtue was not alloyed with corruption, but was cast in its purest form. There was "not another man equal to him in vertue, prudence, courage, industry, reputation and godliness" in all of England.[128] Of Vane's self-control, Sidney observed that he "always preserved the same steady resolution

---

23,254, fols. 99–100; Sidney, "Character of Vane," 279; *Maxims*, 70; *Discourses*, III:9, p. 291; III:12, p. 312.

[125] Sidney to Leicester, 14 July 1660, in Collins, 2:694; Sidney to Leicester, 22 February 1660, in Collins, 2:685.

[126] Sidney to Whitelocke, 4 March 1660, in Blencowe, 178–79. See also: *Discourses*, III:31, p. 400.

[127] Sidney to Leicester, 13 September 1659, in Blencowe, 166–67. See also: Sidney to Whitelocke, 13 November 1659, in Blencowe, 172.

[128] *Maxims*, 188. "Nor can it be imagined our King had any other design when he cut of Vane's head, than to destroy, as in its root, all vertue, wisdom and godliness, since those, who were eminent in any of those qualitys, look'd on him as their Master, and seem'd to have learn't all they knew or practiced by his precepts or example" (ibid.).

of mind, without being ever transported with joy or ruffled and disturbed with Anger; and fearless and unmov'd in danger, so that by obeying reason, he at once seem'd to renounce all kind of unbecoming passions and affections: nay, such was his Magnanimity, that if the frame of the whole world had been dissolv'd and gon to rack about his ears, he would have remained undaunted in the midst of its ruins." Of Vane's martial valor, Sidney recorded: "He was an absolute Master of the Naval affairs, he invented and perfected that kind of vessel, they call, a Frigat, which at this time is so famous all over the world. He zealously promoted the peace with Holland, and helpt to carry on vigorously whatever War was begun by any other Nation. His industry and prudence did not less contribute to the obtaining of Victories than the Valor of the Generals." And of Vane's integrity, Sidney reported that he was "of an inviolable Fidelity; One whom no body ever repented trusting with the most important affairs." In short, "nothing could have devided him from the public Service, except Death."[129]

Death it was that divided Vane from the public service, for in 1662 he was executed by the Crown for his activities during the Civil War. Sidney's sketch of Vane's character, written sometime after 1662, was less an exercise in objective history than an effort at republican mythmaking. The more virtuous Vane was, the more corrupt was the regime that had condemned him.[130] Sidney was not the only republican to engage in hagiography, and the contrast between his sketch of Vane and the sketch drawn by Edmund Ludlow, a fellow republican exile, is instructive. According to Ludlow, Vane was "that renowned patriot . . . who had bin the cheife steeresman of publique affaires during the late wars, and whom the Lord owned as an emynent instrument in his worke." By his execution, Vane had been made a "choyce martyr of Christ."[131] Ludlow's religious interpretation of Vane's life was in keeping with Vane's self-understanding.[132] But the language of religious enthusiasm was entirely absent from Sidney's sketch. Though conscious of Vane's "godliness," Sidney lauded him

---

[129] Sidney, "Character of Vane," 278, 279, 278, 282.

[130] "But how many amongst us have fallen for no other crimes than wisdom valour and fidelity to God & their Countrey? Ah noble Vane, how ample a Testimony hast thou born to this truth, thy condemnation was thy Glory, thy death gave thee a famous victory and a never perishing Crown" (*Maxims*, 42).

[131] Edmund Ludlow, *A Voyce From The Watch Tower*, ed. A. B. Worden, Camden Fourth Series, Vol. 21 (London: Royal Historical Society, 1978), 310, 313. See also: Edmund Ludlow, "A Voyce From The Watch Tower," Bodleian Library, MS. Eng. Hist. C487, fol. 1063.

[132] Sir Henry Vane the younger, "The last sermon My Dearest Father preached at his own house," 1660, Victoria and Albert Museum, Forster MS. 48.D.41, fol. 14.

as a patriot-hero, and not as a saint. His virtue was his unswerving devotion to "the good of his Country."[133]

Sir Henry Vane the younger was one of the leading lights of the Civil War and Interregnum, but Sidney did not restrict the scope of his theory of virtue to great luminaries. The men with whom Sidney's career was most closely associated—Slingsby Bethel, Benjamin Furly, John Hampden the younger, Edmund Ludlow, William Penn, Henry Savile, Sir Henry Vane the younger, and John Wildman—were largely of the second and third tiers of the English social and political hierarchy. In the *Discourses*, Sidney praised the superior virtue of "the *Cliftons, Hampdens, Courtneys, Pelhams, St. Johns, Baintons, Wilbrahams, Hungerfords*, and many others."[134] While the names of Hampden and St. John have survived in English political memory, the others have been lost. The relative obscurity of the men whom Sidney worked with and praised only serves to emphasize the all-embracing scope of his theory.

Once the global reach of Sidney's theory of virtue is recognized, however, a seemingly intractable problem emerges. How is virtue to be cultivated in a republic? Traditionally, virtue was thought to be the product of noble birth and a rigorous education. As noted in Chapter 2, monarchy was frequently justified on the grounds that in the person of the monarch it combined the highest possible birth with the best possible moral and political education. Sidney's whole theory was built on the rejection of the logic of birth; as he crisply stated his position, "Virtues are not entail'd."[135] At the same time, apart from the "precept and example" of a good magistrate, he made no provision for the education of republican citizens to a life of virtue.[136] Though he praised the "discipline" of Roman soldiers, he did not suggest that England be organized like an army, as James Harrington had done.[137] And he said nothing about those instruments designed to create Machiavellian virtue, a great legislator and a civic religion.[138]

Sidney proclaimed the need for virtue, yet provided no specific method for cultivating it. Like many early modern scientists, he appears to have believed that under the correct conditions spontaneous generation was possible. To that extent, Sidney's theory of virtue is radically incomplete and intellectually unsatisfying. But to conclude on that note would be misleading, for it implies that Sidney's chief

---

[133] Sidney, "Character of Vane," 281.

[134] *Discourses*, III:28, p. 385.

[135] *Discourses*, III:26, p. 373. See also: *Maxims*, 24–25.

[136] *Discourses*, III:19, p. 342.

[137] See, for example, *Discourses*, II:28, pp. 217–21.

[138] Machiavelli, *Discourses*, 105, 132, 139–43, 146–52.

failing was his inability to provide a "complete" theory of virtue. Within the confines of his own writings, that would have been an illusory goal. The different accounts of virtue and corruption contained within his theory are logically distinct and frequently at odds with each other. Self-control requires the suppression of nature, while martial valor requires that nature be allowed to flourish; and neither entails the virtue of integrity. More important, Sidney believed that the concepts of virtue and corruption are themselves radically incomplete. As he repeatedly argued, they are both individually and collectively dependent on the concepts of rights, interests, laws, and contracts.

Indeed, Sidney's fusion of the language of virtue with the logic of rights and interests may have made it seem less urgent to provide a method for inculcating virtue. Unlike virtue, interests arise spontaneously and need not be cultivated. This fusion also made it possible to envision the creation of political mechanisms capable of coping with and compensating for the predictable failure of individual virtue. Thus it was that Sidney turned his attention to questions of constitutional design.

FIVE

CONSTITUTIONALISM AND REVOLUTION

> Men can no otherwise be engaged to take care of the
> Publick, than by having such a part in it, as Absolute
> Monarchy dos not allow; for they can neither obtain the
> Good for themselves, Posterity and Friends, that they
> desire, nor prevent the Mischiefs they fear, which are the
> principal Arguments that perswade men to expose
> themselves to labours or dangers.
> *(Algernon Sidney)*[1]

MAN IS naturally free," and consequently "a general consent
. . . is the ground of all just Governments."[2] These two
claims provided the moral foundation for Sidney's theory
of government. But what political superstructure corresponded to
that foundation? To what form of government would free men consent?

Sidney was adamant that there were no natural or universally valid
forms of government. It simply was not true that "God and Nature
have put us into a way from which we are not to swerve."[3] At the same
time, the differences between the various forms of government visible throughout the world were not arbitrary. As the previous two
chapters have revealed, Sidney believed that for a government to receive the consent of a free people it had to meet certain minimum
requirements: it had to be limited in its powers, governing by reason
and law and not by the arbitrary will of man; it had to be capable of
articulating and advancing the public interest; it had to be responsive
to the will of the people; and it had to address the complex problems
caused by human corruption.

So stringent were these requirements that only one form of government had ever proven capable of meeting them: a "regular mixed
Government." Indeed, "there never was a good Government in the
world" that was not mixed.[4] Sidney's praise of mixed government has

---

[1] *Discourses*, II:21, p. 155.

[2] *Discourses*, I:2, p. 5; I:10, p. 23.

[3] *Discourses*, I:1, p. 4. See also: II:20, p. 151; *Maxims*, 32; Algernon Sidney, *The Very
Copy of a Paper Delivered to the Sheriffs* (London: 1683), 2.

[4] *Discourses*, II:20, p. 153; II:16, p. 130. See also: III:21, p. 352; III:43, p. 448.

led previous interpreters to a wide range of conclusions: that he advocated a classical or Machiavellian form of mixed republic;[5] that he advocated a mixed monarchy of the sort that arose in England after the Glorious Revolution of 1688;[6] or that he advocated a constitutional monarchy of the kind that emerged in England during the nineteenth century.[7] Common to all three of these interpretations is the belief that by mixed government Sidney meant a system of rule based either on a mixture of the three principal forms of government (monarchy, aristocracy, and democracy) or on a balance of the three principal estates of the realm (King, Lords, and Commons). The different conclusions they reach are largely a consequence of the way in which they characterize Sidney's fine-tuning of that mixture or balance.

That there should be confusion over Sidney's theory of a "regular mixed Government" is understandable. The term "mixed government" was used to indicate a wide range of ideas and values during the seventeenth century, and its precise meaning in any given text can often prove elusive.[8] This is particularly true of Sidney's *Discourses Concerning Government*, whose argument often resembles a sunken ship: though a few promontories are visible above the surface, the great hulk remains submerged in the depths.

The central purpose of this chapter is to salvage Sidney's concept of a "regular mixed Government." Once it is brought to the surface, it will be clear that the attempt to describe Sidney's theory of government in terms of a mixture of forms or a balance of estates is mis-

[5] Zera Fink, *The Classical Republicans* (Evanston: Northwestern University Press, 1945), chap. 6; Felix Raab, *The English Face of Machiavelli* (London: Routledge & Kegan Paul, 1964), 221; Blair Worden, "Classical Republicanism and the Puritan Revolution," in *History and Imagination: Essays in Honour of H. R. Trevor-Roper*, ed. Hugh Lloyd-Jones, Valerie Pearl, and Blair Worden (London: Duckworth, 1981), 182–88.

[6] Isaac Kramnick, *Bolingbroke and His Circle* (Cambridge, MA: Harvard University Press, 1968), 128, 135, 148, 180; James Conniff, "Reason and History in Early Whig Thought: The Case of Algernon Sidney," *Journal of the History of Ideas* 43 (July–September 1982): 405, 412–13; B. Behrens, "The Whig Theory of the Constitution in the Reign of Charles II," *Cambridge Historical Journal* 7 (1941): 50–55.

[7] Alexander Charles Ewald, *The Life and Times of the Hon. Algernoon Sydney* (London: Tinsley Brothers, 1873), 1:256–67, 2:329–30; George Sabine, *A History of Political Theory* (New York: Henry Holt and Company, 1937), 514.

[8] Transformations in the seventeenth-century concept of mixed government are explored in the following: Corinne Comstock Weston, "The Theory of Mixed Monarchy Under Charles I and After," *English Historical Review* 75 (July 1960): 426–43; Corinne Comstock Weston, *English Constitutional Theory and the House of Lords 1556–1832* (New York: Columbia University Press, 1965), 1–121; W. B. Gwyn, *The Meaning of the Separation of Powers*, Tulane Studies in Political Science, Vol. 9 (New Orleans: Tulane University Press, 1965), 11–81; M.J.C. Vile, *Constitutionalism and the Separation of Powers* (Oxford: The Clarendon Press, 1967), 21–75.

taken. The keel of Sidney's ship of state was provided by the concept of popular sovereignty. As noted before, Sidney's purpose in writing the *Discourses* was to refute the patriarchal absolutism of Sir Robert Filmer. According to Filmer, "we do but flatter ourselves, if we hope ever to be governed without an arbitrary power. No: we mistake; the question is not, whether there shall be an arbitrary power; but the only point is, who shall have that arbitrary power, whether one man or many?"[9] Once properly posed, Filmer argued, this question answered itself: "The supreme power being an indivisible beam of majesty, [it] cannot be divided among, or settled upon a multitude. God would have it fixed in one person."[10] It is against this backdrop that Sidney's constitutional theory must be viewed. In place of a sovereign monarch, Sidney posited the sovereignty of the people; in place of a government that was absolute, unlimited, and arbitrary, he posited the need for a government whose powers were limited, divided, and balanced; in place of a timeless pattern of rule, he posited the right to transform governments by means of popular revolution.

The starting point for Sidney's constitutional theory was the "Gothic Polity," a form of government that held sway in England from the fall of Rome until the sixteenth century. Though Sidney did not adhere to James Harrington's influential description of the Gothic polity, he did accept one of Harrington's key claims: the problems facing seventeenth-century Englishmen could be traced to the collapse of the feudal balance between the king and the nobility. Dramatic historical changes had created a situation in which "new Constitutions" were needed "to repair the breaches made upon the old."[11] Chief among Sidney's proposals was the introduction of a sharp separation between the act of legislation and the enforcement of the law, based on the uniquely representative character of Parliament. Significantly, Sidney viewed England's need for "new Constitutions" in an essentially conservative light. His aim was to eliminate a bad government, not create a new future. Sidney's argument for revolution was far closer to ancient justifications for tyrannicide than it was to modern theories of revolutionary transformation.

The Eclipse of Feudalism

Two different accounts of the political system of feudal England can be found in Sidney's political writings.[12] According to one account,

---

[9] *Patriarcha*, 277.

[10] *Patriarcha*, 189.

[11] *Discourses*, III:37, p. 420.

[12] Sidney did not use the term "feudal England"; but he described a pattern of gov-

England was governed by a representative parliament and elected magistrates; according to the other, it was governed by "boisterous fighting Kings" held in check by "an ancient powerfull virtuous warlike Nobility."[13] Though analytically distinct and frequently contradictory, these two accounts were blended by Sidney in an attempt to explain the origin of the problems and the range of possibilities facing seventeenth-century Englishmen. It was the eclipse of feudalism that made republicanism necessary.

The dominant account of feudal England in Sidney's writings centered on the claim that "the English Nation has always bin governed by it self or its Representatives."[14] According to Sidney's theory of consent, historical arguments were ultimately irrelevant to the moral and political claims of free men.

> But if that Liberty in which God created man, can receive any strength from continuance, and the rights of Englishmen can be render'd more unquestionable by prescription, I say that the Nations whose rights we inherit, have ever enjoy'd the Liberties we claim, and always exercised them in governing themselves popularly, or by such Representatives as have bin instituted by themselves, from the time they were first known in the world.[15]

Sidney adopted this analytically extravagant strategy in order to counter Filmer's assertion that "the King is the sole immediate author, corrector and moderator" of both statute and common laws and that consequently Parliament originated in the "favour and grace" of England's feudal monarchs.[16] Against Filmer's patriarchal absolutism, Sidney posited the historical sovereignty of the English people.

England "lay long concealed under obscure barbarity, and we know nothing of the first Inhabitants, but what is involved in fables that leave us still in the dark."[17] But from the histories of Caesar and Tacitus it was possible to determine that the Germanic tribes that settled England "lived free under such Magistrates as they chose, regu-

---

ernment that held sway roughly from the time of the Anglo-Saxons to the rise of the Tudor dynasty in the late fifteenth century, and hence the term does not seem inappropriate.

[13] *Maxims*, 56–57.

[14] *Discourses*, III:28, p. 379.

[15] *Discourses*, III:28, p. 380. "Our Ancestors were born free, and, as the best provision they could make for us, they left us that Liberty intire, with the best Laws they could devise to defend it" (III:8, p. 288). See also: III:25, p. 369; III:44, p. 453.

[16] *Patriarcha*, 113, 118. Filmer's historical argument is more fully developed in "The Freeholder's Grand Inquest," but there is no evidence that Sidney was familiar with that work.

[17] *Discourses*, III:25, p. 363. See also: III:28, p. 380.

lated by such Laws as they made, and retained the principal powers of the Government in their general or particular Councils. Their Kings and Princes had no other power than was conferred upon them by these Assemblies."[18] When the Saxons came into England, they "retain'd to themselves the same rights."[19] "Sometimes meeting personally in the Micklegemots, sometimes by their Delegates in the Wittenagemots . . . they ordered all things according to their own pleasure."[20] Even the Norman Conquest failed to disrupt the sovereign power of the English people. "Tho the name of Conqueror be odiously given to *William* the *Norman*, he had the same Title to the Crown with his Predecessors, *In magna exultatione a Clero & Populo susceptus, & ab omnibus Rex acclamatus.*" William became king of England not by right of conquest, but by virtue of the election of the people. Like the great Saxon monarchs who had preceded him, "he accepted the Crown upon the conditions offer'd."[21]

On the basis of this historical analysis, Sidney claimed that feudal England had always been governed by representative parliaments and elected kings. The touchstone of his argument, as it had been for Englishmen of almost every stripe since the thirteenth century, was Magna Charta. According to Filmer, Magna Charta had been "granted the rather to flatter the nobility and the people."[22] It created rights that had not previously existed, and, Filmer seemed to imply, it could be withdrawn or revoked at the drop of a hat.[23] To this argument Sidney retorted that Magna Charta was not written in "the language of a Lord treating with such as enjoy'd their liberties by his favour, but with those whom he acknowledged to be the Judges of his performing what had bin stipulated." "*Magna Charta* could give noth-

---

[18] *Discourses*, III:28, p. 381. "The great matters among the *Germans* were transacted *omnium consensu. De minoribus consultant Principes; de majoribus omnes*" (II:5, p. 79). See also: II:30, p. 232; III:28, p. 369. The quotation is from Tacitus, *Germania* (Loeb Classical Library, 1970), par. 11. References to the freedom-loving Goths were a staple of seventeenth-century English radical literature; a wealth of examples can be found in Samuel Kliger, *The Goths in England* (Cambridge, MA: Harvard University Press, 1952), esp. 112–209.

[19] *Discourses*, III:10, p. 296.

[20] *Discourses*, III:28, p. 383. See also: II:5, p. 79; III:25, p. 363; III:28, pp. 382–84, 386–89; III:38, pp. 422–23.

[21] *Discourses*, II:5, p. 82; III:17, pp. 327. See also: III:10, p. 297–98; III:26, p. 375; *Maxims*, 12.

[22] *Patriarcha*, 117.

[23] Filmer never explicitly stated this position, but it follows logically from his theory of patriarchal absolutism. Most royalists would have rejected it. Though unwilling to acknowledge the existence of rights and liberties beyond the four corners of Magna Charta, they accepted it as inviolable. See, for example: *The Nations Interest* (London: 1680), 21; *A Seasonable Address to both Houses* (London: 1681), 10.

ing to the People, who in themselves had all; and only reduced into a small Volume the Rights which the Nation was resolved to maintain; brought the King to confess, they were perpetually inherent, and time out of mind enjoyed, and to swear that he would no way violate them."[24] Magna Charta expressed the nation's sovereign power to define itself and to create and limit the powers of its magistrates. It embodied principles subsequently proclaimed by England's two great feudal jurists, Bracton and Fortescue: that the king rules by law and that the king can change no law.[25] " 'Tis not . . . the King that makes the Law, but the Law that makes the King."[26] And, Sidney added parenthetically, it was Parliament, the representative assembly of the people, that made the law.[27]

Sidney's account of the government of feudal England was idiosyncratic and based on a highly selective reading of the sources available to him. Had it been published during his lifetime, it would have been subject to heated dispute. The unique contours of Sidney's analysis can be highlighted by comparing it to the common-law theory of the ancient constitution and the Leveller theory of the Norman Yoke. Like the common lawyers, Sidney proclaimed the rights of Englishmen to be immemorial, dating from time out of mind; and like the common lawyers, Sidney was committed to the belief that the Norman Conquest had not disrupted those rights. The words of the lawyer Thomas Hedley—"I do not take Magna Charta to be a new grant or statute, but a restoring or confirming of the ancient laws and liberties of the kingdom"—could easily have come from the *Discourses*.[28] But Sidney and the common lawyers parted company over the nature and status of those rights. To men like Sir Edward Coke, the rights and liberties embodied in Magna Charta were fundamental just because they were immemorial. They had received the sanction of time, and they contained the wisdom of the ages.[29] To Sidney, on the other hand, the rights and liberties embodied in Magna Charta were fundamental just because they had been "made according to the will of

[24] *Discourses*, III:17, p. 325; III:28, p. 391. See also: III:8, p. 283; III:14, p. 311; III:15, p. 315; III:26, p. 371; III:27, p. 376; III:45, p. 455.

[25] *Discourses*, III:8, p. 284; III:9, p. 290; III:14, p. 310; III:15, p. 315; III:26, pp. 371–74.

[26] *Discourses*, III:14, p. 310.

[27] "We have had no King since *William* the First more hardy than *Henry* the *8th*, and yet he so intirely acknowledged the power of making, changing and repealing Laws to be in the Parliament, as never to attempt any extraordinary thing otherwise than by their Authority" (*Discourses*, III:26, p. 375). See also: III:15, p. 315.

[28] Quoted in J. P. Sommerville, *Politics and Ideology in England 1603–1640* (London: Longman, 1986), 98.

[29] J.G.A. Pocock, *The Ancient Constitution and the Feudal Law* (Cambridge: Cambridge University Press, 1957), 30–55; Sommerville, *Politics and Ideology*, 86–111.

men."[30] Consent, and not custom, was the cornerstone of his thought. Thus, while the common lawyers deemed it important to prove that the Norman Conquest had not broken the delicate threads of tradition that formed the warp and weft of the common law, Sidney thought it vital to prove that William's power derived from the consent of the people. The chasm separating these two perspectives is virtually unbridgeable.

In many respects Sidney's historical analysis was closer to that of the Levellers. Like Sidney, the Levellers argued that all legitimate governments originate in the consent of the governed; and like Sidney, they believed that the freedom of the English people could be documented by the institutions and practices of the Anglo-Saxons. But in sharp contrast to Sidney, the Levellers argued that that freedom had been destroyed by the Norman Conquest. In the words of Richard Overton, "the History of our Fore-fathers since they were Conquered by the *Normans*, doth manifest that this Nation hath been held in bondage all along ever since."[31] This belief had profound consequences for the Levellers' view of Magna Charta. As William Walwyn explained, "Magna Charta . . . is but a part of the peoples rights and liberties, being no more but what with much striving and fighting, was by the blood of our Ancestors, wrestled out of the pawes of those Kings, who by force had conquered the Nation, changed the lawes, and by strong hand held them in bondage." Far from being an expression of the sovereign power of the English people, Magna Charta was "but a beggerly thing, containing many markes of intollerable bondage."[32]

At stake in the controversy over the Norman Conquest was an explanation for the paucity of political rights in seventeenth-century England. The Levellers adopted the explosive view that England's bondage could be traced to a foreign invasion that had taken place in the year 1066 and that the only way Englishmen could recover the full measure of their liberty was to eradicate every last vestige of the

[30] *Discourses*, III:45, p. 455. "Our Laws were not sent from Heaven, but made by our Ancestors according to the light they had, and their present occasions. We inherit the same right from them, and, as we may without vanity say that we know a little more than they did, if we find our selves prejudic'd by any Law that they made, we may repeal it" (III:25, p. 368). See also: III:18, p. 331; III:25, p. 364; III:28, pp. 380–82.

[31] Richard Overton, "A Remonstrance of Many Thousand Citizens" (1646), 4 (in *Tracts on Liberty in the Puritan Revolution*, ed. William Haller [New York: Columbia University Press, 1934], 3:[354]). Though his analysis is problematic, a wealth of examples of how the myth of the Norman Yoke was used can be found in Christopher Hill, "The Norman Yoke," in *Puritanism and Revolution* (London: Secker & Warburg, 1958), 50–122.

[32] William Walwyn, "Englands Lamentable Slaverie" (1645), 3–4 (in Haller, *Tracts on Liberty*, 3:[313–14]); Overton, "Remonstrance," 15 (in Haller, *Tracts on Liberty*, 3:[365]).

Norman Yoke. For Sidney, on the other hand, the cause of England's bondage was not external, but internal: the breakdown of the balance of power between the king and nobility. In making this argument he drew on a second and very different account of the government of feudal England.

Sidney first described the feudal balance between the king and nobility in the *Court Maxims*:

> A Powerfull gallant Nobility was very useful in those old fashioned Monarchies which were in most parts of Europe till within these last hundred years. Our boisterous fighting Kings of the Plantagenet Race were content with a limited power att home; they endeavour'd to increase the power of the nation by foreign conquests. For such designs it was necessary to have a Nobility great in power & credit, full of virtue and gallantry & exercised in arms that the people might follow them. . . . [If any of the kings] did comitt any irregularities att home they were in danger to be questioned, as Edward and Richard the 2nd, Or if any of their servants did any thing contrary to law either to serve them or make their own fortunes they were not able to protect them from justice, as appears by the Spencers, Tresilian and others; And if any extraordinary burden was laid upon the people as Monopolies or the like the Nobility were the first that exclaimed, talked of laws priviledges and such unpleasing words; If greavances were not redres'd they were presently in Arms and the people looking on them as protectors followed them in all their enterprizes.[33]

When he came to write the *Discourses*, Sidney adopted a less exuberant tone, and in the process he sharpened the focus of his argument:

> [Our ancestors] knew that the Kings of several Nations had bin kept within the limits of the Law, by the virtue and power of a great and brave Nobility; and that no other way of supporting a mix'd Monarchy had ever bin known in the world, than by putting the balance into the hands of those who had the greatest interest in Nations, and who by birth and estate enjoy'd greater advantages than Kings could confer upon them for rewards of betraying their Country.[34]

This was the "Gothic polity," a form of government that held sway throughout Europe from the fall of Rome until the sixteenth century.[35]

[33] *Maxims*, 56–57.

[34] *Discourses*, III:37, p. 419.

[35] *Discourses*, III:8, p. 286; III:21, p. 352. See also: II:16, p. 131. "In all the legal Kingdoms of the North, the strength of the Government has always bin placed in the Nobility; and no better defence has bin found against the encroachments of ill Kings, than by setting up an Order of men, who by holding large Territories, and having

The Gothic polity was, as Sidney acknowledged, a form of mixed government; it rested on a balance between the two leading estates of the realm. During Sidney's lifetime the theory of mixed government enjoyed a renaissance in English political thought. Ironically, it was Charles I who inaugurated this new interest, for it was he who proclaimed in his "Answer to the Nineteen Propositions" that England's government was mixed:

> There being three kinds of Government among Men, Absolute Monarchy, Aristocracy, and Democracy: and all these having their particular Conveniences and Inconveniences. The Experience and Wisdom of your Ancestors, hath so moulded this out of a Mixture of these, as to give to this Kingdom (as far as humane Prudence can provide) the Conveniences of all three, without the Inconveniences of any one, as long as the Balance hangs even between the three Estates, and they run jointly on in their proper Chanel, (begetting Verdure and Fertility in the Meadows on both sides) and the overflowing of either on either side, raise no Deluge or Inundation.[36]

By drawing on the theory of mixed government, Charles I was able to transpose the traditional English doctrine of "balance" into a new key, one whose harmony rested not on a counterpoise of the king's prerogatives and the subjects' liberties, but on a skillful combination of monarchy, aristocracy, and democracy. He was able to do this because he found a perfect parallel to the three primitive forms of government in the three estates of the realm, the King, Lords, and Commons.[37] His promise was that if each estate confined itself to its appointed task then England's government would be regular and limited; his threat was that if they failed to do so all would "end in a dark equal Chaos of Confusion."[38]

Charles I's endorsement of the theory of mixed government was ironic, for almost immediately his argument was "employed by those who for one reason or another sought to limit the power" of the

---

great numbers of Tenants and Dependents, might be able to restrain the exorbitances, that either the Kings or the Commons might run into" (III:28, p. 384). Sidney's reference to the need to restrain the Commons is atypical; as he repeatedly argued, the central purpose of the feudal nobility was to restrain the king.

[36] Charles I, "His Majesty's Answer to the Nineteen Propositions of both Houses of Parliament," 18 June 1642, reprinted in *Historical Collections of Private Passages of State*, ed. J. Rushworth (London: 1659–1701), 5:729.

[37] Only with the appearance of the "Answer" did it become common to refer to the king as one of the estates of the realm; previously, "the term three estates had been used officially and popularly to designate the lords spiritual, the lords temporal, and the commons" (Weston, "Theory of Mixed Monarchy," 431).

[38] Charles I, "Answer to the Nineteen Propositions," in Rushworth, *Historical Collections*, 5:730.

Stuarts.[39] Critics of royal policy frequently invoked the concept of a "Balance . . . between the three Estates" when they felt that the king had exceeded his "proper Chanel." Thus, for example, the moderate parliamentarian Philip Hunton argued in 1643 that the king ought to be deprived of his power to veto legislation on the grounds that it threatened the "compounded and mixed nature" of the constitution; and almost forty years later an anonymous Whig pamphleteer protested the corruption of the House of Commons by placemen and pensioners as an attempt to overthrow England's "mix'd or *Gothick*" form of government.[40] For moderate critics of the Stuarts, the theory of mixed government provided an ideal platform for reform. It was flexible enough to encompass a wide range of changes, yet conservative enough to leave undisturbed the basic institutions of the English government.

Algernon Sidney adopted a very different and much more radical strategy toward the absolutist pretensions of the Stuarts. First, he rejected the notion that each of the three estates of the realm was "naturally" a partner in the government. According to Sidney, "all Nations who have acted freely, have some way or other endeavoured to supply the defects, or restrain the vices of their supreme Magistrates."[41] The primary method adopted to achieve this end has been "dividing and balancing the powers of . . . Government."[42] In the Gothic polity, for example, this technique was used twice: the nobility as a whole provided a check or balance to the power of the king; and within the nobility, each nobleman checked or balanced the defects and vices of the others.[43] The role of the estates in the government of feudal England was instrumental and reflected the right of each nation to allocate the powers of government as it saw fit.[44]

Sidney's second argument built on this claim. While he agreed that England had once had a mixed government, he argued that it was no longer possible. As many commentators have noted, Sidney's nostalgia for the Gothic polity is palpable;[45] without a trace of skepticism

---

[39] Weston, *English Constitutional Theory*, 29.

[40] [Philip Hunton], *A Treatise of Monarchie* (London: 1643), 39; C.B., *An Address to the Honourable City of London* (London: 1681), 4.

[41] *Discourses*, II:30, p. 240. See also: II:11, p. 109.

[42] *Discourses*, III:43, p. 447.

[43] *Discourses*, II:25, p. 200; II:30, p. 241; III:27, pp. 378–79; III:37, pp. 419–20; III:40, pp. 433–34.

[44] "If every People may govern, or constitute and chuse one or more Governors, they may divide the Powers between several men, or ranks of men, allotting to everyone so much as they please, or retaining so much as they think fit" (*Discourses*, II:32, p. 248). See also: II:30, pp. 233–35; III:21, p. 352; III:27, p. 378.

[45] Conniff, "Reason and History," 411–14; Caroline Robbins, *The Eighteenth-Century*

he reported that "the ancient nobility did ever endeavour to preserve the peoples liberties & make them happy." But, he lamented, "these new ones endeavour as much to Impoverish weaken oppresse and destroy them."[46]

What had happened to England's "ancient powerfull virtuous war-like Nobility"? According to Sidney, they had been decimated by a process that began with the death of Henry V (1387–1422).[47] As that king's successors realized, the only way to increase their own power and independence was to decrease those of the nobility. In the *Court Maxims* Sidney focused on the techniques that had been used to corrupt the nobility. Operating on the premise that "all desire to advance their persons and fortunes," England's monarchs devised a system of carrots and sticks centered on the court. As a result, "everyone endeavours to serve the king to the utmost that he may be advanced." Simultaneously, a court culture was fostered in which "those are looked upon as the Gallantest men who spend most on house keeping cloth[e]s liveries Coaches and profuse gameing." Finally, those few hardy members of the ancient nobility who had resisted the temptations of the Court were rendered irrelevant by the creation of an entirely new nobility based on royal patents. As the courtier Philalethos cynically remarked in the *Court Maxims*, "we need not stroke off the highest ears of Corn, we can make others spring out of Dung so, as soon to overtop them."[48]

In the *Discourses* Sidney shifted his attention from corruption to the demise of the feudal system of dependent tenures. The power of the ancient nobility had rested on their private armies; and those armies, in turn, had been created out of the feudal dependents. But at some point after the death of Henry V—Sidney did not specify when—the whole system of dependent tenures had been abolished. As a result, "the Lords have only more mony to spend or lay up than others, but no command of men; and can therefore neither protect the weak, nor curb the insolent. By this means all things have bin brought into

---

Commonwealthman (Cambridge, MA: Harvard University Press, 1959), 45; Blair Worden, "The Commonwealth Kidney of Algernon Sidney," *Journal of British Studies* 24 (January 1985): 17.

[46] *Maxims*, 59. This was, apparently, an international phenomenon; cf. Algernon Sidney to the earl of Leicester, 29 January 1661, in Collins, 2:705.

[47] "Tho we have little reason to commend all the Princes that preceded *Henry* the fifth; yet I am inclined to date the general impairing of our Government from the death of that King, and his valiant Brothers" (*Discourses*, III:46, p. 460). See also: III:46, pp. 461–62.

[48] *Maxims*, 57–58. The final quotation is an allusion to a communication between the tyrants Periander and Thrasybulus, as recorded by both Herodotus (*The Histories*, 92e) and Aristotle (*The Politics*, 1284a).

the hands of the King and the Commoners, and there is nothing left to cement them, and to maintain the union. The perpetual jarrings we hear every day; the division of the Nation into such factions as threaten us with ruin, and all the disorders that we see or fear, are the effects of this rupture."[49] The tripartite balance of King, Lords, and Commons that had given life to the Gothic polity had been destroyed, and " 'tis as impossible to restore it, as for most of those who at this day go under the name of Noblemen, to perform the duties required from the antient Nobility of *England*."[50]

Sidney was not the only seventeenth-century radical to ascribe England's problems to the breakdown of the feudal system of mixed government. Indeed, although he makes no reference to James Harrington, at many points Sidney's argument parallels the much more sophisticated analysis of the "Gothic balance" in *The Commonwealth of Oceana*.[51] To be sure, Harrington's attitude toward the "Gothic balance" was uniformly critical; he considered it to be inherently unstable and, in sharp contrast to Sidney, decried it as "no other than a wrestling match."[52] In this respect Sidney was far closer to the "neo-Harringtonian interpretation" of English history—identified by J.G.A. Pocock with men like Henry Neville—according to which "the nobility's greatness and the people's freedom . . . are inseparable."[53] But like Harrington, Sidney argued that the fires that had destroyed the independence and power of the nobility, fires that had been fueled by the ambitions of the Tudor and Stuart monarchs, had irreversibly altered England's political landscape. It was no longer possible even to imagine that a stable polity could be built on the charred ruins of England's historic mixed constitution.

[49] *Discourses*, III:37, p. 420.

[50] *Discourses*, III:37, pp. 419–20. Sidney considered this to be a European-wide phenomenon; see: II:20, p. 153; II:25, p. 205; III:28, p. 385; *Maxims*, 56–59; Algernon Sidney to the earl of Leicester, 29 January 1661, in Collins, 2:704–5.

[51] James Harrington, "The Commonwealth of Oceana," in *The Political Works of James Harrington*, ed. J.G.A. Pocock (Cambridge: Cambridge University Press, 1977), 191–98. Sidney need not have read Harrington to have picked up the flavor of his arguments; as Pocock's work has amply demonstrated, Harrington's ideas were in the air throughout the second half of the seventeenth century.

[52] Harrington, "Oceana," in *Works*, 196.

[53] Pocock, *Machiavellian Moment*, 416. See generally 415–19. Pocock's argument is vitiated by his failure to take into sufficient account the fact that men like Sidney and Neville believed that the nobility had been permanently eclipsed. The best example of a neo-Harringtonian is Shaftesbury, who argued that "the power of *Peerage*" was the only effective check on a standing army ([Anthony Ashley Cooper], *A Letter From a Person of Quality* [London: 1675], 33). The contrasting perspectives on the nobility held by Sidney and Shaftesbury help to explain the divergent paths they took during the crises of the 1670s and 1680s.

Republicanism was founded on the eclipse of feudalism. But as Sidney explained, it was an eclipse of a unique and limited kind:

> Our Ancestors may evidently appear, not only to have intended well, but to have taken a right course to accomplish what they intended. This had effect as long as the cause continued; and the only fault that can be ascribed to that which they established is, that it has not proved to be perpetual; which is no more than may be justly said of the best human Constitutions that ever have bin in the world. If we will be just to our Ancestors, it will become us in our time rather to pursue what we know they intended, and by new Constitutions to repair the breaches made upon the old, than to accuse them of the defects that will for ever attend the Actions of men.[54]

What remained of the government of "our Ancestors" was a commitment to liberty and the rule of laws and not men; what had been destroyed was the particular set of institutions and techniques designed to ensure the realization of those ends that had constituted the Gothic polity. To prevent Englishmen from becoming slaves, it was necessary to find "new Constitutions to repair the breaches made upon the old."

Constitutionalism and the Separation of Powers

If we are to understand what Sidney meant by a "regular mixed Government," then we must look beyond the Gothic polity to the principles that should guide Englishmen in the creation of a new constitution. We are at a distinct disadvantage in this enterprise, for unlike the Levellers or James Harrington, Sidney did not provide a model for the reconstruction of England's political system. It is not possible to determine the precise contours of Sidney's republic. It is possible, however, to piece together fragmentary observations scattered throughout his writings and to establish the outline of a constitutional theory whose central features are the separation of powers and popular sovereignty.

The authentic note of constitutionalism was struck by Oliver Cromwell in a speech delivered in 1654. Defending the "Instrument of Government" before an increasingly obstructionist Parliament, Cromwell proclaimed that "in every government there must be somewhat fundamental, somewhat like a *Magna Charta*, that should be

---

[54] *Discourses*, III:37, p. 420. See also: II:30, pp. 241–42; III:27, p. 379.

standing and unalterable."[55] By "somewhat fundamental" Cromwell meant something quite different from the "fundamentals" of the ancient constitution so frequently referred to by the common lawyers. The "Instrument of Government" was a human fabrication. It was legislated into existence, not gradually discovered in the fabric of custom and tradition. And though some parts of the "Instrument" were "circumstantial" and could be changed, "some things are fundamental . . . they are not to be parted with."

The things Cromwell declared to be fundamental, and the reasons he did so, were heterodox. "Government by a single person and a Parliament" was fundamental because it defined the basic structure of the political system. "It is the *esse*; it is constitutive." Freedom of religion was fundamental because "liberty of conscience is a natural right." Provisions against "perpetuating of Parliaments" were fundamental because there could be no "security" in the face of a government that controlled its own tenure. Behind each of these fundamentals was the belief that political stability was possible if and only if the frame of government was accepted as given: "The things which shall be necessary to deliver over to posterity, these should be unalterable, else every succeeding Parliament will be disputing to change and alter the government, and we shall be as often brought into confusion as we have Parliaments, and so make our remedy our disease." The fundamentals of a government could be and often were the subject of controversy; but, paradoxically, the very possibility of entertaining controversies and resolving conflicts was contingent upon the acceptance of some things as fundamental. Here Cromwell gave expression to the central insight of constitutionalism, that for a government to be in the public interest it had to be limited.[56]

That Cromwell can be described as a constitutional theorist is fraught with irony, for his power as England's lord protector ultimately rested on his command of the army. The peculiarity of this claim is particularly evident in the context of an analysis of Algernon Sidney's political thought, for Sidney considered Cromwell to be nothing less than a tyrant. But like Cromwell, Sidney thought it im-

---

[55] Oliver Cromwell, "Speech to the Parliament . . . on Tuesday, the 12th of September, 1654," in *The Writings and Speeches of Oliver Cromwell*, ed. Wilber Cortez Abbott (Cambridge, MA: Harvard University Press, 1937–1947), 3:459. All quotations in this and the following paragraph are from this speech, 3:458–60.

[56] This theme is elegantly pursued in Stephen Holmes, "Precommitment and the Paradox of Democracy," in *Constitutionalism and Democracy*, ed. Jon Elster and Rune Slagstad (Cambridge: Cambridge University Press, 1988), 195–240. See also: Charles Howard McIlwain, *Constitutionalism Ancient and Modern*, rev. ed. (Ithaca: Cornell University Press, 1947), 21; Carl J. Friedrich, *Constitutional Government and Democracy*, 4th ed. (Waltham, MA: Blaisdell Publishing Company, 1968), 19–20.

possible for a government to act in the public interest unless it em-bodied certain fundamentals. Chief among these was the separation of powers.

According to Sidney, there are "two Swords" in every nation, "that of War and that of Justice." "The Sword of Justice comprehends the legislative and executive Power; the one is exercised in making Laws, the other in judging Controversies according to such as are made. The military Sword is used by those Magistrates who have it, in mak-ing War or Peace with whom they think fit."[57] Unfortunately, Sidney said nothing more about the "military Sword" than what is contained in this passage. It corresponds roughly to John Locke's "Federative" power, "the Power of War and Peace, Leagues and Alliances, and all the Transactions with all Persons and Communities without the Com-monwealth."[58] We may safely assume that Sidney, like Locke, would have placed this power in the hands of a chief magistrate. But the parallel with Locke cannot be carried too far, for Sidney had a much more restrictive view of the scope of power that could be granted to any magistrate.[59]

Sidney focused his inquiry into the powers of the magistracy by asking whether public officials had the right to act independently of, or in conflict with, the law. Were there any discretionary powers in-herent in the magistracy? Sidney thought not. "The Laws of every place show what the Power of the respective Magistrate is, and by declaring how much is allowed to him, declare what is denied; for he has not that which he has not, and is to be accounted a Magistrate whilst he exercises that which he has."[60] This was true even of that supreme magistrate, the king: "We in *England* know no other King than he who is so by Law, nor any power in that King except that which he has by Law."[61] Sidney quoted with approval Bracton's dic-

---

[57] *Discourses*, III:10, p. 295. See also: II:24, p. 174; III:8, pp. 285–86; III:10, p. 296.

[58] *Two Treatises*, II:146.

[59] According to Locke, "though this *federative Power* in the well or ill management of it be of great moment to the commonwealth, yet it is much less capable to be directed by antecedent, standing, positive Laws, than the *Executive*; and so must necessarily be left to the Prudence and Wisdom of those whose hands it is in, to be managed for the publick good" (*Two Treatises*, II:147). As will be demonstrated below, it is extremely unlikely that Sidney would have accepted this argument.

[60] *Discourses*, II:32, p. 248. As a "legal Magistrate . . . has no other Power than what the Law allows, so the same Law limits and directs the exercise of that which he has" (II:24, p. 176). See also: III:12, pp. 304–5; Sidney, *Very Copy of a Paper* (1683), 2.

[61] *Discourses*, III:21, p. 354. "*Bracton* tells us that *potestas Regis* is *potestis Legis*: It is from the Law that he hath his Power, it is by the Law that he is King, and for the good of the people by whose consent it is made" (Algernon Sidney, Sir William Jones, and Lord John Somers, *A Just and Modest Vindication of the Proceedings of the Two Last Parlia-*

tum that the king was *"singulis major, universis minor"*: though as first magistrate the king was greater in power than every other member of the polity considered individually, he was inferior to them considered collectively.[62]

Sidney's reduction of the king to first magistrate was an extreme version of a common Whig argument. At the heart of many of the political crises that rocked Stuart England were controversies over the nature and extent of the prerogative powers of the Crown, particularly the powers to tax, to create new courts and supervise the personnel of the old, to pardon criminals, to veto legislation, to suspend or dispense with specific laws, and to summon and dismiss Parliament. Though some of these powers were reduced or eliminated during the course of the Civil War, most remained in place after the Restoration and were considered essential to the king's legal and political identity. Opponents of the later Stuarts faced a difficult problem: they could not deny the prerogative without seeming to deny the institution of monarchy itself, and yet the presence of the prerogative made it difficult to guarantee that England's government would remain a government of laws and not men.

During the Exclusion Crisis, many Whig theorists addressed this dilemma by means of an ingenious legal fiction: they acknowledged that the king had extensive prerogative powers, but at the same time they proclaimed that "the king can do no wrong." By this they did not mean that the king had the power to do whatever he wanted, but rather that as king he could act only in ways that cohered with the law. James Tyrrell explained the logic behind this argument in 1681:

> Putting it thus, that the supreme Power (in a limited Monarchy) must be limited by some Law, does not therefore place any coercive power above [the king], who can call him to account for his actions: But a Power that may remonstrate to him where he hath acted contrary to that Law, and may by that law punish, not the Monarch, but his Ministers that have dared to transgress those known laws. For as for the Monarch himself, it is still supposed that he in his own person can do no injury: So that he may still be Supreme, and yet be limited, not by any power Superior to his own, but by his laws (or declared Will) which he himself hath made in the Assembly of his Estates, and which he can not alter, but by the

---

ments [London: 1682], 44). See also: *Discourses*, III:8, p. 284; III:14, p. 310; III:42, p. 443; III:43, p. 445.

[62] *Discourses*, III:9, p. 290; *Maxims*, 9; "The Trial of Colonel Algernon Sidney," in *A Complete Collection of State Trials*, ed. T. B. Howell (London: 1816), 9:855. The role of this concept in seventeenth-century radical thought is traced in Corinne Weston and Janelle Greenberg, *Subjects and Sovereigns* (Cambridge: Cambridge University Press, 1981).

same form by which they were constituted; and this sort of limitation may very well consist with a perfect Monarchy.[63]

Paradoxically, ministerial responsibility could be ensured by means of the legal fiction that the monarch was infallible. The roots of this argument lay in the distinction between the king's "personal" and "political" capacities. Dating to the fourteenth century, this distinction had been used during the early stages of the Civil War to justify Parliament's resistance to the ill-advised "person" of the king in the name of his sovereign "political" powers.[64] The revolutionary implications of this distinction could be avoided only so long as it was possible to believe that the king in his political capacity was in fact doing no wrong and that any untoward actions could be ascribed to his ministers. As both Charles I and Charles II repeatedly demonstrated, that was a very difficult proposition to maintain.

Sidney shared this common Whig desire to confine the powers of the king within legally determinate channels; but in place of their complex legal fiction he asserted a stark and simple claim: neither the king nor any other magistrate had any prerogative powers whatsoever.[65] This claim had no basis in tradition and undoubtedly provided one of the principal reasons for labeling Sidney a "republican." In asserting it he virtually abolished the institution of monarchy. He did much more than that, however, for he also implied that the only way to preserve the government of laws was to eliminate the government of men. The radical nature of this claim can be highlighted by recalling Locke's contemporary defense of the prerogative. According to Locke, "Many things there are, which the Law can by no means provide for, and those must necessarily be left to the discretion of him, that has the Executive Power in his hands. . . . This Power to act according to discretion, for the publick good, without the prescription of the Law, and sometimes even against it, is that which is called

---

[63] [James Tyrrell], *Patriarcha non Monarcha* (London: 1681), 129, second pagination. See also: "An Impartial Account of the Nature and Tendency of the Late Addresses," 1681, in *State Tracts* (London: 1693), 1:429; [Henry Care], *English Liberties* (London: 1682), 1–4; Edmund Hickeringill, "The History of Whiggism," in *The Works of Mr. Edmund Hickeringill* (London: 1716), 1:49, 84; McIlwain, *Constitutionalism*, 131–33.

[64] On the use of this distinction during the Civil War, see Donald Hanson, *From Kingdom to Commonwealth* (Cambridge, MA: Harvard University Press, 1970), 312–17. Hanson overstates the importance of this distinction both to the parliamentary cause and to seventeenth-century English political thought in general.

[65] For Sidney's arguments against various prerogative powers, see: *Discourses*, III:15, pp. 315–16; III:21, pp. 348–49; III:22, pp. 354–58; III:42, pp. 443–45; Algernon Sidney to Henry Savile, 7 April 1679, 28 April 1679, 19 May 1679, in *Letters*, 22–25, 39–41, 70–71; "Letter by a spy for Lord Preston," n.d., in HMC, *Seventh Report* (London: HMSO, 1879), 401.

Prerogative."[66] Locke flatly denied the possibility or desirability of the pure rule of law. No set of rules, no matter how complex or rich it was, was capable of addressing the range of problems faced by every government.[67] That is why, for example, the federative power had to be "left to the Prudence and Wisdom of those hands it is in, to be managed for the publick good." Foreign affairs were not amenable to strict legal control. Sidney's writings do not address this problem; as noted above, he left the conduct of the "military Sword" unanalyzed. But he would undoubtedly have been appalled by Locke's argument.[68] So strong was his commitment to the rule of law, so intense was his fear of corruption, that he permitted no space for discretionary powers in the office of the magistrate. Magistrates were empowered by the people to execute the law, and nothing more.

In sharp contrast to the executive power, the legislative power was by definition "Arbitrary."[69] That did not mean that it was capricious or unrestrained, but that it was discretionary. The content of the law was contingent and variable; apart from the condition that it be "beneficial to the people," no "general rule" had been established by God or nature.[70] As Sidney proudly proclaimed of England: "We know no Laws but our own Statutes, and those immemorial Customs established by the consent of the Nation; which may be, and often are changed by us. The Legislative Power therefore that is exercised by the Parliament . . . must be essentially and radically in the People, from whom their Delegates and Representatives have all that they have."[71] The legislative power was an expression of the sovereign power of the people. To understand it, it is necessary to understand the process by which it was delegated to the representatives of the people assembled in Parliament.

At one time the legislative power in England was exercised by an

---

[66] *Two Treatises*, II:159–60.

[67] John Dunn, *The Political Thought of John Locke* (Cambridge: Cambridge University Press, 1969), 150.

[68] Even in the midst of plotting revolution, he preferred that the conduct of the war be placed in the hands of a council, and not in the hands of a single man (Ford Lord Grey, *The Secret History of the Rye-House Plot* [London: 1754], 56–57).

[69] *Discourses*, III:45, p. 455. See also: III:46, p. 457.

[70] "The various Laws and Governments, that are or have bin in several ages and places, are the product of various opinions in those who had the power of making them. This must necessarily be, unless a general rule be set to all; for the judgments of men will vary if they are left to their liberty, and the variety that is found among them, shews they are subject to no rule but that of their own reason, by which they see what is fit to be embraced or avoided, according to the several circumstances under which they live" (*Discourses*, III:45, p. 455).

[71] *Discourses*, III:44, p. 450. See also: III:46, pp. 457, 462.

assembly of the whole people. In their micklegemots, the Saxons conducted the affairs of government "according to their own pleasure."
But "when they grew to be so numerous that one place could not
contain them, or so far dispersed, that without trouble and danger
they could not leave their habitations, they deputed such as should
represent them."[72] Sidney returned to this argument again and
again: it was the "inconvenience" of large numbers and long distances
that made necessary the innovation of representative government. In
light of these demographic changes, he felt no obligation to defend
"pure Democracy, where the People in themselves, and by themselves, perform all that belongs to Government."[73] As a form of government it was impractical, suited only to "the convenience of a small
Town."[74]

The transition from direct to representative government in feudal
England was momentous, but it did not alter the status of the legislative power. "When a People is, by mutual compact, joined together
in a civil Society, there is no difference as to Right, between that
which is done by them all in their own Persons, or by some deputed
by all, and acting according to the Powers received from all."[75] But
lurking within this argument was a crucial proviso: the equation between direct and representative government held only so long as the
delegates acted "according to the Powers received from all." Sir Robert Filmer had argued that the transfer of power entailed in parliamentary elections was absolute; the electorate "must only choose, and
trust those whom they choose to do what they list."[76] Sidney thought
this

> ingeniously concluded: I take what Servant I please, and when I have
> taken him I must suffer him to do what he pleases. But from whence
> should this necessity arise? Why may not I take one to be my Groom,
> another to be my Cook, and keep them both to the Offices for which I
> took them? What Law dos herein restrain my Right? And if I am free in
> my private capacity to regulate my particular affairs according to my
> own discretion, and to allot to each Servant his proper work, why have
> not I with my Associates the Freemen of *England* the like liberty of di-

[72] *Discourses*, III:28, p. 382; III:38, p. 423. See also: II:5, p. 79; III:28, pp. 382–83, 389.

[73] *Discourses*, II:19, p. 149. See also: I:10, p. 23; III:28, p. 389; *Maxims*, 48.

[74] *Discourses*, II:16, p. 130. See also: II:18, p. 138.

[75] *Discourses*, II:5, p. 79. See also: II:5, pp. 80–83; III:21, p. 349; III:28, p. 389; III:38, pp. 422–23.

[76] *Patriarcha*, 119. Filmer noted with approval that the electorate "may be punished . . . for intermeddling with parliamentary business."

recting and limiting the Powers of the Servants we employ in our publick Affairs?[77]

Why not indeed? By reducing parliamentary representatives to the status of servants, Sidney provided a powerful ideological counter to traditional notions of degree, hierarchy, and order. Temporary market relations replaced the permanent ordering of the universe; MPs were public employees, subject to the commanding will of their electoral masters. At the same time, Sidney intimated that the science of politics was not arcane and that "the Freemen of *England*" were capable of supervising public affairs with the same ease and skill with which they conducted their private lives.

Sidney's analysis of representation was predicated on two distinct but related claims: that "naturally and properly a man is the judg of his own concernments," and that "all men follow that which seems advantagious to themselves."[78] It had long been a maxim of the law that no man ought to be the judge of his own case. Without denying the importance of this principle to the fabric of the law, Sidney rejected its relevance to the determination of private interests. "If I find my self afflicted with hunger, thirst, weariness, cold, heat, or sickness, 'tis a folly to tell me, I ought not to seek meat, drink, rest, shelter, refreshment, or physick, because I must not be the judg of my own case. The like may be said in relation to my house, land, or estate." The same principle applied when a man employed another to assist him:

> A Physician dos not exercise his Art for himself, but for his Patients; and when I am, or think I shall be sick, I send for him of whom I have the best opinion, that he may help me to recover, or preserve my health; but I lay him aside if I find him to be negligent, ignorant, or unfaithful; and it would be ridiculous for him to say, I make my self judg in my own case, for I only, or such as I shall consult, am fit to be the judg of it. . . . If I mistake, 'tis only to my own hurt. The like may be said of Lawyers, Stewards, Pilots, and generally of all that do not act for themselves, but for those who employ them.[79]

Sidney's example is somewhat bizarre; presumably physicians were no more given to treachery or malice in the seventeenth century than they are now.[80] But his point was quite simple: in matters of private

[77] *Discourses*, III:44, p. 450.

[78] *Discourses*, III:41, p. 436; II:28, p. 218. "Man naturally follows that which is good, or seems to him to be so" (II:25, p. 201). See also: I:16, p. 38; II:1, p. 63; III:19, p. 342.

[79] *Discourses*, III:41, pp. 436–37; III:14, p. 313.

[80] Seventeenth-century patients were a different matter. According to the earl of Ailesbury, "Being at Montpelier [Sidney] had like to have killed [the physician] Bar-

interest, the judgment of each man was sovereign. Both morally and intellectually, he and he only was "fit" to judge his own needs and the performance of those he hired to meet them. As a contemporary adage had it, only the wearer knows where the shoe pinches.[81]

The same logic applied collectively: " 'Tis ordinarily said in *France, Il faut que chacon soit servi a sa mode*; Every mans business must be done according to his own mind: and if this be true in particular Persons, 'tis more plainly so in whole Nations."[82] Sidney never explained the precise nature of the connection between the right of men considered individually to judge their private interests and the right of men considered collectively to judge the public interest. Sometimes he implied that knowledge of one's private interests directly contributed to knowledge of the public interest;[83] at other times he implied that the same capacities that served men in judging their private interests— notably common sense—also served them in judging the public interest.[84] But unlike Locke, he did not have a sophisticated epistemology and a robust theory of the law of nature to explain how individual judgment of the public interest was possible. This is an unfortunate gap at a critical point in Sidney's theory, for he acknowledged that the limit to each man's right to pursue his private interests was defined by the public interest:

> I may do what I please with [my house, land, or estate], if I bring no damage upon others. But I must not set fire to my house, by which my neighbour's house may be burnt. I may not erect Forts upon my own Lands, or deliver them to a foreign Enemy, who may by that means infest my Country. I may not cut the banks of the Sea, or those of a River,

---

berai . . . and for what? Because a medicine he had taken by his order had not operated to his mind!" (Thomas Bruce, earl of Ailesbury, *Memoirs of Thomas, Earl of Ailesbury* [Westminster: 1890], 1:136).

[81] "Who will wear a Shoe that hurts him, because the Shoe-maker tells him 'tis well made? or who will live in a House that yields no defence against the extremities of Weather, because the Mason or Carpenter assures him 'tis a very good House? Such as have Reason, Understanding, or common Sense, will, and ought to make use of it in those things that concern themselves and their Posterity" (*Discourses*, I:3, p. 9).

[82] *Discourses*, III:16, p. 318. See also: "The Trial of Colonel Algernon Sidney," in Howell, *State Trials*, 9:855–58.

[83] Concerning a bill for the relief of Nonconformists proposed by Halifax, Sidney wrote: "I could have wished, that intending to oblige above a Million of men, that go under the name of Nonconformists, he had pleased to consult with one of that number, concerning the ways of doing it" (Algernon Sidney to Henry Savile, 31 October 1680, in *Letters*, 165).

[84] "If any man ask, who shall be Judg of that rectitude or pravity which either authorises or destroys a Law? I answer, that as this consists not in formalities and niceties, but in evident and substantial truths, there is no need of any other Tribunal than that of common sense, and the light of nature, to determine the matter" (*Discourses*, III:25, p. 365). See also: I:3, p. 9; III:41, p. 439.

lest my neighbour's ground be overflown, because the Society into which I am incorporated, would by such means receive prejudice. My Land is not simply my own, but upon condition that I shall not thereby bring damage upon the Publick, by which I am protected in the peaceable enjoyment and innocent use of what I possess.[85]

Sidney was groping for a way of distinguishing between private interests that threatened the public interest and private interests that were coherent with the public interest. He provided no independent criteria for making this distinction; as J.A.W. Gunn has argued, Sidney "insisted upon the subjective nature of any concrete formulation of the public good."[86] Instead, Sidney relied on representation itself to mediate between public and private interests. Just as private individuals were the best judge of their own interests, so also were the people as a whole the best judge of the public interest. "They who institute a Magistracy, best know whether the end of the Institution be rightly pursued or not."[87]

Given this premise, the genius of Parliament lay in the fact that it "does ever participate in the present temper of the People."[88] Sidney was particularly interested in three mechanisms by which this was to be ensured: equal subjection to the law, annual parliaments, and the instruction of representatives. The principle of equal subjection to the law was essential to Sidney's conception of the legislative power. It gave vital expression to the principle of equality embodied in the social contract: "The Laws that aim at the publick Good, make no distinction of persons . . . He that will not bend his mind to them, shakes off the equality of a Citizen, and usurps a Power above the Law, to which no man submits upon any other condition, than that none should be exempted from the power of it."[89] Simultaneously, it provided a check on parliamentary malfeasance by linking the interests of representatives and their constituents. As Sidney cynically put it, "the hazard of being ruin'd by those who must perish with us, is not so much to be feared, as by one who may enrich and strengthen himself by our destruction."[90] Neither of these arguments was unique to Sidney; the principle of equal subjection to the law was given a

---

[85] *Discourses*, III:41, p. 437.

[86] J.A.W. Gunn, *Politics and the Public Interest in the Seventeenth Century* (London: Routledge & Kegan Paul, 1969), 303.

[87] *Discourses*, III:31, p. 400. See also: III:41, p. 438.

[88] Sidney, Jones, and Somers, *Just and Modest Vindication*, 6.

[89] *Discourses*, II:18, p. 141. See also: *Maxims*, 141.

[90] *Discourses*, III:45, p. 457. See also: III:43, p. 446; III:45, p. 456.

prominent place in the writings of the Levellers[91] and John Locke.[92] Indeed, this taboo on exemptions from the law was an almost universal feature of seventeenth-century English radical thought and reflected a widespread sense that abuses of power could not be checked unless legal immunities were eliminated.

Alongside equal subjection to the law, Sidney insisted that Parliament convene annually.[93] The contexts within which he stated this claim make it clear that it was directed against both the excessively long Cavalier Parliament, which sat for seventeen and one-half years, and the excessively short Exclusion Parliaments, one of which lasted less than a week. Charles II had proven himself well versed in the art of proroguing and dissolving Parliament, and Sidney considered his actions to be a fundamental violation of the legislative power of the people. The full meaning of this claim emerges in the context of Sidney's discussion of the power of the English electorate to instruct their representatives.

Of the fact that the representatives of the people assembled in Parliament were "accountable to their Principals" there could be no doubt. "The people do perpetually judg of the behaviour of their Deputies. Whensoever any of them has the misfortune not to satisfy the major part of those that chose him, he is sure to be rejected with disgrace the next time he shall desire to be chosen."[94] Paradoxically, the frequency of elections and the conditional nature of political power actually increased the capacity of deputies to act in the public interest, for they dramatically decreased the risks of failure. Defeat and dishonor, not death and destruction, were the consequences of losing a political battle or failing to meet public expectations. Not fearing for their safety, MPs were free to pursue the public interest to the best of their ability.[95]

Electoral accountability also permitted a more sophisticated level of communication concerning the public interest. As a matter of right,

[91] The first "Agreement" mandated "that in all Laws made, or to be made, every person may be bound alike" ("An Agreement of the People," 1647, reprinted in Don Wolfe, *Leveller Manifestoes* [New York: Humanities Press, 1967], 227–28). Each subsequent "Agreement" contained this provision.

[92] "No Man in Civil Society can be exempted from the Laws of it" (*Two Treatises,* II:94).

[93] *Discourses,* II:21, p. 158; II:23, p. 167; II:24, p. 198; III:15, p. 315; III:27, p. 377; Sidney, Jones, and Somers, *Just and Modest Vindication,* 1.

[94] *Discourses,* III:38, pp. 423–24. See also: III:44, p. 451.

[95] Sidney praised the Roman practice of simply removing from office even the most corrupt army commanders: "They thought the mind of a Commander would be too much distracted, if at the same time he should stand in fear both of the Enemy and his own Countrymen" (*Discourses,* III:38, p. 424).

"we always may, and often do give Instructions to our Delegates."[96] This was the logical consequence of thinking of representatives as "Servants we employ in our public Affairs" and gave vital expression to the belief that the exercise of the legislative power was grounded in the judgment of the people. At the same time, Sidney recognized that representatives "cannot foresee what will be proposed when they are altogether; much less resolve how to vote till they hear the reasons on both sides. The Electors must necessarily be in the same ignorance; and the Law which should oblige them to give particular orders to their Knights and Burgesses in relation to every vote, would make the decision of the most important Affairs to depend upon the judgment of those who know nothing of the matters in question, and by that means cast the Nation into the utmost danger of the most inextricable confusion."[97] Strictly relying on instructions would frustrate the purpose of representation. Although the public interest was grounded in the discrete judgments of individual men, it was articulated by means of a complex process of public discussion among the people and Parliament.[98]

Sidney highlighted the complex nature of the process by which public and private interests were mediated through representation by drawing attention to the distinction between the national government of England and the confederated governments of the United Provinces and Switzerland:

> The Powers of every County, City and Borough of *England* are regulated by the general Law to which they have all consented, and by which they are all made Members of one political Body. This obliges them to proceed with their Delegates in a manner different from that which is used in the United Netherlands, or in *Switzerland*. Amongst these every Province, City or Canton making a distinct body independent from any other, and exercising the sovereign Power within it self, looks upon the rest as Allies, to whom they are bound only by such Acts as they themselves have made; and when any new thing not comprehended in them happens to arise, they oblige their Delegates to give them an account of it, and retain the power of determining those matters in themselves. 'Tis not so amongst us: Every County dos not make a distinct Body, having in it self a sovereign Power, but is a Member of that great Body which comprehends the whole Nation. 'Tis not therefore for *Kent* or *Sussex*,

---

[96] *Discourses*, III:44, p. 453. See also: III:38, p. 424.

[97] *Discourses*, III:44, p. 454.

[98] This theme is elegantly discussed in Samuel H. Beer, "The Strengths of Liberal Democracy," in *A Prospect of Liberal Democracy*, ed. William Livingston (Austin: University of Texas Press, 1979), 215–29.

Lewis or *Maidstone*, but for the whole Nation, that the Members chosen in those places are sent to serve in Parliament.[99]

Were representatives confined by the instructions of their electors, they would betray the common bond that had been created in the consensual founding of the nation; were they completely free of instructions, they would betray their dependence on the judgment of their electors. Ideally, the representatives of a free people remained poised between the two poles of dependence and independence.

Sidney's theory of representation almost completes his account of the legislative power. It was an expression of the sovereign power of the nation to make and abrogate binding laws, exercised by parliamentary representatives accountable to the people. But who were "the people" to whom the representatives assembled in Parliament were accountable? Whose voice counted in the determination of the public interest? In modern usage the term "the people" is universal in scope, encompassing all the inhabitants of a nation. This was not true in the seventeenth century, when even radicals tended to restrict the term "the people" to freemen or the "better" sort of men and excluded both the "meaner" sort and the nobility. For example, the first "order" of James Harrington's commonwealth of Oceana distributed "the people into freemen or citizens, and servants, while such; for if they attain unto liberty, that is to live of themselves, they are freemen or citizens. This order needeth no proof, in regard of the nature of servitude, which is inconsistent with freedom or participation of government in a commonwealth." That Harrington felt no obligation to justify this distinction speaks volumes concerning contemporary sensibilities. It was self-evident to seventeenth-century observers that men living on the lowest rungs of the social ladder lacked the moral, intellectual, and economic independence necessary to take part in the political life of the nation. Even a man as unlike Harrington as James Tyrrell shared this view: "I desire always to be understood, that when I make use of the word People, I do not mean the vulgar or mixt multitude."[100] In light of this prevailing sense of the meaning of the term "the people," two key questions must be posed of Sidney's theory: What was the extent of the franchise? And why

[99] *Discourses*, III:44, p. 451. The "Constitutions" of the United Provinces "seem to have a more particular regard to the preservation of the Libertys and priviledges of each town and Province, than to the welfare of the whole"; "their Commonwealth seems to be a vast building of loose stones, which not well cemented threatens ruine" (*Maxims*, 173). For a more favorable assessment of the governments of the Low Countries and Switzerland, see: *Discourses*, II:22, pp. 162–64.

[100] Harrington, "Oceana," in *Works*, 212; [James Tyrrell], *Bibliotheca Politica* (London: 1694), "Preface." See also: Tyrrell, *Patriarcha non Monarcha*, 83.

were the boundaries set where they were? The answers to these questions have bearing not only on our understanding of Sidney's radicalism, but also on an important debate in the history of political thought.

From the closing years of Sidney's life come two hints concerning his conception of "the people." Appearing before Parliament after a contested election in the borough of Amersham in the fall of 1680, Sidney declared that "of common Right those only ought to have Voices in Elections who pay Scot and Lot." That is to say, he favored the narrower scot and lot franchise over the broader franchise of inhabitant householders. It is not clear whether he was motivated by principle or by expediency, however, for he was subsequently defeated in a reelection held on the household franchise.[101] More revealing were Sidney's comments on the jurors who convicted him of treason three years later. They were "a rabble of men of the meanest callings, ruined fortunes, lost reputation, and hardly endowed with such understanding, as is required for a jury in a nisi prius court for a businesse of five pounds."[102] It can hardly be imagined that the man who uttered these words would have extended the franchise to the "meaner" sort of men. At the same time, these words must be understood in their context: Sidney was quite literally fighting for his life. Alongside his aristocratic disdain for the lower classes was an argument concerning independence of judgment. Sidney objected to his jury because he believed that it had been corrupted (or railroaded) into convicting him.[103] He was, in fact, willing to accept a jury composed of "the most eminent men for quality and understanding, reputation and virtue, who lived in the county, though they had not freeholds."[104] Such men could be trusted to recognize the truth. But he preferred men of property for the simple reason that they were less likely to succumb to the suasive tactics of the prosecution.

The association of independence with the status of a freeman carried over into the argument of the *Discourses*. Echoing Harrington, Sidney declared that "the difference between *Civis* and *Servus* is irreconcilable; and no man, whilst he is a Servant, can be a Member of a

---

[101] Algernon Sidney, *The Case of Algernon Sidney Esq* [1680], 1; Basil Duke Henning, *The House of Commons 1660–1690*, 3 vols. (London: Secker & Warburg, 1983), 1:137–38.

[102] "Apology," 9. See also: Algernon Sidney, *To the KING's Most Excellent Majesty* (London: 1683).

[103] "Many of the king's servants now in pay, from whome impartiall justice could not be expected whilst I was prosecuted at the king's suite, were returned upon the panell, and many whoe were not freeholders, and somme lewd and infamous persons, who deserve not to be of any jury" ("Apology," 28). See also: 9, 25–28.

[104] "Apology," 8.

Commonwealth; for he that is not in his own power, cannot have a part in the Government of others."[105] Sidney's argument was inseparable from his analysis of corruption, and in that sense the whole range of topics discussed in Chapter 4 might be taken as a commentary on it. Unfortunately, there is little more that can be said on the basis of his writings, for he rarely addressed the link between independence and citizenship directly. Because Sidney's premises were widely shared by his contemporaries, however, it is possible to use a unique historical lens to focus on the kinds of concerns that led men to restrict the franchise to freemen: Whig pamphlets advising the English electorate how to vote during the three parliamentary elections held between 1679 and 1681.[106]

Concern over the corruption of Parliament by placemen and pensioners was at the heart of the Whig ideology that emerged during the 1670s. As Andrew Marvel complained in his inflammatory pamphlet *An Account of the Growth of Popery, and Arbitrary Government*, "it is too notorious to be concealed, that near a third part of the House have Beneficial Offices under his Majesty."[107] Compounding the problem of parliamentary corruption was the corruption of elections by candidates bearing gifts to magistrates and electors altogether too willing to receive them. Mercenary behavior threatened the foundations of the polity. Failing to regulate these abuses legislatively,[108] Whig pamphleteers had to rely on exhortation: "Upon your *well* or *ill Choosing*, depends your *well* or *ill Being* . . . your Fate will not suffer you to offend *twice* in this *one particular*." Above all else it was necessary to avoid placemen and pensioners, for "they are not their own

---

[105] *Discourses*, II:5, p. 79. "They who place the Power in a Multitude, understand a Multitude composed of Freemen" (II:5, p. 75); "In the Counties, which make up the Body of the Nation, all Freeholders have their Votes: these are properly *Cives*, Members of the Commonwealth, in distinction from those who are only *Incolae*, or Inhabitants, Vilains, and such as being under their Parents, are not yet *sui juris*" (III:38, p. 423). See also: III:28, p. 389.

[106] The four urtexts for the following analysis are: William Penn [Philanglus, pseud.], *Englands Great Interest In The Choice of this New Parliament* [1679?]; *A Seasonable Warning to the Commons of England* [1679]; *Sober and Seasonable Queries* [1679]; C.B., *An Address to the Honourable City of London* (1681). These texts were recycled in later pamphlets: *Englands Great Interest* and *A Seasonable Warning* were plagiarized in *A Certain Way to Save England* (1681); and subsequently it, along with *An Address to the Honourable City*, was plagiarized in [Care], *English Liberties*.

[107] Andrew Marvel, *An Account of the Growth of Popery, and Arbitrary Government in England* (Amsterdam: 1677), 24.

[108] During the First Exclusion Parliament, "A Bill for Regulating the Abuses of Elections" was unsuccessfully introduced in the Commons (reprinted in John Somers, ed., *A Collection of Scarce and Valuable Tracts* [London: 1748], 1:63–66).

men."[109] For the same reason, indigents, "Ambitious men," and "Prodigal or Voluptuous Persons" were to be rejected: "The *Representative* of a Nation ought to consist of the most Wise, Sober and Valiant of the People, not Men of mean Spirits or sordid *Passions*, that would sell the *Interest* of the People that chuse them to advance their own, or be at the Beck of some great Man, in hopes of a *Lift* to a good Employ; pray beware of these."[110] In their place were to be elected "men of Courage," men who feared "God, and not the Faces of Great ones."[111] Men who were cowed by the disapproval of others were a hindrance, and not a help, to the public interest; independence was the watchword of the Whig campaign.

The same qualities that were called for in representatives were required in the people. As William Penn memorably put it in 1679: "Let neither Fear, Flattery, nor Gain *Byass* us. We must not make our *Publick Choice*, the Recompence of *Private Favours* from our Neighbours, they must excuse us from that: the Weight of the Matter will very well bear it. This is our Inheritance; all depends upon it: Men don't use to lend their Wives, or give their Children to satisfie *Personal Kindnesses*; nor must we make a *Swop* of our *Birth-right*, (and that of our Posterities too) for a Mess of Pottage, a *Feast*, or a *Drinking bout; there can be no Proportion here*."[112] The franchise was a trust, and its proper exercise required men to be free from the corrupting influence of others. It is important to note that Penn and his fellow Whig pamphleteers did not argue that honest voting required men to renounce private interests *simpliciter*. Indeed, a blend of public and private motives was the best possible guarantee of a person's integrity.[113] There were, however, certain kinds of interests, interests that created "places of profit in the commonwealth," that were destructive of the legislative power.

Whig arguments for restricting the franchise to freemen tread between the poles established by Colonel Thomas Rainborough and Henry Ireton at the Putney debates in 1647. According to Rainborough, "The poorest he that is in England hath a life to live, as the greatest he; and therefore truly, sir, I think it's clear, that every man that is to live under a government ought first by his own consent to

[109] *A Seasonable Warning*, 1; *A Certain Way*, 15.

[110] Penn, *Englands Great Interest*, 3.

[111] *A Seasonable Warning*, 4.

[112] Penn, *Englands Great Interest*, 1.

[113] This was true even in religious matters: as "private Interest" was "the string in the *Bears* Nose," it was "not amiss" in choosing representatives to "seek for those, whose spiritual interest is seconded by a temporal one" (C.B., *An Address*, 7, 10). On Penn's concept of interests, see: Gunn, *Politics and the Public Interest*, 169–90.

put himself under it." To this ringing declaration of democratic principles, Ireton responded: "I think that no person hath a right to an interest or share in the disposing of the affairs of the kingdom, and in determining or choosing those that shall determine what laws we shall be ruled by here—no person hath a right to this, that hath not a permanent fixed interest in this kingdom."[114] In principle the Whigs agreed with Rainborough: the franchise was a right to which every inhabitant of a nation was entitled. But in practice they were unwilling to endorse a universal franchise. They were keenly sensitive to the corrupting influence of personal dependence and sought to restrict the franchise to men they thought capable of acting autonomously. At the same time, they displayed little interest in Ireton's defense of the representation of property in Parliament. Property was relevant to Whig arguments concerning the franchise only to the extent that its possession enabled men to exercise independence of judgment.

When placed in this context, Sidney's restriction of the franchise to freemen acquires new meaning.[115] Like these Whig pamphleteers, he believed that the survival of liberty required men to be free from corrosive forms of personal dependency. Individualism fostered collective strength. In this regard servants were no different from the despised pensioners of the court: both were at the beck and call of others. These arguments render implausible C. B. Macpherson's contention that the freehold franchise was a paradigmatic expression of "the political theory of possessive individualism." The key problem associated with the franchise was not the defense of capitalism by reference to the "differential rationality" of social classes, but the unequal susceptibility of individuals to the enslaving powers of corruption.[116] This widespread fear of mercenary voting also casts doubt on Richard Ashcraft's recent claim that the "radical resonance" of Whig arguments presumptively favored a universal franchise.[117] Sidney

---

[114] "The Putney Debates," 29 October 1647, in *Puritanism and Liberty*, ed. A.S.P. Woodhouse (Chicago: University of Chicago Press, 1951), 53–54.

[115] I do not mean to imply that these pamphlets permit us to know Sidney's intentions, but rather that they form an ideological context that is coherent with the logic of Sidney's arguments. The plausibility of this strategy is enhanced by noting that William Penn was Sidney's campaign manager at the time that he wrote *Englands Great Interest*; indeed, there are earmarks of Sidney's style in the pamphlet itself.

[116] C. B. Macpherson, *The Political Theory of Possessive Individualism* (Oxford: Oxford University Press, 1962), esp. 232–38. Macpherson's analysis of the logic of a freehold franchise focuses on the Levellers, but his argument as a whole pivots on the claim that there existed a common structure of ideas in seventeenth-century radical thought.

[117] Richard Ashcraft, *Revolutionary Politics & Locke's Two Treatises of Government* (Princeton: Princeton University Press, 1986), 594. For a penetrating analysis of Ash-

and his cohorts had no qualms about restricting the franchise in order to preserve its integrity. Indeed, at precisely the moment when Shaftesbury's parliamentary power was at its peak, the House of Commons voted overwhelmingly to support the narrow scot and lot franchise in Sidney's controversial Amersham election.[118]

The equation of freehold and independence can and ought to be questioned; the pensioners and placemen so loudly complained of frequently were, after all, freemen themselves. Sidney himself recognized that freeholders were not capable of sustaining liberty in the face of certain pervasive forms of corruption, and that is why he thought the preservation of constitutional government required a right of revolution.

Revolution

Algernon Sidney's name is inseparable from the theory and practice of revolution. During his life he was associated with the trial and execution of Charles I in 1649, various aborted republican uprisings during the early 1660s, and the Rye House Plot of 1682–83. After his death, his *Discourses* became, in the words of one scholar, a "textbook of revolution."[119] But in Sidney's political theory, revolution was not the centerpiece of a just political order, but a consequence of its failure:

> No human condition being perfect, such a one is to be chosen, which carries with it the most tolerable inconveniences. . . . But as no rule can be so exact, to make provision against all contestations; and all disputes about Right do naturally end in force when Justice is denied (ill men never willingly submitting to any decision that is contrary to their passions and interests) the best Constitutions are of no value, if there be not a power to support them. This power first exerts it self in the execution

craft's argument concerning the meaning of "the people," see Gordon Schochet, "Radical Politics and Ashcraft's Treatise on Locke," *Journal of the History of Ideas* 50 (July–September 1989): 503–6.

[118] As the record of the debate makes clear, MPs considered their decision to be of national significance (Anchitell Grey, ed., *Debates of the House of Commons*, 10 vols. [London: T. Becket and P. A. DeHonde, 1769], 7:127–28). For this reason I am unable to accept Ashcraft's contention that "the Whigs had every reason to support the broadest possible interpretation of a freeman's right to vote . . . as a guarantee against the corruption of Court pensions or the bribery of large landowners" (Ashcraft, *Revolutionary Politics*, 169). A similar mistake is made by J. H. Plumb in "The Growth of the Electorate in England from 1600 to 1715," *Past and Present* 45 (November 1969): 109.

[119] Caroline Robbins, "Algernon Sidney's *Discourses Concerning Government*: Textbook of Revolution," *William and Mary Quarterly*, 3rd ser., 4 (July 1947): 267–96.

of justice by the ordinary Officers: But no Nation having bin so happy, as not sometimes to produce such Princes as *Edward* and *Richard* the Seconds, and such Ministers as *Gaveston*, *Spencer*, and *Tresilian*, the ordinary Officers of Justice often want the will, and always the power to restrain them. So that the Rights and Liberties of a nation must be utterly subverted and abolished, if the power of the whole may not be employed to assert them, or punish the violation of them. But as it is the fundamental Right of every Nation to be governed by such Laws, in such manner, and by such persons as they think most conducing to their own good, they cannot be accountable to any but themselves for what they do in that most important affair.[120]

Implicit in this argument are answers to three key questions, questions that must be explored if Sidney's theory of revolution is to be fully understood: What justifies revolution? Who judges when revolution is necessary? And what actions can or must be taken in the name of revolution?

Sir Robert Filmer had argued that subjects, like servants and slaves, have "no authority or liberty," no "commission" or "power," to judge the commands and actions of their master.[121] Kings were not to be resisted, regardless of what they said or did. During the 1670s and 1680s this doctrine of passive obedience gained wide acceptance among royalists, particularly within the Anglican clergy.[122] But in the history of seventeenth-century political thought it was an aberration, and not the norm. Most royalists, and virtually all critics of the Crown, accepted the proposition that under certain circumstances resistance to the king was legitimate. As the moderate parliamentarian Philip Hunton explained in 1643, even in an absolute monarchy if the king "should so degenerate into Monstrous unnaturall Tyranny as apparently to seek the destruction of the whole community, subject to him in the lowest degree of vassallage, then such a community may negatively resist such subversion: yea, and if constrained to it by the last necessity, positively resist and defend themselves by force."[123] Like individuals, nations had a right to resist enslavement and destruction. Two of the most widely cited "sources" for this view were Bracton and William Barclay: Bracton because he was a venerable jurist, and Barclay because his credentials as a royalist were impeccable. Sidney drew on both of these authorities, the latter indirectly and

---

[120] *Discourses*, III:36, p. 417.

[121] *Patriarcha*, 105.

[122] Mark Goldie, "John Locke and Anglican Royalism," *Political Studies* 31 (1983): 61–85.

[123] [Hunton], *A Treatise of Monarchie*, 9.

by way of Grotius, in constructing his theory of revolution.[124] Sidney's use of Grotius in this context was not accidental; he once suggested that *De Jure Belli ac Pacis* was the most important book in political theory.[125] Indeed, from an analytic point of view, Sidney's theory of revolution might best be seen as the fruit of a creative misreading of Grotius's arguments concerning the right of resistance.

In the fourth chapter of the first book of *De Jure Belli*, Grotius undertook an examination of the right of "war of subjects against superiors." His analysis, as Richard Tuck has argued, is divided against itself.[126] On the one hand, Grotius sharply curtailed the right of resistance: "By nature all men have the right of resisting in order to ward off injury. . . . But as civil society was instituted in order to maintain public tranquillity, the state forthwith acquires over us and our possessions a greater right, to the extent necessary to accomplish this end. The state, therefore, in the interest of public peace and order, can limit that common right of resistance."[127] "In particular," Tuck notes, "men no longer have a right to defend themselves against the person of the sovereign."[128] When in this mood, Grotius lauded the virtues of endurance, patience, and obedience. On the other hand, he acknowledged that in certain cases resistance was legitimate. One such case was in the face of "extreme and imminent peril."[129] Citing Barclay, Grotius argued that "the kingdom is forfeited if a king sets out with a truly hostile intent to destroy a whole people. . . . The will to govern and the will to destroy cannot coexist in the same person." A second case was when "the sovereign power is held in part by the king, in part by the people or senate . . . [and the king] attempts to usurp that part of the sovereign power which does not belong to him."[130] In these and a number of similar cases, Grotius argued, the right of resistance overrode the duty of obedience.

Sidney paid no attention to the absolutist dimensions of *De Jure Belli*, but he was deeply impressed by Grotius's arguments justifying resistance. In the process of adapting them to his own purposes, how-

---

[124] For Bracton, see: *Discourses*, III:9, pp. 289–90; III:14, p. 310; III:15, p. 315; III:26, pp. 373–74; Sidney, Jones, and Somers, *Just and Modest Vindication*, 43–44. For Barclay-Grotius, see: *Discourses*, II:27, p. 211.

[125] Algernon Sidney, "Conversations with Lantin in 1677," Bibliotheque Nationale, Fr. MS. 23,254, fol. 100.

[126] "The book is Janus-faced, and its two mouths speak the language of both absolutism and liberty" (Tuck, *Natural Rights Theories*, 79).

[127] Hugo Grotius, *De Jure Belli Ac Pacis*, trans. Francis Kelsey (Oxford: The Clarendon Press, 1925), I.iv.2, p. 139.

[128] Tuck, *Natural Rights Theories*, 79.

[129] Grotius, *De Jure Belli*, I.iv.7, p. 148. On the principle of "interpretive charity" that supports this conclusion, see Tuck, *Natural Rights Theories*, 79–80.

[130] Grotius, *De Jure Belli*, I.iv.11, pp. 157–58; I.iv.13, p. 158.

ever, he significantly changed their meaning. Grotius's first case had been designed to justify "the right of self-defence against atrocious cruelty."[131] Sidney accepted this argument, but he redefined the underlying notions of cruelty and destruction to include any attempt to govern by will and not law. A "truly hostile intent" was signaled by the desire to act arbitrarily, and not necessarily by the desire to act cruelly.[132] Similarly, he transformed Grotius's second case, which had been designed to provide a nation with the tools necessary to preserve a system of divided or concurrent sovereignty, into an argument justifying resistance to any "legal Magistrate, who takes upon him . . . to exercise a Power which the Law dos not give."[133] The cumulative effect of these changes in Grotius's analysis was a single argument much more radical than Grotius himself would have accepted: resistance was justified whenever it was directed against those who would replace the freedom of consent and law with the slavery of force and will. Sidney explained this right in terms of the ends of government:

> Has every man given up into the common store his right of avenging the injuries he may receive, that the publick Power which ought to protect or avenge him, should be turned to the destruction of himself, his Posterity, and the Society into which they enter, without any possibility of redress? . . . Surely if this were the condition of men living under Government, Forests would be more safe than Cities; and 'twere better for every man to stand in his own defence, than to enter into Societies. He that lives alone might encounter such as should assault him upon equal terms, and stand or fall according to the measure of his courage and strength; but no valour can defend him, if the malice of his enemy be upheld by a publick Power. There must therefore be a right of proceeding judicially or extrajudicially against all persons who transgress the Laws; or else those Laws, and the Societies that should subsist by them, cannot stand; and the ends for which Governments are constituted, together with the Governments themselves, must be overthrown.[134]

The right of revolution was a necessary component of any theory of legitimate government, for in certain circumstances only rebellion

---

[131] Grotius, *De Jure Belli*, I.iv.7, p. 130.

[132] *Discourses*, II:27, pp. 211–12.

[133] *Discourses*, II:24, p. 176. See also: II:24, p. 177; II:30, p. 236; III:1, p. 258; *Maxims*, 115. For Sidney's use of Grotius's distinction between a power that is *Summum Imperium summo modo* and a power that is *modo non summo* to support this argument, see: *Discourses*, II:7, p. 89; II:24, p. 176; III:31, p. 402.

[134] *Discourses*, II:24, p. 180. See also: II:24, pp. 177–78; II:30, p. 237; III:4, pp. 266–67; III:36, pp. 413–17; III:41, pp. 437–40; *Maxims*, 11, 48.

was capable of ensuring that the power of magistrates was limited and exercised according to law and not will.

The range of Sidney's argument for the right of revolution can be highlighted by comparing it to similar arguments in the writings of John Locke and John Milton. According to Locke, *"Tyranny* is *the exercise of Power beyond Right. . . .* And whosoever in Authority exceeds the Power given him by the law, and makes use of the Force he has under his Command, to compass that upon the Subject, which the Law allows not, ceases in that to be a Magistrate, and acting without Authority, may be opposed, as any other Man, who by force invades the Right of another."[135] This argument flowed from Locke's conception of the end of civil society, which was the advancement of the public good through the rule of known and impartial laws.[136] In strikingly similar language, both Sidney and Locke argued that tyranny could be opposed because it replaced law with force and introduced a state of war between magistrates and the people.[137] Milton's description of the right of revolution, on the other hand, was much more expansive: "Since the King or Magistrate holds his authoritie of the people, both originaly and naturally for their good in the first place, and not his own, then may the people, as oft as they shall judge it for the best, either choose him or reject him, retaine him or depose him, though no Tyrant, meerly by the liberty and right of free born Men, to be govern'd as seems to them best."[138] Like those of Sidney and Locke, Milton's argument was designed to justify rebellion against a tyrant. But it encompassed a great deal more, for it implied that changing a government was no different from buying a new suit of clothes: either was justified when the old one was frayed at the edges, no longer fit, or was simply out of style. Sidney and Locke were much more conservative or restrictive in their arguments concerning the right of revolution. A magistrate could be resisted only when he had actually violated his trust.

The parallels between Locke and Sidney run deeper than this general perspective on the right of resistance. Both men argued that the term "rebel" properly applied to a magistrate who acted outside the

---

[135] *Two Treatises*, II:199, 202.

[136] *Two Treatises*, II:123–31, 134, 222.

[137] " 'Tis the *unjust use of force* then, that *puts a Man into the state of War* with another, and thereby he, that is guilty of it, makes a forfeiture of his Life. For quitting reason, which is the rule given between Man and Man, and using force the way of Beasts, he becomes liable to be destroyed by him he uses force against, as any savage ravenous Beast, that is dangerous to his being" (*Two Treatises*, II:181). See also: Dunn, *Political Thought of John Locke*, 165–86.

[138] John Milton, "The Tenure of Kings and Magistrates," in *Complete Prose Works*, ed. Don M. Wolfe, 8 vols. (New Haven: Yale University Press, 1953–82), 3:206.

law, and not to the men who opposed him. To Sidney, "the general revolt of a Nation cannot be called a Rebellion," for the Latin word *rebellare* implied "a superiority in them against whom it is, as well as the breach of an establish'd Peace," and both of these conditions were lacking in the case of a people resisting the illegal actions of a magistrate.[139] Locke made the same point in a characteristically more precise way: "When Men by entering into Society and Civil Government, have excluded force, and introduced Laws for the preservation of Property, Peace, and Unity amongst themselves; those who set up force again in opposition to the Laws, do *Rebellare*, that is, bring back again the state of War, and are properly Rebels."[140] From one perspective, this was simply the application of the logic of self-defense to political affairs: thieves in the night, and not the innocents who fend them off, are the true criminals in society. But the effect of this argument was quite radical, for it inverted the traditional relationship between government and the people and permanently placed the magistrates who wield public power on the defensive. It was they, and not the people, who constantly threatened the nation with rebellion.

Both Sidney and Locke applied two constraints to this generalized right of resistance. First, it could be invoked only in extremis, when all forms of legal recourse had been exhausted. "Where the injured Party may be relieved, and his damages repaired by Appeal to the Law," Locke argued, "there can be no pretence for Force."[141] (By implication, armed resistance was justified against those who, like Charles and James Stuart, either ignored or overawed the regular proceedings of the law.) Second, it should be invoked only in the face of a pattern of abuse; as Sidney explained in the *Court Maxims*:

> He were contentious, who should so nicely criticize upon the administration [of the law], as to deny the validity of the law for every errour committed in the administration thereof. We ought not to be too quick-sighted in other mens faults. We have our own: much is to be imputed to human frailty: we ought not to blame every mote we see in our brother's eye. But if the ill administration be such as proceeds not from ignorance but malice; not in some small circumstances, but in such as destroy the end, for which the Law was made, so that the people, which sought justice thereby, falls under oppression; the trust is broke; all acts done

[139] *Discourses*, III:36, p. 413. See also: II:14, p. 122; II:24, pp.179–80; III:19, p. 343; III:36, pp. 413–17; *Maxims*, 141–42.

[140] *Two Treatises*, II:226. See also: II:227–31.

[141] *Two Treatises*, II:207. Sidney consistently described revolution as following on the heels of the failure of appeals to the law: *Discourses*, II:24, pp. 174–82; II:30, p. 237; III:15, p. 315; III:36, p. 417; III:40, pp. 434–35.

upon pretence of powers given are void; and those that exercise them become enemys and traytors to their masters that intrusted them.[142]

Locke concurred: "he that *appeals to Heaven*, must be sure he has Right on his side."[143] Recognizing the frailty of this normative claim, both men reinforced it with an empirical observation: though revolutions might follow on the heels of mismanagement or abuses touching only a few men, they were not likely to do so. Most men were sufficiently insensitive to the welfare of others that only "a long train of Abuses, Prevarications, and Artifices, all tending the same way" and all touching the generality of men, would actually meet with resistance.[144]

Implicit in this last observation was an answer to the question "Who decides when revolution is necessary?" In sharp contrast to most previous theories of resistance, which lodged this power with the people's representatives, Locke and Sidney acknowledged the right of private individuals to determine this question. Locke was unambiguous: "*every Man* is *Judge* for himself . . . whether another hath put himself into a State of War with him, and whether he should appeal to the Supreme Judge, as *Jeptha* did."[145] Sidney was less explicit, but the collective weight of various observations and arguments in his writings tips the balance in favor of the conclusion that he, too, assigned this momentous right to private individuals.

Sidney frequently invoked Tertullian's dictum that "against men guilty of treason and against public enemies every man is a soldier."[146] This notorious justification of tyrannicide would seem to be dispositive of the question of individual resistance, but in fact it leaves open the central question of who determines whether or not a given magistrate is a public enemy. We can come somewhat closer to answering this question by asking what criteria and capacities were involved in making such a determination. According to Sidney, judgments concerning the "rectitude or pravity" of constitutional arrangements consist "not in formalities and niceties, but in evident and substantial

---

[142] *Maxims*, 116. See also: *Discourses*, III:15, p. 315.

[143] *Two Treatises*, II:176.

[144] *Two Treatises*, II:225. See also: II:208–10, 223–24, 230; *Discourses*, II:14, p. 312.

[145] *Two Treatises*, II:241. "The *injured Party must judge* for himself, when he will think fit to make use of that Appeal [to Heaven], and put himself on it" (II:242). Cf. *Discourses*, II:30, p. 237: "Wrongs will be done, and when they that do them cannot or will not be judged publicly, the injur'd Persons become Judges in their own case, and executioners of their own sentence."

[146] *Maxims*, 11; *Discourses*, II:24, pp. 175, 181. The quotation is from Tertullian's *Apology*, chap. 2; Sidney may have known it through Grotius (*De Jure Belli*, I.iv.16, p. 160).

truths, [and hence] there is no need of any other Tribunal than that of common sense, and the light of nature, to determine the matter."[147] Stronger yet: "Such as have Reason, Understanding, or common Sense, will, and ought to make use of it in those things that concern themselves and their Posterity."[148] Sidney's argument concerning revolution precisely paralleled his argument concerning representation. Royalist claims to the contrary notwithstanding, there was nothing esoteric about the business of government. As every man was possessed of common sense and the light of nature, so every man could and ought to judge the conduct of his magistrates.

Evidence to support this conclusion can be found in an unexpected location: Sidney's theory of the function of juries. According to Sidney, grand and petit juries had the power to judge questions of law as well as questions of fact.[149] This claim was made with increasing frequency by Whig pamphleteers during the early 1680s.[150] With Parliament stymied through repeated prorogations and dissolutions, and city corporations falling victim to a Tory campaign of corruption, juries appeared to many Whigs to be their last refuge against the revenge of the Stuarts. So long as juries remained independent, and were considered competent to judge matters of law as well as matters of fact, they could prevent the courts from being used as an instrument of oppression: in the event of a political trial, the facts could be judged insufficient and the law could be judged inapplicable. The political expediency of this claim should not be allowed to overshadow its radical intellectual foundation, however. Each member of the jury, it was being claimed, had the capacity to judge the rectitude of the law. This was the very antithesis of the view of the common lawyers, who argued that the law could be understood only by those who had cultivated an "artificial" form of reason through years of disciplined study. Sidney did not deny that judges might assist juries with the finer points of the law but he insisted that common sense was all that was required to judge the law's rectitude.[151] It is worth

---

[147] *Discourses*, III:25, p. 365. "They who had felt the smart of the vices and follies of their Princes, knew what remedies were most fit to be applied, as well as the best time of applying them" (III:41, p. 439).

[148] *Discourses*, I:3, p. 9.

[149] "Grand and petit juries . . . are not only Judges of matters of fact, as whether a man be kill'd, but whether he be kill'd criminally" (*Discourses*, III:22, p. 354). On the place of juries, see also: III:15, p. 315; III:22, pp. 355–58; III:26, pp. 370–71.

[150] Leading examples include: [John Hawles], *The English-mans Right* (London: 1680), 10–11; [John Somers], *The Security of English-Mens Lives* (London: 1681), 10–11; [Care], *English Liberties*, 220–23; [Robert Ferguson], *The Second Part of No Protestant Plot* (London: 1682), 19–32.

[151] *Discourses*, III:26, pp. 370–71; III:25, pp. 365–66. Needless to say, Sidney be-

recalling in this context that Sidney, like the Levellers before him, harshly criticized the complexity of the English law, and argued that a drastically simplified legal system would be more just.

Taken together, these pieces of Sidney's theory lend credence to the claim that he believed that every man had the right to determine when revolution was necessary. Precisely how this highly atomized right would be put into practice is not clear, however. By temperament Sidney was a loner, and not given to political organization.[152] His frequent praise for biblical and classical examples of tyrannicide,[153] and his involvement in the Rye House Plot, may be symptomatic of his revolutionary vision: a single providential act of liberation. Here was Sidney at his most violent and anarchic, raising a cry that had not been heard in England since the notorious pamphlet *Killing, No Murder* had called for the assassination of Oliver Cromwell.[154]

At the same time, Sidney refused to believe that tyrannicide in and of itself could successfully reform a nation's government. According to Gilbert Burnet, Sidney frequently said that "it was all one to him whether James duke of York or James duke of Monmouth was to succeed."[155] Much more than disdain for the character of these two men was involved in this observation, for the whole point of both the Exclusion movement and the Rye House Plot had been to ensure that

---

lieved that his own jury lacked the minimum degree of independence necessary for common sense to hold sway. Freeholder restrictions on the franchise applied to juries as well.

[152] As he protested at his trial, "for my part, I do not know where to raise five men" for purpose of a rebellion ("The Trial of Colonel Algernon Sidney," in Howell, *State Trials*, 9:865).

[153] "In those Ages and Parts of the World, where there hath bin any thing of Vertue and Goodness, we may observe a . . . sort of Men, who would neither do Villanies, nor suffer more than the Laws did permit, or the consideration of the publick Peace did require. Whilst Tyrants with their Slaves, and the Instruments of their Cruelties, were accounted the Dregs of Mankind, and made the objects of detestation and scorn, these Men who delivered their Countries from such Plagues were thought to have something of Divine in them, and have bin famous above all the rest of Mankind to this day. Of this sort were *Pelopidas, Epaminondas, Thrasibulus, Harmodius, Aristogiton, Philopemen, Lucius Brutus, Publius Valerius, Marcus Brutus, C. Cassius, M. Cato*, with a multitude of others amongst the antient Heathens. Such as were Instruments of the like Deliverances amongst the Hebrews, as *Moses, Othniel, Ehud, Barac, Gideon, Sampson, Jeptha, Samuel, David, Jehu, the Maccabees* and others" (*Discourses*, I:3, p. 11). See also: II:24, pp. 175, 181; *Maxims*, 11, 52–53, 87ff.

[154] Edward Sexby and Silius Titus [William Allen, pseud.], *Killing, No Murder* (London: 1657).

[155] Gilbert Burnet, *Bishop Burnet's History of His Own Time*, ed. M. J. Routh, 2nd ed. (Oxford: Oxford University Press, 1833), 2:353.

Monmouth, and not York, assumed the throne on the death of Charles II. As Sidney recognized, "destroying the immediate instruments" of the nation's oppression could at most provide "a respite from ruin"; with the form of government left unchanged, the reign of the tyrant's successor could prove to be "no more than a lucid interval."[156] Failure to recognize that fact had been the mistake of

> all the Kingdoms of the *Arabians, Medes, Persians, Moors*, and others of the East. . . . Common sense instructs them, that barbarous pride, cruelty and madness grown to extremity, cannot be born: but they have no other way than to kill the Tyrant, and to do the like to his Successor if he fall into the same crimes. . . . But those Nations that are more generous, who set a higher value upon Liberty, and better understand the ways of preserving it, think it a small matter to destroy a Tyrant, unless they can also destroy the Tyranny. They endeavour to do the work thoroughly, either by changing the Government intirely, or reforming it according to the first institution, and making such good Laws as may preserve its integrity when reformed.[157]

Without constitutional change, tyrannicide was incapable of bringing an end to the government of will and force and introducing the government of law and consent.

Only in this context is it possible to evaluate Sidney's frequently stated claim that "all human Constitutions are subject to corruption, and must perish, unless they are timely renewed, and reduced to their first principles."[158] Though Sidney nowhere mentions them, this argument alludes to the classical theories of Polybius and Machiavelli. It was Polybius who first identified "the cycle of political revolution, the law of nature according to which constitutions change, are transformed, and finally revert to their original form." With an eye to this cycle, Machiavelli proclaimed that for a state to survive it had to "frequently be restored to its original principles"; "for it is clearer than daylight that, without renovation, these bodies do not last."[159] To slow or delay the inevitable corruption of governments, it was necessary to return them periodically to the purity of their original constitution.

---

[156] *Discourses*, III:41, pp. 439–40. Sidney was referring to the Roman Empire in these remarks; see also: III:4, p. 269.

[157] *Discourses*, III:41, p. 440.

[158] *Discourses*, II:13, p. 117. See also: II:30, p. 241; III:25, p. 366; III:27, p. 378; III:41, pp. 439–40.

[159] Polybius, *The Rise of the Roman Empire*, trans. Ian Scott-Kilvert (Harmondsworth: Penguin Books, 1979), 309; Niccolò Machiavelli, *The Discourses*, trans. Leslie Walker, ed. Bernard Crick (Harmondsworth: Penguin Books, 1970), 385.

It would be tempting to view Sidney's theory of revolution in this light and to see classical colors in his republican landscape. J.G.A. Pocock has attempted to do so with parallel arguments in the writings of James Harrington and his followers.[160] But unlike Harrington's argument, Sidney's vision of returning a government to its "first principles" had little more to do with Machiavelli's concept of *rinnovazione* than a similarity of words. The "first principles" to which he referred were drawn from a moral theory describing the foundations of legitimate governments, and not from a historical theory describing the movement of states between the six pure forms of government. As a result, Sidney took a very different attitude toward the relationship between corruption and change. To Machiavelli, these concepts were synonymous; all change was movement away from the perfect form of a mixed republic. Only by constantly returning a government to its perfect form could the debilitating spread of corruption be halted. To Sidney, on the other hand, change was often the necessary and proper response to the growth of corruption:

> Some men . . . have proposed a necessity of reducing every State once in an age or two, to the integrity of its first principle: but they ought to have examined, whether that principle be good or evil, or so good that nothing can be added to it, which none ever was; and this being so, those who will admit of no change would render Errors perpetual, and depriving Mankind of the benefits of Wisdom, Industry, Experience, and the right use of Reason, oblige all to continue in the miserable barbarity of their Ancestors, which sutes better with the name of a Wolf than that of a Man.[161]

Without changing the form or structure of a government, it was not possible to preserve the ends—the "first principles"—for which it had been created. When Sidney looked at the government of seventeenth-century England, he saw that "new Constitutions" were needed "to repair the breaches made upon the old." Without a radical departure from England's original constitution, freedom would soon be replaced by slavery. Such a belief was inconceivable within the Polybian-Machiavellian theory of history. As was so often the case in his writings, Sidney clothed new arguments within the respectable garb of classical concepts.

[160] J.G.A. Pocock, *The Machiavellian Moment* (Princeton: Princeton University Press, 1975), 407, 420. See also: *Politics, Language and Time* (New York: Atheneum, 1971), 129–32.

[161] *Discourses*, III:25, p. 366.

Conclusion

With his theory of revolution in place, Sidney's argument came full circle. As governments were instituted to preserve liberty, so changes in governments were sometimes necessary to cope with new threats to liberty. The purpose of revolution was to restore the rule of law; constitutional government and the separation of powers, in turn, were designed to facilitate this restoration by checking corruption, facilitating change, and advancing the public interest. It was Sidney's sincere hope that by adopting "new Constitutions" Englishmen might "repair the breaches" that had been "made upon the old." The passing of the Gothic polity posed many problems, but it also presented a great opportunity.

PART THREE

THE RADICAL HERITAGE

SIX

ALGERNON SIDNEY AND THE AMERICAN

REVOLUTION

For myself, I can hardly consider the name of Algernon
Sidney as anything other than an American name—
American in all its associations, and American in all its
influences.
(Robert C. Winthrop)[1]

THROUGHOUT the eighteenth century Algernon Sidney
was revered by radicals in Europe and America as a martyr
to liberty.[2] He was "the British Brutus," a man who had selflessly devoted his life to the cause of freedom. Perhaps nowhere was
Sidney's fame and influence more strongly felt than in revolutionary
America.[3] Writing in a London newspaper in 1765, Benjamin Franklin proclaimed that the Americans' refusal to accept the Stamp Act
was motivated by "a strong sense of liberty, a public spirit that de-

[1] *Algernon Sidney: A Lecture, Delivered Before the Boston Mercantile Association, December 21, 1853* (Boston: S. K. Whipple, 1854), 43.

[2] During the eighteenth century the *Discourses Concerning Government* was translated twice into French, twice into German, and reprinted eight times in England (see Bibliography). There are no studies of Sidney's place in German thought. French reactions to the *Discourses* are briefly noted in Paulette Carrive, *La pensée politique d'Algernon Sidney* (Paris: Méridiens Klincksieck, 1989), 219–22. Sidney's role in eighteenth-century English thought is discussed in Caroline Robbins, *The Eighteenth-Century Commonwealthman* (Cambridge, MA: Harvard University Press, 1959), and Blair Worden, "The Commonwealth Kidney of Algernon Sidney," *Journal of British Studies* 24 (January 1985): 1–40.

[3] Previous studies of Sidney's place in American thought are: Chester Greenough, "Algernon Sidney and the Motto of the Commonwealth of Massachusetts," *Proceedings of the Massachusetts Historical Society* 51 (1917–1918): 259–82; Caroline Robbins, "Algernon Sidney's *Discourses Concerning Government*: Textbook of Revolution," *William and Mary Quarterly*, 3rd ser., 3 (July 1947): 267–96; Peter Karsten, *Patriot-Heroes in England and America* (Madison: University of Wisconsin Press, 1978). I have also profited from: H. Trevor Colbourn, *The Lamp of Experience: Whig History and the Intellectual Origins of the American Revolution* (Chapel Hill: University of North Carolina Press, 1965); Bernard Bailyn, *The Ideological Origins of the American Revolution* (Cambridge, MA: Harvard University Press, 1967); Bernard Bailyn, *The Origins of American Politics* (New York: Vintage Books, 1967); Gordon Wood, *The Creation of the American Republic, 1776–1787* (New York: W. W. Norton, 1972).

spises all selfish private considerations, and thence a determination to risque everything rather than submit voluntarily to what they deem an unconstitutional exertion of power. If they are mistaken, 'tis their misfortune, not their fault. Your most celebrated writers on the constitution, your *Seldens*, your *Lockes*, and your *Sidneys*, have reasoned them into this mistake."[4] Franklin's invocation of Sidney's name in connection with the American cause was not idiosyncratic. Sidney's writings and the story of his life were staples in the literary diet of eighteenth-century Americans.[5] During the decades of political and intellectual turmoil surrounding the Revolution, they were repeatedly turned to for example, inspiration, and instruction.

To the colonists, the single most important fact about Sidney's life was the manner of his death. By his unselfish devotion to liberty, Sidney set a standard against which men repeatedly measured themselves; by his martyrdom, he graphically demonstrated the evils of unchecked power. Colonial Americans also read the *Discourses Concerning Government* with care and precision. They cited Sidney on a wide range of issues, from the corruption of men to the rule of law, and from the representative nature of government to the right of revolution. The distinction between these two facets of Sidney's impact on American thought—his fame as a martyr and his influence as a political theorist—has not previously been noted. But it is vital to an understanding of the ideologically problematic role he played in eighteenth-century America. Sidney's fame and his influence generally reinforced each other. But on occasion they did not, as when opponents of the Revolution and the Constitution attempted to capitalize on his fame in order to counter the influence of his ideas. When attention is restricted to those cases in which the influence of Sidney's ideas was strongest, a striking conclusion emerges: virtually all of the

[4] Benjamin Franklin, " 'F.B': Second Reply to Tom Hint," in *The Papers of Benjamin Franklin*, ed. Leonard Labaree (New Haven: Yale University Press, 1960–), 12:413.

[5] The evidence based on colonial library-holdings and book purchases is presented in Colbourn, *Lamp of Experience*, and summarized in Karsten, *Patriot-Heroes*, 34–37. Regard for the *Discourses* can be seen in the fact that Franklin ordered a copy for the Library Company of Philadelphia in 1732 and later recommended that it be used in the curriculum of the Academy of Philadelphia, while Jefferson frequently included the *Discourses* in his syllabi for legal education (Edwin Wolf, "The First Books and Printed Catalogues of the Library Company of Philadelphia," *Pennsylvania Magazine of History and Biography* 78 [January 1954]: 45–70; Benjamin Franklin, "Proposals Relating to the Education of Youth in Pennsylvania," 1749, in *Papers*, 3:405–7; Thomas Jefferson to Robert Skipwith, 3 August 1771, in *The Papers of Thomas Jefferson*, ed. Julian P. Boyd [Princeton: Princeton University Press, 1950–], 1:76–81; Thomas Jefferson to Bernard Moore, c.1772, in *The Writings of Thomas Jefferson*, ed. Paul Leicester Ford [New York: 1892–99], 9:480–85).

"republican" principles drawn from Sidney's writings were perfectly compatible with Lockean liberalism. Indeed, the only salient difference between Sidney and Locke in the minds of most colonists was that Sidney's violent opposition to the Stuarts made him a much more "radical" figure than the esteemed author of *An Essay Concerning Human Understanding*. This conclusion casts doubt on the widely held view that there existed a distinct and coherent "republican" language of politics in revolutionary America that was distinct from and in tension with Lockean liberalism.[6]

Interpreting Sidney's Place in American Thought

The task of measuring Sidney's impact on eighteenth-century American thought presents a number of difficult interpretive problems. American reactions to Sidney's writings and the story of his life were complex and wide-ranging. Three examples help chart the perimeter of the political and intellectual terrain that will be mapped in this chapter. First, there is Benjamin Rush, newly arrived in Edinburgh in 1766 for his medical studies. In the course of a conversation with John Bostock, a Scotsman and fellow student, Rush learned that one of Bostock's forefathers had

> commanded a company under Oliver Cromwell. I told him that my first American ancestor held the same rank in Cromwell's army. This was like a discovery of relationship between persons who had previously behaved as strangers to each other. He now opened his mind fully to me, and

[6] The foundation for the "republican synthesis" was laid in Robbins's *Eighteenth-Century Commonwealthman* and Bailyn's *Ideological Origins*, though Bailyn in particular was careful to note the importance of Lockean ideas to eighteenth-century Americans. The scope of this interpretive movement is staggering; among the most important contributions are: Wood, *Creation of the American Republic*; J.G.A. Pocock, *The Machiavellian Moment* (Princeton: Princeton University Press, 1975); J.G.A. Pocock, ed., *Three British Revolutions* (Princeton: Princeton University Press, 1980); Lance Banning, *The Jeffersonian Persuasion* (Ithaca: Cornell University Press, 1978); Rowland Berthoff, "Independence and Attachment, Virtue and Interest: From Republican Citizen to Free Enterprise, 1787–1837," in *Uprooted Americans*, ed. Richard Bushman, Neil Harris, et al. (Boston: Little, Brown and Co., 1979), 97–124; Drew McCoy, *The Elusive Republic* (Chapel Hill: University of North Carolina Press, 1980); Robert Shalhope, "Toward a Republican Synthesis: The Emergence of an Understanding of Republicanism in American Historiography," *William and Mary Quarterly*, 3rd ser., 29 (January 1972): 49–80; Robert Shalhope, "Republicanism and Early American Historiography," *William and Mary Quarterly*, 3rd ser., 39 (April 1982): 334–56. As befits such a powerful current of ideas, the list of critics of republican revisionism is equally long; see in particular the works by Joyce Appleby, John P. Diggins, and Isaac Kramnick cited in the Bibliography.

declared himself to be an advocate for the Republican principles for which our ancestors had fought. He spoke in rapture of the character of Sidney, and said that he once got out of his carriage in passing by Sidney's country house, and spent several hours in walking in the wood in which he was accustomed to meditate when he composed his famous treatise upon government. Never before had I heard the authority of Kings called in question. I had been taught to consider them nearly as essential to political order as the Sun is to the order of our Solar System. For the first moment in my life I now exercised my reason upon the subject of government. I renounced the prejudices of my education upon it; and from that time to the present, all my reading, observations, and reflexions have tended more and more to shew the absurdity of hereditary power, and to prove that no form of government can be rational but that which is derived from the Suffrages of the people who are the subjects of it.[7]

Rush's exuberant conversion to Sidney's republican doctrines was matched only by his reluctance to act on his newfound beliefs. "The change produced in my political principles . . . had no effect on my conversation or conduct. I considered the ancient order of things with respect to government as fixed and perpetual, and I enjoyed in theory only the new elevating system of government I had adopted."[8] Here was a most peculiar form of influence, a complete conversion in theory with "no effect on . . . conversation or conduct."

Rush's conversion to republicanism was virtually complete before he became involved in colonial politics. In the case of John Adams, this order was reversed. As Adams recalled after the Revolution, "I

---

[7] Benjamin Rush, *The Autobiography of Benjamin Rush*, ed. George W. Corner (Princeton: Princeton University Press, 1948), 46. The leveling and liberating potential of Sidney's ideas did not go unnoticed by his eighteenth-century critics, as revealed in the following satirical letter: "There was a time, my lord, when I thought that a bastard kind of liberty, that did permit a multitude of Catos, Brutuses, Senecas, and Socrateses, to call Johnson a hireling, Warburton an atheist, Burke a Jesuit, Mansfield an ass, Wilkes a saint. . . . But my long meditations upon Machiavel, together with a careful perusal of Algernon Sidney's works, and Molesworth's Account of Denmark, have turned me into so genuine a liberty man, that I now think it very pretty to curse a king's mother when dead, after having poured on her all kind of abuse when alive. I push even so far the liberality of my new notions, that though I know nothing of any queen, I am vastly pleased when I listen to a ballad, as I go along, in which a fair queen is called a damned____without the least ceremony. Huzza, my boys! Wilkes and liberty for ever! and a plague upon my former apathy about politics!" (Giuseppe Baretti to James, earl of Charlemont, 25 February 1772, in HMC, *12th Report, Appendix, Part X: Manuscripts and Correspondence of James, first earl of Charlemont* [London: HMSO, 1891], 1:310).

[8] Rush, *Autobiography*, 46.

had read Harrington, Sydney, Hobbs, Nedham and Lock, but with very little Application to any particular Views: till these Debates in [the Continental] Congress and these Interrogations in public and private, turned my thoughts to those Researches, which produced the *Thoughts on Government*, the Constitution of Massachusetts, and at length the *Defence of the Constitutions of the United States* and the *Discourses on Davila*."[9] Without his experience in colonial politics, particularly in the wake of the Stamp Act, the Townshend Duties, and the garrisoning of Boston, it is unlikely Adams would ever have seen the need to embrace the theories of Sidney, Locke, and others; on the other hand, it is equally unlikely he would have experienced these events as he did had he not been steeped in the literature of English radicalism. As he observed in a rough draft of his 1776 *Thoughts on Government*, "In my early youth, the Works of Sidney, Harrington, Lock, Milton, Nedham, Neville, Burnet, Hoadley, were put into my Hands; and the miserable Situation of our Country, for fifteen Years past, has frequently reminded me of their Principles and Reasonings. They have convinced me that there is no good Government but what is Republican."[10] Adams was a careful student of Sidney's writings—perhaps the most careful in all the American Revolution—and his reflections on his political education give testimony to the complex interplay of ideas and events during this period.

Not every colonist who revolted against the British empire did so on the basis of his or her reading of Sidney or Locke, however. In 1842 a young judge interviewed Captain Preston, a ninety-one-year-old veteran of the Concord fight:

"Did you take up arms against intolerable oppressions?" he asked.

"Oppressions?" replied the old man. "I didn't feel them."

"What, were you not oppressed by the Stamp Act?"

"I never saw one of those stamps. I certainly never paid a penny for one of them."

"Well, what then about the tea tax?"

"I never drank a drop of the stuff; the boys threw it all overboard."

"Then I suppose you had been reading Harrington or Sidney and Locke about the eternal principles of liberty?"

"Never heard of 'em. We read only the Bible, the Catechism, Watt's Psalms and Hymns, and the Almanac."

[9] John Adams, *Diary and Autobiography of John Adams*, ed. L. H. Butterfield (Cambridge, MA: Harvard University Press, 1961), 3:358–59.

[10] John Adams to William Hooper, ante 27 March 1776, in *Papers of John Adams*, ed. Robert Taylor (Cambridge, MA: Harvard University Press, 1977–), 4:74.

"Well then, what was the matter? And what did you mean in going to the fight?"

"Young man, what we meant in going for those redcoats was this: *we always had governed ourselves, and we always meant to. They didn't mean we should.*"[11]

Captain Preston's experience was the inverse of Benjamin Rush's: he brought about a revolution in his conduct without bothering to adopt a "new and elevating system of government." The story of this chapter is the story of men like Benjamin Rush and John Adams; and Captain Preston's recollections help draw attention to the fact that that is not the same thing as a history of the American Revolution.

Even when attention is restricted to men like Rush and Adams, the task of measuring the precise nature of Sidney's influence is fraught with difficulties. Like their English cousins, eighteenth-century American writers were habitual list-makers, fortifying every argument with a litany of respected authorities. These lists gave additional weight and importance to an author's claims and reflect the deeply conservative cast of Anglo-American political writing at this time. Consequently, we must be cautious in evaluating John Adams's claim that the Massachusetts constitution of 1780 was "Locke, Sidney, and Rousseau and DeMably reduced to practice" or Thomas Jefferson's assertion that the authority of the Declaration of Independence rested on "the harmonizing sentiments of the day, whether expressed in conversation, in letters, printed essays, or in the elementary books of public right, as Aristotle, Cicero, Locke, Sidney, &c."[12] As John Dunn has observed in an analysis of John Locke's influence on eighteenth-century English and American thought, "It was not that Locke meant nothing to those who favoured the different litanies; merely that there is no reason to suppose that anything Locke ever wrote caused the least deflection of their political behaviour from the paths it would otherwise have followed."[13] Dunn's skepticism concerning the causal efficacy of Locke's political writings should be applied to Sidney's as well. In many cases, the invocation of Sidney's name may

---

[11] Quoted in Samuel Eliot Morrison, *The Oxford History of the American People* (New York: Oxford University Press, 1965), 212–13.

[12] John Adams to Edmund Jenings, 7 June 1780, in *The Works of John Adams*, ed. Charles Francis Adams (Boston: Little and Brown, 1850–56), 4:216; Thomas Jefferson to Henry Lee, 8 May 1825, in *The Writings of Thomas Jefferson*, ed. Andrew Lipscomb and Albert Burgh (Washington, DC: Thomas Jefferson Memorial Association, 1907), 16:116–17.

[13] John Dunn, "The Politics of Locke in England and America in the Eighteenth Century," in *John Locke: Problems and Perspectives*, ed. John W. Yolton (Cambridge: Cambridge University Press, 1969), 60.

signify little more than the desire of a writer to tap its affective power, much as contemporary American politicians invoke the names of Lincoln or Roosevelt to validate their actions.

At the same time, the standard used to measure whether or not Sidney had an influence on American thought should not be unattainably high. It might be possible to deconstruct each and every invocation of Sidney's name or writings, proving that no behavioral or intellectual changes were associated with them.[14] But this would be no more satisfactory than naively assuming that every invocation gave proof of Sidney's influence. Eighteenth-century Americans read the *Discourses* with great care and frequently referred to its influence on their ideas and values. When Jonathan Mayhew proclaims of his education in the principles of civil government that "excepting what I learnt from nature, from the ancient greeks & romans, & from the holy Scriptures, I own I learnt them from such writers as Sidney, Locke and Hoadley,"[15] or when Andrew Eliot states that Sidney "was the first who taught me to form any just sentiments on government,"[16] we must at some level simply take them at their word. Though we may lack sufficient evidence to prove the causal efficacy of Sidney's ideas on men like Mayhew and Eliot, it would immeasurably impoverish our understanding of American political thought to discount their professions as simple window dressing.

Two further problems complicate the story of Sidney's influence on American thought. First, to understand Sidney's significance for eighteenth-century thought, it is not enough to recover the seventeenth-century meaning of his arguments. The paradigm of intentional explanation, so crucial to understanding the original meaning of a text, can be misleading when applied to the interpretation of a

[14] The "fallacy of decomposition" entailed by such an undertaking stems in part from the almost unbridgeable gap between the evidential standards of a causal analysis and our (relatively) scanty knowledge of the evolution of ideas in eighteenth-century America.

[15] Jonathan Mayhew, Mayhew Papers No. 61, fols. 54–55, quoted in Charles W. Akers, *Called Unto Liberty: A Life of Jonathan Mayhew 1720–1766* (Cambridge, MA: Harvard University Press, 1964), 18. As Mayhew reflected in 1766, "Having been initiated, in youth, in the doctrines of civil liberty, as they were taught by such men as Plato, Demosthenes, Cicero, and other renowned persons among the ancients; and such as Sidney and Milton, Locke and Hoadley, among the moderns; I liked them; they seemed rational. Having, earlier still learnt from the holy scriptures, that wise, brave and vertuous men were always friends to liberty . . . I would not, I cannot now, tho' past middle age, relinquish the fair object of my youthful affections, Liberty" (Jonathan Mayhew, *The snare broken. A Thanksgiving-Discourse, Preached . . . May 23, 1766* [Boston: 1766], 35).

[16] Andrew Eliot to Thomas Hollis, 13 May 1767, in *Massachusetts Historical Society—Collections*, 4th ser., 4 (1858): 403.

text's later influence.[17] When placed in political and intellectual contexts unlike those within which it was originally conceived, a text may assume a whole new range of meanings and have implications unintended by its author. Indeed, "misreadings" of a text may be the most powerful readings, for they often permit an author to speak with a simplicity and directness foreign to his or her original intention. Marx is not "Marxism," Rousseau is not "Rousseauism" and the thought of Algernon Sidney is not (necessarily) the same as the ideas his readers obtained from him. As a result, the network of claims and arguments developed in the previous chapters of this book provides but a first clue to the ways Sidney may have influenced eighteenth-century Americans. The focus of this chapter is interpretation, not composition.

The second problem complicating any analysis of Sidney's influence on American thought arises from his place in the writings of the "true," "real," or "independent" Whigs of England. Though of marginal importance in their own country, these men—Walter Moyle, Robert viscount Molesworth, John Trenchard, James Gordon, Benjamin Hoadley, James Burgh, and others—had a profound influence on colonial Americans.[18] Of particular importance in this context is the fact that the "true" Whigs drew their inspiration from the writings of three seventeenth-century English radicals: James Harrington, John Milton, and Algernon Sidney. Consequently, alongside direct encounters with the text of the *Discourses*, colonial Americans indirectly encountered Sidney's ideas through the writings of the "true" Whigs. This means that any study of Sidney's influence on American thought may be subject to two errors: it may overstate Sidney's influence, by giving him credit for ideas whose importance lay in the fact that they were held in common by a large group of respected pamphleteers; or it may understate his influence, by failing to recognize the indirect impact his writings had by way of the tracts of the "true" Whigs. Both of these problems are associated with the difficulty of extricating the influence of one (albeit central) member

[17] According to John Dunn, the aim of interpretation should be "grasping the point of the original intellectual enterprise" (John Dunn, "The Identity of the History of Ideas," *Philosophy* 43 [April 1968]: 99). Dunn's commitment to this principle significantly weakens his analysis of Locke's place in eighteenth-century American thought, however, for his methodological premise seems to be that Locke could have had influence only at those times when the intellectual needs of Americans precisely mirrored the needs that Locke himself sought to address (Dunn, "Politics of Locke in England and America," esp. 74–80). As Sidney's influence on American political thought clearly demonstrates, this is an untenable hypothesis.

[18] The writings of the "true" Whigs "dominated the colonists' miscellaneous learning and shaped it into a coherent whole" (Bailyn, *Ideological Origins*, 34).

of a family of related theorists. Unfortunately, neither can be completely eliminated, and thus an element of indeterminacy dogs any attempt to chart Sidney's influence on American thought. A striking example of this problem is presented by the writings of Tom Paine. Though Paine's arguments closely resemble Sidney's, he makes no direct reference to him in any of his works. Indeed, the only known connection between them is Burgh's *Political Disquisitions*, cited by Paine and chock-full of quotations from Sidney.[19] In the absence of dramatic biographical or textual discoveries, we simply have no way of accurately measuring the influence Sidney had on Paine.

Given the wide range of reactions to Sidney's writings and the story of his life, and the difficult methodological problems facing any interpretation of them, the aim of this chapter is necessarily modest: to determine when literate eighteenth-century Americans found Sidney of interest or importance, and to suggest some reasons why those responses took the form that they did. As an account of the ideological contours of the American Revolution, it is necessarily incomplete. Tracing the story of Sidney's influence is much like following a single path through a complex landscape: though many landmarks may be revealed, a large number are also left hidden and out of sight. Fortunately, there is ample evidence indicating that Sidney provided an important point of reference for eighteenth-century Americans as they gradually moved toward independence and the creation of a new form of government.

Sidney's Influence before 1760

Copies of Sidney's *Discourses Concerning Government* made their way to America soon after its publication in 1698.[20] According to a recent study, only Trenchard and Gordon's *Cato's Letters* and Locke's *Two Treatises* could be found with greater frequency in colonial libraries.[21] But Sidney's impact on America before 1760 was largely a consequence of the events of his life, and not the content of his writings. To colonial Americans, the single most important fact about Sidney's

[19] Tom Paine, "Common Sense," in *The Complete Writings of Thomas Paine*, ed. Philip S. Foner, 2 vols. (New York: Citadel Press, 1945), 1:38. Burgh's *Disquisitions* was printed in Philadelphia in 1775; for quotations from Sidney, see: 1:vii, 21, 191–92; 3:65, 444, 451–52, 456–57.

[20] William Penn received two copies of the *Discourses* in 1700, though he apparently experienced great difficulty selling them (Edwin Wolf, "A Parcel of Books for the Province in 1700," *Pennsylvania Magazine of History and Biography* 89 [1965]: 429–46).

[21] Karsten, *Patriot-Heroes*, 34–35.

life was that he had been tried and executed by those men of blood, Charles and James Stuart; less well known, but also of interest, was Sidney's contribution to William Penn's constitution for the province of Pennsylvania.

Sidney's role in the drafting of Penn's "Fundamental Constitutions" provides the clearest and strongest example of his influence on American politics. Until recently, however, the only evidence we had concerning Sidney's contribution to Pennsylvania's provincial charter was a letter written by William Penn on 13 October 1681. Penn had been Sidney's campaign manager in the parliamentary elections of 1679 and may have collaborated with him in the writing of political tracts at that time.[22] But in 1681 Penn wrote Sidney with the scorching anger of a man who had been betrayed:

> I have been askt by severall since I came last to town if Coll Sydney & I were fallen out, and when I deny'd it, and laught at it; they told me I was mistaken, & to Convince me, told me that he had used me very ill to severall persons, if not Companys; saying, I had a good County [Pennsylvania] but the basest laws in the world, not to be endured or lived under, and that the Turk was not more absolute than I. This made me remember the discours we had at my house about my drawing Constitutions, not as proposals but as if fixt to the hand: And that as my Act, to which the rest were to comply if they would be Concerned with me. But withall I could not but call to mind that thy objections were presently complyed with both by my verball denyall of all such Construction as the words might bear as if they were imposed, and not yet free from debate, and also that I took my Pen & immediately alter'd the Termes so as they Corresponded (and truly I thought more properly) with thy objection & sense. Upon this thou didst draw a draught as to the Frame of the Government gave it me to read, & we discourst it, with a considerable agreement: it was afterwards Called for back by thee, to finish and polish. I suspended proceeding in the Business of the Government, ever since (that being to be done after other Matters) instead of any farther Conference about it.[23]

The precise meaning of Penn's letter is elusive, but when first published in 1834 it sparked a heated controversy over the nature and extent of Sidney's influence on Penn's constitutional endeavors. After

[22] Both *Englands Great Interest In The Choice of this New Parliament* and *One Project for the Good of England*, published in 1679 under the pseudonym Philanglus and widely attributed to Penn, bear earmarks of Sidney's style and ideas.

[23] William Penn to [Algernon Sidney], 13 October 1681, in *The Papers of William Penn*, ed. Richard Dunn and Mary Maples Dunn (Philadelphia: University of Pennsylvania Press, 1982), 2:124–25.

surveying these arguments and the evidence on which they are based, Peter Karsten concluded that Sidney's influence must have been minimal. As Penn moved from the quite radical "Fundamental Constitutions of Pennsylvania" to the economically and politically more conservative "Frame of Government," he was abandoned by Sidney.[24]

Evidence recently made available in *The Papers of Benjamin Franklin* places the question of Sidney's influence on the provincial constitution of Pennsylvania in an entirely different light, however. In his marginal notes to Allan Ramsey's *Thoughts on the Origin and Nature of Government* (1769), Franklin responded to Ramsey's charge that "the assertion that [colonial] charters are not charters, but Pacta conventa, is brim-full of absurdity": "[Ramsey] does not know that both Sidney and Locke were concerned in drawing up two of those Charters, viz. that for Carolina and that for Pennsylvania. This paragraph is all mere Banter."[25] Sixty-five years before Penn's letter was made public, Franklin was trumpeting Sidney as one of the authors of Pennsylvania's charter. While it is possible Franklin had access to the original manuscript of Penn's letter during his sojourn in London, it is far more likely that his statement reflected a widely held belief and that Sidney's role in the drafting of the charter was part of the lore of Pennsylvania's government.

This belief, regardless of its basis in fact, is central to an appreciation of Sidney's place in pre-revolutionary thought. Like many British-Americans, Pennsylvanians recognized that the surviving colonial charters "had become defensive bulwarks against the misuse of power."[26] At the same time, many Pennsylvanians—Franklin included—felt that the proprietary charter gave inordinate power to the heirs of William Penn and that it had to be either drastically changed or abolished. In waging this fight, these men invoked Sidney as a witness to the corruption of Pennsylvania's government.[27] The

[24] Peter Karsten, "Who was 'Colonel Sidney'?: A Note on the Meaning of the October 13, 1681, Penn-Sidney Letter," *Pennsylvania Magazine of History and Biography* 91 (April 1967): 193–98.

[25] Franklin, "Marginalia," in *Papers*, 16:319–20.

[26] Bailyn, *Ideological Origins*, 192.

[27] In a satiric letter attributed to William Smith, an Anglican clergyman and tool of Thomas Penn's, Smith described how he would teach students at the College of Philadelphia: "I will teach them to spurn at *magna charta* charters of priviledges and the laws of the English constitution and if ever I find Lock, Sidney, or *Cato's Letters* within the walls of my jurisdiction, they shall be instantly condemned to the flames, their notions of the liberties of the English constitution carefully eradicated, and *machiavel* shall be the study of my pupils in their rooms. Thus will I instruct the rising generation in the principles of slavery, and in an implicit obedience to their superiors" (*Pennsylvania Journal*, 6 April 1758, quoted in Franklin, *Papers*, 8:46 n. 2).

very form of the charter, a compact between king and colonists that had been revised over time, encouraged Pennsylvanians to think in terms of the constituent power of the people and to view changes in the charter as acts of restoration. These ideas were central to the development of constitutional thought in America; and though they cannot be attributed to Sidney alone, not even in Pennsylvania, they help shed light on the matrix of ideas to which he contributed.

To the vast majority of colonists, however, the most important fact about Sidney's life was not that he had played a role in the drafting of Pennsylvania's colonial charter, but that he had been tried and executed at the express command of Charles II. The first extended treatment of Sidney's martyrdom appeared in the course of James Alexander's successful defense of John Peter Zenger against the charge of seditious libel. In Zenger's habeas corpus hearing of 23 November 1734, Alexander drew attention to the "well-known" fact that Sidney had been "attainted of treason for writing a book, which since the Revolution has been esteemed one of the best books of government in the English language. . . . From whence I would infer that in times when men were murdered by colour of law for doing & asserting the liberty of the subject against the arbitrary power which was then brought and fast bringing upon the nation, I say precedents of those times are rather to be looked on as rocks to avoid splitting on rather than as precedents to follow."[28] Three years later Alexander returned to these themes in a series of articles published in Franklin's *Pennsylvania Gazette*. "Sidney, the sword foe of tyranny, was a gentleman of noble birth, of sublime understanding and exalted courage," while "King Charles II aimed at the subversion of the government, but concealed his designs under a deep hypocrisy."[29] Sidney's trial—in which the manuscript of the *Discourses* was introduced as a second witness to his treason on the principle that "scribere est agere"[30]—was "a pregnant instance of the danger that attends a law for punishing words; and of the little security the most valuable men have for their lives in that society where a judge by remote inferences and distant innuendoes may construe the most innocent expressions into capital crimes. Sidney, the British Brutus, the warm, the steady friend of liberty, who from a diffusive love to mankind left them that invalu-

[28] James Alexander, "Notes for Zenger's Habeas Corpus Hearing, 23 November 1734," in *A Brief Narrative of the Case and Trial of John Peter Zenger*, ed. Stanley Katz, 2nd ed. (Cambridge, MA: Harvard University Press, 1972), 210.

[29] Alexander, *Pennsylvania Gazette*, 17–24 November 1737, in *Brief Narrative*, 188, 186.

[30] "The Trial of Colonell Algernon Sidney," in *A Complete Collection of State Trials*, ed. T. B. Howell (London: 1816), 9:889.

able legacy, his immortal discourses on government, was for those very discourses MURDERED by the hands of lawless power."[31] Alexander's portrait contains three elements that can be found in virtually every eighteenth-century sketch of Sidney's trial and execution: the resolute conduct of Algernon Sidney, author of the "immortal" *Discourses Concerning Government* and a "steady friend of liberty"; the unconscionable behavior of Lord Chief Justice Jeffreys, who used "remote inferences and distant innuendoes" to condemn innocent men; and the despotic plans of Charles II, a tyrant who would stop at nothing to augment his "lawless power." The last of these elements was all-important, for Sidney's fame as a martyr was intimately connected to the fact that he had been killed as part of a conspiracy to enslave England.

Sidney's martyrdom was the most powerful piece of evidence that could have been given to verify the truth of his writings. As the latter preached, so the former graphically demonstrated the consequence of permitting one man to enjoy arbitrary and unlimited power. Had Sidney not been a martyr, it is unlikely the *Discourses* would have been as widely read in eighteenth-century America; had he not written the *Discourses*, on the other hand, it is unlikely his death would have received the attention it did.

When focusing on Sidney's death, the colonists tended to highlight his innocence and the injustice of his execution. Thus in *Poor Richard Improved* for 1750, Franklin noted that on 7 December 1683 "was the honourable Algernon Sidney, Esq; beheaded, charg'd with a pretended Plot, but whose chief Crime was the Writing an excellent Book, intituled, *Discourses on Government*. A Man of admirable Parts, and great Integrity."[32] But like many Americans, Franklin was of two minds concerning Algernon Sidney: he was the innocent victim of Stuart despotism, but he was also a militant defender of liberty. Thus five years later, Franklin's *Pennsylvania Gazette* drew attention to Sidney's motto: "Manus haec inimica tyrannis / Ense petit placidam sub libertate quietem." The same article included two "extracts" from the *Discourses* that "deserve Notice, and will exact it at this melancholy Juncture":

I. "He that builds a city, and does not intend it should increase, commits as great an Absurdity, as if he should desire his Child might ever continue under the same weakness in which he is born. If it do not grow, it

---

[31] Alexander, *Pennsylvania Gazette*, 17–24 November 1737, in *Brief Narrative*, 189. See also: *Pennsylvania Gazette*, 24 November–1 December 1737, in *Brief Narrative*, 190–92.
[32] Franklin, "Poor Richard Improved, 1750," in *Papers*, 3:455.

must pine and perish; for in this World nothing is permanent; that which does not grow better will grow worse."

II. "That Government which ought to be valued, *above all*, in Point of Wisdom as well as Justice, is the Government given by GOD to the *Hebrews*, which *chiefly* fitted them for War, and to make Conquests. . . . Every Man was obliged to go out to War, except such as had married a Wife, or upon other special Occasions were *for a Time* excused."[33]

The context for these quotations is critical. In 1754 Franklin had unsuccessfully advocated "The Albany Plan of Union," a quasi-federal system of government designed for the colonies' "Mutual Defence and Security, and for Extending the British Settlements in North America."[34] By mid-1755 the colonies were reeling under the impact of Braddock's defeat in the French and Indian War, and Franklin undertook the responsibility of both moving a militia act through the Pennsylvania Assembly and organizing the colony's frontier defenses.[35] Under such circumstances, Sidney's militancy, his whole-hearted embrace of the use of political power to expand the sphere of liberty, and his endorsement of militias must have resonated powerfully with Franklin's sense of the needs of colonial America.

1760–1768

Before the Stamp Act crisis, no mention was made of Sidney's justification of resistance and revolution. When Franklin's *Pennsylvania Gazette* quoted Sidney's incendiary motto in 1755, it was meant to mobilize the colonists against the French, not the British. But as the tensions between England and her American colonies mounted, Sidney was read more carefully, and his arguments were used in new and different ways. There is no evidence to suggest that reading the *Discourses* "caused" the Revolution; colonial Americans were the most reluctant of revolutionaries, and it is hard to imagine any theory of government "causing" them to rebel. But like Locke's *Two Treatises*, Sidney's *Discourses* situated men and women within a matrix of ideas that made rebellion not only conceivable, but under certain circum-

[33] *Pennsylvania Gazette*, 20 November 1755. The passages are from *Discourses*, II:23, p. 165; II:22, p. 162.

[34] Franklin, "The Albany Plan of Union," in *Papers*, 5:387.

[35] Franklin, "Autobiography," in *Writings*, ed. Lemay, 1440–52. See also Franklin's "Dialogue . . . Concerning the Present State of Affairs in Pennsylvania," 18 December 1755, in *Papers*, 6:295–306.

stances obligatory. In this way it encouraged the colonists to see themselves in ways they otherwise might not have.

John Adams gave powerful expression to Sidney's expanding role in American political thought in his 1765 *Dissertation on the Canon and the Feudal Law*:

> Let us dare to read, think, speak and write. . . . In a word, let every sluice of knowledge be open'd and set a flowing. The encroachments upon liberty, in the reigns of the first James and the first Charles, by turning the general attention of learned men to government, are said to have produced the greatest number of consummate statesmen, which has ever been seen in any age, or nation. Your Clarendons, Southamptons, Seldens, Hampdens, Faulklands, Sidneys, Locks, Harringtons, are all said to have owed their eminence in political knowledge, to the tyrannies of those reigns. The prospect, now before us, in America, ought in the same manner to engage the attention of every man of learning to matters of power and of right, that we may be neither led nor driven blindfolded to irretrievable destruction.[36]

A "direct and formal design . . . to enslave all America" was on foot in England, and its chief instruments were those twin engines of destruction, the canon law of the Church and the feudal law of absolute monarchy. But "the true source of our sufferings, has been our timidity," for the simple fact was that "wherever a general Knowledge and sensibility have prevailed among the People, Arbitrary Government and every kind of oppression, have lessened and disappeared in Proportion."[37] As Sidney, Locke, and others had dared to challenge the forces of despotism in the seventeenth century, so Americans must do in the eighteenth century.

Adams's argument rested on the belief that the principles of liberty uncovered by Sidney, Locke, and their fellow "illuminators" were embodied in the English constitution. The conflicts between England and her American colonies were aberrations, the foul fruit of ministerial factions, misunderstandings, and inadequately articulated imperial relations. Consequently, the "true" principles of the English constitution could be invoked against the practices of the English government.

Adams's use of Sidney, Locke, and others to explain the "true" meaning of the English constitution was typical of American pamphlets written during the 1760s. In *The Rights of Colonies Examined*,

[36] John Adams, "Dissertation on the Canon and the Feudal Law," 1765, in *Papers*, 1:126–27.

[37] Adams, "Canon and Feudal Law," in *Papers*, 1:127, 122, 108.

for example, Stephen Hopkins proposed to "consider the British constitution as it at present stands, on Revolution principles, and from thence endeavor to find the measure of the magistrate's power and the people's obedience." What were those principles? According to Hopkins,

> This glorious constitution, the best that ever existed among men, will be confessed by all to be founded by compact and established by consent of the people. By this most beneficent compact British subjects are to be governed only agreeable to laws to which themselves have some way consented, and are not to be compelled to part with their property but as it is called for by the authority of such laws. The former is truly liberty; the latter is really to be possessed of property and to have something that may be called one's own.
>
> On the contrary, those who are governed at the will of another, or of others, and whose property may be taken from them by taxes or otherwise without their own consent and against their will, are in the miserable condition of slaves. "For liberty solely consists in an independency upon the will of another; and by the name of slave we understand a man who can neither dispose of his person or god, but enjoys all at the will of his master," says Sidney on government.[38]

In precisely the same manner, Landon Carter invoked the names of "*Locke, Sydney, Selden* and Others" to justify the claim that "Representation in Parliament was evidently inherent by Birth, in every *Englishman*,"[39] and James Otis defended the right of the colonists not to be taxed without the consent of their representatives by reference to the writings of Locke and Sidney.[40]

The structure of American arguments did not go unnoticed in En-

---

[38] Stephen Hopkins, "The Rights of Colonies Examined," 1765, in *Pamphlets of the American Revolution 1750–1776*, ed. Bernard Bailyn (Cambridge, MA: Harvard University Press, 1965), 1:507–8. The passage quoted is from *Discourses*, I:5, p. 12.

[39] Landon Carter, September 1765, in " 'Not to be Governed or Taxed, but by . . . Our Representatives': Four Essays in Opposition to the Stamp Act by Landon Carter," ed. Jack P. Greene, *Virginia Magazine of History and Biography* 76 (July 1968): 271. See also: 281.

[40] James Otis, *A Vindication of the Conduct of the House of Representatives of the Province of the Massachusetts-Bay* (Boston: 1762), 20. Otis's pamphlet also highlights the extent to which Sidney was perceived to be a more radical figure than Locke: "It is possible there are a few . . . that can't bear the names of Liberty and Property, much less that the things signified by those terms, should be enjoyed by the vulgar. These may be inclined to brand some of the principles advanced in the vindication of the house, with the odious epithets *seditious* and *levelling*. Had any thing to justify them been quoted from Col. *Algernon Sidney*, or other British Martyrs, to the liberty of the country, an outcry of rebellion would not be surprising. The authority of Mr. *Locke* has therefore been preferred to all others" (ibid.).

gland. As one critic noted in 1768, the colonists "adopted, as unanswerable, all the arguments of Sidney, Lock, and other venerable names."[41] English pamphleteers deflected American claims by arguing that they were idiosyncratic and out of keeping with accepted English practice. If Manchester and Birmingham were taxed without representation in Parliament, then why not the colonies? "All *British* Subjects are really in the same [situation]; none are actually, all are virtually represented in Parliament; for every Member of Parliament sits in the House, not as Representative of his own Constituents, but as one of that august Assembly by which all the Commons of *Great Britain* are represented."[42] According to the English, the "Revolution principles" of Locke and Sidney had no place in the English frame of government. Thus arose a situation familiar to students of English history, where two opposing camps each claimed possession of the "true" constitution.

The colonists frequently attributed the rejection of their constitutional claims to the spread of corruption in the English government. Here, too, they turned to Sidney for instruction. For example, in a furious attack on Soame Jenyns's 1765 defense of British imperial policies, James Otis cried out that you "may, if you please, look back to the most infamous times of the Stuarts, ransack the history of all their reigns, examine the conduct of every debauchee who counted for one in that parliament, which Sidney says, 'drunk or sober' passed the five mile act, and you will not find any expressions equal in absurdity to those of Mr. J——s."[43] Otis's implication was clear: only corrupt men, men fit for the company of Charles II and his Cavalier Parliament, could hold the views then current in England.

It is sometimes argued that the eighteenth-century American concept of corruption owed its origin to the literature of classical republicanism and the writings of the "true" Whigs in England.[44] Otis's

[41] *The Constitutional Right of the Legislature of Great Britain, to Tax the British Colonies in America, Impartially Stated* (London: 1768), vii. "I am well aware, that I shall hear *Lock, Sidney, Selden,* and many other great Names quoted, to prove that every *Englishman,* whether he has a Right to vote for a Representative or not, is still represented in the *British* Parliament" ([Soame Jenyns], *The Objections to the Taxation of Our American Colonies . . . Briefly Consider'd* [London: 1765], 7).

[42] [Thomas Whately], *The Regulations Lately Made concerning the Colonies, and the Taxes Imposed upon Them, considered* (London: 1765), 109.

[43] [James Otis], *Considerations on Behalf of the Colonists in a Letter to a Noble Lord* (Boston: 1765), 13. The passage quoted is from *Discourses*, III:45, p. 457. According to Otis, the ideas of Sidney, Locke, and Selden "will not quadrate with the half-born sentiments of a courtier. Their views will never center in the *paricranium* of a modern politician" (*Considerations*, 7–8).

[44] The most vigorous proponent of this view is J.G.A. Pocock; see, for example, *The Machiavellian Moment*, 506–52. See also the works cited above in note 6.

quotation from Sidney's *Discourses* gives proof of this connection; but it is also worth recalling the example of Jonathan Mayhew in this context. Mayhew was an ardent admirer of Sidney's writings and frequently quoted from them.[45] He was also a New England clergyman, and when he came to preach a sermon of thanksgiving on the repeal of the Stamp Act in 1766, he took his text not from the *Discourses*, but from the Bible: "Our soul is escaped as a bird out of the snare of the fowlers: the snare is broken, and we are escaped."[46] Mayhew was careful to explain why he had chosen this text:

> When I speak of that pernicious act as a *snare*, and those who prepared it for us as *fowlers*, greedy of their prey, let it be particularly observed, that I intend not the least reflexion on our gracious Sovereign or the Parliament. . . . No! I apply this, as I conclude you will, only to some evil-minded individuals in Britain, who are true friends neither to her nor us; and who accordingly spared no wicked arts, no deceitful, no dishonorable, no dishonest means, to push on and obtain, as it were by *surprize*, an act so prejudicial to both; and, in some sort, to the *ensnaring* of his Majesty and the Parliament, as well as the good people of America.[47]

The image of snares, of traps set by corrupt men and women to lure the innocent to their destruction, had long exercised a powerful influence over the English moral and political imagination. It was integral to the Whig ideology developed in the 1670s and 1680s, when it was feared that hypocrisy, deceit, and ministerial intrigue ruled all; and examples of its use can be found throughout Sidney's writings.[48] Mayhew's sermon of 1766 is important because it draws attention to the fact that the language of virtue and corruption had Christian as well as classical roots. Indeed, its strength and resiliency rested on its capacity to draw nourishment from a wide variety of sources.

Though willing to endorse the use of force in the struggle against the Stamp Act, Mayhew was no root-and-branch radical; he was eager to restore relations between England and her American colonies as quickly as possible. His sole aim was the reestablishment of the rights

[45] For example, the heart of Mayhew's sermon of 26 August 1765, "the most famous—or infamous—sermon ever preached" in Boston's West Church, was "a succinct summation of the political philosophy of Locke, Milton and Sidney" (Akers, *Called Unto Liberty*, 202–3).

[46] Psalm 124:7.

[47] Mayhew, *Snare Broken*, 8–9.

[48] See, for example: *Maxims*, 41, 105, 121, 128; *Discourses*, II:18, p. 143; II:19, p. 149; II:27, pp. 214–15; III:19, pp. 344–45. Contemporary Whig usage is illustrated by: [Anthony Ashley Cooper], *A Letter From a Person of Quality, To His Friend In the Country* (1675), 8; and William Penn [Philanglus, pseud.], *One Project for the Good of England* (1679), 8.

of freeborn Englishmen living in America. But the distinction between revolution and restoration could be maintained only as long as it was possible to believe that England was willing and able to respect the rights of colonial Americans. The Declaratory Act of 1766 and the Townshend Duties of 1767 made that increasingly difficult. So too did the vocabulary used by the colonists to frame their arguments. The language of traps and snares, of corruption and slavery, lent itself to the search for hidden causes and magnified the significance of seemingly minor events. It was this language of conspiracy that gave John Dickinson's *Letters from a Farmer in Pennsylvania* such power: "To console ourselves with the *smallness* of duties, is to walk deliberately into the snare that is set for us, praising the *neatness* of the workmanship." The duties imposed by Great Britain were intended "to establish a *precedent* for future use."[49] For all that, Dickinson was no revolutionary, and he flatly rejected the possibility of independence: "Torn from the body, to which we are united by religion, liberty, laws, affections, relation, language and commerce, we must bleed at every vein."[50]

In the hands of some men, however, the language of corruption began to assume a more radical meaning. This is particularly evident in Arthur Lee's "Monitor" articles, written in defense of the nonimportation agreements and first published in the *Virginia Gazette* early in 1768. Lee confessed that "the more I reflect on the nature of man, or read the histories of nations; the more fully am I convinced of the truth of this observation of the illustrious *Sidney's*, That liberty produces virtue, order and stability; while slavery is of necessity accompanied with vice, weakness and misery."[51] Without a trace of irony or self-consciousness, Lee wondered—in a colony of slaveholders—"Is any imagination capable of conceiving a people more absolute, more abject slaves, than when they are taxed, not only without their consent, but directly contrary to their express will?" And yet that was precisely what the British were attempting to do in America. "The *question* now is, whether we shall be *slaves or freemen*, whether *we* shall

[49] John Dickinson, "Letters from a Farmer in Pennsylvania," 1768, in *The Writings of John Dickinson*, ed. Paul Leicester Ford (Philadelphia: Historical Society of Pennsylvania, 1895), 1:355. The language of conspiracy is brilliantly explored in Gordon Wood, "Conspiracy and the Paranoid Style: Causality and Deceit in the Eighteenth Century," *William and Mary Quarterly*, 3rd ser., 39 (July 1982): 401–41.

[50] Dickinson, "Letters from a Farmer," in *Writings*, 1:326. "Let us behave like dutiful children, who have received unmerited blows from a beloved parent" (1:327).

[51] [Arthur Lee], "Monitor II," *Virginia Gazette* (Rind), 3 March 1768. The passage quoted is from *Discourses*, II:11, p. 104.

bequeath bondage or liberty to our children."[52] Lee did not hesitate to answer this question: "There would not be wanting some, who would stile [resistance to the English government] rebellion; but (I speak the words of Mr. Sidney), 'they who seek after truth will find, that there can be no such thing in the world as the rebellion of a whole nation against its Magistrates.' "[53] English corruption justified American resistance. Lee concluded his series of articles with a call to arms:

It is now that every man ought to grave upon his free heart, this noble *Roman* determination.

—Manus haec inimica tyrannis
Ense petit placidam sub libertate quietem.

To tyrants and to tyranny a foe, I will maintain my liberty at the hazard of my life.[54]

Thirteen years earlier Franklin's *Pennsylvania Gazette* had invoked Sidney's motto to steel colonists against the invasion of the French; in Lee's "Monitor" articles it was used for the first time to harden resistance to the British. Lee did not call for independence; but the moral and political sensibility expressed by his quotations from Sidney made accommodation with England increasingly difficult.

1769–1773

The year 1768 saw the dissolution of the Massachusetts House of Representatives and the arrival of British troops in Boston, but unlike the Stamp Act these traumatic events did not initiate a new wave of reflection and writing in the colonies.[55] Relatively few pamphlets

[52] [Arthur Lee], "Monitor VI," *Virginia Gazette* (Rind), 31 March 1768; "Monitor IX," ibid., 21 April 1768.

[53] [Arthur Lee], "Monitor III," *Virginia Gazette* (Rind), 10 March 1768. The passage quoted is from *Discourses*, III:36, p. 413.

[54] [Arthur Lee], "Monitor X," *Virginia Gazette* (Rind), 28 April 1768.

[55] Though the crisis surrounding the arrival of the troops was exacerbated by American pamphleteering and, significantly, connected with Sidney's name: "Governor Bernard['s] . . . nerve held until early September, when an article in the [Boston] *Gazette* 'containing a System of Politicks, exceeding all former Exceedings,' forced him into a strategic mistake. The article, actually a series of queries by 'Clericus Americanus,' purported to deal with the various grievances long discussed by Americans. What caught Bernard's eye was the answer to 'Sidney's' question: What shall we do if troops are sent to Boston? Clericus Americanus answered with horrifying bluntness: the colonies must declare their independence. Bernard had received word on August 27 that troops had been dispatched to Boston. Dreading an 'insurrection' should they arrive unannounced—and convinced by Clericus Americanus that the situation would be explo-

were printed between 1768 and 1774, and thus the resources for studying Sidney's influence during this period are limited. Nonetheless, it is possible to trace Sidney's expanding influence on both the iconography and the ideology of American radicalism.

To American colonists, the name of John Wilkes was associated with belief in the true principles of the English constitution and opposition to the corrupt policies of the government in London. The colonists had enormous faith in Wilkes's capacity to restore order to Parliament; as the Boston Sons of Liberty wrote him in the summer of 1768, "your perseverance in the *good old cause* may still prevent the great system from dashing to pieces. 'Tis from your endeavors we hope for a royal 'Pascite, ut ante, boves,' and from our attachment to 'peace and good order' we wait for a constitutional redress: being determined that the King of Great Britain shall have subjects but not slaves in these remote parts of his dominions."[56] According to Bernard Bailyn, "by February 1769 it was well known that *'the fate of Wilkes and America must stand or fall together.'* " It is thus of special significance that the colonists linked Wilkes with Algernon Sidney. A "Report from London" printed in the *Virginia Gazette* on 30 March 1769 passed on the following piece of information: "It is said to be a fact that the house in the Old Bailey built for the great Algernon Sidney, is taken for the residence of Mr. Alderman Wilkes; and as soon as Mr. Wilkes resides there, his friends propose to call the Old Bailey by the name of Sidney street, an alteration which will be extremely pleasing to the inhabitants." "The house in the Old Bailey" was Newgate prison, to which Wilkes had been committed for his political activities; that Sidney had been imprisoned in the Tower of London seems never to have crossed the reporter's mind. It was at Newgate that Benjamin Rush "had the pleasure of dining" with Wilkes, and in a letter printed in the *Pennsylvania Journal*—coincidentally, also on the 30th of March—Rush paid Wilkes the highest of accolades: "I heard a number of sentiments from him that would have done honor to a Sidney or a Hamden." There was no doubt in the minds of the colonists that Wilkes and Sidney suffered for a common cause: the defense of liberty against the encroachment of arbitrary power.[57]

---

sive—on September 9 he leaked the information he had of the troops' coming and thereby made more trouble for himself. . . . In seeking to forestall opposition, Bernard helped spread it" (Robert Middlekauff, *The Glorious Cause: The American Revolution 1763–1789* [New York: Oxford University Press, 1982], 171).

[56] Quoted in Bailyn, *Ideological Origins*, 111.

[57] Bailyn, *Ideological Origins*, 111; *Virginia Gazette* (Purdie & Dixon), 30 March 1769;

The colonists' tendency to wrap their English allies in the mantle of Sidney's reputation can also be seen in a painting of William Pitt, earl of Chatham, commissioned for the courthouse of Westmoreland County in Virginia. According to a contemporary description, Chatham's "countenance appears full of ire and expression, and he looks as if he was waiting for an answer to some forcible argument he had just used, being represented in the habit of a Roman orator speaking in the Forum. His right hand is extended naked to the elbow, his left hanging down, and holding Magna Charta. Close by him stands an alter, supported by the busts of Sidney and Hampden, with the flame sacred to Liberty burning bright on it."[58] Almost everywhere they turned, the colonists saw reflections of Sidney's "Roman" spirit.

Not every use of Sidney's name was symbolic, however. In 1770 John Adams defended two British soldiers who had participated in the Boston Massacre on March 5 of that year. The bulk of Adams's defense rested on a series of legal maxims culled from the writings of the great English jurist Sir Matthew Hale and designed to establish that acquittal was called for when the evidence was inconclusive or uncertain.[59] But in the conclusion of his argument, Adams directly addressed the enormous popular pressure on the jury; the authority he chose to assist him was Algernon Sidney.

> The law, in all vicissitudes of government, fluctuations of the passions, or flights of enthusiasm, will preserve a steady undeviating course; it will not bend to the uncertain wishes, imaginations, and wanton tempers of men. To use the words of a great and worthy man, a patriot, and an hero, and enlightened friend of mankind, and a martyr to liberty; I mean ALGERNON SIDNEY, who from his infancy sought a tranquil retirement under the shadow of the tree of liberty, with his tongue, his pen, and his sword, "The Law (says he), no passion can disturb. Tis void of Desire and Fear, Lust and Anger. Tis *Mens Sine affectu*, written Reason, retaining Some Measure of divine Perfection. It does not enjoin that which pleases a weak, frail Man, but without any Regard to Persons, commands that which is good, and punishes evil in all whether rich or poor, high or low. Tis deaf, inexorable, inflexible." On the one hand it is inexorable to the cries and lamentations of the prisoners; on the other it is deaf, deaf as an adder to the clamours of the populace.[60]

Benjamin Rush, *The Letters of Benjamin Rush*, ed. L. H. Butterfield (Princeton: Princeton University Press, 1951), 1:72.

[58] *Virginia Gazette* (Purdie & Dixon), 20 April 1769.

[59] John Adams, *Legal Papers of John Adams*, ed. L. K. Wroth and H. B. Zobel (Cambridge, MA: Harvard University Press, 1965), 3:81–82, 242–43.

[60] Adams, *Legal Papers*, 3:269–70. See also: 3:82. The passage quoted is from *Discourses*, III:15, p. 316.

Adams's invocation of Sidney was a brilliant rhetorical move, for it enabled him to use one of the heroes of "the populace" to demonstrate why they must not be permitted to influence the outcome of the soldiers' trials. The jury must strictly adhere to the law, refusing to be influenced either by their sympathy for the accused or by their fear of the mob, for justice to be done. The law's virtue lay in its freedom from corrupt—that is to say partial or biased—human passions.

Adams's association of Sidney's name with arguments for the preservation of legal order was modified in an important way by Josiah Quincy. In 1770 Ebeneezer Richardson, a colonist who had provided information to the customs office concerning Boston merchants, shot and killed an eleven-year-old boy. Twice convicted of murder, Richardson was pardoned by the king because of the inordinate popular pressure on his juries; yet in 1772 he still languished in jail. It was to this latter fact, and the legal mechanism that permitted it, that Quincy objected:

> Is Richardson kept in gaol in order to recommend him to mercy? . . . The *honour* of magistracy ought openly to avow it:—the wisdom of the recommenders ought to justify it. . . . Let not the infamy of the man give origin to an acquiescence in unjustifiable confinement. . . . What is law for a *Richardson* is law for a *Sidney*. If oppression is warranted by law, the Patriot is much more likely to fall a victim than the pimp and pander. *Hampdens* will stain the scaffold with blood, while a robber or murderer finds a city of refuge. *No tyranny so secure, no so intolerable, no so dangerous, none so remediless, as that of Executive Courts.*[61]

While Adams feared the arbitrariness of the passions, Quincy feared the power of courts whose discretionary powers were unchecked by popular will. This was a well-established theme in the writings of colonial Americans: without public accountability, even the law could become an instrument of oppression.[62] As Quincy reminded his readers, the fact that Richardson deserved imprisonment should not be allowed to mask the fact that *they* were at risk.

The colonists' belief that tyranny could be avoided only by subjecting public powers to popular control blended easily with their fear of corruption and their growing commitment to rebellion: according to the "true" principles of the English constitution, political power was

[61] Josiah Quincy [Calisthenes, pseud.], *Boston Gazette*, 10 February 1772.

[62] Thus the colonists feared the decision to make judicial salaries dependent on the Crown, and not on the provincial assemblies; and thus they feared the rise of admiralty or "prerogative" courts. For an early example of these fears, see: *A Letter to the People of Pennsylvania* (1760), in Bailyn, *Pamphlets of the American Revolution*, 1:248–72.

legitimate only when it originated in the consent of the people; only pervasive corruption could explain the betrayal of this fundamental principle by the English government; thus good English subjects must do everything in their power to resist the spread of corruption. The links in this argument were hammered out by Benjamin Franklin in an article published in London in 1770: "When it is remembered that it is an old Artifice of the Enslavers of Kingdoms to begin with the more distant Parts, surely every freeborn Subject on this Island ought to be alarmed at the late bold Attempt on the Liberties of our brave Fellow-Subjects in America, and to think, with Horror, of the bare Possibility of its Success. For, should an encroaching Administration prevail in enslaving the Colonies, would they not thence be emboldened to subject the Mother-Country to their Iron Rod?" Franklin posed a decisive either/or: either Englishmen joined the colonists in checking the spread of "an encroaching Administration," or the entire British empire would be enslaved by it. Lest Franklin's own views be mistaken, he made them explicit:

> I will conclude this Paper with the Words of the great Sidney's *Discourse on Government*: "Asiatic Slaves usually pay such Tributes as are imposed on them. We own none but what we freely give, none is or can be imposed on us, unless by ourselves. We measure our Grants according to our Will, or the present Occasion, for our own Safety. The Happiness of those who enjoy the like Liberty, and the shameful Misery they lie under who have suffered themselves to be forced, or cheated out of it, may persuade, and the justice of the Cause encourage us to think nothing too dear to be hazarded in Defence of it."[63]

Franklin made no mention of revolution or independence, but they were implicit in Sidney's name and the uncompromising claims he made. To a growing number of colonists, nothing—not even the bonds of faith and family, of economy and society, that united the British empire—was "too dear to be hazarded in Defence of" liberty.

1774–1776

As the colonists inched their way toward a declaration of independence, Sidney's martyrdom grew in significance. To Josiah Quincy, writing in 1774, Sidney's ardent devotion to liberty was the promise latent in every colonist's breast: "America hath in store her Bruti and

[63] Franklin, "The Colonist's Advocate: VI," 29 January 1770, in *Papers*, 17:47–48. The passage quoted is from *Discourses*, III:8, p. 288.

Casii—her Hampdens and Sydneys—patriots and heroes, who will form a band of brothers: men who will have memories and feelings—courage and swords:—courage shall inflame their ardent bosoms, till their hands cleave to their swords—and their swords to their enemies' hearts."[64] To Hugh Henry Brackenridge, writing after the battle of Bunker Hill, Sidney's heroic self-sacrifice had been matched by America's fallen. As Joseph Warren proclaimed in Brackenridge's commemorative poem,

> Weep not for him who first espoused the cause,
> And risking life, hath met the enemy
> In fatal opposition—but rejoice!
> For now I go to mingle with the dead—
> Great Brutus, Hampden, Sidney, and the rest,
> Of old or modern memory, who lived
> A mound to tyrants, and a strong hedge to kings,
> Bounding the inundation of their rage
> Against the happiness and peace of man.
>
> . . . .
>
> I come, I come, ye first-born of true fame.
> Fight on, my countrymen, be free, be free![65]

The colonists' enthusiastic identification with Sidney's militant devotion to liberty reached a peak in Massachusetts in the summer of 1775, when the second line of Sidney's motto ("Ense petit placidam sub libertate quietem") was adopted as the motto of the commonwealth.[66]

Not every colonist found solace in Sidney's death, however. On the eve of the first Continental Congress, John Adams wrote James Warren that "there is one ugly Reflection—Brutus and Cassius were conquered and slain. Hampden died in the field, Sydney on the Scaffold, Harrington in gaol, &c. This is cold Comfort. Politics are an ordeal Path, among red hot Ploughshares. Who then would be a Politician for the Pleasure of running about barefoot among them?" Adams's dark view of politics contrasted sharply with his sense of "all the Pleasures Profits and Prospects of Life . . . all the Sweets of Society." Accordingly, he wrote Warren that "the arduous Duties of the Times

[64] Josiah Quincy, "Observations on . . . the Boston Port-Bill," 1774, in *Memoir of the Life of Josiah Quincy* (Boston: 1825), 469.

[65] Hugh Henry Brackenridge, "The Battle of Bunker's Hill," 1776, in Moses Coit Tyler, *Literary History of the American Revolution: 1763–1783* (New York: G. P. Putnam's Sons, 1897), 2:216.

[66] Greenough, "Motto of Massachusetts," passim.

ought to be discharged in Rotation—and I never will engage more in Politicks but upon this System."[67]

Once the decision for independence had been made, however, Adams changed his tune and sang the praises of Sidney's death. As he wrote his wife in early 1777, in a letter castigating the British commanders in America,

> I would not be an Howe, for all the Empires of the Earth, and all the Riches, and Glories thereof.
>
> Who would not rather be brave, even though unfortunate, in the Cause of Liberty? Who would not rather be Sydney, than Monk?[68]

Adams's memory of Monk—the general in the parliamentary army who had facilitated the restoration of Charles II in 1660—bolstered his own commitment to the "ordeal Path" of politics. For all its horrors, Sidney's martyrdom was a sufficiently plastic concept that Adams could use it to justify a commitment to as well as a withdrawal from the political life of the new nation.

Sidney's name also surfaced in a number of ways unconnected with his martyrdom. He was a mythic figure, "a man or an angel," who helped uncover the fact that "the real interest" of England was "totally disregarded" by its government in favor of a plot to introduce "arbitrary power, and the Roman Catholick religion," throughout the empire.[69] He was the pseudonymous author of newspaper articles calling on the towns in Massachusetts to "resolve, that no Tea of any Kind, shall be sold or used amongst Them,"[70] and reminding the colonists that the Low Countries had gained their freedom only by uniting with each other.[71] So powerful was Sidney's name that a pamphlet critical of the colonists could be rejected solely on the grounds that its English author had once attempted to discredit Sidney's reputation as an incorruptible patriot.[72]

---

[67] Adams to Warren, 25 June 1774, in Adams, *Papers*, 2:100. Once before Adams had linked Sidney's martyrdom with his own decision to "meddle not with public Affairs of Town or Province" (Adams, *Diary and Autobiography*, 22 September–5 October 1772, 2:63).

[68] John Adams to Abigail Adams, 13 April 1777, in *Adams Family Correspondence*, ed. L. H. Butterfield, W. Garrett, and M. Sprague (Cambridge, MA: Harvard University Press, 1963), 2:208.

[69] *Virginia Gazette* (Pinkney), 18 May 1775.

[70] "Sydney," *Boston Evening Post*, 17 January 1774.

[71] "Sidney," *Virginia Gazette* (Dixon & Hunter), 7 January 1775.

[72] "A pamphlet having lately made its appearance in this country, entitled *The address of the people of Great Britian to the inhabitants of America*, it may not be amiss to inform the publick that this pamphlet is wrote by sir John Dalrymple . . . [who] some time ago, wrote and published his *Memoirs of Great Britain and Ireland*, calculated almost solely to

Moving closer to the actual content of Sidney's writings, colonial pamphleteers continued to cite him as a proponent of the "true" principles of the English constitution. In a paraphrase of Locke, Arthur Lee declared that "the supreme powers cannot take from any man any part of his property, without his own consent,"[73] then noted that "the reasoning of Mr. Locke is so clear and conclusive, and his authority so great, that it is not necessary to give the words of Sidney and Milton, whose opinions were precisely the same."[74] Addressing his audience in Great Britain as one Englishman speaking to another, Lee argued that "upon these principles our own constitution stands; upon these principles the American claim is founded. If they are fallacious, then were our own claims usurpations upon the crown, and the glorious revolution itself was nothing more than a successful rebellion; Hampden, Pym, Sidney and Russell, than whom Greece with all her patriots, and Rome with all her heroes, produced no men who trod this mortal stage with more dignity, or quitted it with greater lustre, were sturdy traitors."[75] To renounce the claims of the Americans was to renounce the principles on which the revolution of 1688—and every English government since then—had been founded. On the eve of revolution, the colonists continued to portray themselves as conservatives, preserving the "true" principles of the English constitution against the radical practices of the English government.

The revolutionary origin of the colonists' principles was not lost on them, however, and it was in making the transition to independence that they drew most heavily on Sidney's writings. The clearest example of this can be found in John Adams's "Novanglus" essays, first published in early 1775 in the *Boston Gazette*. Adams's stated aim was to prove that the American colonies constituted distinct legislative authorities and hence that the only point of contact between the govern-

---

extirpate the very idea of patriotism, by endeavouring to condemn to infamy the memory of two of the most celebrated patriots mentioned in British history, the illustrious and celebrated *Russell* and *Sidney*" (*Virginia Gazette* [Purdie], 22 September 1775). See also: Samuel Adams to James Warren, 14 October 1778, in *The Writings of Samuel Adams*, ed. Harry Alonzo Cushing (New York: G. P. Putnam's Sons, 1904–1908), 4:73.

[73] *Two Treatises*, II:139.

[74] [Arthur Lee], *An Appeal to the Justice and Interests of the People of Great Britain, in the Present Disputes with America* (London: 1774), 25–26. William Stearns thought that this point could be established by "producing only one authority from a writer who understood the nature of civil government, as well (at least) as any writer, ancient or modern—the famous Algernon Sydney—Says he, 'No man can give that which is another's' " (William Stearns, *A View of the Controversy* [Watertown: 1775], 17–18). The quotation, which varies from the original, is from *Discourses*, III:29, p. 392.

[75] [Lee], *An Appeal*, 28.

ments of the colonies and the government of England was the person of the king.[76] He flatly denied the charge that American Whigs favored independence.[77] But in the process of defending the legislative rights of the colonies, Adams deployed a range of arguments that fully justified revolution.

The starting point for Adams's analysis was a statement of political principles: "That all men by nature are equal; that kings are but the ministers of the people; that their authority is delegated to them by the people, for their good, and they have a right to resume it, and place it in other hands, or keep it themselves, whenever it is made use of to oppress them. . . . These are what are called revolution principles. They are the principles of Aristotle and Plato, of Livy and Cicero, and Sydney, Harrington and Locke. The principles of nature and eternal reason. The principles on which the whole government over us, now stands."[78] From these principles Adams extracted two maxims. First, "there are tumults, seditions, popular commotions, insurrections and civil wars, upon just occasions, as well as unjust." Adams briefly quoted Grotius to verify this claim; but he clinched his argument with a lengthy (approximately a thousand words) extract from Sidney's *Discourses*. According to Sidney,

> The ways of preventing or punishing injuries are judicial or extra-judicial. Judicial proceedings are of force against those who submit, or may be brought to trial, but are of no effect against those who resist, and are of such power that they cannot be constrained. It were absurd to cite a man to appear before a tribunal, *who can awe the judges, or has armies to defend him*; and impious to think that he who has added treachery to his other crimes, and usurped a power above the law, should be protected by the enormity of his wickedness. Legal proceedings, therefore, are to be used when the delinquent submits to the law; *and all are just, when he will not be kept in order by the legal*. . . . If the laws of God and Men, are therefore of no effect, when the magistracy is left at liberty to break them; and if the lusts of those who are too strong for the tribunals of justice, cannot be otherwise restrained than by sedition, tumults and war; those seditions, tumults and wars, are justified by the laws of God and man.[79]

[76] John Adams and Daniel Leonard [erroneously, Jonathan Sewall], *Novanglus and Massachusettensis* (Boston: Hews & Goss, 1819), 89–118. The "imperial" context of Revolutionary thought is explored in Randolph Greenfield Adams, *Political Ideas of the American Revolution* (Durham, NC: Trinity College Press, 1922).

[77] Adams, *Novanglus and Massachusettensis*, 41, 45.

[78] Adams, *Novanglus and Massachusettensis*, 12. See also: 66.

[79] Adams, *Novanglus and Massachusettensis*, 62, 63–64. The quotation is from *Discourses*, II:24, pp. 174–75.

The emphases in this quotation were added by Adams to encourage the colonists to recognize their own condition in it. In Massachusetts the judges had been corrupted, and a standing army held sway. Lacking all means of legal recourse, the colonists were justified in turning to extralegal means for preserving their liberty.

Second, Adams argued that nations need not wait until they are actually enslaved to use force against unjust magistrates; they need only observe a clear pattern of abuse. Once again Adams quoted Sidney: "Neither are subjects bound to stay till the prince has entirely finished the chains which he is preparing for them, and put it out of their power to oppose. It is sufficient that all the advances which he makes are manifestly tending to the oppression, that he is marching boldly on to the ruin of the state."[80] He also quoted Locke: "How can a man any more hinder himself from believing in his own mind, which way things are going, or from casting about to save himself, than he could from believing the captain of the ship he was in, was carrying him and the rest of his company to Algiers, when he found him always steering that course, though cross winds, leaks in his ship and want of men and provisions, did often force him to turn his course another way for some time, which he steadily returned to again, as soon as the winds, weather, and other circumstances would let him?"[81] The conclusion Adams drew from these maxims was quite simple: "Opposition, nay open, avowed resistance by arms, against usurpation and lawless violence, is not rebellion by the law of God, or the land. Resistance to lawful authority makes rebellion."[82] This was precisely the conclusion Sidney and Locke had reached ninety years before: unjust magistrates, not restive citizens, are the true rebels in society.

Of the fact that England's magistrates were rebels against the law and the "true" principles of the constitution there could be no doubt. Working by "cautious cunning" and "deep dissimulation," a "Junto" in England—Adams did not name its principals, but he identified Governors Shirley, Hutchinson, and Bernard as its instruments—was plotting to enslave the colonies.[83] As a student of history with a par-

---

[80] Adams, *Novanglus and Massachusettensis*, 65. The quotation is a paraphrase of *Discourses*, III:36, which Adams drew from Barbeyrac's edition of Grotius.

[81] Adams, *Novanglus and Massachusettensis*, 65. See also: 12–13. The quotation is from *Two Treatises*, II:210.

[82] Adams, *Novanglus and Massachusettensis*, 45. "Hampden, Russell, Sydney, Somers, Holt, Tillotson, Burnet, Hoadley, &c. were no tyrants nor rebels, although some of them were in arms, and the others undoubtedly excited resistance against the tories" (ibid.). See also: 10–11.

[83] Adams, *Novanglus and Massachusettensis*, 15–17.

ticularly Tacitean view of human affairs, Adams knew that "the same game, with the same success, has been played in all ages and countries. . . . When a favorable conjuncture has presented, some of the most intriguing and powerful citizens have conceived the design of enslaving their country, and building their own greatness on its ruins."[84] With England itself consumed by corruption,[85] and the "cancer" of "encroachment upon [the] American constitution" growing "faster and faster every hour," there could be no delay. *"Obsta principiis*—Nip the shoots of arbitrary power in the bud, is the only maxim which can ever preserve the liberties of any people. When the people give way, their deceivers, betrayers and destroyers press upon them so fast that there is no resisting afterwards."[86] Though Adams repeatedly denied it, his arguments left little alternative to a declaration of independence.

Adams's argument in the "Novanglus" essays provides a clear illustration of one of the most important functions of the concept of corruption in American political thought. According to the "true" principles of the English constitution, rebellion was legitimate if and only if there existed a settled design against liberty on the part of the nation's magistrates. The concept of corruption enhanced the colonists' ability to identify such a design in the policies of the English government. It unified discrete events, placing them within a coherent and purposive whole; and it magnified the significance of events, such that even minor threats to liberty were the harbingers of total enslavement. Daniel Leonard, the Boston loyalist whose "Massachusettensis" essays had prompted Adams to write his "Novanglus" responses, protested the hyperbole of the colonial radicals: "Where are the traces of the slavery that our patriots would terrify us with? The effects of slavery are as glaring and obvious in those countries that were cursed with its abode, as the effects of war, pestilence or famine. Our land is not disgraced by the wooden shoes of France, or the uncombed hair of Poland: we have neither racks nor inquisitions, tortures or assassinations: the mildness of our criminal jurisprudence is proverbial, 'a man must have many friends to get hanged in New England.' "[87] Leonard's assessment of America's condition was essentially correct; there was something odd in describing the colonists as

[84] Adams, *Novanglus and Massachusettensis*, 11.

[85] "Is not the British constitution arrived nearly to that point, where the Roman republic was, when Juguertha left it, and pronounced it a venal city ripe for destruction, if it can only find a purchaser?" (Adams, *Novanglus and Massachusettensis*, 43). See also: 23.

[86] Adams, *Novanglus and Massachusettensis*, 34.

[87] Daniel Leonard, *Novanglus and Massachusettensis*, 216.

slaves. But he completely failed to understand the power of a theory that combined an intense devotion to liberty with a pervasive fear of corruption.[88] As the former provided the colonists with an account of the moral and political foundations of all just governments, so the latter heightened their sense that those foundations were being mined and sapped by clever politicians in England and America.

Not every loyalist was blind to the ideological contours of radical thought, however, and it was during the years immediately preceding the Declaration of Independence that an effort was made to prove that Sidney's arguments were consistent with and conducive to continued British rule. Sidney's mantle as a martyr to liberty was claimed by loyalists bent on countering the influence of his ideas. For example, in 1774 Jonathan Boucher—perhaps the only man in America to take Filmer's patriarchalism seriously—attempted to deflate the colonists' hopes for remaining within the British empire without being subject to parliamentary rule by denying the possibility of divided sovereignty: "That no political society can subsist, unless there be an absolute supreme power lodged somewhere in the society, has been universally held as an uncontrolable maxim in theory, by all writers on government, from Aristotle down to Sidney and Locke, and has been universally adopted in practice." That no evidence to support this view could be found in either Sidney's *Discourses* or Locke's *Two Treatises* seems not to have bothered Boucher. He simply assumed that they contained what he knew to be correct; and if they didn't, well, they were "beautiful theor[ies]" but had no bearing on the conduct of "good subjects."[89]

A far more serious attempt to enlist Sidney in the loyalist cause was made by William Smith in early 1776. In response to Tom Paine's *Common Sense*, Smith—Anglican clergyman, provost of the College of Philadelphia, and "spokesman for the wealthy aristocracy" in Pennsylvania[90]—published a series of articles in the *Pennsylvania Gazette* under the pseudonym Cato. Paine had argued that the institution of monarchy was explicitly rejected by God in I Samuel 8, that the English constitution was fundamentally flawed, and that a republic was the only legitimate form of government. Against each of these claims Smith produced a wealth of authorities, from Grotius and

[88] Additional examples of Sidney's influence on the colonists' perceptions of the links between liberty and corruption can be found in: *Virginia Gazette* (Rind), 8 September 1774; and Demophilus, *The Genuine Principles of the Ancient Saxon, or English Constitution* (Philadelphia: 1776).

[89] [Jonathan Boucher], *A Letter from a Virginian to the Members of the Congress to be held at Philadelphia* (Boston: 1774), 13–14, 27.

[90] In Paine, *Complete Writings*, 2:60.

Montesquieu to Sidney and Locke. According to Smith, Sidney had argued that God did not reject the institution of monarchy,[91] that the historic English constitution was essentially sound,[92] and that popular or democratic government was impossible in a large state.[93] At a time when many colonists were electrified by Paine's call for independence and republicanism, Smith produced Sidney as a witness for continued British rule.

Smith's essays were a mockery of colonial pieties; an almost audible smirk accompanied his report that the "immortal" Sidney, that "martyr to liberty," would have wholeheartedly embraced the eighteenth-century English constitution. Paradoxically, however, they provoked no response. No one—not even Paine, who wrote a series of essays defending *Common Sense* against Smith's accusations—thought it necessary to "correct" Smith's interpretations.[94] This may have been a reflection of the belief that Smith's references to Sidney were superficial and patently wrong; or it may have been a consequence of the almost overwhelming flow of events after the signing of the Declaration of Independence. But it is puzzling nonetheless, particularly since Americans vigorously defended Sidney's reputation as a man who had selflessly given his life in the cause of freedom. Unfortunately, there is no reliable way of interpreting the silence following the publication of Smith's essays. The one thing Smith's essays show with certainty is that there were sufficient ambiguities in Sidney's

[91] "*Sidney* (that great martyr to liberty) adopts the same explanation [as Grotius]. '*Samuel's* words (says he) are acknowledged by all interpreters who were not malicious or mad, to be a disuasion of the *Jews* from their wicked purpose, not a description of what a King might justly do, by virtue of his office' " (William Smith, "To the People of Pennsylvania: Letter VI," 10 April 1776, in *American Archives*, 4th ser., ed. Peter Force [Washington, DC: 1844], 5:841). The quotation is from *Discourses*, III:3, p. 266.

[92] "The author of *Common Sense* stands singular in his rage for condemning the *English* Constitution in the lump, and the administration of it from the beginning. The immortal *Sydney* himself gives it a different character, and speaks with reverence of the wisdom of our ancestors. 'They evidently appear, (says he), not only to have intended well, but to have taken a right course to accomplish what they intended' " (Smith, "To the People of Pennsylvania: Letter VII," 11 April 1776, in Force, *American Archives*, 4th ser., 5:851–52). The quotation is from *Discourses*, III:37, p. 420.

[93] "The great *Sydney* never meant more, by his celebrated work, than to reform the abuses of mixed Government, and to restrain the rapid progress which the nation was making, in his time, towards absolute Monarchy. . . . If *Sydney* understood anything of the matter, we see that every Colony in *America* is already too unwieldy for such a Government [pure democracy], and therefore it cannot be a model for an immense Continent" (Smith, "To the People of Pennsylvania: Letter VIII," April 1776, in Force, *American Archives*, 4th ser., 5:1050–51). In support of these claims, Smith quoted *Discourses*, II:16, p. 130; II:19, p. 148; II:19, p. 149; II:21, p. 154.

[94] Paine's "Forrester's Letters" are reprinted in his *Complete Writings*, 2:60–87. They contain no reference to Sidney.

writings for a crafty conservative to find evidence in them to support his views. As will be shown below, this phenomenon resurfaced in the debates over the proposed constitution in 1787–88.

1777–1786

Despite Sidney's wide-ranging influence before 1776, Americans found few occasions to reflect on his writings or the story of his life during the decade between the signing of the Declaration of Independence and the drafting of the Constitution. The rare instances where Sidney was referred to suggest that he was viewed in an increasingly diffuse and unfocused light. For example, when the marquis de Lafayette commissioned a portrait of George Washington, it was captioned with Sidney's defiant motto.[95] Sidney was a militant defender of the faith of liberty, and Washington was his spiritual descendant. On the other hand, when Congress deprived General Horatio Gates of the command of the Southern Army in October 1780, he protested in a draft letter to Thomas Jefferson that "Columbus was rewarded with Chains for adding a World to His Masters Dominions. The Great Raleigh was Sacrificed to Gondomar, and Sydney for His patriotism. You see Congress have Great Examples before their Eyes of the Corruption of all Good Government."[96] Here Sidney did not represent liberty in arms, but virtue disarmed. Gates's implication was clear: he was no less an innocent victim of corrupt forces than Sidney, Raleigh, or Columbus. Like the triumphant Lafayette, Gates in his humiliation found ways to identify with the story of Sidney's life.

A similar example of the way Sidney's influence began to sheer off in different directions can be seen in the writings of the two Adamses, Samuel and John. Samuel was shocked and frightened by the reception given Massachusetts' new constitution in 1780:

> I am affraid there is more Pomp & Parade than is consistent with those sober Republican Principles, upon which the Framers of it thought they had founded it. Why should this new Era be introduced with Entertainments expensive & tending to dissipate the Minds of the People? Does it

[95] In the portrait Washington "is depicted with the French treaty and the Declaration of Independence in his hand and the edicts and proclamations of His Britannic Majesty under his feet. Beneath it one reads the famous lines, 'Manus haec inimica tyrannis, &c.' " (Lafayette to the comte de Vergennes, 1 July 1779, in *Lafayette in the Age of the American Revolution: Selected Letters and Papers, 1776–1790*, ed. Stanley Idzerda [Ithaca: Cornell University Press, 1979], 2:285).

[96] Horatio Gates to Thomas Jefferson, 2 August 1781, in Jefferson, *Papers*, 6:111.

become us to lead the People to such publick Diversions as promote su-
perfluity of Dress & Ornament, when it is as much as they can bear to
support the Expense of cloathing a naked Army? . . . I love this People
of Boston. I once thought, that City would be the *Christian* Sparta. But
Alas! Will men never be free! They will be free no longer than while
they remain virtuous. Sidney tells us, there are times when People are
not worth saving. Meaning when they have lost their Virtue. I pray God,
this may never be truly said of my beloved Town.[97]

Samuel Adams's Bostonians were the best of men for having the capacity to be free, and the worst of men for not having lived up to
their potential. Sidney's republicanism held out the promise of freedom so long as they remained virtuous, but it threatened them with
slavery as soon as they succumbed to the temptations of corruption.

On the other hand, John Adams believed that the new state constitution—of which he was the principal author—was sufficient to preserve liberty in part because it contained the essence of Sidney's
teachings. "There never was an example of such precautions as are
taken by this wise and jealous people in the formation of their government. None was ever made so perfectly upon the principles of the
people's rights and equality. It is Locke, Sidney, and Rousseau and
DeMably reduced to practice, in the first instance."[98] Here Sidney was
a prophet of mixed government, the separation of powers, and the
rule of law.

These two interpretations of Sidney's writings—a republicanism of
virtue, designed to reflect and realize man's highest qualities, and a
republicanism of stability, designed to prevent anarchy and civil
war—were both founded on an intense fear of corruption. But their
implications, like the careers of Samuel and John Adams, led in very
different directions. While Samuel called on men to reform their
manners and emphasized the need for a rigorous education in "the
exalted virtues of the Christian system," John focused his attention
on the creation and preservation of political systems capable of containing the explosive powers of man's passions and interests. Like David Hume, he thought systems of government founded on extraordinary degrees of virtue to be "chimerical."[99]

Prior to 1776 Sidney's influence had centered on the problems of
resistance, rebellion, and revolution: under what circumstances were

[97] Samuel Adams to John Scollay, 30 December 1780, in Samuel Adams, *Writings*,
4:236, 238.

[98] John Adams to Edmund Jenings, 7 June 1780, in John Adams, *Works*, 4:216.

[99] Samuel Adams to John Adams, 4 October 1790, and John Adams to Samuel Adams, 18 October 1790, in John Adams, *Works*, 6:414, 415.

they legitimate, and how might colonial Americans be encouraged to act them out? After 1776 these were moot questions, and the relative lack of attention to Sidney's writings and the story of his life during this period must in large measure be ascribed to a diminished sense of his relevance to American politics. A new direction for Sidney's influence, however, was signaled by an article published in the *Providence Gazette* in 1779. According to "The American Whig," the writings of Pufendorf

> as well as those of the learned and ingenious Mr. Locke, Mr. Sidney, and others, clearly demonstrates that these three things are essentially necessary in the structure or civil constitution of every State, viz., First, an agreement or covenant to unite and form the society or State. Secondly, an agreement or covenant to submit to the form of government which shall be agreed upon by the majority. And thirdly, the constitution or form of government itself, which when once established cannot be altered or changed, by any man or set of men, without the consent of the whole body of the people.[100]

But what constitution best met these criteria? This was the central question in the debates over the ratification of the Constitution in 1787–88, and it was then that Sidney reemerged as a major influence on American political thought.

1787–1788

During the debates over the ratification of the Constitution, Sidney was most visibly associated with men who either did not understand or refused to accept the American commitment to popular sovereignty or the new federal system with its ideal of extended republics. Like John Locke, Sidney's name appears nowhere in the *Federalist*. Indeed, in the collected writings of Alexander Hamilton, James Madison, and John Jay, Sidney is referred to only once, in 1825, and then only to suggest that he was no longer relevant to American politics. This is not to say that Sidney was unfamiliar to the supporters of the Constitution; he was, for example, carefully studied by Benjamin Franklin and Thomas Jefferson. Nor is it to say that his republican ideals were inconsistent with the new national system. But Sidney figured most prominently in the writings of men who were at odds with the proposed constitution. In particular, Sidney's influence can be

[100] "The American Whig. No. II," *Providence Gazette and Country Journal*, 20 March 1779.

seen in John Adams's *Defence of the Constitutions of the United States* and in the writings of the Antifederalists.

This pattern of influence reflects a general feature of Sidney's writings and the story of his life: they were most at home among "opposition" writers. It was no accident that both the Federalists and the Antifederalists turned from Locke and Sidney to Montesquieu during the debates over the ratification of the Constitution,[101] for the *Spirit of the Laws* provided a wealth of detail concerning historical constitutions and a well-stocked chest of intellectual tools that could be used to analyze specific political institutions. In this respect Sidney's writings were much more like those of Tom Paine. They provided explosive arguments for the general framework of liberty—popular sovereignty, political representation, the rule of law, and so forth—but very few details concerning the precise mechanisms with which those goals could be put into practice. As a result, they were better suited to the needs of men attacking an existing (or proposed) system of government than of men attempting to solve the concrete problem of organizing a nation for freedom.

Prefiguring Sidney's influence on the constitutional debates was the role his writings played in a controversy that engulfed the state of Maryland in 1787. After the Maryland Senate had turned down a series of paper-money bills, the House of Delegates appealed to the people to instruct their senators to approve them. In so doing, they "precipitated the longest and most important constitutional debate of the Confederation period prior to the meeting of the Philadelphia Convention."[102]

Samuel Chase initiated the argument for instructions with a statement of principle: "All *lawful* authority originates from the people, and their power is like the light of the sun, native, original, inherent, and unlimited by human authority." Because the people are sovereign, both branches of the legislature, not just the lower house, are "equally the *representatives, trustees,* and *servants* of the people." History verified this claim: "Our law books, and treatises by Sydney, and many other celebrated writers on the English government, inform us, 'that not only particular members but the whole body of the House of Commons *often* refused to grant money, or to agree to requisitions from the Crown, *before they consulted with their constituents*; and that

---

[101] The statistical basis for this claim is presented in Donald Lutz, "The Relative Influence of European Writers on Late Eighteenth-Century American Political Thought," *American Political Science Review* 78 (March 1984): 189–97.

[102] Wood, *Creation of the American Republic*, 369–70. See also: 251–54.

they often adjourned for *this* purpose.' "[103] Chase's invocation of English practice was a brilliant tactical move, not so much for what it said as for what it implied: if Maryland's senators were not subject to instructions, then they were much more like a hereditary House of Lords than an elected House of Commons. As Gordon Wood has observed, the opponents of instructions "wisely avoided any attempt to define the upper house . . . as an aristocracy immune from popular dictation" and concentrated instead on the question of whether the people had a right to instruct *either* branch of the legislature.[104]

As the controversy over instructions sharpened, it came to hinge on an interpretation of Sidney's theory of representation. According to William Paca, who published a series of articles in the *Maryland Journal* under the pseudonym Publicola, Sidney "expressly maintains the peoples right to instruct."[105] Sidney had mocked Sir Robert Filmer's assertion that the English electorate "must only chuse, and trust those whom they chuse, to do what they list." That was like saying that though a man could hire a servant he could not assign him specific tasks to perform. No one denied him that right. "And if I am free in my private capacity to regulate my particular affairs according to my own discretion, and to allot to each Servant his proper work, why have not I with my Associates the Freemen of *England* the like liberty of directing and limiting the Powers of the Servants we employ in our publick Affairs?" After citing this passage, Paca concluded: "If this is not an explicit assertion of the people's right to *direct* and *control* their delegates, I am mistaken indeed."[106]

Paca's arguments were countered by Alexander Hanson in a series of articles published under the pseudonym Aristides. Hanson admitted that he had not read Locke or Sidney before the controversy over instructions had erupted. But under the prompting of "Publicola's" essays he did so, and he was "utterly astonished to find both these writers pointedly" opposed to instructions. To prove his point, Hanson quoted from Sidney's *Discourses*:

> Every County dos not make a distinct Body, having in it self a sovereign Power, but is a Member of that great Body which comprehends the

[103] Samuel Chase, *Maryland Journal and Baltimore Advertiser*, 13 February 1787. The passage quoted is a paraphrase of *Discourses*, III:38, p. 424.

[104] Wood, *Creation of the American Republic*, 370.

[105] William Paca [Publicola, pseud.], *Maryland Journal*, 18 May 1787.

[106] *Patriarcha*, 119; *Discourses*, III:44, p. 450; Paca, *Maryland Journal*, 18 May 1787. Paca also quoted *Discourses*, III:44, p. 451 ("Every County dos not make a distinct Body, having in itself a sovereign Power, but is a Member of that great Body which comprehends the whole Nation"), and III:44, p. 453 ("We always may, and often do give Instructions to our Delegates").

whole Nation. 'Tis not therefore for *Kent* or *Sussex*, *Lewis* or *Maidstone*, but for the whole Nation, that the Members chosen in those places are sent to serve in Parliament. . . . [Thus] they are not strictly and properly obliged to give account of their actions to any, unless the whole body of the nation for which they serve, and who are equally concerned in their resolutions, could be assembled. This being impracticable, the only punishment to which they are subject if they betray their trust, is scorn, infamy, hatred, and an assurance of being rejected, when they shall again seek the same honor.[107]

"That a representative should yield [the people] blind obedience . . . is denied by Mr. Sydney, one of the greatest advocates for equal liberty that England ever produced."[108]

The heart of the conflict between Paca and Hanson lay in their different conceptions of the social contract. According to Paca, Sidney and Locke had irrefutably proven that all mankind was "originally" in a state of nature, where "every man stood upon an equal footing." Consequently, "they never could be rightfully removed out of that state but by their own consent. And therefore . . . all rightful government is founded upon *compact*."[109] Thus far Hanson would have agreed; but Paca went on to argue that the people permanently retained the right to judge whether the government they had created was fulfilling its public trust.[110] As Tom Paine once put it, "the Nation is the paymaster of every thing, and every thing must conform to its general will."[111] The sovereign people, like any employer, were free to instruct or cashier their servants and employees at will.

But to Hanson, "the idea of people being masters is one of the most incongruous and absurd, that ever entered into a human brain." "In every free government, founded on a real compact, neither the governing nor the governed are to be considered on the footing of either master or slave; they both are possessed of certain rights, which ought to be held inviolable."[112] Hanson's argument contained two key claims: that the people have only those rights explicitly embodied in

---

[107] Alexander Hanson [Aristides, pseud.], *Maryland Journal*, 22 June 1787. The quotation is from *Discourses*, III:44, p. 451. Hanson also quoted III:44, p. 453: "We always may, and often do give Instructions to Delegates; but the less we fetter them, the more we manifest our own rights."

[108] Hanson, *Maryland Journal*, 13 April 1787.

[109] Paca, *Maryland Journal*, 31 August 1787.

[110] "I maintain that the people have a right to *instruct* both branches and *demand* redress; for they are the *constitutional judges* of what is *public oppression*" (Paca, *Maryland Journal*, 20 February 1787).

[111] Paine, "Rights of Man," in *Complete Writings*, 1:321.

[112] Hanson, *Maryland Journal*, 3 August 1787, 22 June 1787.

the social contract or constitution; and that the system of elections entails the complete but temporary transfer of sovereignty from the people to their representatives. Between elections, the government had a "right' to the legislative power. Even the whole people, speaking with one voice, had no "right" to instruct the government in the use of its power. None of these claims could be traced to Sidney or Locke, but Hanson made a valiant attempt to bend their writings to his purposes.

At the same time that Paca and Hanson were debating the "true" meaning of Sidney's theory of representation, an author using the pseudonym Sidney was calling attention to "the opportune publication and arrival of Mr. John Adams's book upon government in America." "[Adams's] arguments in favor of two or three legislative branches and a powerful executive, drawn from history, from reason, and even from the works of nature, are unanswerable, and will probably serve, joined with the melancholy experience we have had of the folly, instability, and tyranny of single legislatures, to banish those dangerous experiments in government out of our country. It is to be hoped every freeman in the United States will furnish himself with a copy of this invaluable book."[113] "Sidney's" endorsement was appropriate, for Adams's *Defence of the Constitutions of the United States of America* drew extensively on the *Discourses Concerning Government*. Sidney was more than an intellectual resource to Adams, however; he was also a source of inspiration and an object of emulation and comparison. According to Adams, Sidney had written during the third period in English history when the threat of tyranny led men to reflect on the foundations of freedom.[114] Adams clearly believed that he was living and writing during a fourth such period. Indeed, he compared his own efforts to overturn the doctrine that all political authority ought to be concentrated in a single body to the "labored reasonings" of Locke and Sidney to refute Sir Robert Filmer's patriarchal absolutism.[115]

The central problem Adams addressed in the *Defence* was the apparently inescapable conflict between the facts of human nature and society and the moral and political ambitions of good government. Adams accepted as a providential fact that every nation was divided

---

[113] "Sidney," *Independent Gazetteer* (Philadelphia), 6 June 1787.

[114] John Adams, "Defence of the Constitutions of the United States of America," in *Works*, 6:4. The three periods, and the theorists of liberty Adams associated with them, were: the Reformation (Machiavelli, John Poynet), the Interregnum (Milton, Harrington), and the Glorious Revolution (Sidney, Locke, Trenchard, Gordon, Neville, Hoadley). See also: Adams, "Canon and Feudal Law," in *Papers*, 1:127.

[115] Adams, "Defence of the Constitutions," in *Works*, 4:302.

between the few and the many, between the rich, talented, and well connected and the poor, less talented, and unconnected.[116] He also believed that the passions of men led these two "orders" of society to war with each other constantly. The poverty and "indolence" of the many led them to assault the property of the few, while the ambition and "passion for distinction" of the few led them to tyrannize and enslave the many.[117] These facts of human nature and society were true of all nations at all times. And they posed a constant threat to stability and peace, without which freedom and happiness were not possible.[118] Consequently, the question facing Americans in 1787 was not "Are we sufficiently free of the baneful features of past societies to found a nation on freedom?"—there could be no American exceptionalism—but rather "How can we best cope with these permanent threats to freedom and happiness?"

In his search for a "science of government" that could cope with "the nature of man [and] the necessities of society,"[119] Adams cited Sidney as an authority on two issues: the primacy of the rule of law, and the superiority of mixed government. According to Adams, the term "republic" properly signified "only a government, in which all men, rich and poor, magistrates and subjects, officers and people, masters and servants, the first citizen and the last, are equally subject to the laws."[120] He approved of James Harrington's distinction between government de jure, which is "the empire of laws and not of men," and government de facto, which is "the empire of men and not of laws."[121] But he was even more strongly impressed by Sidney's arguments demonstrating that no government was well constituted unless the law prevailed against the arbitrary commands of men. For it was Sidney who had proven that ambitious men are impatient of restraint, that there can be no freedom in a kingdom where there is no law but the prince's will, and that the loss of liberty in Rome could be attributed to the rise of men whose power was above the law.[122] Sid-

---

[116] Adams, "Defence of the Constitutions," in *Works*, 4:392–98, 6:68.

[117] Adams, "Defence of the Constitutions," in *Works*, 4:290, 5:426, 6:9–10, 89–90; Adams, "Discourses on Davila," in *Works*, 6:232.

[118] "The form of government, which communicates ease, comfort, security, or in one word happiness to the greatest number of persons, and in the greatest degree, is the best" (Adams, "Thoughts on Government," in *Papers*, 4:86).

[119] Adams, "Defence of the Constitutions," in *Works*, 4:299.

[120] Adams, "Defence of the Constitutions," in *Works*, 5:453.

[121] Adams, "Defence of the Constitutions," in *Works*, 4:404. The quotations are from James Harrington, "The Commonwealth of Oceana," in *The Political Works of James Harrington*, ed. J.G.A. Pocock (Cambridge: Cambridge University Press, 1977), 161.

[122] Adams, "Defence of the Constitutions," in *Works*, 4:403–5. Adams quoted from *Discourses*, I:5, p. 12 ("Liberty solely consists in an independency upon the Will of an-

ney had said nothing about a universal conflict between the few and the many—here Adams was closer to Machiavelli than to any of the leading English republicans—but he had demonstrated both historically and theoretically that good government was inseparable from the rule of law.[123]

The second issue on which Adams cited Sidney's authority was the superiority of mixed government. In light of the destructive potential of inequality and the sovereignty of the passions, Adams argued that the rule of law could be ensured only by establishing "a complication of forces" in government.[124] The many should be represented in a lower house, the few should be isolated in an upper house, and an independent executive with a legislative veto should be created to maintain a balance between them.[125] To prove the advantages of this arrangement, Adams turned once again to Sidney. For it was Sidney who had argued that "pure Democracy"—which Adams took to mean government by a single assembly—"can never be good, unless for a small Town"; and it was Sidney who had demonstrated that "there never was a good Government in the world, that did not consist of [a mixture of] the three simple Species of Monarchy, Aristocracy and Democracy."[126] Adams also drew on the testimony of Machiavelli, Harrington, and Montesquieu; and he ransacked the history of Eu-

---

other"); II:14, p. 120 ("No Sedition was hurtful to Rome, till through their Prosperity some men gained a Power above the Laws"); II:20, p. 152 (quoting Livy on the "dissolute crew that us'd to be companions to the Tarquins"); III:16, p. 317 ("if there be no other Law in a Kingdom than the will of a Prince, there is no such thing as Liberty").

[123] Adams's use of Sidney's arguments for the rule of law provides a good example of how seventeenth-century radicalism was transformed to fit an eighteenth-century context. Sidney had argued that by universalizing the logic of corruption, by recognizing the common humanity of monarchs and their subjects, it was possible to see the folly of giving monarchs power to act above the law. Adams inverted this argument: the known corruption of monarchs shed light on what could be expected of any man in a position of power. Sidney's argument undercut any claims to special virtue on the part of monarchs; Adams's argument undercut any claims to special virtue on the part of republican citizens.

[124] Adams, "Defence of the Constitutions," in *Works*, 4:391. "I think a people cannot be long free, nor ever happy, whose government is in one Assembly" (Adams, "Thoughts on Government," in *Papers*, 4:88).

[125] Adams, "Defence of the Constitutions," in *Works*, 4:290, 398, 579; 6:43.

[126] Adams, "Defence of the Constitutions," in *Works*, 4:420–23, 559. The quotations are from *Discourses*, II:18, p. 138; II:16, p. 130. Adams also quoted I:10, p. 23 ("the wisest, best, and far the greatest part of mankind . . . did form Governments mixed or composed of the three [simple Species]"); II:19, p. 149 ("As to Popular Government in the strictest sense . . . I know of no such thing"); II:21, p. 154 ("no way concerned in the defence of Democracy"); II:30, p. 238 ("more ignorance cannot be express'd, than by giving the name of Democracy" to mixed governments).

rope to prove in painful detail that the failure to establish a proper "balance" or "equilibrium" in the constitution of a government had always led to chaos and destruction.[127]

Adams's *Defence of the Constitutions* was a one-man campaign against the doctrine of popular sovereignty and the concept of a single, omnicompetent legislature he associated with it. He was harshly criticized for his failure to understand the difference between American and European inequality, and hence for his confused defense of mixed government. Almost immediately his arguments were overshadowed by the emerging *Federalist* doctrines of the separation of powers and checks and balances. Ironically, many of the strongest critics of the new Constitution drew on the same sources as John Adams but used them to reach the opposite conclusion. Thus it was that the Antifederalists, who thought of themselves as the defenders of popular sovereignty, also relied on the writings of Algernon Sidney.

Like John Adams and a great many other eighteenth-century Americans, the Antifederalists identified their own struggles with those Sidney had endured. In a series of articles published in early 1788 under the pseudonym Sidney, the author—probably Abraham Yates—proclaimed: "For my own part, I adopt the sentiments of Sidney: 'While I live I shall endeavor to preserve my liberty, or at least not consent to the destroying of it: I hope I shall die in the same principle in which I lived, and will no longer live than they can preserve me.' "[128] Not coincidentally, "Sidney" began this essay with a similar quotation from Marcus Junius Brutus. As had been the case before 1776, Sidney's "Roman" spirit provided a model for the self-understanding of Americans who felt themselves to be the victims of plots against their liberties.

The Antifederalists were, in the words of Cecilia Kenyon, "men of little faith": they were suspicious of the nature of man, they feared the corrupting influence of power, and they distrusted large, distant, and loosely supervised governments.[129] In Algernon Sidney they

[127] "Saint Bartholomew's Days are the natural, necessary, and unavoidable effect and consequence of diversities in opinion, the spirit of party, unchecked passions, emulation, and rivalry, where there is not a power always ready and inclined to throw weights into the lightest scale, to preserve or restore the equilibrium" (Adams, "Discourses on Davila," in *Works*, 6:394).

[128] "Sidney," "Essay II," *Albany Gazette*, 21 February 1788, reprinted in Herbert J. Storing, ed., *The Complete Anti-Federalist* (Chicago: University of Chicago Press, 1981), 6:97. The quotation is from Algernon Sidney, "Letter to a Friend," in Blencowe, 200. This letter—now known to be a forgery—was reprinted in full in the *Virginia Gazette* (Rind), 8 September 1774.

[129] Cecilia Kenyon, "Men of Little Faith: The Anti-Federalists on the Nature of Representative Government," *William and Mary Quarterly*, 3rd ser., 12 (1955): 3–46.

found a kindred spirit. As "Cincinnatus" wrote in a sarcastic attack on James Wilson's defense of the absence of a bill of rights in the Constitution,

> Do you indeed suppose, Mr. Wilson, that if the people give up their privileges to these new rulers they will render them back again to the people? . . . If we throw away suspicion—to be sure, the thing will go smoothly enough, and we shall deserve to continue a free, respectable, and happy people. Suspicion shackles rulers and prevents good government. All great and honest politicians, *like yourself*, have reprobated it. . . . But such men as Milton, Sidney, Locke, Montesquieu, and Trenchard, have thought it essential to the preservation of liberty against the artful and persevering encroachments of those with whom power is trusted.[130]

"Cincinnatus" apparently believed that Wilson's naïve trust in the new Constitution was a mask for more sinister views. In the writings of Sidney and others, he found an unobstructed view of the corrupt reality that lay behind that facade.

The Antifederalists used Sidney's writings to highlight three deficiencies in the proposed constitution. First, it did not contain a bill of rights; and as "A Farmer" in Maryland remonstrated, "If a citizen of Maryland can have no benefit of his own bill of rights in the confederal courts, and if there is no bill of rights of the United States—how could he take advantage of a natural right founded in reason, how could he plead it and produce Locke, Sydney, or Montesquieu as authority?"[131] One might wonder how Montesquieu could ever be cited as an "authority" on natural rights; and Locke and Sidney had never suggested that they be embodied in or protected by a bill of rights. But the "Farmer's" confusion should not be allowed to mask his central point: without a bill of rights, the personal and political liberties that had come to be associated with the names of Sidney, Locke, and Montesquieu could not be protected.

Second, the proposed constitution provided insufficient checks on the power of the executive. As "Tamony" protested to the readers of the *Virginia Independent Chronicle*, "Do not contemn the declarations of Locke, Sydney, Montesquieu, Raynal, whose writings are legacies to the present and future ages, they unite in asserting that annual supplies and an annual mutiny law, are the chief dykes man's sagacity can raise against that torrent of despotism, which continually at-

---

[130] Cincinnatus, "Letter II," *New York Journal*, 8 November 1787, reprinted in Storing, *Complete Anti-Federalist*, 6:11.

[131] A Farmer, "Letter I," *Maryland Gazette* (Baltimore), 15 February 1788, reprinted in Storing, *Complete Anti-Federalist*, 5:13.

tempts to deluge the rights of individuals."[132] By "an annual mutiny law" "Tamony" meant an annual or provisional grant to the executive of control over the army. As with the concept of a bill of rights, there is no clear source for this argument in Sidney's writings. But it was a plausible interpolation, for Sidney had made his distrust of standing armies and unsupervised power abundantly clear.

Finally, the Antifederalists believed that the drafters of the Constitution had abandoned "the safe democratical principles of annual" elections. In an important series of essays "Cato"—possibly George Clinton of New York—argued that this significantly weakened both the nation and the government:

> If annual elections were to exist in this government, and learning and information to become more prevalent, you never will want men to execute whatever you could design—Sidney observes "that a well governed state is as fruitful to all good purposes as the seven headed serpent is said to have been in evil; when one head is cut off, many rise up in the place of it." He remarks further, that "it was thought, that free cities by frequent elections of magistrates became nurseries of great and able men, every man endeavoring to excel others, that he might be advanced to the honor he had no other title to, than what might arise from his merit or reputation," but the framers of this *perfect government*, as it is called, have departed from this democratical principle, and established bienniel elections for the house of representatives . . . and sextenniel for the senate.[133]

This passage is of particular interest because it illustrates the danger of viewing the Antifederalists as nothing but "men of little faith." John Adams had defended annual elections in 1776 on the grounds that they would teach representatives "the great political virtues of humility, patience, and moderation, without which every man in power becomes a ravenous beast of prey."[134] The Antifederalists shared Adams's overwhelming fear of corruption. But as "Cato's" quotations from Sidney indicate, they also believed that annual elections were a vital source of energy and strength in the nation.

On each of these issues—a bill of rights, control of the executive, and annual elections—the Antifederalists invoked a large number of authorities, only one of whom was Algernon Sidney. And on many

---

[132] Tamony, *Virginia Independent Chronicle*, 9 January 1788, reprinted in Storing, *Complete Anti-Federalist*, 5:147.

[133] Cato, "Letter V," *New York Journal*, September 1787–January 1788, reprinted in Storing, *Complete Anti-Federalist*, 2:118–19. The passages quoted are from *Discourses*, II:23, p. 167; II:28, p. 216.

[134] Adams, "Thoughts on Government," in *Papers*, 4:90.

issues of concern to them they did not quote Sidney at all. But as with the Maryland debate over instructions, and John Adams's *Defence of the Constitutions*, the arguments of the Antifederalists demonstrate that Sidney's writings and the story of his life were vital parts of the political heritage brought to bear on the constitutional debates of 1787–88.

EPILOGUE

AFTER THE ratification of the Constitution, the men who had fomented the American Revolution found relatively few occasions on which to refer to Algernon Sidney. Benjamin Franklin decried the decline of English in favor of Greek and Latin in the Academy of Philadelphia and renewed his commitment to the teaching of English through the writings of "Tillotson, Addison, Pope, Algernon Sidney, Cato's Letters, &c."[1] Benjamin Rush was led to the conclusion that war with England was preferable to the continuation of vice-ridden "funding systems, banks, embargoes, and nonintercourse laws" after reflecting on Sidney's maxim that slavery was worse than civil war.[2] John Adams alternately regretted having "wasted" so much time reading Sidney's *Discourses*[3] and proclaimed the need to publish "as splendid an Edition of it, as the art of printing can produce, as well for the intrinsick merit of the work, as for the proof it brings of the bitter sufferings of the advocates of Liberty from that time to this."[4] Thomas Jefferson sought pictures and busts of "Newton, [Locke, Bacon, Syd]ney, Hampden, Shakespeare," endorsed the *Discourses* as "a rich treasure of republican principles" and "probably the best elementary book of the principles of government, as founded in natural right which has ever been published in any language," and ascribed the "authority" of the Declaration of Independence to "the harmonizing sentiments of the day, whether ex-

---

[1] Benjamin Franklin, "Observations Relative to the Intentions of the Original Founders of the Academy of Philadelphia," June 1789, in *The Writings of Benjamin Franklin*, ed. Albert Henry Smyth (New York: Macmillan, 1905–1907), 10:10, 31.

[2] Benjamin Rush to John Adams, 13 March 1809, in *The Letters of Benjamin Rush*, ed. L. H. Butterfield (Princeton: Princeton University Press, 1951), 2:997–98.

[3] "Oh that I had devoted to Newton and his Fellows that time which I fear has been wasted on Plato and Aristotle, Bacon, Acherly, Bolinbrooke, DeLolme, Harrington, Sidney, Hobbes, Plato Redivivus, Marchamont Nedham, with twenty others upon Subjects which Mankind is determined never to Understand, and those who do Understand them are resolved never to practice, or countenance" (John Adams to Thomas Jefferson, 3 February 1812, in *The Adams-Jefferson Letters*, ed. Lester J. Cappon [Chapel Hill: University of North Carolina Press, 1959], 2:294–95).

[4] John Adams to Thomas Jefferson, 18 September 1823, in *Adams-Jefferson Letters*, 2:598. See also: John Adams to John Taylor of Caroline, 1814, in *The Works of John Adams*, ed. Charles Francis Adams (Boston: Little and Brown, 1850–1856), 6:481–82; and John Adams to J. H. Tiffany, 31 March 1819, in *Works*, 10:377.

pressed in conversation, in letters, printed essays, or in the elementary books of public right, as Aristotle, Cicero, Locke, Sidney, &c."[5]

That Sidney continued to play a role in the intellectual lives of these men is a reflection of the profound influence that he had on them. None would have hesitated to list him among their favorite authors. At the same time, their references to Sidney are scattered and often retrospective, and they lack the concentrated energy and purpose with which his writings and the story of his life were greeted before 1789.

Sidney's changing role in American political thought was captured in an exchange between Thomas Jefferson and James Madison in 1825. Jefferson, as "Father of the University of Virginia"[6] and rector of its Board of Visitors, proposed a set of basic texts to be taught to all students in the school of law. While the "distinctive principles" of the governments of Virginia and the United States were to be taught by the Declaration of Independence, the *Federalist*, and the Virginia Resolutions of 1799, "the general principles of liberty and the rights of man, in nature and in society," were to be taught by Locke's *Second Treatise* and Sidney's *Discourses Concerning Government*.[7] Given Jefferson's lifelong concern for education, this was the highest accolade he could have given Sidney's writings.

On learning of Jefferson's proposal, Madison demurred. He was skeptical of the very idea of attempting to instill a political creed in Virginia's law students: "In framing a political creed, a like difficulty occurs in the case of religion. . . . If the Articles be in very general terms, they do not answer the purpose; if in very particular terms, they divide & exclude where meant to unite & fortify." Moreover, Madison doubted whether reading Sidney or Locke would adequately prepare young Virginians to defend their freedom. "Sidney & Locke are admirably calculated to impress on young minds the right of Nations to establish their own Governments, and to inspire a love of free ones; but afford no aid in guarding our Republican

---

[5] Thomas Jefferson to John Trumbull, 18 January 1789, in *The Papers of Thomas Jefferson*, ed. Julian P. Boyd (Princeton: Princeton University Press, 1950), 14:467–68; Thomas Jefferson to Mason Locke Weems, 13 December 1804, in *Catalogue of the Library of Thomas Jefferson*, ed. W. Millicent Sowerby (Washington, DC: Library of Congress, 1953), 3:13; Thomas Jefferson to Henry Lee, 8 May 1825, in *The Writings of Thomas Jefferson*, ed. Andrew Lipscomb and Albert Burgh (Washington, DC: Thomas Jefferson Memorial Association, 1907), 16:116–17.

[6] Thomas Jefferson, "Epitaph," in *Writings*, ed. Merrill D. Peterson (New York: Library of America, 1984), 706.

[7] Thomas Jefferson, "Minutes of the Board of Visitors of the University of Virginia," 4 March 1825, in *Writings*, ed. Lipscomb and Burgh, 19:460–61. See also: Thomas Jefferson to John Norvell, 11 June 1807, ibid., 11:222–23.

Charters against constructive violations." Even the *Federalist* "did not foresee all the misconstructions which have occurred; nor prevent some that it did foresee."[8] Having adopted a constitution, America had fundamentally altered its political landscape. While some problems had been solved, others had been created. New institutions brought changed distributions of power, novel claims of right, and unprecedented forms of opposition. Ever the practical politician, Madison refused to lose sight of those facts. Without trivializing the importance of Sidney and Locke, he implied that they were no longer immediately relevant to the conduct of American politics. There was a world of difference between fomenting revolution and defending an institutional order. New problems demanded new solutions.

Despite his opposition to Jefferson's educational proposals, Madison implicitly acknowledged the extent to which republican ideals had been incorporated into the new state and federal constitutions. In some cases they were embedded in new practices and spawned indigenous vocabularies. Republican opposition to standing armies bore fruit in constitutional and political provisions for the civilian control of the military, and republican fear of corruption and the abuse of executive power was reflected in the congressional power of impeachment. In other cases the original language of republicanism was preserved intact. Election, representation, instruction, the separation of powers, the rule of law: each expressed a key republican ideal. Though it would be a mistake to view these concepts and the political practices associated with them as exclusively "republican" in origin, their resonance with Sidney's doctrines cannot be gainsaid. As an anonymous author put it in the *North American Review* of 1822, "what was considered by Sydney's contemporaries as a fanciful theory, has long been [a] matter of experience. . . . [Sydney's principles] are adopted and acted upon in their fullest extent, in our own admirable constitutions."[9]

Ironically, the very success of republicanism permanently altered Sidney's place in American political thought. During the debates over the ratification of the Constitution, Sidney's republicanism had been most influential among men opposed to the new national order. After 1789 that tendency both intensified and was transformed. What remained influential from Sidney's writings and the story of his life can only be described as "rump republicanism," the remnant of a set

[8] James Madison to Thomas Jefferson, 8 February 1825, in *The Writings of James Madison*, ed. Gaillard Hunt (New York: G. P. Putnam's Sons, 1901–1910), 9:220, 218–19.

[9] Review of Meadley, *Memoirs of Algernon Sidney*, in *North American Review* 14 (January 1822): 86.

of ideals and arguments whose principle objectives had been achieved. Sidney's republicanism was originally and essentially anti-monarchical. He wrote with the express purpose of countering the "slavish" principles and practices of the Stuarts. Against the moral claim that men are born into relationships of rule and subjection, command and obedience, inequality and dependence, Sidney argued that men were by nature free and equal. Against the political claim that the greatest strength, stability, and order were found in monarchy, and monarchy alone, Sidney argued for the superiority of a self-governing republic. The revolutionary events of 1776–89 decisively resolved the place of monarchy in America's future, and in so doing transformed the moral, political, and intellectual contexts within which Sidney's writings and the story of his life were viewed.

After 1789 Sidney's republicanism provided less a coherent language than a fragmented vocabulary. Cut loose from its intellectual and political moorings, it was captive to increasingly diverse ideological currents. Jeffersonian Republicans claimed to be the spiritual heirs of Sidney and Locke[10] and employed the heroic martyr's name as a pseudonym in an effort to reconcile Federalists to their rule.[11] Jacksonian Democrats invoked Sidney as an apostle of popular sovereignty and an expansive franchise,[12] while anti-Jacksonians appealed to Sidney as a critic of executive power and unchecked majorities.[13]

[10] In addition to the quotations from Jefferson cited in note 5 above, see: Edmund Randolph, "Edmund Randolph's Essay on the Revolutionary History of Virginia (1774–1782)," *Virginia Magazine of History and Biography* 43 (April 1935): 122–23; James Cheetham, *The Life of Thomas Paine* (New York: Southwick and Pelsue, 1809), 131n.

[11] Gideon Granger [Algernon Sidney, pseud.], *A Vindication of the Measures of the Present Administration* (Wilmington: James Wilson, 1803); Gideon Granger [Algernon Sidney, pseud.], *An Address to the People of New England* (Washington, DC: Dinmore and Cooper, 1808).

[12] Frances Harriet Whipple Green [A Rhode Islander, pseud.], *Might and Right* (Providence: A. H. Stillwell, 1844), 62, 132–34, 150, 197–98, 257; Benjamin F. Hallett, "The Right of the People to Establish Forms of Government," 1848, in *Social Theories of Jacksonian Democracy*, ed. Joseph L. Blau (New York: Liberal Arts Press, 1954), 113. In the Virginia Constitutional Convention debates of 1829, John Cooke contended that the principle of equal representation had been "illustrated by the genius of Locke, and Sydney, and Milton," and Chapman Johnson declared that the " 'Declaration of Rights [of the people of Virginia],' which proclaims the principles pertaining to the Government of a free people . . . faithfully embodies the doctrines, which gave to Algernon Sydney his crown of martyrdom, and to John Locke imperishable fame" (*Proceedings and Debates of the Virginia State Convention of 1829–1830* [Richmond: Samuel Shepherd, 1830], 54, 260).

[13] Surrounded by "greedy and corrupt adherents," exerting his influence through "satellites," Jackson "made his own will and pleasure, the sole rule and guide of all his

Sidney's fragmented influence on nineteenth-century American political thought was nowhere more evident than in his contribution to debates over the nature and significance of slavery. Though America was no longer enslaved to the British monarch, slavery—as metaphor and reality—persisted on American soil. It was here, in his concern for the interplay of freedom, slavery, virtue, and corruption, that Sidney spoke loudest to nineteenth-century Americans. As symbols of the contest between liberty and tyranny, Sidney's writings and the story of his life seemed uniquely relevant to men and women who felt themselves to be the victims of distant unseen, unknown, or uncontrolled powers. And as the original location of those powers—the British monarchy—was permanently eclipsed, Sidney's opposition to slavery took on an increasingly wide range of meanings.

Sidney was frequently invoked in the struggle against chattel slavery. His writings were early favorites of William Lloyd Garrison's. In 1837 Garrison was given the opportunity to demonstrate his devotion to Sidney when an opponent of the First Amendment rights of abolitionists had "the rare audacity" to publish his views under the pseudonym Algernon Sidney. Garrison responded to this "bold and shameless" abuse of the heroic martyr's name in a series of letters to the Boston *Courier*. Using extensive quotations from the *Discourses*, "that exhaustless treasury of free thoughts," Garrison sought to prove that Sidney was "an uncompromising enemy of slavery under every phase and color," "the father of modern Abolitionism," and "an immediate emancipationist, in the strictest sense."[14] Others may have been less well-versed in Sidney's writings, but they were equally certain that he would have been opposed to chattel slavery. In 1850 Wil-

---

actions" (Benjamin Watkins Leigh [Algernon Sydney, pseud.], *The Letters of Algernon Sydney, in Defence of Civil Liberty* [Richmond: T. W. White, 1830], vi, 18). Henry Clay wished "Sidney's" views "everywhere diffused" (Henry Clay to Francis Brook, 23 May 1830, in *The Papers of Henry Clay*, ed. James Hopkins [Lexington: University of Kentucky Press, 1959–], 8:211). For a similar use of Sidney to attack Jackson's enhancement of the executive power, see: [John Pendleton Kennedy], *Defence of the Whigs* (New York: Harper & Brothers, 1844), 14–15. In 1837 Noah Webster published a series of letters under the pseudonym Sidney designed to prove that "the people . . . are just as bad as kings" (Noah Webster [Sidney, pseud.], "To William Leete Stone," 29 August 1837, in *Letters of Noah Webster*, ed. Harry Warfel [New York: Library Publishers, 1953], 505; see generally 504–13).

[14] *William Lloyd Garrison, 1805–1879: The Story of His Life Told by His Children* (New York: Negro Universities Press, 1969), 4:314; "To the Editor of the Boston *Courier*," 4 March 1837 and 11 March 1837, in *The Letters of William Lloyd Garrison*, ed. Louis Ruchames (Cambridge, MA: Harvard University Press, 1971–), 2:217, 219, 224. See also: "To the Editor of the Newburyport 'Herald,'" 11 June 1830, in *William Lloyd Garrison, 1805–1879*, 1:187.

liam H. Seward, a leader in the fight against the Compromise of 1850, stood on the floor of the Senate and proclaimed that "Algernon Sidney expiated with his life the offence of writing as mere abstractions the fundamental principles of our own Constitution; and among them was the Wilmot Proviso, thus expressed by that immortal patriot: 'The liberty of one man cannot be limited or diminished by one or any number of men, and none can give away the right of another.' " Between freedom and slavery there could be no compromise. As Sidney declared and Seward seconded, no law or constitution should be followed unless it was rightly made, and it could not have been rightly made if it violated "the universal law of God and nature."[15] With no less vehemence Wendell Phillips invoked Sidney's "immortal book" in defense of the legal rights of John Brown, and Theodore Parker drew attention to the parallels between Sidney's martyrdom and his own persecution for abolitionist agitation.[16]

The concept of slavery also served as a metaphor, and Sidney's fate at the hands of the Stuarts provided a powerful symbol for the consequences of despotism. As during the Revolution, Sidney's name carried particular weight against violations of the rule of law. Both during and after Aaron Burr's trial for treason in 1805, for example, Burr's attorneys were subjected to heated public abuse. Henry Clay sought to quell this public outcry by suggesting that the same spirit that was attempting to silence Burr's defenders would have condemned the supporters of "Sidney and Hampden." Burr's guilt or innocence was not the issue; before the law, every man deserved to be heard.[17]

Herman Melville added an important twist to the symbolic importance of Sidney's martyrdom when, in his novel *White-Jacket*, he un-

[15] William H. Seward, "Freedom in the New Territories: The Compromise Bill," 2 July 1850, in *The Works of William H. Seward*, ed. George Baker (New York: Redfield, 1853–1884), 1:102, 108.

[16] Wendell Phillips, "John Brown and the Spirit of Fifty-Nine," 1859, in *Modern Eloquence*, ed. Thomas Reed (Philadelphia: John Morris, 1900–1903), 14:1598; Theodore Parker, *The Trial of Theodore Parker*, 1855 (New York: Negro Universities Press, 1970), 54. See also: Wendell Phillips, "The Scholar in a Republic," 30 June 1881, in *Speeches, Lectures and Letters*, 2nd ser. (Boston: Lee and Shepard, 1891), 359.

[17] " 'Regulus' to the People," ca. 9 July 1808, in Clay, *Papers*, 1:364–65. Burr's attorneys were not unaware of the power of Sidney's name; according to the prosecution, during the trial they trumpeted Burr as "a persecuted patriot: a Russell or a Sidney, bleeding under the scourge of a despot, and dying for virtue's sake!" (*Reports of the Trials of Colonel Aaron Burr . . . For Treason* [Philadelphia: Hopkins and Earle, 1808], 1:144).

dertook to explain how the cruel "Articles of War" came to form "the ark and constitution of the penal laws of the American Navy."

> Whence came they? . . . They are an importation from abroad, even from Britain, whose laws we Americans hurled off as tyrannical, and yet retained the most tyrannical of all. But we stop not here; for these Articles of War had their congenial origin in a period of the history of Britain when the Puritan Republic had yielded to a monarchy restored; when a hangman like Judge Jeffreys sentenced a world's champion like Algernon Sidney to the block; when one of a race—by some deemed accursed of God—even a Stuart, was on the throne; and a Stuart, also, was at the head of the Navy, as Lord High Admiral.[18]

The rage of Judge Jeffreys and the despotic ambitions of the Stuarts had been staples of American political thought since the 1730s, when they were cited as proof of a widespread conspiracy against liberty.[19] But unlike his polemical predecessors, Melville chose to emphasize the uniquely and distinctively "British" nature of Stuart absolutism. The scourge of despotism could be removed only when America had purged itself of all remnants of British legal practices.[20]

The metaphoric power of the concept of slavery permitted Sidney to be invoked by Southerners as well. In *McCulloch v. Maryland* (1819) and again in *Cohens v. Virginia* (1821) the Supreme Court rendered decisions that sent Virginians running back to the conservative "principles of '98," strict construction and states' rights. In *McCulloch* the Court sustained the constitutionality of the Bank of the United States and barred states from taxing it; in *Cohens* it decided that the Court had jurisdiction to review state criminal judgments. In the eyes of many Southerners, both decisions threatened state sovereignty and, by implication, the preservation of slavery. Judge Spencer Roane of Virginia hoisted the Old Republican banner in a series of public letters written under the pseudonyms Hampden and Algernon Sidney. According to Roane, "the Union was no more than a league of sovereign states that had delegated only certain specific powers to the

---

[18] Herman Melville, *White-Jacket* (Boston: The Page Company, 1892), 278.

[19] This tradition continued into the nineteenth century; see: James Parton, "Life, Trial, and Execution of Algernon Sidney," in *Triumphs of Enterprise, Ingenuity, and Public Spirit* (New York: Virtue & Yorston, 1874), 601–13; and S. P. Scott, "Algernon Sidney," *Potter's American Magazine* 6 (1876): 333–41.

[20] Here, too, Sidney was relevant. For all their glory, England's "illustrious heroes"— Hampden, Russell, and Sidney—paled next to George Washington, the founder of a new empire of freedom and virtue (Thomas Condie, "George Washington," *Philadelphia Monthly Magazine* 1 [June 1798]: 307–8).

central government." As any but "a deplorable idiot" could see, the decisions of the Court had violated this fundamental premise of the republic.[21] Thomas Jefferson was pleased by Roane's efforts and proclaimed that they "appeared to . . . pulverize every word which had been delivered by Judge Marshall."[22] Once again Old Republicanism rose up to do battle with the corrupt forces of centralization.[23]

This strange marriage between Sidney and chattel slavery was sanctified by John Calhoun in 1843. Calhoun's argument is striking and warrants lengthy quotation:

> The truth is, the Government of the uncontrolled numerical majority, is but the *absolute and despotic form of popular government*—just as that of the uncontrolled will of one man, or a few, is of monarchy or aristocracy. . . . Hence it is that it would be the death-blow of constitutional democracy, to admit the right of the numerical majority, to alter or abolish constitutions at pleasure. . . . This would be, to attribute to the simple numerical majority, an inherent, absolute, and paramount power, derived not from agreement, compact or constitution, either expressed or implied, but a higher source. It would be, in short, to attribute to it the same divine right to govern, which Sir Robert Filmer claimed for kings; and against which, Locke and Sydney so successfully combated. The argument, in both cases, is drawn from the same source, and leads to the same consequence.[24]

Calm, rational, and perfectly in keeping with the libertarian spirit of Locke and Sidney—except that Calhoun's "doctrine of the concurrent majority" was designed in part to protect southern states against northern assaults on chattel slavery. Calhoun's argument was extraordinarily disingenuous. But it was also extremely clever in its mobilization of traditional republican arguments linking corruption and the "uncontrolled will" of a man or group of men.[25] Like many

---

[21] Norman K. Risjord, *The Old Republicans: Southern Conservatism in the Age of Jefferson* (New York: Columbia University Press, 1965), 223. Sidney's appeal to Old Republicans ran deep; cf. John Taylor of Caroline, *An Inquiry into the Principles and Policy of the Government of the United States*, 1814 (New Haven: Yale University Press, 1950), 83.

[22] Thomas Jefferson to William Johnson, 27 October 1822, in *The Writings of Thomas Jefferson*, ed. Paul Leicester Ford (New York: 1892–1899), 12:255.

[23] Cf. Lance Banning, "Republican Ideology and the Triumph of the Constitution, 1789 to 1793," *William and Mary Quarterly*, 3rd ser., 31 (April 1974): 167–88.

[24] John Calhoun to William Smith, 3 July 1843, in *The Papers of John C. Calhoun* (Columbia: University of South Carolina Press, 1959–), 17:284–85.

[25] Not all who invoked Sidney's name in defense of slavery possessed Calhoun's acumen; see, for example, D. K. Whitaker [Sidney, pseud.], *Sidney's Letters to William S. Channing* (Charleston, SC: Edward C. Councell, 1837).

Southerners, Calhoun saw no contradiction between his commitment to republicanism and his defense of "the peculiar institution."[26]

Sidney's complex and seemingly contradictory influence on American conceptions of freedom and slavery persisted throughout the Civil War era. Northerners and Southerners alike found reason to praise him. In 1866 Senator Charles Sumner, a Radical Republican, quoted Sidney and Locke in a speech defending the political rights of former slaves, while in 1867 General Richard Taylor, an officer in the Confederate army, argued that the "names and characters" of rebel leaders in Louisiana "should be reverenced as are those of Hampden and Sidney."[27] As the nineteenth century came to a close, however, Americans found fewer and fewer occasions on which to refer to Sidney's writings and the story of his life. New problems arose, educational practices were modified, and intellectual tastes changed. The distinguished jurist Oliver Wendell Holmes undoubtedly spoke for many Americans when, in 1919, he half-jokingly referred to his inability to "assimilat[e] the dull books of the past, such as Harrington's *Oceana* or Sydney."[28] Holmes felt no kinship with England's seventeenth-century radicals and saw no reason to study them. Sidney's republicanism has proven more resilient than Holmes imagined, however, and during the second half of the twentieth century it has once again influenced the moral and political imaginations of Americans. During the 1960s the Pacifica radio network sought to undermine the prosecution of radical activists by producing "a sixty-minute dramatization of the 'conspiracy trial' of 'a left-winger named Algernon Sidney,'" and in 1990 the Liberty Fund, a foundation "established to encourage study of the ideal of a society of free and responsible individuals," issued the first new edition of Sidney's *Discourses* in 185 years.[29] As heroic martyr and revered author, Sidney remains a vital figure in the intellectual life of America.

[26] Cf. Lacy K. Ford, "Republican Ideology in a Slave Society: The Political Economy of John C. Calhoun," *Journal of Southern History* 54 (August 1988): 412–13, and the sources cited there.

[27] Charles Sumner, "The Equal Rights of All," in *Charles Sumner, His Complete Works* (New York: Negro Universities Press, 1969), 1:155–56; Richard Taylor, *Destruction and Reconstruction*, ed. Richard Harwell, 1879 (New York: Longmans, Green and Co., 1955), 129.

[28] Oliver Wendell Holmes to Sir Frederick Pollock, 21 August 1919, in *Holmes-Pollock Letters*, ed. Mark DeWolfe Howe (Cambridge, MA: Harvard University Press, 1941), 2:22. See also: Holmes to Pollock, 19 September 1919, 2:24.

[29] Peter Karsten, *Patriot-Heroes in England and America* (Madison: University of Wisconsin Press, 1978), 199 n. 31; Algernon Sidney, *Discourses Concerning Government*, ed. Thomas G. West (Indianapolis: Liberty Press, 1990).

For three decades the concept of republicanism has played an important role in the study of history and political theory. Historians have found it a useful tool for understanding early modern English and American politics, while political theorists have turned to it for a theory of citizenship capable of reviving America's seemingly torpid public life. These studies of the rise, transmission, decline, and revival of republicanism have assumed that the defining characteristic of republicanism is a classical theory of virtue and that the republican language of virtue is distinct from and in tension with the liberal logic of rights and interests. It would be imprudent to overgeneralize from the analysis of a single figure. But a careful consideration of the range, structure, and influence of Algernon Sidney's political writings suggests that these assumptions, and the conclusions based on them, are unwarranted. Sidney's republicanism was complex and extraordinarily sophisticated. Through the concepts of freedom and slavery, he sought to describe the moral foundations of free governments; through the concepts of virtue and corruption, he sought to demonstrate the flawed character of monarchy and establish the psychological bases of republican citizenship; through the concepts of constitutionalism and revolution, he sought to describe the political forms most likely to preserve liberty and the conditions under which a free people could revolt against its government. Sidney frequently drew on the same intellectual resources as John Locke. Though fragments of his arguments may be used to criticize liberalism, they do not constitute a distinct and coherent alternative to it.[30] Many of Sidney's most cherished aims are embedded in the practices of constitutional government. Some, including economic restrictions on the franchise, have been decisively rejected. Others, like his commitment to militant expansion, continue to be debated. Fragments of his arguments concerning freedom and slavery, or virtue and corruption, remain vital undercurrents in American political thought. This is as one should expect. It would be surprising to discover that Sidney's once-influential ideas had disappeared completely. On the other hand, it would be positively bizarre to imagine that the needs and aspirations of late twentieth-century men and women are canonically expressed by a set of arguments intended to counter the principles

---

[30] Recent studies of the American Revolution have tended to confirm these conclusions. See, for example: Isaac Kramnick, "The 'Great National Discussion': The Discourse of Politics in 1787," *William and Mary Quarterly*, 3rd ser., 45 (January 1988): 3–32; Lance Banning, "Some Second Thoughts on Virtue and the Course of Revolutionary Thinking," in *Conceptual Change and the Constitution*, ed. Terence Ball and J.G.A. Pocock (Lawrence: University of Kansas Press, 1988), 194–212.

and practices of seventeenth-century English monarchs. Sidney undoubtedly would have understood both the vitality and the limitations of his arguments. As he insisted some three hundred years ago, "new Constitutions" are needed "to repair the breaches made upon the old."[31]

[31] *Discourses*, III:37, p. 420.

APPENDIX I

SIDNEY FAMILY TREE

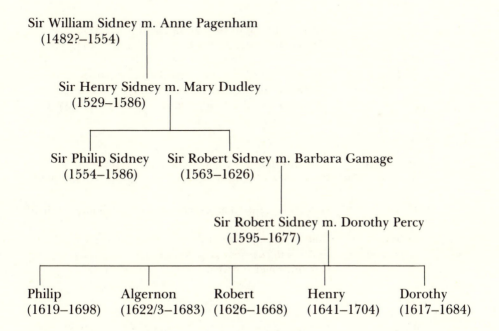

Sir William Sidney m. Anne Pagenham
(1482?–1554)

Sir Henry Sidney m. Mary Dudley
(1529–1586)

Sir Philip Sidney
(1554–1586)

Sir Robert Sidney m. Barbara Gamage
(1563–1626)

Sir Robert Sidney m. Dorothy Percy
(1595–1677)

Philip
(1619–1698)

Algernon
(1622/3–1683)

Robert
(1626–1668)

Henry
(1641–1704)

Dorothy
(1617–1684)

APPENDIX II

SIDNEY'S PARLIAMENTARY ACTIVITY

1647

25 May	Teller: business of George Mynne (*CJ*, 5:182)
	Teller: dissolution of Fairfax's troops (*CJ*, 5:183)
2 June	Committee to investigate Perceval (*CJ*, 5:195)
23 June	Commissioner for Glamorgan (Firth, 1:979)
1 November	Committee on Irish affairs (*CJ*, 5:347)
27 November	Teller: propositions for treating with king (*CJ*, 5:371)

1648

16 February	Commissioner for Glamorgan (Firth, 1:1097)
3 May	Committee of both houses for Irish affairs (*CSPI*, 1647–60:15)
12 May	Committee for Glamorgan for settling militia (Firth, 1:1136)
26 May	Teller: perpetuation of Presbyterian Church (*CJ*, 5:574)
2 December	Teller: king's response to Newmarket Treaty (*CJ*, 6:93)
	Commissioner for Kent for militia (Firth, 1:1238)

1649

6 January	Commissioner for trial of Charles I (Firth, 1:1254)
6 February	Committee to abolish Lords (*CJ*, 6:132)
7 February	Committee to abolish monarchy (*CJ*, 6:133)
22 February	Opposes oath of engagement for Council of State (Blencowe, 238–39)
5 March	Teller: pardon of John Lord Paulett (*CJ*, 6:156)
7 April	Commissioner for Kent and Glamorgan in assessment bill (Firth, 2:36)
10 May	Reports for Committee on Irish affairs (*CJ*, 6:206)
15 May	Committee to consider future Parliaments (*Perfect Diurnall*, 303 [14–21 May])
26 September	Governor of school and almshouses of Westminster (Firth, 2:257)
11 October	Teller: disputed election of Neville (*CJ*, 6:305)
7 December	Commissioner for Kent and Glamorgan in assessment bill (Firth, 2:300, 314)

1650

10 October	Teller: Hutchinson as treasurer of navy (*CJ*, 6:482)
21 November	Teller: supply bill for hospitals (*CJ*, 6:500)
26 November	Commissioner for Kent and Glamorgan in assessment bill (Firth, 2:469, 483)

1651

21 May	Committee to investigate king's property (*CJ*, 6:576)
12 June	Teller: sale of delinquent estates (*CJ*, 6:587)
8 July	Teller: naming of surveyor general (*CJ*, 6:599)
1 October	Committee to draft bill to end Rump (*CJ*, 7:23)
24 November	Teller: elections to Council of State (*CJ*, 7:41)
26 November	Teller (3 divisions): tenure of committee chairs (*CJ*, 7:43)
23 December	Committee to consider private petition (*CJ*, 7:55)
26 December	Committee for bill for treasurers, army (*CJ*, 7:58)
	Committee for law reform (*CJ*, 7:58, 67, 73, 74)
31 December	Teller: election of treasurers at war (*CJ*, 7:61)

1652

6 January	Teller: naming commissioner of excise (*CJ*, 7:63)
8 January	Committee regulating foreign relations (*CJ*, 7:64)
10 February	Committee to consider ministers' petition (*CJ*, 7:86)
30 March	Teller: disposal of Crown/Church lands (*CJ*, 7:112)
6 April	Teller: disposal of Dover Pier (*CJ*, 7:115)
9 April	Teller: fen drainage (*CJ*, 7:118)
2 July	Teller: private bill (*CJ*, 7:148)
15 July	Teller: private petition (*CJ*, 7:154)
20 July	Committee on sales of delinquent estates (*CJ*, 7:156)
22 July	Teller: sale of delinquent papist estates (*CJ*, 7:157)
27 July	Committee to consider reform of Treasury (*CJ*, 7:159)
6 August	Committee to resolve Irish problems (*CJ*, 7:161–62)
11 August	Teller: private bill (*CJ*, 7:163)
27 August	Committee to receive petitions for relief (*CJ*, 7:171)
16 September	Committee for Irish estate of Lord Loftus (HMC, *Various Collections*, 3)
7 October	Committee uniting England and Scotland (*CJ*, 7:189)
15 October	Teller: sale of manor of The Maze (*CJ*, 7:191)
22 October	Teller: private bill (*CJ*, 7:193)
18 November	Teller: private bill (*CJ*, 7:218)
25 November	Elected to Council of State (*CJ*, 7:220)
26 November	Teller: election of judges of admiralty (*CJ*, 7:221)
	Teller: sale of Somerset House (*CJ*, 7:222)
2 December	Committee for Ireland and Scotland (*CSPD*, 1652–53:2)
	Committee for trade (*CSPD*, 1652–53:2)
	Committee for plantations (*CSPD*, 1652–53:2)

4 December	Commissioner to Portuguese ambassador (*CSPD*, 1652–53:9)
8 December	Committee for examinations (*CSPD*, 1652–53:16)
10 December	Commissioner for Kent and Glamorgan in assessment bill (Firth, 2:665, 680)
18 December	Committee for the fleet (*CSPD*, 1652–53:39)
24 December	Teller: acts at sea against allies (*CJ*, 7:234)
29 December	Committee to minister from Spain (*CSPD*, 1652–53:62)
30 December	Teller: sale of Wallingford House (*CJ*, 7:238)

1653

1 January	To report on soldiers in Ireland (*CJ*, 7:241)
3 January	Reports on Portuguese treaty (*CSPD*, 1652–53:77)
4 January	Reports on soldiers in Ireland (*CJ*, 7:242)
6 January	Reports on paper from Louis XIV (*CSPD*, 1652–53:83)
19 January	Reports on Spanish ambassador (*CSPD*, 1652–53:112)
25 January	To report on Spanish ambassador (*CJ*, 7:250)
27 January	Reports on answer to Spanish ambassador (*CJ*, 7:251)
28 January	Reports on ambassador to Sweden (*CSPD*, 1652–53:130)
1 February	To confer with Cromwell on fleet (*CSPD*, 1652–53:137)
2 February	Gathering intelligence (*CSPD*, 1652–53:140)
9 February	To study supply of rope, pitch, tar (*CSPD*, 1652–53:155)
10 February	Committee to French agent (*CSPD*, 1652–53:157)
11 February	Committee to examine four ministers (*CSPD*, 1652–53:160)
17 February	Teller (2 divisions): poor law (*CJ*, 7:260)
22 February	To present private petition (*CSPD*, 1652–53:178)
1 March	Committee to examine Mr. Denham (*CSPD*, 1652–53:193)
4 March	Funding for ambassador to Sweden (*CSPD*, 1652–53:198)
11 March	To report on private petitions (*CSPD*, 1652–53:210)
14 March	To present letters from Ireland (*CSPD*, 1652–53:212)
19 March	To report on John Dury (*CSPD*, 1652–53:220–21)
22 March	Reports on ambassador to Sweden (*CJ*, 7:269–70)
	Reports on messengers from Holland, West-Frizland (*CJ*, 7:271)
1 April	To report on John Dury (*CSPD*, 1652–53:250)
4 April	To report on John Dury (*CSPD*, 1652–53:254)
13 April	Committee on abuses of officers, clerks (*CJ*, 7:277)
20 April	Present at dissolution of Rump (Blencowe, 139–41)

1659

13 May	Committee for prisoners of conscience (*CJ*, 7:650)
14 May	Teller: election of Council of State (*CJ*, 7:653)
	Chosen to sit on Council of State (*CJ*, 7:653–54)
	Committee for Act of Indemnity (*CJ*, 7:654–55)

16 May	Committee for bill constituting Council of State (*CJ*, 7:656)
21 May	Committee on laws/ordinances under Protectorate (*CJ*, 7:661)
23 May	Committee on property in Whitehall, etc. (*CJ*, 7:663)
25 May	Committee for pension for Richard Cromwell (*CJ*, 7:665)
6 June	Supports bill to regulate army commissions (Ludlow, *Memoirs*, 2:88–89)
7 June	Teller: election of commissioners for Ireland (*CJ*, 7:674)
9 June	Named commissioner to the Sound (*CJ*, 7:677)
	Reports from Council on Irish Affairs (*CJ*, 7:678)
17 June	Recommends promotion for soldier (*CSPD*, 1658–59:378)
18 June	Committee on continuation of taxes (*CJ*, 7:689)
22 June	Committee on impressing of sailors (*CJ*, 7:691)
1 July	Reports from Council on Irish Affairs (*CJ*, 7:700)
26 July	Commissioner of militia for Kent (Firth, 2:1371)

1660

26 January	Commissioner for Kent and Glamorgan in assessment bill (Firth, 2:1371, 1383)

BIBLIOGRAPHY

THE WRITINGS AND CORRESPONDENCE OF ALGERNON SIDNEY

Sources for Sidney's Writings

1680 *The Case of Algernon Sidney Esq.; as it appeared before the Committee, Novemb. 10th.* [London].

1682 *A Just and Modest Vindication of the proceedings of the Two last Parliaments of King Charles the Second.* [Attribution uncertain; see Chapter 1, note 159.] London.

1683a *To the KING's Most Excellent Majesty. The Humble Petition of Algernoon Sidney, Esq.* London.

1683b *The Very Copy of a Paper Delivered to the Sheriffs, Upon the Scaffold on Tower-Hill, on Friday Decemb. 7. 1683.* London: R.H.J.B. and J.R.

1683c *The Very Copy of a Paper Delivered to the Sheriffs, Upon the Scaffold on Tower-Hill, on Friday Decemb. 7. 1683.* Dublin: Joseph Ray.

1683d *An Exact Account of the Tryal of Algernon Sidney, esq.* London: E. Mallet.

1684a *The Arraignment, Tryal & Condemnation of Algernon Sidney, Esq; for High Treason.* London: Benj. Tooke.

1684b *Laatse redenen van . . . colonel S., Behandigt aan den sheriff, voor sign executie op Tower-Hill, tol London.* Amsterdam.

1689a *A Copy of a Prophecy, Sent by the late Honourable Algernoon Sydney Esq; in the Year 1666, from Montpelliers, to B. Furley of Rotterdam, and by him accidentally found among old Papers.* London: 18 February.

1689b *Sidney Redivivus: Or The Opinion Of the Late Honourable Collonel Sidney As to Civil Government.* London: H. Smith.

1689c *The Design of Enslaving England Discovered In the Incroachments upon the Powers and Privileges of Parliament, by K. Charles II.* [Attribution uncertain; see Chapter 1, note 159.] London: Richard Baldwin.

1697 *Familiar Letters: Written by the Right Honourable John late Earl of Rochester And several other Persons of Honour and Quality.* London: W. Onley for Sam Briscoe.

1698 *Discourses Concerning Government.* London.

1702 *Discours sur le gouvernement, par Algernon Sidney.* Translated by P. A. Sanson. 3 vols. La Haye: L. & H. van Dole.

1704 *Discourses Concerning Government.* The Second Edition. London: J. Darby.

1705a *Algernon Sidneys Betrachtungen über der Regierungsformen.* Edited by Ludwig Heinrich Jakob. Erfurt: H. G. Vollmer.

1705b *Discourses Concerning Government.* London: J. D. for T. Atkinson.

1725 *Brieven, Geschreven ende gewisselt tusschen de Heer Johan DeWitt.* 7 vols. Gravenhage: Hendrick Scheurleer.

1730 *Discourses Concerning Government.* 2 vols. London.

1742a   *A Collection of the State Papers of John Thurloe.* 7 vols. London.

1742b   *Letters of the Honourable Algernon Sydney, to the Honourable Henry Savile ambassador in France.* London: R. Dodsley.

1742c   *Letters of the Honourable Algernon Sydney, to the Honourable Henry Savile ambassador in France.* Dublin: S. Powell, for George Ewing.

1746   *Letters and Memorials of State.* Edited by Arthur Collins. 2 vols. London: T. Osborne.

1750   *Discourses Concerning Government.* 2 vols. Edinburgh: G. Hamilton and J. Balfour.

1751   *Discourses Concerning Government.* The Third Edition. London: A. Millar.

1754   *The Works of Sir William Temple.* 4 vols. Edinburgh.

1763   *Discourses Concerning Government.* London: A. Millar.

1772   *The Works of Algernon Sydney.* Edited by Joseph Robertson. London: W. Strahan Iun. for T. Becket, T. Cadell, T. Davies, and T. Evans.

1793   *Algernon Sidneys Betrachtungen über der Regierungsformen nach der neuesten von Robertson besorgten Ausgabe.* Translated and edited by Christian Daniel Erhard. 2 vols. Leipzig: Weygand.

1794a   *Discours sur le gouvernement, par Algernon Sidney.* Translated by P. A. Sanson. New Edition. 3 vols. La Haye: L. & H. van Dole.

1794b   *Political Classics,* vols. 1, 2. London.

1795   *The Essence of Algernon Sidney's Work on Government, To Which Is Annexed, His Essay On Love.* London: J. Johnson.

1797   *The Essence of Algernon Sidney's Work on Government, To Which Is Annexed, His Essay On Love.* The Second Edition. London: J. Johnson.

1805a   *Discourses Concerning Government.* 3 vols. New York: Richard Lee.

1805b   *Discourses Concerning Government.* 2 vols. Philadelphia: Printed and Published by G. P. Wayne for the Rev. M. L. Weems.

1812   *A Collection of Scarce and Valuable Tracts . . . Particularly that of the Late Lord Somers.* Edited by Sir Walter Scott. The Second Edition. London.

1816   *A Complete Collection of State Trials.* Edited by T. B. Howell. 21 vols. London.

1825   *Sidney Papers, Consisting of a Journal of the Earl of Leicester, and Original Letters of Algernon Sydney.* Edited by Robert Willis Blencowe. London: John Murray.

1830   *Original Letters of Locke; Algernon Sidney; and Anthony Lord Shaftesbury.* Edited by T. Forster. London: J. B. Nichols and Son.

1834   *Memoirs of the Historical Society of Pennsylvania,* vol. 3, part 1. Edited by Joshua Fisher. Philadelphia.

1847   *Original Letters of Locke; Algernon Sidney; and Anthony Lord Shaftesbury.* Edited by T. Forster. The Second Edition. London: J. B. Nichols and Son.

1872a   *Calendar of Clarendon State Papers Preserved in the Bodleian Library.* 5 vols. Oxford: The Clarendon Press.

1872b   *HMC. Third Report, Appendix*. London.
1882   *History of the Irish Confederation and the War in Ireland, 1641–1649*. Edited by John Gilbert. 7 vols. Dublin: M. H. Gill & Son.
1898   H. C. Foxcroft. *The Life and Letters of Sir George Savile, Bart. First Marquess of Halifax*. 2 vols. London: Longmans, Green and Co.
1925   *HMC. Report on the Manuscripts of Lord De L'Isle and Dudley Preserved at Penshurst Place*. 6 vols. London: HMSO.
1960   *Kentish Sources*. Vol. 2, *Kent and the Civil War*. Edited by Elizabeth Melling. Maidstone: Kent County Council.
1970   Violet A. Rowe. *Sir Henry Vane the Younger*. London: Athlone Press.
1981   *The Papers of William Penn*. Edited by Mary Dunn and Richard Dunn. Philadelphia: University of Pennsylvania Press.
1990   *Discourses Concerning Government*. Edited by Thomas G. West. Indianapolis: Liberty Press.
AN   Archives Nationales
BL   British Library
BOD   Bodleian Library
CH   Chatsworth House
DUL   Durham University Library
ESRO   East Sussex Record Office
HRO   Hertfordshire Record Office
KAO   Kent Archives Office
LH   Longleat House
PRO   Public Record Office
SL   Sevenoaks Library
VA   Victoria and Albert Museum Library
WRO   Warwickshire Record Office

Sidney's Writings and Correspondence

1643

18 June   Letter to Countess of Leicester, from Dublin (1882)

1645

14 May   Letter to Fairfax (BL)

1648

17 July   Letter to Sir Michael Livesey, from Dover (KAO; 1960)
19 July   Letter to Fairfax, from Dover (DUL)
4 October   Letter to W. Aylesbury, from London (1872a)

1649

10 January   Letter to Leicester, from Leicester House (BL; 1746; 1763; 1772)

1650

2 April — Letter to Whitelocke (LH)
16 July — Letter to Corporation of Sandwich, from Dover (KAO)

1652

5 January — Letter from Edward, Marquis of Worcester, to Sidney (1746; 1763; 1772)

1653

4 January — Letter to Sydenham (BL)
25 January — Letter to Fee-farm Trustees, Worcester House (BL)

1654

23 January — Letter from van Beverningk to Sidney (BOD)
3 June — Letter from John Kellerby to Sidney (BL)
8 August — Letter to Myn Heer Beverning, from the Hague (BOD; 1742a; 1772)
14 August — Letter to Leicester, from the Hague (BOD; 1742a; 1772)
6 October — Letter to Mr. Spencer, from the Hague (BOD; 1742a; 1772)

1656

June — Petition to subpoena Henry Canon (PRO)

1658

7 April — Letter to Leicester, from Leicester House (KAO; 1746; 1763; 1772)

1659

16 July — Letter from Commissioners in the Sound to President of Council of State (BOD; 1742a; 1772)
28 July — Letter to Whitelocke (LH)
29 July — Letter from Commissioners in the Sound to President of Council of State, from Elsenore (BOD; 1742a; 1772)
9 August — Letter from Commissioners in the Sound to the King of Sweden, from Fredericiburgi (1742a; 1772)
10 August — Letter from the English Commissioners in the Sound, from Elsenore (BL; 1742a; 1772)

21 August	Letter to the Council of State, from Copenhagen (1742a; 1772)
24 August	Letter from Commissioners in the Sound to Secretary Thurloe, from Copenhagen (BL; 1742a; 1772)
	Letter to Whitelocke (LH)
12 September	Letter from Commissioners in the Sound to Secretary Thurloe, from Copenhagen (BL; 1742a; 1772)
13 September	Letter to Leicester, from Copenhagen (SL; 1825)
18 September	Letter from Commissioners in the Sound to De Witt (1725)
5 November	Letter to Leicester, from Copenhagen (KAO; 1746; 1763; 1772)
13 November	Letter to Whitelocke, from Elsinore (1825)
14 November	Letter from Commissioners in the Sound to De Witt, from Elsinore (1725)
4 December	Letter to Whitelocke (LH)

1660

22 February	Letter to Leicester, from Copenhagen (KAO; 1746; 1763; 1772; 1825)
23 February	Letter from Commissioners in the Sound to De Witt, from Copenhagen (1725)
25 February	Letter from Commissioners in the Sound to Thurloe (BOD)
	Letter from English Plenipotentiaries in Denmark to the Speaker of Parliament, from Copenhagen (1742a)
4 March	Letter to Whitelocke, from Copenhagen (VA; 1825)
2 April	Letter to Thurloe, from Copenhagen (BOD; 1742a; 1772)
7 April	Letter to Downing, from Copenhagen (1742a; 1772)
20 April	Notes on conference with Slingelandt (BOD)
22 May	Letter to Leicester, from Copenhagen (1746; 1763; 1772)
28 May	Letter to Leicester, from Copenhagen (SL; 1825)
16 June	Letter to Leicester, from Stockholm (KAO; 1746; 1763; 1772)
23 June	Letter to Leicester, from Stockholm (KAO; 1763; 1772)
27 June	Letter to Leicester, from Stockholm (KAO; 1746; 1763; 1772)
14 July	Letter to Leicester, from Copenhagen (KAO; 1746; 1763; 1772)

22 July	Letter to Leicester, from Copenhagen (KAO; 1746; 1763; 1772)
28 July	Letter to Leicester, from Copenhagen (SL; 1825)
30 August	Letter to Leicester, from Hamburg (SL; 1825)
	Letter from Leicester to Sidney, from London (SL; 1697; 1812; 1825)
8 September	Letter to Leicester, from Frankfurt-am-Main (KAO; 1746; 1763; 1772)
	Letter to Leicester, from Frankfurt-am-Main (KAO; 1925)
21 September	Letter to Leicester, from Augsburg (SL; 1825)
26 September	Letter to Leicester, from Augsburg (SL; 1825)
12 October	Letter to Leicester, from Venice (SL; 1825)
19 November	Letter to Leicester, from Rome (KAO; 1746; 1763; 1772; 1825)
12 December	Letter to Leicester, from Rome (KAO; 1746; 1763; 1772)
29 December	Letter to Leicester, from Rome (KAO; 1746; 1763; 1772)

1661

29 January	Letter to Leicester, from Rome (KAO; 1746; 1763; 1772)
18 February	Letter to Leicester, from Rome (KAO; 1746; 1763; 1772)
12 March	Letter to Leicester, from Rome (KAO; 1746; 1763; 1772)
8 April	Letter to Leicester, from Rome (KAO; 1746; 1763; 1772)
15 April	Letter to Leicester, from Rome (KAO; 1746; 1763; 1772)
22 April	Letter to Leicester, from Rome (KAO; 1746; 1763; 1772)
3 June	Letter to Leicester, from Frascati (KAO; 1746; 1763; 1772)
23 June	Letter to Leicester, from Frascati (KAO; 1746; 1763; 1772; 1825)
14 July	Letter to Leicester, from Frascati (KAO; 1746; 1763; 1772; 1825)

1663

1 December	Letter to Leicester, from Brussels (KAO; 1746; 1763; 1772; 1825)
	Letter to Leicester, from Brussels (KAO; 1925)

1666

"A Copy of a Prophecy" (BOD; 1689a)

1667

29 April   Letter from Sir William Temple to Sidney, from Brussels (1754)

1676

14 November   Letter to Savile, from Paris (CH; 1742b; 1742c; 1763; 1772)

18 December   Letter to Savile, from Nerac (CH; 1742b; 1742c; 1763; 1772)

1677

January   Letter to Bafoy (AN)
5 February   Letter to Savile (LH)
16 April   Letter from Henry Coventry to Sidney (LH; BL)
4 May   Letter to Henry Coventry, from Nerac (LH; 1872b)

29 November   Letter to Furly, from Leicester House (1830; 1847)

10 December   Letter to Strangford (KAO)

1678

3 January   Letter to Furly, from London (1830; 1847)
4 January   Statement of Suit with Strangford (PRO)
29 January   Letter to Furly, from London (1830; 1847)
3 April   Letter to Furly, from London (1830; 1847)
19 August   Letter to Furly, from London (1830; 1847)

1679

1 January   Letter from William Penn to Sidney (1746; 1981)
31 January   Letter to Furly, from London (1830; 1847)
15 February   Letter to Furly, from London (1830; 1847)
1 March   Account of election defeat in Guildford (1746)
9 March   Letter to Furly, from London (BOD; 1830; 1847)
23 March   Letter to Furly, from London (BOD; 1830; 1847)
7 April   Letter to Savile, from London (1742b; 1742c; 1763; 1772)

16 April   Letter to Lord Halifax (1898)
21 April   Letter to Savile, from London (CH; 1742b; 1742c; 1763; 1772)

28 April   Letter to Savile, from London (CH; 1742b; 1742c; 1763; 1772)

5 May	Letter to Savile, from London (CH; 1742b; 1742c; 1763; 1772)
12 May	Letter to Savile, from London (CH; 1742b; 1742c; 1763; 1772)
19 May	Letter to Savile, from London (CH; 1742b; 1742c; 1763; 1772)
29 May	Letter from William Penn to Sidney, from Wiston (1746; 1981)
2 June	Letter to Savile, from London (1742b; 1742c; 1763; 1772)
9 June	Letter to Savile, from London (CH; 1742b; 1742c; 1763; 1772)
16 June	Letter to Savile, from London (CH; 1742b; 1742c; 1763; 1772)
23 June	Letter to Savile, from London (CH; 1742b; 1742c; 1763; 1772)
30 June	Letter to Savile, from London (CH; 1742b; 1742c; 1763; 1772)
10 July	Letter to Savile, from London (CH; 1742b; 1742c; 1763; 1772)
16 July	Letter to Savile, from London (CH; 1742b; 1742c; 1763; 1772)
1 August	Letter to Savile, from London (CH)
8 September	Letter to Savile, from London (CH; 1742b; 1742c; 1763; 1772)
29 October	Letter to Savile, from London (CH; 1742b; 1742c; 1763; 1772)

1680

14 May	Letter to Furly, from London (1830; 1847)
26 July	Letter to Savile, from London (CH; 1742b; 1742c; 1763; 1772)
13 October	Letter to Furly, from London (1830; 1847)
31 October	Letter to Savile, from London (CH; 1742b; 1742c; 1763; 1772)
10 November	"The Case of Algernon Sidney Esq." (1680)

1681

3 February	Letter to Savile, from London (1742b; 1742c; 1763; 1772)
10 February	Letter to Savile, from London (CH; 1742b; 1742c; 1763; 1772)
13 October	Letter from William Penn to Sidney (1834; 1981)

1682

*A Just and Modest Vindication of the Proceedings of the
Two Last Parliaments* (1682; 1689c)

1683

<17 July	Petition to the King (PRO; *CSPD*)
[October?]	Letter to John Hampden, from the Tower (ESRO)
[October?]	Letter to John Hampden, from the Tower (ESRO)
[October?]	Letter to John Hampden, from the Tower (ESRO)
6 October	Letter to John Hampden, from the Tower (ESRO)
[October?]	Letter to John Hampden, from the Tower (ESRO)
18 October	Letter to John Hampden, from the Tower (ESRO)
[October?]	Letter to John Hampden, from the Tower (ESRO)
31 October	Letter to John Hampden, from the Tower (ESRO)
5 November	Letter to John Hampden, from the Tower (ESRO)
7–26 November	*The Trial of A. Sydney* (1684a; 1689b; 1763; 1772; 1794b; 1805a; 1805b; 1816)
<21 November	Petition to the King (PRO; *CSPD*)
22 November	Letter to [?], from the Tower (ESRO)
25 November	*To the KING's Most Excellent Majesty. The Humble Petition of Algernoon Sidney, Esq.* (PRO; 1683a; 1816; *CSPD*)
7 December	*The Very Copy of a Paper Delivered to the Sheriffs, Upon the Scaffold* (1683b; 1683c; 1689b; 1704; 1750; 1816)
	"The Apology of Algernon Sidney, In the Day of his Death" (1751; 1763; 1772; 1794b; 1805a; 1805b; 1816)

Undated Writings

	"Of Love" (BL; 1795; 1797; 1812)
c.1665–66	*Court Maxims, discussed & refelled* (WRO)
c.1664–65	Letter to Benjamin Furly (1825)
c.1666–77	"The Character of Sir Henry Vane" (HRO; 1970)
c.1677–79	Letter to Lord Strangford (KAO)
c.1679–82	"Case of Algernone and Henry Sydney" (BL)
c.1679–82	Notes concerning action in Chancery (KAO)
c.1681–83	*Discourses Concerning Government* (1698; 1702; 1704; 1705a; 1705b; 1730; 1750; 1751; 1763; 1772; 1793; 1794a; 1794b; 1795; 1797; 1805a; 1805b; 1990)

Erroneously Attributed
to Sidney

Letter to a Friend (1697; 1772; 1812; 1825)
Discorso Politico (KAO)
Commonplace Book (KAO)

Notes in Italian, regarding miracles (KAO)
Poem on education (LH)

MANUSCRIPTS

Archives Nationales
  R2/82   Sidney to Bafoy, January [1677]

Bibliotheque Nationale
  Fr. MS. 23,254   Sidney, conversations with Lantin, 1677

Bodleian Library
  8° Rawl 432   James Tyrrell, annotations in personal copy
                  of *Patriarcha non Monarcha*

  MS. Carte
    216, fol. 86   Longford to [?], 27 June 1682
  MS. Clarendon
    60, fol. 332   Sidney, notes of conference with Slingelandt,
                20 April [1660]

  MS. English History
    C487   Edmund Ludlow, "A Voyce from the Watch
                Tower"

  MS. English Letters
    C12, fol. 159   Bohun to Hickes, 5 November 1683
    C200, fol. 22   Sidney to Benjamin Furly, 9 March [1679]
    C200, fol. 23   Sidney to Benjamin Furly, 23 March [1679]
    C200, fol. 24   Sidney, "A Prophesy of St. Thomas the
                Martyr"

  MS. Locke
    c.28   John Locke, "Ethica: 'Morality' "
  MS. Rawlinson
    A10, fol. 211   H. Beverningk to Sidney, 23 January 1654
    A16, fol. 467   Sidney to Beverningk, 8 August 1654 (copy)
    A17, fol. 88   Sidney to Leicester, 4 August 1654 (copy)
    A19, fol. 121   Sidney to Spencer, 6 October [1654] (copy)
    A65, fol. 227   Commissioners in Sound, 16 July 1659
    A65, fol. 259   Commissioners in Sound, 29 July 1659
    A67, fol. 82   Commissioners in Sound, 25 February 1660
    A67, fol. 324   Sidney to John Thurloe, 2 April 1660
    A67, fol. 378   General Monck to States General, 26 April
                1660

    C719, fol. 263 John Hawles, "Remarks"
  MS. Smith
    31, fol. 30   "Mr. F[erguson's] account of books"

British Library
  Additional Manuscripts
    4,158, fol. 164 Sidney to John Thurloe, 10 August 1659
    4,158, fol. 170 Sidney to John Thurloe, 24 August 1659

4,158, fol. 185	[?] to John Thurloe, 10 September 1659
4,158, fol. 193	Sidney to John Thurloe, 12 September 1659
4,197, fol. 192	Warrant, Council of State, June 1659
6,399 A., fol. 28	Satirical epitaph on Sidney's death
15,914, fol. 118	John Kellerby to Sidney, 3 June 1654
21,426, fols. 7, 189	Correspondence of Captain Adam Baynes [1651?]
21,506, fol. 55	Sidney to Leicester, 10 January 1648/9
25,124, fol. 122	Henry Coventry to Sidney, 16 April 1677
28,875, fols. 311–22	Letters to John Ellis, December 1683
31,984	Whitelocke's History of the forty eighth year of his Age
32,352, fol. 32	Portrait of Sidney, 1 December 1819
32,518, fol. 121	Lord Guildford, "A Discourse of High Treason"
32,680, fol. 9	Leicester, notes on Sidney's views, 1660
32,683, fol. 75	Leicester, codicil to will
34,100	Sidney, "Of Love"
35,683	Proceedings of Hale Committee for Law Reform
38,847, fols. 88–121	Robert West, "Full Confession—Rye House Plot"
44,729, fol. 19	W. E. Gladstone, reading notes on "Discourses"
47,126, fol. 32	John Perceval, character sketch of Sidney
53,727, fols. 53–64	Bulstrode Whitelocke, "Diary," 4 September 1653
63,057	Gilbert Burnet, "History of My Own Times"
Additional Charters	
70777	Sidney, deed on sale of stock in East India Company, 28 March 1648
Egerton MS.	
1049, fol. 9	Sidney, "Case of Algernone and Henry Sydney"
2618, fol. 140	Warrant to seize Sidney's papers, 25 June 1683
Harleian MS. 6845	Nathaniel Wade, "Confession"
Northumberland MS., vol. 16, fol. 59 (Micro Reel 286)	Northumberland to [?], [September 1643?]
Sloane MS. 1519, fol. 112	Sidney to Lord Fairfax, 14 May 1645
Stowe MS.	
154, fol. 14	Charles II to Clarendon, June 1662
184, fol. 269	Sidney to Richard Sydenham, 4 January 1652/3
184, fol. 272	Sidney to Worcester House, 25 January 1652/3

376, fol. 142   "A Short Disquisition of High Treason"
758, fol. 3   Sidney, "Speech delivered to the Sheriffs"
Printed Books
C.142.e.13   Robert Sidney, annotations to Tacitus

Chatsworth House
Du Moulin Letters
21.9   Du Moulin to Halifax, 21 October 1676
21.12   Du Moulin to Halifax, 21 November 1676
Halifax Collection
A.1–14   Halifax, notes on Rye House Plot, 1689
C.13a   Henry Savile to [Halifax], [1682?]
E.1   Sidney to Savile, 14 November [1676]
.2   Sidney to Savile, 18 December [1676]
.3   Sidney to Savile, 7 April [1679]
.4   Sidney to Savile, 21 April [1679]
.5   Sidney to Savile, 28 April [1679]
.6   Sidney to Savile, 5 May [1679]
.7   Sidney to Savile, 12 May [1679]
.8   Sidney to Savile, 19 May [1679]
.9   Sidney to Savile, 9 June [1679]
.10   Sidney to Savile, 16 June [1679]
.11   Sidney to Savile, 23 June [1679]
.12   Sidney to Savile, 30 June [1679]
.13   Sidney to Savile, 10 July [1679]
.14   Sidney to Savile, 16 July [1679]
.15   Sidney to Savile, 26 July [1680]
.16   Sidney to Savile, 1 August [1679]
.17   Sidney to Savile, 8 September [1679]
.18   Sidney to Savile, 29 October [1679]
.19   Sidney to Savile, 31 October [1680]
.20   Sidney to Savile, 10 February [1681]

East Sussex Record Office
Glynde Place Papers 794

Sidney to [John Hampden?], [October?] 1683
Sidney to [John Hampden?], [October?] 1683
Sidney to [John Hampden?], [October?] 1683
Sidney to [John Hampden?], 6 October 1683
Sidney to [John Hampden?], [October?] 1683
Sidney to [John Hampden?], 18 October 1683
Sidney to [John Hampden?], [October?] 1683

Sidney to [John Hampden?], 31 October
1683

Sidney to [John Hampden?], 5 November
1683

Sidney to [?], 22 November 1683

Hertfordshire Record Office
D/EP F45   "The Character of Sir Henry Vane"

Kent Archives Office
De L'Isle MSS.
U1475

A74/1	Note of work done for Sidney, April–July 1654
A74/2–5	Receipts for payments of Strangford's debts, February 1654
C83/18	Philip Sidney to Leicester, 18 December 1649
C84/	
1	Sidney to Leicester, 7 April 1658
2	Sidney to Leicester, 5 November 1659
3	Sidney to Leicester, 22 February 1660
4	Sidney to Leicester, 16 June 1660
5	Sidney to Leicester, 23 June 1660
6	Sidney to Leicester, 27 June 1660
7	Sidney to Leicester, 14 July 1660
8	Sidney to Leicester, 22 July 1660
9	Sidney to Leicester, 8 September 1660
10	Sidney to Leicester, 8 September 1660
11	Sidney to Leicester, 19 November 1660
12	Sidney to Leicester, 12 December 1660
13	Sidney to Leicester, 29 December 1660
14	Sidney to Leicester, 8 February 1661
15	Sidney to Leicester, 18 February 1661
16	Sidney to Leicester, 12 March 1661
17	Sidney to Leicester, 8 April 1661
18	Sidney to Leicester, 15 April 1661
18a	Sidney to Leicester, 22 April 1661
19	Sidney to Leicester, 3 June 1661
20	Sidney to Leicester, 23 June 1661
21	Sidney to Leicester, 4 July 1661
22	Sidney to Leicester, 1 December 1663
23	Sidney to Leicester, 1 December 1663
C97/1	Mark Duncan to Leicester, 30 August 1636
E28/5	Sidney, transactions with Strangfords
L5	Sidney, notes concerning action in chancery
O101/1–6	Sidney, official documents
T332	Leicester, grant of money to Sidney, 1672

Z1/1–11   1st and 2nd earls of Leicester, commonplace books

Z22   "Discorso politico"

Z33   Notes in Italian, regarding miracles

Z45/2   Catalog, Penshurst library

U1500

  A14/9, 11–13   Receipts for bills for Sidney, 1634

  A14/16   Accounts of John Kellerby

  C2/4   Sidney to Lord Strangford, 10 December 1677

Q/JC 4   Sidney named J.P. for Kent, 20 October 1651

Q/SB 1/45   Sidney to Kent Quarter Sessions, 17 July [1648?]

Sa/ZB2/114   Sidney to Borough of Sandwich, 16 July [1648?]

Longleat House

Coventry Papers

  LXXXIII, fol. 125   Henry Coventry to Sidney, 16 April 1677

  App., Vol. II, fol. 105   Sidney to Henry Coventry, 4 May 1677

  App., Vol. II, fol. 134   Sidney to Henry Savile, 5 February [1677]

Whitelocke Papers

  XIX, fol. 66   Sidney to Bulstrode Whitelocke, 28 July [1659]

  XIX, fol. 74   Sidney to Bulstrode Whitelocke, 24 August [1659]

  XIX, fol. 94   Sidney to Bulstrode Whitelocke, 4 December [1659]

  XIX, fol. 96   William Nieupoort to Bulstrode Whitelocke, 8 December [1659]

  XX, fol. 176   Sidney, petition to King, 1683

  XXVI, fol. 250   Sidney to Bulstrode Whitelocke, 2 April [1650]

Portland Papers

  XVII, fol. 65   Poem on education, erroneously attributed to Sidney

Ministere des Affaires Étrangeres

Correspondence Politique

  Angleterre 99, fol. 270   Louis XIV to Colbert, 29 July 1670

Public Record Office

PRO 31/3/

  125, fol. 227   Colbert to Louis XIV, 4 August 1670

  150, fol. 261b   Barillon to Louis XIV, September 1681

C6/244/2   Sidney, Chancery petition re Agmondesham, 1682

C7/325/2	Sidney, petition to subpoena Henry Canon, 1656
C7/327/50	Sidney, suit with Strangford, 4 January 1678
SP25/138	Committee on Anglo-Scottish Union, 1652
SP29/	
426	Information concerning the Rye House Plot
429, part 1, fol. 5	Sidney, petition to King, 1683
429, part 1, fol. 144–49	Russell, dying speech
434, fol. 85	Sidney, petition to King, 1683
434, fol. 97	Sidney, petition to King, 1683
434, fol. 116	Sidney, petition to King, 1683
SP77/36	
fol. 205	[?] to Sam Cottington, 26 April 1667
fol. 208	Temple to [Arlington], 29 April 1667

Sevenoaks Library
  U1000/7 Z1/

2	Sidney to Leicester, 13 September 1659
3	Sidney to Leicester, 30 August 1660
4	Leicester to Sidney, 30 August 1660
5	Sidney to Leicester, 28 May 1660
6	Sidney to Leicester, 28 July 1660
7	Sidney to Leicester, 21 September 1660
8	Sidney to Leicester, 26 September 1660
9	Sidney to Leicester, 12 October 1660

University of Durham Library
  Mickleton & Spearman
  MSS.

| 46, fols. 103–6 | Sidney to Fairfax, 19 July [1648] |

Victoria and Albert Museum
  Forster MSS.

| 48.D.41, fols. 1–14 | Vane, sermon |
| 48.G.26 | Sidney to Whitelocke, 4 March 1660 |

Warwickshire Record Office
  CR 1886   Sidney, *Court Maxims, discussed & refelled*

PRIMARY SOURCES

Adams, Charles Francis. *The Diary of Charles Francis Adams.* Edited by Marc Friedlaender and L. H. Butterfield. Cambridge, MA: Harvard University Press, 1968.

Adams Family Correspondence. Edited by L. H. Butterfield, W. Garrett, and M. Sprague. 4 vols. Cambridge, MA: Harvard University Press, 1963.

Adams, John. *Diary and Autobiography of John Adams.* Edited by L. H. Butterfield. 4 vols. Cambridge, MA: Harvard University Press, 1961.

Adams, John. *Legal Papers of John Adams*. Edited by L. K. Wroth and H. B. Zobel. 3 vols. Cambridge, MA: Harvard University Press, 1965.

——. *Papers of John Adams*. Edited by Robert Taylor. Cambridge, MA: Harvard University Press, 1977–.

——. *The Works of John Adams*. Edited by Charles Francis Adams. 10 vols. Boston: Little and Brown, 1850–1856.

Adams, John, and Thomas Jefferson. *The Adams-Jefferson Letters: The Complete Correspondence Between Thomas Jefferson and Abigail and John Adams*. Edited by Lester J. Cappon. 2 vols. Chapel Hill: University of North Carolina Press, 1959.

Adams, John, and Daniel Leonard [erroneously, Jonathan Sewall]. *Novanglus and Massachusettensis*. Boston: Hews & Goss, 1819.

Adams, John Quincy. *Memoirs of John Quincy Adams*. Edited by Charles Francis Adams. 12 vols. Philadelphia: J. B. Lippincott, 1876.

Adams, Samuel. *The Writings of Samuel Adams*. Edited by Harry Alonzo Cushing. 4 vols. New York: G. P. Putnam's Sons, 1904–1908.

Ailesbury, Thomas Bruce, earl of. *Memoirs of Thomas, Earl of Ailesbury*. 2 vols. Westminster: Nichols and Sons, 1890.

Alexander, James. *A Brief Narrative of the Case and Trial of John Peter Zenger*. Edited by Stanley N. Katz. 2nd ed. Cambridge, MA: Harvard University Press, 1972.

Algernoon Sidneys Farewell. London: T. Davis, [1683].

American Archives, 4th ser. Edited by Peter Force. Washington, DC: 1844.

The American Magazine and Monthly Chronicle for the British Colonies. Philadelphia: William Bradford, 1758.

An Appeal from the Country to the City, For the Preservation of His Majesties Person, Liberty, Property, and the Protestant Religion [1679]. In *State Tracts*, 1:401–11. London: 1693.

Aristotle. *The Complete Works of Aristotle*. Edited by Jonathan Barnes. Princeton: Princeton University Press, 1984.

Ascham, Anthony. *Of the Confusions and Revolutions of Governments*. 2nd ed. London: W. Wilson, 1649.

Aubrey, John. *Aubrey's Brief Lives*. Edited by Oliver Lawson Dick. London: Secker and Warburg, 1950.

Bailyn, Bernard, editor. *The Pamphlets of the American Revolution, 1750–1776*. Cambridge, MA: Harvard University Press, 1965.

[Bethel, Slingsby.] *The Interest of Princes and States*. London: John Wickins, 1680.

——. *The Present Interest of England Stated. By a Lover of his King and Countrey*. London: D. B., 1671.

——. *The Vindication of Slingsby Bethel Esq. . . . Against the several Slanders Cast upon him*. London: Francis Smith, 1681.

——. *The World's Mistake in Oliver Cromwell; Or, A Short Political Discourse Shewing, That Cromwell's Maladministration . . . layed the Foundation of Our present Condition, in the Decay of Trade*. London: 1668.

A Bill for Regulating the Abuses of Elections, 5 April 1679. In *A Collection of Scarce and Valuable Tracts,* edited by John Somers, 1:63–66. London: F. Cogan, 1748.

Blencowe, Robert Willis, editor. *Diary of the Times of Charles the Second by the Honourable Henry Sydney.* 2 vols. London: Henry Colburn, 1843.

———. *Sydney Papers, Consisting of a Journal of the Earl of Leicester, and Original Letters of Algernon Sydney.* London: John Murray, 1825.

[Bohun, Edmund.] *An Address to the Free-Men and Free-Holders of the Nation.* London: George Wells, 1682.

———. *A Defence of Sir Robert Filmer, Against the Mistakes and Misrepresentations of Algernon Sidney, Esq; In A Paper Delivered by him to the Sheriffs upon the Scaffold.* London: W. Kettilby, 1684.

———. *The Diary and Autobiography of Edmund Bohun.* Beccles: Read Crisp, 1853.

———. "Preface to the Reader." In *Patriarcha: or the Natural Power of Kings. By the Learned Sir Robert Filmer,* edited by Edmund Bohun. 2nd ed. London: 1685.

Boston Evening Post.

The Boston Gazette, and Country Journal.

[Boucher, Jonathan.] *A Letter from a Virginian to the Members of the Congress to be held at Philadelphia.* Boston: 1774.

Brackenridge, Hugh Henry. "The Battle of Bunker's Hill," 1776. In Moses Coit Tyler, *Literary History of the American Revolution: 1763–1783,* 2:216. New York: G. P. Putnam's Sons, 1897.

[Brady, Robert.] *The Great Point of Succession Discussed. With a Full and Particular Answer to a late Pamphlet, intituled, A Brief History of Succession, &c.* London: H. Rodes, 1681.

[Burgh, James.] *Political Disquisitions: or, An Enquiry into public Errors, Defects, and Abuses.* 3 vols. London: 1774–1775.

Burnet, Gilbert, bishop of Salisbury. *Bishop Burnet's History of His Own Time.* Edited by M. J. Routh. 2nd ed. 6 vols. Oxford: Oxford University Press, 1833.

———. *A Supplement to Burnet's History of My Own Time.* Edited by H. C. Foxcroft. Oxford: The Clarendon Press, 1902.

C.B. *An Address to the Honourable City of London, and all other Cities, Shires, and Corporations, Concerning their Choice of a New Parliament.* London: Allen Banks, 1681.

Calendar of State Papers, Colonial Series, America and West Indies.

Calendar of State Papers, Domestic.

Calendar of State Papers, Ireland.

Calendar of State Papers, Venetian.

Calhoun, John C. *The Papers of John C. Calhoun.* Columbia: University of South Carolina Press, 1959–.

Captain Thorogood His Opinion of the Point of Succession, To a Brother of the Blade in Scotland. 3 January 1679.

[Care, Henry.] *English Liberties: Or, The Free-Born Subject's Inheritance.* London: George Larkin, 1682.

Carter, Landon. " 'Not to be Governed or Taxed, but by . . . Our Representatives': Four Essays in Opposition to the Stamp Act by Landon Carter." Edited by Jack P. Greene. *Virginia Magazine of History and Biography* 76 (July 1968): 258–300.

A Certain Way to Save England; Not only Now, but in Future Ages, by a Prudent Choice of Members to Serve in the next ensuing Parliament. London: Richard Baldwin, 1681.

The Character of a Rebellion, and what England may expect from one, Or, The Designs of Dissenters Examined by Reason, Experience, and the Laws and Statutes of the Realm. London: Benj. Tooke, 1681.

Charles I. "His Majesty's Answer to the Nineteen Propositions of both Houses of Parliament." In *Historical Collections of Private Passages of State*, edited by J. Rushworth, 5:725–35. 8 vols. London: 1659–1701.

———. *King Charles His Speech made upon the Scaffold at Whitehall Gate, Immediately before his Execution.* London: Peter Cole, 1649.

Charles II. *His Majesties Declaration To all His Loving Subjects, Touching The Causes & Reasons That moved Him to Dissolve The Two last Parliaments.* London: John Bill, Thomas Newcomb, Henry Hills, 1681.

Cheetham, James. *The Life of Thomas Paine.* New York: Southwick and Pelsue, 1809.

Churchill, Charles. *The Poetical Works of Charles Churchill.* Edited by Douglas Grant. Oxford: The Clarendon Press, 1956.

Cicero. *De Officiis.* Loeb Classical Library. 1975.

Clarendon, Edward Hyde, earl of. *Calendar of the Clarendon State Papers Preserved in the Bodleian Library.* 5 vols. Oxford: The Clarendon Press, 1872–1970.

———. *The History of the Rebellion and Civil Wars in England Begun in the Year 1641.* Edited by W. Dunn Macray. 6 vols. Oxford: Oxford University Press, 1888.

Clay, Henry. *The Papers of Henry Clay.* Edited by James F. Hopkins. Lexington: University of Kentucky Press, 1959–.

Collins, Arthur, editor. *Letters and Memorials of State in the Reigns of Queen Mary, Queen Elizabeth, King James, King Charles the First, Part of the Reign of Charles the Second, and Oliver's Usurpation.* 2 vols. London: T. Osborne, 1746.

The Condemnation, Behaviour, Last Dying Words and Execution of Algernon Sidney, Esq. London: L.S., 1683.

Condie, Thomas. "George Washington." *Philadelphia Monthly Magazine* 1 (June 1798): 303–8.

The Constitutional Right of the Legislature of Great Britain, to Tax the British Colonies in America, Impartially Stated. London: 1768.

[Cooper, Anthony Ashley.] *The Compleat Statesman, Demonstrated in the Life, Actions, and Politicks, Of that great Minister of State, Anthony Earl of Shaftesbury.* London: Benjamin Alsop and Thomas Malthus, 1683.

———. *A Letter From a Person of Quality, To His Friend In the Country.* London: 1675.

————. *The Right Honourable the Earl of Shaftesbury's Speech in the House of Lords, March 25, 1679.* In *State Tracts*, 2:71–72. London: 1693.

————. *A Speech Lately Made by a Noble Peer of the Realm* [23 December 1680]. London: F.S., 1681.

Cromwell, Oliver. *The Writings and Speeches of Oliver Cromwell.* Edited by Wilber Cortez Abbott. 4 vols. Cambridge, MA: Harvard University Press, 1937–1947.

Daille, John. *A Treatise Concerning the Right Use of the Fathers, in the Decision of the Controversies that are at this Day in Religion.* London: John Martin, 1675.

Dalrymple, Sir John. *Memoirs of Great Britain and Ireland.* 2nd ed. 2 vols. London: 1771.

D'Avaux, Jean Jacques de Mesmes, Count. *The Negotiations of Count D'Avaux.* 4 vols. London: A. Millar, D. Wilson, T. Durham, 1754.

[Dean, J.] *The Wine-Cooper's Delight.* London: 1681.

Demophilus. *The Genuine Principles of the Ancient Saxon, or English Constitution, Carefully collected from the best Authorities.* Philadelphia: Robert Bell, 1776.

Dering, Sir Edward. *The Diaries and Papers of Sir Edward Dering, Second Baronet 1644 to 1684.* Edited by Maurice F. Bond. London: HMSO, 1976.

De Witt, Johan. *Brieven, Geschreven ende gewisselt tusschen de Heer Johan De Witt.* 7 vols. Gravenhage: Hendrick Scheurleer, 1725.

————. *Brieven van Johan de Witt. Eerste Deel 1650–1657 (1658).* Edited by Robert Fruin. Amsterdam: Johannes Müller, 1906.

De Witt, Johan, [and Pieter de la Court]. *The True Interest and Political Maxims of the Republick of Holland and West-Friesland.* London: 1702.

A Dialogue Between the Pope and a Phanatick, Concerning Affairs in England. London: 1680.

Dickinson, John. *The Writings of John Dickinson.* Edited by Paul Leicester Ford. Philadelphia: Historical Society of Pennsylvania, 1895.

[Digges, Dudley.] *An Answer to a Printed Book, Intituled, Observations Upon Some of His Majesties Late Answers and Expresses.* Oxford: Leonard Lichfield, 1642.

————. *The Unlawfulnesse of Subjects taking up Armes against their Soveraigne, in what case soever.* 1643.

[Dryden, John?] *His Majesties Declaration Defended: In a Letter to a Friend.* London: T. Davies, 1681.

Du Plessis Mornay, Philip. *A Woorke concerning the trewnesse of the Christian Religion.* Translated by Sir Philip Sidney and Arthur Golding. London: Thomas Cadman, 1587.

E.F. *A Letter From A Gentleman of Quality In The Country, To His Friend, Upon His being Chosen a Member to serve in the Approaching Parliament.* 1679.

An Elegy, On the Death of Algernon Sidney Esq; Who was found Guilty of High-Treason, and Beheaded at Tower-Hill on Friday the 7th of December, 1683. London: George Croom, 1683.

Eliot, Andrew. *A Sermon Preached Before His Excellence Francis Bernard, Esq. . . . May 29th 1765. Being the Anniversary for the Election of His Majesty's Council for the Province.* Boston: Green and Rusell, 1765.

Elton, G. R., editor. *The Tudor Constitution*. Cambridge: Cambridge University Press, 1960.

Evelyn, John. *The Diary of John Evelyn*. Edited by Austin Dobson. 3 vols. London: Macmillan and Co., 1906.

An Exact Account of the manner of the Execution of Algernon Sidney Esq. London: E. Mallet, 1683.

An Exact Account of the Tryal of Algernon Sidney, Esq; Who was Tryed at the Kings-Bench-Bar at Westminster. London: E. Mallet, 1683.

[Ferguson, Robert.] "Concerning the Rye House Business." In *Robert Ferguson the Plotter*, by James Ferguson, 409–37. Edinburgh: David Douglas, 1887.

———. *An Enquiry Into, And Detection of the Barbarous Murther of the Late Earl of Essex*. 1684.

———. *A Letter to a Person of Honour, concerning the Black Box*. London: 15 May 1680.

———. *No Protestant Plot: Or the present pretended Conspiracy of Protestants against the King and Government, Discovered to be a Conspiracy of the Papists*. London: R. Lett, 1681.

———. *The Second Part of No Protestant Plot*. London: R. Smith, 1682.

———. *The Third Part of No Protestant Plot*. London: Richard Baldwin, 1682.

Ferne, Henry. *Conscience Satisfied. That there is no warrant for the Armes now taken up by Subjects*. Oxford: Leonard Lichfield, 1643.

A Few Words Among Many, About the touchy point of Succession, Humbly Proposed to Timely Consideration against the Session of Parliament. [1679?].

Filmer, Sir Robert. *Patriarcha and Other Political Works of Sir Robert Filmer*. Edited by Peter Laslett. Oxford: Basil Blackwell, 1949.

Firth, C. H., and R. S. Rait. *Acts and Ordinances of the Interregnum, 1642–1660*. 3 vols. London: HMSO, 1911.

Fountainhall, Sir John Lauder of. *Historical Observes of Memorable Occurrents in Church and State, From October 1680 to April 1686*. Edinburgh: Thomas Constable, 1840.

Franklin, Benjamin. *Benjamin Franklin. Writings*. Edited by J. A. Leo Lemay. New York: Library of America, 1987.

———. *The Papers of Benjamin Franklin*. Edited by Leonard W. Labaree. New Haven: Yale University Press, 1960–.

———. *The Writings of Benjamin Franklin*. Edited by Albert Henry Smyth. 10 vols. New York: Macmillan, 1905–1907.

Free-men Inslaved: Or, Reasons humbly offered . . . for the taking off the Excise upon Beer, and Ale. [1660?].

A Funeral Sermon on the Occasion of the Death of Algernon Sidney, Esq. London: J. Smith, 1683.

Gardiner, Samuel Rawson. *The Constitutional Documents of the Puritan Revolution 1625–1660*. 3rd ed. Oxford: The Clarendon Press, 1906.

Garrison, William Lloyd. *The Letters of William Lloyd Garrison*. Edited by Louis Ruchames. Cambridge, MA: Harvard University Press, 1971–.

Granger, Gideon [Algernon Sidney, pseud.]. *An Address to the People of New England*. Washington, DC: Dinmore and Cooper, 1808.

———. *A Vindication of the Measures of the Present Administration*. Wilmington: James Wilson, 1803.

Great and Weighty Considerations Relating to the D., Or Successor of the Crown. [1679].

Green, Frances Harriet Whipple [A Rhode Islander, pseud.]. *Might and Right*. Providence: A. H. Stillwell, 1844.

Grey, Anchitell, editor. *Debates of the House of Commons, From the Year 1667 to the Year 1694*. 10 vols. London: T. Becket and P. A. DeHonde, 1769.

Grey, Ford Lord. *The Secret History of the Rye-House Plot: And of Monmouth's Rebellion. Written by Ford Lord Grey in MDCLXXXV*. London: Andrew Millar, 1754.

Grotius, Hugo. *De Jure Belli Ac Pacis*. Translated by Francis W. Kelsey. 4 vols. The Classics of International Law, edited by James Brown Scott. 1925. Reprint. New York: Oceana Publications, 1964.

Haller, William, editor. *Tracts on Liberty in the Puritan Revolution*. 3 vols. New York: Columbia University Press, 1934.

Hallett, Benjamin F. "The Right of the People to Establish Forms of Government." In *Social Theories of Jacksonian Democracy*, edited by Joseph Blau, 100–128. New York: Liberal Arts Press, 1954.

Hamilton, Alexander, John Jay, and James Madison. *The Federalist Papers*. Edited by Clinton Rossiter. New York: New American Library, 1961.

Hancock, John. *An Oration Delivered March 5, 1774 . . . To Commemorate the Bloody Tragedy of the Fifth of March 1770*. Boston: Edes and Gill, 1774.

Harrington, James. *The Political Works of James Harrington*. Edited by J.G.A. Pocock. Cambridge: Cambridge University Press, 1977.

Hawles, John. *The English-mans Right. A Dialogue between a Barrister at Law, and a Jury-man: Plainly setting forth, I. The Antiquity, II. The excellent designed use, III. The Office and just Priviledges of Juries, by the Law of England*. London: Richard Janeway, 1680.

———. *Remarks Upon the Tryals of Edward Fitzharris, Stephen Colledge, Count Coningsmark, The Lord Russel, Collonel Sidney, Henry Cornish, and Charles Bateman. As also on the Earl of Shaftesbury's Grand Jury, Wilmore's Homine Replegiando, And the Award of Execution against Sir Thomas Armstrong*. London: Jacob Tonson, 1689.

Hickeringill, Edmund. "The History of Whiggism: In A Dialogue between a Tantivy-Tory and a Trimmer," 1682. In *The Works of Mr. Edmund Hickeringill*, 1:1–170. London: John Baker and R. Burleigh, 1716.

[Hickes, George.] *The Harmony of Divinity and Law, In a Discourse About Not Resisting of Soveraign Princes*. London: R.E., 1684.

———. *Jovian. Or, An Answer to Julian the Apostate*. London: Sam. Roycroft, 1683.

[Hicks, William.] *Considerations upon the Rights of the Colonists to the Privileges of British Subjects*. New York: John Holt, 1766.

Historical Manuscripts Commission. *Calendar of the Manuscripts of the Marquess of Ormonde, K.P., Preserved at Kilkenny Castle.* New Series. vols. 1, 4, 6, 7. London: HMSO, 1902–1912.

———. *Fifteenth Report, Appendix, Part VIII. Manuscripts of His Grace the Duke of Buccleuch and Queensberry, K.G., K.T., Preserved at Drumlanrig Castle.* London: HMSO, 1897.

———. *Fifth Report of the Royal Commission on Historical Manuscripts.* London: HMSO, 1876.

———. *Fourteenth Report, Appendix, Part IV. Manuscripts of Lord Kenyon.* London: HMSO, 1894.

———. *Fourteenth Report, Appendix, Part VII. Manuscripts of the Marquis of Ormonde, Preserved at the Castle, Kilkenny.* Vol. 1. London: HMSO, 1895.

———. *Fourth Report of the Royal Commission on Historical Manuscripts.* London: 1874.

———. *Report on Manuscripts in Various Collections.* London: HMSO, 1904.

———. *Report on the Manuscripts of Lord De L'Isle and Dudley Preserved at Penshurst Place.* 6 vols. London: HMSO, 1925–1966.

———. *Report on the Manuscripts of the Earl of Egmont.* Vol. 1, Part 2. London: HMSO, 1905.

———. *Seventh Report of the Royal Commission on Historical Manuscripts.* London: HMSO, 1879.

———. *Thirteenth Report, Appendix, Part I. Manuscripts of his Grace the Duke of Portland, Preserved at Welbeck Abbey.* Vol. 1. London: HMSO, 1891.

———. *Thirteenth Report, Appendix, Part IV. Manuscripts of the Rye and Hereford Corporations; Captain Loder-Symonds, Mr. E. R. Wodehouse, M.P., and Others.* London: HMSO, 1892.

———. *Thirteenth Report, Appendix, Part VI. Manuscripts of Sir William Fitzherbert, Bart., and Others.* London: HMSO, 1893.

———. *Twelfth Report, Appendix, Part X. Manuscripts and Correspondence of James, first earl of Charlemont.* Vol. 1. London: HMSO, 1891.

Hobbes, Thomas. *De Cive: The English Version.* Edited by Howard Warrender. Oxford: The Clarendon Press, 1983.

———. *Leviathan.* Edited by C. B. Macpherson. Harmondsworth: Penguin Books, 1981.

Hollis, Thomas. *Memoirs of Thomas Hollis, Esq.* 2 vols. London: 1780.

Holloway, James. *The Free and Voluntary Confession and Narrative of James Holloway.* London: Robert Horn, John Baker and John Redmayne, 1684.

Holmes, Oliver Wendell. *Holmes-Pollock Letters.* Edited by Mark DeWolfe Howe. 2 vols. Cambridge, MA: Harvard University Press, 1941.

Howell, T. B., editor. *A Complete Collection of State Trials.* London: 1816.

Hunt, Thomas. *A Defence of the Charter, And Municipal Rights of the City of London.* London: Richard Baldwin, [1683?].

———. *The Great and Weighty Considerations, Relating to the Duke of York.* London: 1680.

———. *Mr. Hunt's Postscript for Rectifying some Mistakes in some of the Inferiour Clergy, Mischievous to our Government and Religion.* London: 1682.

[Hunton, Philip.] *A Treatise of Monarchie*. London: John Bellamy and Ralph Smith, 1643.

An Impartial Account of the Nature and Tendency of the Late Addresses, 28 June 1681. In *State Tracts*, 1:425–39. London: 1693.

Independent Gazetteer (Philadelphia).

J.D. *A Word without Doors Concerning the Bill for Succession*. [1679].

James I. *Political Works of James I*. Edited by C. H. McIlwain. Cambridge, MA: Harvard University Press, 1918.

James II. "The Life of James the Second, Written by Himself." In *Original Papers*, edited by James Macpherson, 1:17–262. London: W. Strahan and T. Cadell, 1776.

Jefferson, Thomas. *The Papers of Thomas Jefferson*. Edited by Julian P. Boyd. Princeton: Princeton University Press, 1950–.

———. *Thomas Jefferson: Writings*. Edited by Merrill D. Peterson. New York: Library of America, 1984.

———. *The Writings of Thomas Jefferson*. Edited by Paul Leicester Ford. 10 vols. New York: 1892–1899.

———. *The Writings of Thomas Jefferson*. Edited by Andrew Lipscomb and Albert Burgh. 20 vols. Washington, DC: Thomas Jefferson Memorial Association, 1907.

[Jenyns, Soame.] *The Objections to the Taxation of Our American Colonies, By the Legislature of Great Britain, Briefly Consider'd*. London: 1765.

[Johnson, Stephen.] *Some Important Observations, Occasioned by . . . The Publick Fast . . . December 18th, AD 1765*. Newport: Samuel Hall, 1766.

Journals of the House of Commons.

Journals of the House of Lords.

[Kennedy, John Pendleton.] *Defence of the Whigs. By a Member of the Twenty-Seventh Congress*. New York: Harper & Brothers, 1844.

Kenyon, J. P. *The Stuart Constitution*. Cambridge: Cambridge University Press, 1966.

Lafayette, Marquis de. *Lafayette in the Age of the American Revolution: Selected Letters and Papers, 1776–1790*. Edited by Stanley J. Idzerda. Ithaca: Cornell University Press, 1979.

Lawrence, William. *The Right of Primogeniture, In Succession to the Kingdoms of England, Scotland, and Ireland*. London: 1681.

[Lee, Arthur.] *An Appeal to the Justice and Interests of the People of Great Britain, in the Present Disputes with America*. London: J. Almon, 1774.

Leicester, Robert Sidney, earl of. "Diary of Events 1636–1650." In *Report on the Manuscripts of Lord De L'Isle and Dudley Preserved at Penshurst Place*, 6:554–59. London: HMSO, 1966.

———. "Journal of the Earl of Leicester." In *Sydney Papers, Consisting of a Journal of the Earl of Leicester, and Original Letters of Algernon Sydney*, edited by R. W. Blencowe, 1–161. London: John Murray, 1825.

Leigh, Benjamin Watkins [Algernon Sydney, pseud.] *The Letters of Algernon Sydney, in Defence of Civil Liberty and against the Encroachments of Military Despotism*. Richmond: T. W. White, 1830.

[L'Estrange, Roger.] *An Account of the Growth of Knavery, Under the Pretended Fears of Arbitrary Government and Popery*. London: H.H. for Henry Brome, 1678.

———. *Citt and Bumpkin. In a Dialogue over a Pot of Ale, Concerning Matters of Religion and Government*. London: Henry Brome, 1680.

———. *The Free-born Subject: Or, The Englishman's Birthright: Asserted against all Tyrannical Usurpations in Church or State*. London: Henry Brome, 1679.

———. *The Observator, in Dialogue*. 2 vols. London: J. Bennet, 1684, 1687.

A Letter from a Person of Quality to his Friend, concerning His Majesty's late Declaration, touching the Reasons which moved Him to Dissolve the Two last Parliaments, 1681. In *State Tracts*, 1:187–92. London: 1693.

A Letter to the People of Pennsylvania; Occasioned by the . . . Act for Constituting the Judges . . . During Good Behaviour. 1760. In *The Pamphlets of the American Revolution, 1750–1776*, edited by Bernard Bailyn, 1:248–72. Cambridge, MA: Harvard University Press, 1965.

[Lilburne, John.] "Englands Birth-Right Justified." In *Tracts on Liberty in the Puritan Revolution*, edited by William Waller, 3:257–308. New York: Columbia University Press, 1934.

Locke, John. *The Correspondence of John Locke*. Edited by E. S. De Beer. 8 vols. Oxford: Oxford University Press, 1976.

———. *An Essay concerning Human Understanding*. Edited by Peter Nidditch. Oxford: The Clarendon Press, 1975.

———. *A Letter Concerning Toleration*. Edited by James Tully. Indianapolis: Hackett Publishing Company, 1983.

———. "Some Thoughts Concerning Education." In *The Educational Writings of John Locke*, edited by James Axtell, 109–325. Cambridge: Cambridge University Press, 1968.

———. "Some Thoughts Concerning Reading and Study for a Gentleman." In *The Works of John Locke*, 3:291–301. 10 vols. London: 1823.

———. *Two Treatises of Government*. Edited by Peter Laslett. Cambridge: Cambridge University Press, 1960.

The London Gazette. Published by Authority.

Louis XIV. *Memoires Pour les années 1661 et 1666*. Paris: Editions Bossard, 1923.

Ludlow, Edmund. *The Memoirs of Edmund Ludlow, Lieutenant-General of the Horse in the Army of the Commonwealth of England, 1625–1672*. Edited by C. H. Firth. 2 vols. Oxford: The Clarendon Press, 1894.

———. *A Voyce From The Watch Tower. Part Five: 1660–1662*. Edited by A. B. Worden. Camden Fourth Series, Vol. 21. London: Royal Historical Society, 1978.

Luttrell, Narcissus. *A Brief Historical Relation of State Affairs from September 1678 to April 1714*. 6 vols. Oxford: Oxford University Press, 1857.

Machiavelli, Niccolò. *The Discourses*. Edited by Bernard Crick. Translated by Leslie Walker. Harmondsworth: Penguin Books, 1970.

———. *The Prince*. Translated by George Bull. Harmondsworth: Penguin Books, 1981.

Mackenzie, Sir George. *Jus Regium: Or, the Just and Solid Foundations of Monarchy In General . . . Maintain'd against Buchannan, Napthali, Dolman, Milton &c.* London: Richard Chiswel, 1684.

———. *Observations Upon the Laws and Customs of Nations, as to Precedency.* Edinburgh: 1680.

Madison, James. *The Writings of James Madison.* Edited by Gaillard Hunt. 9 vols. New York: G. P. Putnam's Sons, 1901–1910.

Marvel, Andrew. *An Account of the Growth of Popery, and Arbitrary Government in England.* Amsterdam: 1677.

The Maryland Journal and Baltimore Advertiser.

[Maseres, Francis.] *Considerations on the Expediency of Admitting Representatives from the American Colonies into the British House of Commons.* London: 1770.

Massachusetts Historical Society—Collections.

Massachusetts Historical Society—Proceedings.

Mayhew, Jonathan. *A Discourse Concerning Unlimited Submission and Nonresistance to the Higher Powers.* 1750. In *Pamphlets of the American Revolution 1750–1776,* edited by Bernard Bailyn, 1:203–47. Cambridge, MA: Harvard University Press, 1965.

———. *Memoir of the Life and Writings of Rev. Jonathan Mayhew.* Edited by Alden Bradford. Boston: C. C. Little, 1838.

———. *A Sermon Preached in the Audience of His Excellency William Shirley . . . May 29, 1754. Being the Anniversary for the Election of His Majesty's Council for the Province.* Boston: Samuel Kneeland, 1754.

———. *The snare broken. A Thanksgiving-Discourse, Preached . . . May 23, 1766. Occasioned by the Repeal of the Stamp-Act.* Boston: 1766.

———. "Thomas Hollis and Jonathan Mayhew Their Correspondence, 1759–1766." Edited by Bernhard Knollenberg. *Proceedings of the Massachusetts Historical Society,* 3rd series, 69 (1947–1950): 102–93.

Melville, Herman. *White-Jacket, or, The World in a Man-of-War.* Boston: The Page Company, 1892.

Mercurius Politicus, Comprising the summe of all Intelligence, with the Affairs and Designs now on foot in the three Nations of England, Ireland, and Scotland.

Milton, John. *Complete Prose Works.* Edited by Don M. Wolfe. 8 vols. New Haven: Yale University Press, 1953–1982.

A Ministerial Catechise, Suitable to be Learned by all Modern Provincial Governors, Pensioners, Placemen, &c. Boston: 1771.

The Moderate Intelligencer. Impartially communicating Martiall Affairs to the Kingdom of England.

A Modest Account of the Present Posture of Affairs in England, With particular Reference to the Earl of Shaftesburies Case. [1682].

[Molesworth, Lord.] *An Account of Denmark, as It was in the Year 1692.* London: 1694.

Monarchy Asserted to be the Best, most Antient and Legall Form of Government. In a Conference held at Whitehall, with Oliver, Lord Protector, and a Committee of Parliament. London: 1742.

Montesquieu, Baron de. *The Spirit of the Laws*. Translated by Thomas Nugent. New York: Hafner Press, 1949.

Morton, A. L., editor. *Freedom in Arms*. New York: International Publishers, 1975.

Mountagu, Edward. *The Journal of Edward Mountagu First Earl of Sandwich*. Edited by R. C. Anderson. London: Navy Records Society, 1929.

Nalson, John. *The Common Interest of King and People: Shewing the Original, Antiquity and Excellency of Monarchy*. London: Jonathan Edwin, 1677.

———. *The Complaint of Liberty & Property Against Arbitrary Government*. London: Robert Steel, 1681.

———. *Reflections Upon Coll. Sidney's Arcadia; The Old Cause, Being Some Observations Upon his Last Paper*. London: Thomas Dring, 1684.

———. *The True Liberty and Dominion of Conscience Vindicated, from the Usurpations and Abuses of Opinion, and Persuasion*. 2nd ed. London: Jonathan Edwin, 1678.

The Nations Interest: In Relation to the Pretentions of his Royal Highness the Duke of York. London: James Vade, 1680.

[Nedham, Marchamont.] *The Case of the Commonwealth of England, Stated*. Edited by Philip A. Knachel. Folger Shakespeare Library. 1969.

———. *Interest will not Lie, Or, a View of England's True Interest: In reference to the Papist, Royalist, Presbyterian, Baptised, Neuter, Army, Parliament, City of London*. London: Tho. Newcomb, 1659.

———. *A Pacquet of Advices and Animadversions, Sent from London To the Men of Shaftesbury*. London: 1676.

[Neville, Henry.] "Nicholas Machiavel's Letter to Zanobius Buondelmontius in Vindication of Himself and his Writings." In *The Works of the Famous Nicolas Machiavel, Citizen and Secretary of Florence*. [Translated by Henry Neville.] London: J.S., 1675.

———. "Plato Redivivus: Or, A Dialogue Concerning Government." In *Two Republican Tracts*, edited by Caroline Robbins, 61–200. Cambridge: Cambridge University Press, 1969.

North, Roger. *Examen: or, an Enquiry into the Credit and Veracity of a Pretended Complete History*. London: Fletcher Gyles, 1740.

North American Review.

[Northleigh, John.] *Remarks Upon the most Eminent of our Antimonarchical Authors and their Writings*. London and Westminster, 1699. [Originally published as *The Triumph Of Our Monarchy*, 1685].

Osborne, Dorothy. *The Letters of Dorothy Osborne to William Temple*. Edited by G. C. Moore Smith. Oxford: The Clarendon Press, 1928.

Otis, James. *Considerations on Behalf of the Colonists in a Letter to a Noble Lord*. Boston: 1765.

———. *A Vindication of the Conduct of the House of Representatives of the Province of the Massachusetts-Bay*. Boston: Edes & Gill, 1762.

Paine, Thomas. *The Complete Writings of Thomas Paine*. Edited by Philip S. Foner. 2 vols. New York: Citadel Press, 1945.

[Parker, Henry.] *Jus Populi. Or, A Discourse Wherein clear satisfaction is given, as well concerning the Right of Subjects, as the Right of Princes.* London: Robert Bostock, 1644.

————. *Observations upon some of his Majesties late Answers and Expresses.* 1642.

Parker, Theodore. *The Trial of Theodore Parker, for the "Misdemeanor" of a Speech in Faneuil Hall against Kidnapping.* 1855. Reprint. New York: Negro Universities Press, 1970.

The Parliament Scout Communicating His Inteligence To The Kingdome.

The Parliamentary Intelligencer Comprising the Sum of Forraign Intelligence, with the Affairs now in Agitation in England, Scotland, and Ireland.

Parton, James. "Life, Trial, and Execution of Algernon Sidney." In *Triumphs of Enterprise, Ingenuity, and Public Spirit*, 601–13. New York: Virtue & Yorston, 1874.

Pemberton, Ebenezer. *A Catalogue of Curious and Valuable Books, Belonging to the late Reverend & Learned, Mr. Ebenezer Pemberton.* Boston: 1717.

Penn, William. *An Address to Protestants upon the Present Conjuncture.* [London]: 1679.

————. *England's Present Interest Discover'd With Honour to the Prince and Safety to the People.* [London]: 1675.

————. *The Papers of William Penn.* Edited by Mary Maples Dunn and Richard S. Dunn. 2 vols. Philadelphia: University of Pennsylvania Press, 1981–1982.

————. [Philanglus, pseud.]. *Englands Great Interest In The Choice of this New Parliament, Dedicated to all her Free-holders and Electors.* [1679?].

————. [Philanglus, pseud.]. *One Project for the Good of England: That is, Our Civil Union is our Civil Safety.* [1679].

————. [Philo-Britannicus, pseud.]. *The Great Question to be Considered by the King, and this approaching Parliament.* [1680].

The Pennsylvania Gazette.

Pepys, Samuel. *The Diary of Samuel Pepys.* Edited by Robert Latham and William Matthews. 11 vols. Berkeley and Los Angeles: University of California Press, 1971.

A Perfect Diurnall Of Some Passages in Parliament, And from other parts of this Kingdome.

Philanglus. *The Protestants Remonstrance Against Pope and Presbyter: in an Impartial Essay upon the Times, or a Plea for Moderation.* London: N.T. for Walter Davis, 1684.

Phillips, Wendell. "John Brown and the Spirit of Fifty-Nine." 1859. Reprinted in *Modern Eloquence*, edited by Thomas Reed, 14:1588–1602. Philadelphia: John Morris, 1900–1903.

————. *Speeches, Lectures and Letters.* 2nd series. Boston: Lee and Shepard, 1891.

Pluto, the Prince of Darkness, His Entertainment of Coll. Algernoon Sidney, Upon His Arrival at the Internal Palace. With the Congratulations of the Fanatick Cabal for his Arrival There. To the Tune of, "Hail to the Mirtle shade," &c. London: 1684.

Poems on Affairs of State. Augustan Satirical Verse, 1660–1714. Edited by George Lord (and others). New Haven: Yale University Press, 1963–1975.

Pownall, Thomas. *The Administration of the Colonies.* 3rd ed. London: 1766.

Price, Richard. *Richard Price and the Ethical Foundations of the American Revolution.* Edited by Bernard Peach. Durham, NC: Duke University Press, 1979.

Proceedings and Debates of the Virginia State Convention of 1829–1830. Richmond: Samuel Shepherd, 1830.

The Proceedings to Sentence of Death Against Algernon Sidney Esq. London: Langley Curtis, 1683.

The Providence Gazette and Country Journal.

Pufendorf, Samuel von. *The Compleat History of Sweden, from its Origin to this Time.* London: 1702.

———. *De Jure Naturae Et Gentium Libri Octo.* Translated by C. H. Oldfather and W. A. Oldfather. Oxford: The Clarendon Press, 1934.

———. *Histoire du Regne de Charles Gustave Roy de Suede.* 2 vols. Nuremberg: 1697.

Quincy, Josiah. *Memoir of the Life of Josiah Quincy Jun. . . . By his Son.* Boston: Cummings, Hilliard, 1825.

Randolph, Edmund. "Edmund Randolph's Essay on the Revolutionary History of Virginia (1774–1782)." *Virginia Magazine of History and Biography* 43 (April 1935): 113–38.

Reasons for His Majesties Passing the Bill of Exclusion. London: J.W., 1681.

Reports of the Trials of Colonel Aaron Burr . . . For Treason. 2 vols. Philadelphia: Hopkins and Earle, 1808.

Reresby, Sir John. *Memoirs of Sir John Reresby.* Edited by Andrew Browning. Glasgow: Jackson, Son & Co., 1936.

[Rider, Matthew.] *The Power of Parliaments in the Case of Succession; Or, A Seasonable Address to the High Court of Parliament.* London: M.R., 1680.

[Rokeby, Matthew Robinson-Morris, Lord.] *Considerations on the Measures Carrying on with respect to the British Colonies in North America.* London: 1774.

Rousseau, Jean-Jacques. *On The Social Contract.* Translated by Judith R. Masters. Edited by Roger D. Masters. New York: St. Martin's Press, 1978.

The Roxburghe Ballads: Illustrating the last Years of the Stuarts. Edited by J. Woodfall Ebsworth. Hertford: Stephen Austin and Sons, 1885.

The Royal Apology: Or, An Answer To the Rebels Plea . . . With a Parallel between Doleman, Bradshaw, Sidney and other of the True-Protestant Party. London: T.B. for Robert Clavel, 1684.

Rush, Benjamin. *The Autobiography of Benjamin Rush.* Edited by George W. Corner. Princeton: Princeton University Press, 1948.

———. *The Letters of Benjamin Rush.* Edited by L. H. Butterfield. 2 vols. Princeton: Princeton University Press, 1951.

Rushworth, J. *Historical Collections of Private Passages of State.* 8 vols. London: 1659–1701.

Russell, William Lord. *The Speech of the late Lord Russel, To the Sheriffs, Together with the Paper delivered by him to them, at the Place of Execution, on July 21, 1683*. London: John Darby, 1683.

Savile, George. *Halifax: Complete Works*. Edited by J. P. Kenyon. Harmondsworth: Penguin Books, 1969.

Scott, S. P. "Algernon Sidney." *Potter's American Magazine* 6 (1876): 113–38.

A Seasonable Address to both Houses of Parliament Concerning the Succession. London: 1681.

A Seasonable Answer to . . . The Vindication of Slingsby Bethel Esq. London: T. Davies, 1681.

A Seasonable Warning to the Commons of England; Discovering to them Their Present Danger. [1679].

Selden, John. *Table-Talk: Being the Discourses of John Selden Esq*. London: E. Smith, 1689.

[Settle, Elkanah.] *The Character of a Popish Successor, and What England May Expect From Such a One*. London: T. Davies, 1681.

——. *Remarks on Algernoon Sidney's Paper, Delivered to the Sheriffs at his Execution*. London: W.C., 1683.

Seward, William H. *The Works of William H. Seward*. Edited by George Baker. New York: Redfield, 1853–1884.

Sexby, Edward, and Silius Titus [William Allen, pseud.]. *Killing, No Murder: With Some Additions Briefly Discourst . . . To deter and prevent Single Persons, and Councils, from Usurping Supream Power*. London: 1659. [1st edition, 1657].

Sharp, Granville. *A Declaration of the People's Natural Right to a Share in the Legislature; Which is the Fundamental Principle of the British Constitution of State*. London: 1774.

Sherlock, William. *The Case of Resistance of the Supreme Powers Stated and Resolved, According to the Doctrine of the Holy Scriptures*. London: Fincham Gardiner, 1684.

[Skillman, the Rev. Isaac.] *The American Alarm, or the Bostonian Plea, for the Rights, and Liberties of the People*. Boston: Kneeland and Davis, 1773.

——. *An Oration Upon the Beauties of Liberty, Or the Essential Rights of the Americans*. Boston: Kneeland and Davis, 1773.

Sober and Seasonable Queries Humbly offered to all Good Protestants In England. [1679].

Some Animadversions on the Paper Delivered to the Sheriffs . . . By Algernon Sidney, Esq. London: G.C. for John Cox, 1683.

Some Reflections on the Paper Delivered unto the Sheriffs of London by James Holloway at the time of his Execution. London: W. Davis, 1684.

[Somers, John.] *A Brief History of the Succession, Collected out of the Records, and the most Authentick Historians*. [London: 1680].

——. *The Security of English-Mens Lives, Or the Trust, Power, and Duty of the Grand Jurys of England*. London: T. Mitchel, 1681.

South Carolina Gazette.

[Sprat, Thomas.] *A True Account and Declaration of the Horrid Conspiracy Against the late King, His Present Majesty, and the Government.* 2nd ed. London: Thomas Newcomb, 1685.

Stearns, William. *A View of the Controversy subsisting between Great-Britain and the American Colonies. A Sermon Preached . . . May 11, 1775.* Watertown, MA: Benjamin Edes, 1775.

Storing, Herbert J., editor. *The Complete Anti-Federalist.* 7 vols. Chicago: University of Chicago Press, 1981.

Stubbe, Henry. *An Essay in Defence of the Good Old Cause, or A Discourse concerning the Rise and Extent of the power of the Civil Magistrate in reference to Spiritual Affairs.* London: 1659.

————. *Malice Rebuked, or A Character of Mr. Richard Baxter's Abilities. And a Vindication of the Honourable Sr. Henry Vane.* London: 1659.

Sumner, Charles. *Charles Sumner: His Complete Works.* 20 vols. New York: Negro Universities Press, 1969.

Tacitus. *Germania.* Loeb Classical Library. 1970.

Taylor, John, of Caroline. *An Inquiry into the Principles and Policy of the Government of the United States.* 1814. Reprint. New Haven: Yale University Press, 1950.

Taylor, Richard. *Destruction and Reconstruction.* Edited by Richard Harwell. 1879. New York: Longmans, Green and Co., 1955.

Temple, William. *The Works of Sir William Temple, Bart.* 4 vols. Edinburgh: 1754.

Terlon, Chevalier Hugues de. *Memoires.* 2 vols. Paris: 1681.

Thomson, James. *The Complete Poetical Works of James Thomson.* Edited by J. L. Robertson. Oxford: Oxford University Press, 1908.

Three Great Questions Concerning the Succession and the Dangers of Popery, Fully Examin'd. London: M.R., 1680.

Thurloe, John. *A Collection of the State Papers of John Thurloe.* 7 vols. London: 1742.

The True Protestant Subject, or, the Nature, and Rights of Sovereignty Discuss'd, and Stated. London: 1680.

The Tryal and Process of High-Treason and Doom of Forfaulture against Mr. Robert Baillie of Jerviswood Traitor. Edinburgh: 1685.

The Tryal of Thomas Pilkington, Samuel Shut, Henry Cornish, Ford Lord Grey of Werk, Sir Thomas Player, Slingsby Bethel . . . for the Riot at Guild-Hall on Midsommer-Day 1682. London: Thomas Dring, 1682.

The Tryals of Thomas Walcot, William Hone, William Lord Russell, John Rouse & William Blagg, For High-Treason. London: Richard Royston, Benjamin Took and Charles Mearn, 1683.

[Tyrrell, James.] *Bibliotheca Politica: Or, An Enquiry into the Ancient Constitution of the English Government . . . in Thirteen Dialogues.* London: R. Baldwin, 1694.

————. *Patriarcha non Monarcha. The Patriarch Unmonarch'd: Being Observations on a Late Treatise and diverse other Miscellanies, Published under the Name of Sir Robert Filmer Baronet.* London: Richard Janeway, 1681.

Vane, Henry. *The Cause of the People of England Stated.* London: Richard Baldwin, 1689.

————. *A Healing Question Propounded and Resolved, Upon occasion of the late publique and seasonable Call to Humiliation.* London: T. Brewster, 1656.

————. *A Needful Corrective or Ballance in Popular Government, Expressed in a Letter to James Harrington, Esquire, Upon Occasion of a late Treatise of his.* [London: 1660].

————. *The Retired Mans Meditations, or the Mysterie and Power of Godliness Shinning forth in the Living Word.* London: R.W., 1655.

Vernon, James. *Letters Illustrative of the Reign of William III. From 1696 to 1708. Addressed to the Duke of Shrewsbury by James Vernon, Esq. Secretary of State.* Edited by G.P.R. James. 3 vols. London: Henry Colburn, 1841.

Vicars, John. *Gods Arke Overtopping the Worlds Waves, or The Third Part of the Parliamentary Chronicle.* London: M. Simons and J. Macock, 1646.

Virginia Gazette (Dixon & Hunter, Hunter, Pinkney, Purdie, Purdie & Dixon, Rind).

Vox Patriae: Or, the Resentments and Indignation of the Free-born Subjects of England . . . being a true collection of the Petitions and Addresses [1681]. In *State Tracts,* 2:125–46. London: 1693.

Vox Populi: Or the Peoples Claim to their Parliaments Sitting, To Redress Grievances, and Provide for the Common Safety. London: Francis Smith, 1681.

W.L. *The Two Questions, Whereon this present Juncture of Affairs . . . Depend.* London: A.C., 1681.

W.W. *Antidotum Britannicum; Or, A Counter-Pest Against the Destructive Principles of Plato Redivivus; Wherein His Majestie's Royal Prerogatives are Asserted, and the Ancient Rights of the Imperial Crown of England are Vindicated, Against All Innovators.* London: Richard Sare, 1681.

[Walwyn, William.] "The Compassionate Samaritane." In *Tracts on Liberty in the Puritan Revolution,* edited by William Haller, 3:49–104. New York: Columbia University Press, 1934.

————. "A Helpe to the right understanding of a Discourse concerning Independency." In *Tracts on Liberty in the Puritan Revolution,* edited by William Haller, 3:189–202. New York: Columbia University Press, 1934.

————. "A Pearle in a Dounghill," July 1646. In *Freedom in Arms,* edited by A. L. Morton, 77–85. New York: International Publishers, 1975.

Ward, S. *The Animadversions and Remarks upon Collonel Sydney's Paper Answered.* London: 1684.

Webster, Noah. *Letters of Noah Webster.* Edited by Harry Warfel. New York: Library Publishers, 1953.

[Whately, Thomas.] *The Regulations Lately Made concerning the Colonies, and the Taxes Imposed upon Them, considered.* London: 1765.

Whitaker, D. K. [Sidney, pseud.]. *Sidney's Letters to William S. Channing, D.D., Occasioned by his Letter to Hon. Henry Clay, on the Annexation of Texas.* Charleston, SC: Edward C. Councell, 1837.

Whitelocke, Bulstrode. *Memorials of the English Affairs from the Beginning of the*

Reign of Charles the First to the Happy Restoration of King Charles the Second. 4 vols. Oxford: Oxford University Press, 1853.

[Wildman, John?] *A Declaration of the Free-born people of England, now in Armes against the Tyrannie and Oppression of Oliver Cromwell Esq*. [Thomason dates: 16 March 1654/5].

———— [?] "The Leveller: Or, the Principles and Maxims concerning Government and Religion, which are asserted by those that are commonly called 'Levellers.'" In *The Harleian Miscellany*, edited by William Oldys and Thomas Park, 4:543–50. London: 1809.

William Lloyd Garrison, 1805–1879: The Story of His Life Told by His Children. 4 vols. 1885. Reprint. New York: Negro Universities Press, 1969.

Witt, Johan De. "Brieven van Johan De Witt, Erste Deel." Edited by Robert Fruin. *Historisch Genootschap*, 3rd series, vol. 18 (1906).

Wittgenstein, Ludwig. *Philosophical Investigations*. Translated by G.E.M. Anscombe. 3rd ed. New York: Macmillan, 1958.

Wolseley, Sir Charles. *Liberty of Conscience Upon its true and proper Grounds Asserted & Vindicated*. 2nd ed. London: 1668.

[Womock, Laurence?] *A Short Way To A Lasting Settlement . . . With A Warning to All Loyal Gentlemen and Freeholders*. London: Robert Clavel, 1683.

Woodhouse, A.S.P., editor. *Puritanism and Liberty; Being the Army Debates (1647–9) from the Clarke Manuscripts*. Chicago: University of Chicago Press, 1951.

A Word within-doors: Or, A Reply To A Word without-doors. [1679].

SECONDARY SOURCES

Adams, Randolph Greenfield. *Political Ideas of the American Revolution: Britannic-American Contributions to the Problem of Imperial Organization*. Durham, NC: Trinity College Press, 1922.

Akers, Charles W. *Called Unto Liberty: A Life of Jonathan Mayhew 1720–1766*. Cambridge, MA: Harvard University Press, 1964.

Appleby, Joyce. "Commercial Farming and the 'Agrarian Myth' in the Early Republic." *Journal of American History* 68 (March 1982): 833–49.

————. "The New Republican Synthesis and the Changing Political Ideas of John Adams." *American Quarterly* 25 (December 1973): 578–95.

————. "Republicanism and Ideology." *American Quarterly* 37 (Fall 1985): 461–73.

————. "Republicanism in Old and New Contexts." *William and Mary Quarterly*, 3rd ser., 43 (January 1986): 20–34.

————. "The Social Origins of American Revolutionary Ideology." *Journal of American History* 64 (March 1978): 935–58.

Ashcraft, Richard. *Locke's Two Treatises of Government*. London: Unwin Hyman, 1987.

————. "On the Problem of Methodology and the Nature of Political Theory." *Political Theory* 3 (February 1975): 5–25.

————. "Political Theory and the Problem of Ideology." *Journal of Politics* 42 (August 1980): 687–721.

———. "Revolutionary Politics and Locke's Two Treatises of Government." *Political Theory* 8 (November 1980): 429–85.

———. *Revolutionary Politics & Locke's Two Treatises of Government*. Princeton: Princeton University Press, 1986.

Ashley, Maurice. *John Wildman, Plotter and Postmaster: A Study of the English Republican Movement in the Seventeenth Century*. London: Jonathan Cape, 1947.

Ashton, Robert. *The English Civil War: Conservatism and Revolution 1603–1649*. New York: W. W. Norton, 1978.

Bailyn, Bernard. "The Central Themes of the American Revolution." In *Essays on the American Revolution*, edited by Stephen Kurtz and James Hutson, 3–31. Chapel Hill: University of North Carolina Press, 1973.

———. *The Ideological Origins of the American Revolution*. Cambridge, MA: Harvard University Press, 1967.

———. *The Origins of American Politics*. New York: Vintage Books, 1967.

Banning, Lance. "Jeffersonian Ideology Revisited: Liberal and Classical Ideas in the New American Republic." *William and Mary Quarterly*, 3rd ser., 43 (January 1986): 3–19.

———. *The Jeffersonian Persuasion: Evolution of a Party Ideology*. Ithaca: Cornell University Press, 1978.

———. "Republican Ideology and the Triumph of the Constitution, 1789 to 1793." *William and Mary Quarterly*, 3rd ser., 31 (April 1974): 167–88.

———. "Some Second Thoughts on Virtue and the Course of Revolutionary Thinking." In *Conceptual Change and the Constitution*, edited by Terence Ball and J.G.A. Pocock, 194–212. Lawrence: University of Kansas Press, 1988.

Beer, Samuel H. "The Strengths of Liberal Democracy." In *A Prospect of Liberal Democracy*, edited by William Livingston, 215–29. Austin: University of Texas Press, 1979.

Behrens, B. "The Whig Theory of the Constitution in the Reign of Charles II." *Cambridge Historical Journal* 7 (1941): 42–71.

Berlin, Isaiah. *Four Essays on Liberty*. Oxford: Oxford University Press, 1969.

Berry, Mary. *Some Account of the Life of Rachel Wriothesley Lady Russell*. London: 1819.

Blackburne, Gertrude. *Algernon Sidney: A Review*. London: Kegan Paul, Trench & Co., 1885.

Blickle, Peter. "Kommunalismus, Parlamentarismus, Republikanismus." *Historische Zeitschrift* 242 (June 1986): 529–56.

Blitzer, Charles. *An Immortal Commonwealth: The Political Thought of James Harrington*. New Haven: Yale University Press, 1960.

Bloch, Ruth H. "The Gendered Meanings of Virtue in Revolutionary America." *Signs: Journal of Women in Culture and Society* 13 (1987): 37–58.

Borgeaud, Charles. *Histoire de l'Universite de Geneve. L'Academie de Calvin, 1559–1748*. Geneva: George & Co., 1900.

Bradford, Alan T. "Stuart Absolutism and the 'Utility' of Tacitus." *Huntington Library Quarterly* 46 (Winter 1983): 127–55.

Brailsford, H. N. *The Levellers and the English Revolution*. Edited by Christopher Hill. Stanford: Stanford University Press, 1961.

Brown, Irene Coltman. "Algernon Sidney, the Noble Republican." *History Today* 34, no. 2 (February 1984): 11–17.

Browning, Andrew. *Thomas Osborne Earl of Danby and Duke of Leeds 1632–1712*. 3 vols. Glasgow: Jackson, Son & Co., 1951.

Burke, Peter. "Tacitism." In *Tacitus*, edited by T. A. Dorey, 149–71. London: Routledge & Kegan Paul, 1969.

Cameron, W. J. *New Light on Aphra Behn*. Auckland: University of Auckland Monograph No. 5, 1961.

Carrive, Paulette. *La pensée politique d'Algernon Sidney*. Paris: Méridiens Klincksieck, 1989.

Carswell, John. "Algernon Sidney's 'Court Maxims': The Biographical Importance of a Transcript." *Historical Research* (February 1989): 98–103.

———. *The Porcupine: The Life of Algernon Sidney*. London: John Murray, 1989.

Cartwright, Julia. *Sacharissa; Some Account of Dorothy Sidney, Countess of Sunderland, Her Family and Friends, 1617–1684*. New York: Charles Scribner's Sons, 1893.

Colbourn, H. Trevor. *The Lamp of Experience: Whig History and the Intellectual Origins of the American Revolution*. Chapel Hill: University of North Carolina Press, 1965.

Conniff, James. "Reason and History in Early Whig Thought: The Case of Algernon Sidney." *Journal of the History of Ideas* 43 (July–September 1982): 397–416.

Cotterell, Mary. "Interregnum Law Reform: The Hale Commission of 1652." *English Historical Review* 83 (October 1968): 689–704.

Cranston, Maurice. *John Locke: A Biography*. Oxford: Oxford University Press, 1985.

Daly, James. "The Idea of Absolute Monarchy in Seventeenth-Century England." *Historical Journal* 21 (1978): 227–50.

———. *Sir Robert Filmer and English Political Thought*. Toronto: University of Toronto Press, 1979.

———. "Some Problems in the Authorship of Sir Robert Filmer's Works." *English Historical Review* (October 1983): 737–62.

Davis, David Brion. *The Problem of Slavery in Western Culture*. Ithaca: Cornell University Press, 1966.

Dictionary of National Biography.

Diggins, John Patrick. "Comrades and Citizens: New Mythologies in American Historiography." *American Historical Review* 90 (June 1985): 614–38.

———. *The Lost Soul of American Politics: Virtue, Self-Interest, and the Foundations of Liberalism*. Chicago: University of Chicago Press, 1984.

Dumbauld, Edward. "Algernon Sidney on Public Right." *University of Arkansas at Little Rock Law Journal* 10 (1987–88): 317–38.

Dunn, John. "The Identity of the History of Ideas." *Philosophy* 43 (April 1968): 85–104.

————. *Locke*. Oxford: Oxford University Press, 1984.

————. *The Political Thought of John Locke: An Historical Account of the Argument of the 'Two Treatises of Government'*. Cambridge: Cambridge University Press, 1969.

————. "The Politics of Locke in England and America in the Eighteenth Century." In *John Locke: Problems and Perspectives*, edited by John Yolton, 45–80. Cambridge: Cambridge University Press, 1969.

Dunn, Mary Maples. *William Penn: Politics and Conscience*. Princeton: Princeton University Press, 1967.

Etter, Else-Lilly. *Tacitus in der Geistesgeschichte des 16. und 17. Jahrhunderts*. Basel and Stuttgart: Von Helbing & Lichtenhahn, 1966.

Everitt, Alan. *The Community of Kent and the Great Rebellion 1640–1660*. Leicester: Leicester University Press, 1966.

Ewald, Alexander Charles. *The Life and Times of the Hon. Algernoon Sydney, 1622–1683*. 2 vols. London: Tinsley Brothers, 1873.

Feiling, Keith. *A History of the Tory Party, 1640–1714*. Oxford: The Clarendon Press, 1924.

Ferguson, James. *Robert Ferguson the Plotter*. Edinburgh: David Douglas, 1887.

Fink, Zera. *The Classical Republicans: An Essay in the Recovery of a Pattern of Thought in Seventeenth Century England*. Evanston: Northwestern University Press, 1945.

Foley, Henry. *Records of the English Province of the Society of Jesus*. 7 vols. London: Burns and Oates, 1880.

Ford, Lacy K. "Republican Ideology in a Slave Society: The Political Economy of John C. Calhoun." *Journal of Southern History* 54 (August 1988): 405–24.

Fox Bourne, H. R. *The Life of John Locke*. 2 vols. New York: Harper & Brothers, 1876.

Foxcroft, H. C. *The Life and Letters of Sir George Savile, Bart. First Marquis of Halifax, &c.* 2 vols. London: Longmans, Green, and Co., 1898.

Franklin, Julian H. *John Locke and the Theory of Sovereignty*. Cambridge: Cambridge University Press, 1978.

Fraser, Andrew. "Legal Amnesia: Modernism vs. the Republican Tradition in American Legal Theory." *Telos* 60 (1984): 18.

Friedrich, Carl J. *Constitutional Government and Democracy*. 4th ed. Waltham, MA: Blaisdell Publishing Company, 1968.

Furly, O. W. "The Whig Exclusionists: Pamphlet Literature in the Exclusion Campaign, 1679–81." *Cambridge Historical Journal* 13 (1957): 19–36.

Gardiner, Samuel Rawson. *History of England from the Accession of James I to the Outbreak of the Civil War 1603–1642*. 10 vols. London: Longmans, Green and Co., 1909.

————. *History of the Commonwealth and Protectorate 1649–1656*. 4 vols. London: 1903.

————. *History of the Great Civil War 1642–1649*. 4 vols. London: 1893.

Geyl, Pieter. *The Netherlands in the Seventeenth Century: Part Two, 1648–1715.* New York: Barnes and Noble, 1964.

Goldie, Mark. "Danby, the Bishops, and the Whigs." In *Conscience and Authority,* edited by T. Harris, P. Seaward, and M. Goldie. Oxford: Blackwell, 1990.

———. "Edmund Bohun and *Jus Gentium* in the Revolution Debate, 1689–1693." *Historical Journal* 20 (1977): 569–86.

———. "John Locke and Anglican Royalism." *Political Studies* 31 (1983): 61–85.

Gough, J. W. "James Tyrrell, Whig Historian and Friend of John Locke." *Historical Journal* 19 (1976): 581–610.

Gray, John N. "On Negative and Positive Liberty." *Political Studies* 28 (September 1980): 507–26.

Greenleaf, W. H. *Order, Empiricism and Politics: Two Traditions of English Political Thought 1500–1700.* Oxford: Oxford University Press, 1964.

Greenough, Chester N. "Algernon Sidney and the Motto of the Commonwealth of Massachusetts." *Proceedings of the Massachusetts Historical Society* 51 (1917–18): 259–82.

Gunn, J.A.W. *Politics and the Public Interest in the Seventeenth Century.* London: Routledge & Kegan Paul, 1969.

Gwyn, W. B. *The Meaning of the Separation of Powers.* Tulane Studies in Political Science, Vol. 9. New Orleans: Tulane University Press, 1965.

Haakonssen, Knud. "Hugo Grotius and the History of Political Thought." *Political Theory* 13 (May 1985): 239–65.

Haitsma Mulier, Eco O. G. *The Myth of Venice and Dutch Republican Thought in the Seventeenth Century.* Assen, The Netherlands: Van Gorcum, 1980.

Haley, K.H.D. *The First Earl of Shaftesbury.* Oxford: The Clarendon Press, 1968.

Handlin, Oscar, and Mary Handlin. "James Burgh and American Revolutionary Theory." *Proceedings of the Massachusetts Historical Society* 73 (1961): 38–57.

Hanson, Donald W. *From Kingdom to Commonwealth: The Development of Civic Consciousness in English Political Thought.* Cambridge, MA: Harvard University Press, 1970.

Harris, F. R. *The Life of Edward Mountagu, K.G., First Earl of Sandwich (1625–1672).* 2 vols. London: John Murray, 1912.

Harrison, John, and Peter Laslett, editors. *The Library of John Locke.* 2nd ed. Oxford: The Clarendon Press, 1971.

Hatch, Orrin G. "Civic Virtue: Wellspring of Liberty." *National Forum* 64 (Fall 1984): 34–38.

Havighurst, A. F. "The Judiciary and Politics in the Reign of Charles II." *The Law Quarterly Review* 66 (January 1950): 63–78, 229–52.

Haydon, Brigid. "Algernon Sidney, 1623–1683." *Archaeologia Cantiana* 76 (1961): 110–33.

Henning, Basil Duke. *The House of Commons 1660–1690.* 3 vols. London: Secker & Warburg, 1983.

Herzog, Don. *Happy Slaves: A Critique of Consent Theory*. Chicago: University of Chicago Press, 1989.

———. "Some Questions for Republicans." *Political Theory* 14 (August 1986): 473–93.

Hexter, J. H. "Review Essay: *The Machiavellian Moment*, by J.G.A. Pocock." *History and Theory* 16 (1977): 306–37.

Higgonet, Patrice. *Sister Republics: The Origins of French and American Republicanism*. Cambridge, MA: Harvard University Press, 1988.

Hill, Christopher. "The Norman Yoke." In *Puritanism and Revolution*, 50–122. London: Secker & Warburg, 1958.

Hirschman, Albert O. *The Passions and the Interests: Political Arguments for Capitalism before Its Triumph*. Princeton: Princeton University Press, 1977.

Holmes, Stephen. *Benjamin Constant and the Making of Modern Liberalism*. New Haven: Yale University Press, 1984.

———. "Precommitment and the Paradox of Democracy." In *Constitutionalism and Democracy*, edited by Jon Elster and Rune Slagstad, 195–240. Cambridge: Cambridge University Press, 1988.

Hont, Istvan, and Michael Ignatieff. "Needs and Justice in the *Wealth of Nations*: An Introductory Essay." In *Wealth and Virtue: The Shaping of Political Economy in the Scottish Enlightenment*, edited by Hont and Ignatieff, 1–44. Cambridge: Cambridge University Press, 1983.

Hull, William I. *Benjamin Furly and Quakerism in Rotterdam*. Swarthmore, PA: Swarthmore College Monograph on Quaker History No. 5, 1941.

Hutton, Ronald. *The Restoration: A Political and Religious History of England and Wales 1658–1667*. Oxford: The Clarendon Press, 1985.

Jaszi, Oscar, and John D. Lewis. *Against the Tyrant: The Tradition and Theory of Tyrannicide*. Glencoe, IL: The Free Press, 1957.

Johnston, David. *The Rhetoric of Leviathan: Thomas Hobbes and the Politics of Cultural Transformation*. Princeton: Princeton University Press, 1986.

Jones, J. R. *Britain and Europe in the Seventeenth Century*. London: Edward Arnold, 1966.

———. *Country and Court: England, 1658–1714*. Cambridge, MA: Harvard University Press, 1979.

———. *The First Whigs: The Politics of the Exclusion Crisis 1678–1683*. London: Oxford University Press, 1961.

———. "The Green Ribbon Club." *Durham University Journal* 49 (December 1956): 17–20.

Judson, Margaret. *The Crisis of the Constitution*. New York: Octagon Books, 1976.

———. *The Political Thought of Sir Henry Vane the Younger*. Philadelphia: University of Pennsylvania Press, 1969.

Karsten, Peter. *Patriot-Heroes in England and America: Political Symbolism and Changing Values over Three Centuries*. Madison: University of Wisconsin Press, 1978.

———. "Who was 'Colonel Sidney'? A Note on the Meaning of the October

13, 1681, Penn-Sidney Letter." *Pennsylvania Magazine of History and Biography* 91 (April 1967): 193–98.

Kenyon, Cecilia. "Men of Little Faith: The Anti-Federalists on the Nature of Representative Government." *William and Mary Quarterly*, 3rd ser., 12 (1955): 3–46.

Kenyon, John. *The Popish Plot*. Harmondsworth: Pelican Books, 1974.

Keohane, Nannerl O. *Philosophy and the State in France: The Renaissance to the Enlightenment*. Princeton: Princeton University Press, 1980.

Kishlansky, Mark. *The Rise of the New Model Army*. Cambridge: Cambridge University Press, 1979.

Kitchen, George. *Sir Roger L'Estrange; A Contribution to the History of the Press in the Seventeenth Century*. London: Kegan Paul, Trench, Trübner & Co., 1913.

Kliger, Samuel. *The Goths in England: A Study in Seventeenth and Eighteenth Century Thought*. Cambridge, MA: Harvard University Press, 1952.

Kossmann, E. H. "The Development of Dutch Political Theory in the Seventeenth Century." In *Britain and the Netherlands*, edited by J. S. Bromley and E. H. Kossmann, 91–110. London: Chatto and Windus, 1960.

———. "Dutch Republicanism." In *L'età dei lumi: Studi storici sul settecento europeo in onore di Franco Venturi*, 1:453–86. Naples: Jovene, 1985.

———. *In Praise of the Dutch Republic: Some Seventeenth-Century Attitudes*. London: H. K. Lewis, 1963.

Kramnick, Isaac. *Bolingbroke and His Circle: The Politics of Nostalgia in the Age of Walpole*. Cambridge, MA: Harvard University Press, 1968.

———. "The 'Great National Discussion': The Discourse of Politics in 1787." *William and Mary Quarterly*, 3rd ser., 45 (January 1988): 3–32.

———. "Republican Revisionism Revisited." *American Historical Review* 87 (June 1982): 629–64.

Laslett, Peter. Introduction to *Patriarcha and Other Political Works of Sir Robert Filmer*. Oxford: Basil Blackwell, 1949.

———. Introduction to *Two Treatises of Government*, by John Locke. Cambridge: Cambridge University Press, 1960.

———. *The World We Have Lost—Further Explored*. 3rd ed. London: Methuen, 1983.

Lienesch, Michael. *New Order of the Ages: Time, the Constitution, and the Making of Modern American Political Thought*. Princeton: Princeton University Press, 1988.

Lister, T. H. *Life and Administration of Edward, First Earl of Clarendon*. 3 vols. London: Longman, Orme, Brown, Green, and Longmans, 1837.

Lovejoy, Arthur O. *The Great Chain of Being*. Cambridge, MA: Harvard University Press, 1964.

Lutz, Donald S. *The Origins of American Constitutionalism*. Baton Rouge: Louisiana State University Press, 1988.

———."The Relative Influence of European Writers on Late Eighteenth-Century American Political Thought." *American Political Science Review* 78 (March 1984): 189–97.

MacCallum, Gerald. "Negative and Positive Freedom." *Philosophical Review* 76 (July 1967): 312–34.

McCoy, Drew. *The Elusive Republic: Political Economy in Jeffersonian America*. Chapel Hill: University of North Carolina Press, 1980.

McIlwain, Charles Howard. *Constitutionalism Ancient and Modern*. Rev. ed. Ithaca: Cornell University Press, 1947.

MacInnes, C. M. *England and Slavery*. Bristol: Arrowsmith, 1934.

Macpherson, C. B. *The Political Theory of Possessive Individualism: Hobbes to Locke*. Oxford: Oxford University Press, 1962.

Meadley, George Wilson. *Memoirs of Algernon Sidney*. London: Cradock and Joy, 1813.

Middlekauff, Robert. *The Glorious Cause: The American Revolution 1763–1789*. New York: Oxford University Press, 1982.

Miller, John. *Popery and Politics in England 1660–1688*. Cambridge: Cambridge University Press, 1973.

Miller, Perry. "From the Covenant to the Revival." In *Nature's Nation*, 90–120. Cambridge, MA: Harvard University Press, 1967.

———. *The New England Mind: The Seventeenth Century*. Cambridge, MA: Harvard University Press, 1954.

Milne, Doreen J. "The Results of the Rye House Plot and Their Influence upon the Revolution of 1688." *Transactions of the Royal Historical Society*, 5th ser., 1 (1951): 91–108.

Morrison, Samuel Eliot. *The Oxford History of the American People*. New York: Oxford University Press, 1965.

Oestreich, Gerhard. *Neostoicism and the Early Modern State*. Translated by David McLintock. Edited by Brigitta Oestreich and H. G. Koenigsberger. Cambridge: Cambridge University Press, 1982.

Ogg, David. *England in the Reign of Charles II*. 2 vols. Oxford: Oxford University Press, 1934.

Pitkin, Hanna Fenichel. *The Concept of Representation*. Berkeley and Los Angeles: University of California Press, 1967.

———. *Fortune Is a Woman: Gender and Politics in the Thought of Niccolo Machiavelli*. Berkeley and Los Angeles: University of California Press, 1984.

Plumb, J. H. "The Growth of the Electorate in England from 1600 to 1715." *Past and Present* 45 (November 1969): 90–116.

Pocock, J.G.A. *The Ancient Constitution and the Feudal Law: A Study of English Historical Thought in the Seventeenth Century*. Cambridge: Cambridge University Press, 1957.

———. "Between Gog and Magog: The Republican Thesis and the *Ideologia Americana*." *Journal of the History of Ideas* 48 (April–June 1987): 325–46.

———. "Machiavelli in the Liberal Cosmos." *Political Theory* 13 (November 1985): 559–74.

———. *The Machiavellian Moment: Florentine Political Thought and the Atlantic Republican Tradition*. Princeton: Princeton University Press, 1975.

———. "The Machiavellian Moment Revisited: A Study in History and Ideology." *Journal of Modern History* 53 (March 1981): 49–72.

Pocock, J.G.A. "The Myth of John Locke and the Obsession with Liberalism." In *John Locke*, by J.G.A. Pocock and Richard Ashcraft, 3–24. Los Angeles: William Andrews Clark Memorial Library, 1980.

————. *Politics, Language and Time: Essays on Political Thought and History*. New York: Atheneum, 1971.

————. *Three British Revolutions*. Princeton: Princeton University Press, 1980.

————. *Virtue, Commerce, and History: Essays on Political Thought and History, Chiefly in the Eighteenth Century*. Cambridge: Cambridge University Press, 1985.

Pole, J. R. *Political Representation in England and the Origins of the American Republic*. Berkeley and Los Angeles: University of California Press, 1971.

Raab, Felix. *The English Face of Machiavelli: A Changing Interpretation 1500–1700*. London: Routledge & Kegan Paul, 1964.

"Return. Members of Parliament. Part I: Parliaments of England, 1213–1702." *Parliamentary Papers*, vol. 62. London: HMSO, 1872.

Richter, Melvin. "Despotism." In *Dictionary of the History of Ideas*, edited by Philip Wiener, 2:1–18. New York: Charles Scribner's Sons, 1973.

Risjord, Norman K. *The Old Republicans: Southern Conservatism in the Age of Jefferson*. New York: Columbia University Press, 1965.

Robbins, Caroline. "Algernon Sidney's *Discourses Concerning Government*: Textbook of Revolution." *William and Mary Quarterly*, 3rd ser., 4 (July 1947): 267–96.

————. *The Eighteenth-Century Commonwealthman: Studies in the Transmission, Development and Circumstance of English Liberal Thought from the Restoration of Charles II to the War with the Thirteen Colonies*. Cambridge, MA: Harvard University Press, 1959.

Rowe, Violet A. *Sir Henry Vane the Younger: A Study in Political and Administrative History*. London: Athlone Press, 1970.

Rowen, Herbert. *John De Witt, Grand Pensionary of Holland, 1625–1672*. Princeton: Princeton University Press, 1978.

————. "Kingship and Republicanism in the Seventeenth Century: Some Reconsiderations." In *From the Renaissance to the Counter-Reformation: Essays in Honor of Garrett Mattingly*, edited by Charles H. Carter, 420–31. New York: Random House, 1965.

Rowse, A. L. *The England of Elizabeth*. Madison: University of Wisconsin Press, 1978.

Russell, Conrad. "Arguments for Religious Unity in England, 1530–1650." *Journal of Ecclesiastical History* 18 (October 1967): 201–26.

Sabine, George. *A History of Political Theory*. New York: Henry Holt and Company, 1937.

Salmon, J. H. "Algernon Sidney and the Rye House Plot." *History Today* 4 (1954): 698–705.

————. *The French Religious Wars in English Political Thought*. Oxford: The Clarendon Press, 1959.

Schellhase, Kenneth. *Tacitus in Renaissance Political Thought*. Chicago: University of Chicago Press, 1976.

Schlaifer, Robert. "Greek Theories of Slavery from Homer to Aristotle." *Harvard Studies in Classical Philology* 47 (1934): 165–204.

Schneewind, J. B. "Pufendorf's Place in the History of Ethics." *Synthese* 72 (July 1987): 123–55.

Schochet, Gordon. *Patriarchalism in Political Thought: The Authoritarian Family and Political Speculation and Attitudes Especially in Seventeenth-Century England.* Oxford: Basil Blackwell, 1975.

———. "Radical Politics and Ashcraft's Treatise on Locke." *Journal of the History of Ideas* 50 (July–September 1989): 491–510.

———. "Sir Robert Filmer: Some New Bibliographical Discoveries." *The Library* 26 (1971): 154–60.

Schwoerer, Lois G. *The Declaration of Rights, 1689.* Baltimore: Johns Hopkins University Press, 1981.

———. *"No Standing Armies!" The Antiarmy Ideology in Seventeenth-Century England.* Baltimore: Johns Hopkins University Press, 1974.

———. "William, Lord Russell: The Making of a Martyr, 1683–1983." *Journal of British Studies* 24 (January 1985): 41–71.

Scott, Jonathan. *Algernon Sidney and the English Republic 1623–1677.* Cambridge: Cambridge University Press, 1988.

Shackleton, Robert. "Montesquieu and Machiavelli: A Reappraisal." *Comparative Literature Studies* 1 (1964): 1–13.

Shalhope, Robert E. "The Ideological Origins of the Second Amendment." *Journal of American History* 69 (December 1982): 599–614.

———. "Republicanism and Early American Historiography." *William and Mary Quarterly*, 3rd ser., 39 (April 1982): 334–56.

———. "Toward a Republican Synthesis: The Emergence of an Understanding of Republicanism in American Historiography." *William and Mary Quarterly*, 3rd ser., 29 (January 1972): 49–80.

Shipley, John. "Franklin Attends a Book Auction." *Pennsylvania Magazine of History and Biography* 80 (1956): 37–45.

Shklar, Judith N. "Ideology Hunting: The Case of James Harrington." *American Political Science Review* 53 (September 1959): 662–92.

———. *Legalism: Law, Morals, and Political Trials.* Cambridge, MA: Harvard University Press, 1964.

———. *Men and Citizens: A Study of Rousseau's Social Theory.* Cambridge: Cambridge University Press, 1969.

———. *Ordinary Vices.* Cambridge, MA: Harvard University Press, 1984.

Skinner, Quentin. "Conquest and Consent: Thomas Hobbes and the Engagement Controversy." In *The Interregnum*, edited by G. E. Aylmer, 79–98. London: Macmillan, 1972.

———. *The Foundations of Modern Political Thought.* 2 vols. Cambridge: Cambridge University Press, 1978.

———. "The Idea of Negative Liberty: Philosophical and Historical Perspectives." In *Philosophy in History*, edited by Richard Rorty, J. B. Schneewind, and Quentin Skinner, 193–221. Cambridge: Cambridge University Press, 1984.

Skinner, Quentin. "The Ideological Context of Hobbes's Political Thought." *Historical Journal* 9 (1966): 286–317.

———. *Machiavelli.* Oxford: Oxford University Press, 1981.

———. "Meaning and Understanding in the History of Ideas." *History and Theory* 8 (1969): 3–53.

———. "The Paradoxes of Political Liberty." In *Tanner Lectures on Human Values,* edited by Sterling McMurrin, 7:225–50. Salt Lake City: University of Utah Press, 1986.

Sommerville, J. P. "From Suarez to Filmer: A Reappraisal." *Historical Journal* 25 (1982): 525–40.

———. *Politics and Ideology in England 1603–1640.* London: Longman, 1986.

Sowerby, W. Millicent. *Catalogue of the Library of Thomas Jefferson.* 6 vols. Washington, DC: Library of Congress, 1953.

Sprunger, Keith. *Dutch Puritanism: A History of English and Scottish Churches of the Netherlands in the Sixteenth and Seventeenth Centuries.* Leiden: E. J. Brill, 1982.

Stone, Lawrence. *The Crisis of the Aristocracy 1558–1641.* Oxford: The Clarendon Press, 1965.

Tarlton, Charles D. "The Exclusion Controversy, Pamphleteering, and Locke's *Two Treatises.*" *Historical Journal* 24 (1981): 49–68.

Thirsk, Joan. "Younger Sons in the Seventeenth Century." *History* 54 (October 1969): 358–77.

Thomas, Keith. *Religion and the Decline of Magic.* Harmondsworth: Penguin, 1973.

———. "The Social Origins of Hobbes's Political Thought." In *Hobbes Studies,* edited by K. C. Brown, 185–236. Oxford: Blackwell, 1965.

Thompson, Martyn P. *Ideas of Contract in English Political Thought in the Age of John Locke.* New York: Garland Publishing, 1987.

Thornton, A. P. "The Organization of the Slave Trade in the English West Indies, 1660–1685." *William and Mary Quarterly,* 3rd ser., 12 (1955): 399–409.

Tillyard, E.M.W. *The Elizabethan World Picture.* New York: Vintage Books, n.d.

Tuck, Richard. *Hobbes.* Oxford: Oxford University Press, 1989.

———. "The 'Modern' Theory of Natural Law." In *The Languages of Political Theory in Early-Modern Europe,* edited by Anthony Pagden, 99–119. Cambridge: Cambridge University Press, 1987.

———. *Natural Rights Theories: Their Origin and Development.* Cambridge: Cambridge University Press, 1979.

———. "A New Date for Filmer's Patriarcha." *Historical Journal* 29 (1986): 183–86.

Tully, James. *A Discourse on Property: John Locke and His Adversaries.* Cambridge: Cambridge University Press, 1980.

Underdown, David. "Party Management in the Recruiter Elections, 1645–1648." *English Historical Review* 83 (April 1968): 235–64.

——. *Pride's Purge: Politics in the Puritan Revolution.* 2nd ed. London: George Allen & Unwin, 1985.

——. *Revel, Riot, and Rebellion:Popular Politics and Culture in England 1603–1660.* Oxford: The Clarendon Press, 1985.

Van Santvoord, G. *Life of Algernon Sidney; With Sketches of Some of His Contemporaries, and Extracts from His Correspondence and Political Writings.* New York: Charles Scribner, 1851.

Vile, M.J.C. *Constitutionalism and the Separation of Powers.* Oxford: The Clarendon Press, 1967.

Walker, James. "The English Exiles in Holland During the Reigns of Charles II and James II." *Transactions of the Royal Historical Society,* 5th ser., 30 (1948): 111–25.

Wallace, John M. "The Date of Sir Robert Filmer's Patriarcha." *Historical Journal* 23 (1980): 155–65.

Walzer, Michael. *Exodus and Revolution.* New York: Basic Books, 1985.

——. *Regicide and Revolution: Speeches at the Trial of Louis XVI.* Cambridge: Cambridge University Press, 1974.

——. *The Revolution of the Saints: A Study in the Origins of Radical Politics.* Cambridge, MA: Harvard University Press, 1965.

Warkentin, Germaine. "Ins and Outs of the Sidney Family Library." *Times Literary Supplement* 4,314 (6 December 1985): 1394.

Wedgwood, C. V. *A Coffin for King Charles: The Trial and Execution of Charles I.* New York: Macmillan, 1964.

——. *The King's Peace 1637–1641.* New York: Macmillan, 1956.

Weston, Corinne Comstock. *English Constitutional Theory and the House of Lords 1556–1832.* New York: Columbia University Press, 1965.

——. "The Theory of Mixed Monarchy Under Charles I and After." *English Historical Review* 75 (July 1960): 426–43.

Winthrop, Robert C. *Algernon Sidney: A Lecture, Delivered Before the Boston Mercantile Association, December 21, 1853.* Boston: S. K. Whipple & Co., 1854.

Wirszubski, Chaim. *Libertas as a Political Idea at Rome During the Late Republic and Early Principate.* Cambridge: Cambridge University Press, 1960.

Wolf, Edwin. "The First Books and Printed Catalogues of the Library Company of Philadelphia." *Pennsylvania Magazine of History and Biography* 78 (January 1954): 45–70.

——. "A Parcel of Books for the Province in 1700." *Pennsylvania Magazine of History and Biography* 89 (1965): 429–46.

Wood, Gordon S. "Conspiracy and the Paranoid Style: Causality and Deceit in the Eighteenth Century." *William and Mary Quarterly,* 3rd ser., 39 (July 1982): 401–41.

——. *The Creation of the American Republic, 1776–1787.* New York: W. W. Norton, 1972.

Wood, Neal. "The Value of Asocial Sociability: Contributions of Machiavelli, Sidney and Montesquieu." In *Machiavelli and the Nature of Political Thought,* edited by Martin Fleisher, 282–307. New York: Atheneum, 1972.

Woolrych, A. H. "The Good Old Cause and the Fall of the Protectorate." *Cambridge Historical Journal* 13 (1957): 133–61.

Wootton, David. Introduction to *Divine Right and Democracy: An Anthology of Political Writing in Stuart England*. Harmondsworth: Penguin Books, 1986.

Worden, Blair. "Classical Republicanism and the Puritan Revolution." In *History and Imagination: Essays in Honour of H. R. Trevor-Roper*, edited by Hugh Lloyd-Jones, Valerie Pearl, and Blair Worden, 182–200. London: Duckworth, 1981.

———. "The Commonwealth Kidney of Algernon Sidney." *Journal of British Studies* 24 (January 1985): 1–40.

———. "Edmund Ludlow: The Puritan and the Whig." *Times Literary Supplement* 3,904 (7 January 1977): 15–16.

———. *The Rump Parliament 1648–1653*. Cambridge: Cambridge University Press, 1974.

———. "Toleration and the Cromwellian Protectorate." *Studies in Church History* 21 (1984): 199–233.

Wrightson, Keith. *English Society 1580–1680*. New Brunswick: Rutgers University Press, 1982.

Zagorin, Perez. *A History of Political Thought in the English Revolution*. London: Routledge & Kegan Paul, 1954.

INDEX